Abundance from the Desert

Middle East Literature in Translation
Michael Beard and Adnan Haydar, *Series Editors*

Abundance from the Desert

Classical Arabic Poetry

Raymond Farrin

SYRACUSE UNIVERSITY PRESS

First Paperback Edition 2017

17 18 19 20 21 22   6 5 4 3 2 1

∞ The paper used in this publication meets the minimum requirements
of the American National Standard for Information Sciences—Permanence
of Paper for Printed Library Materials, ANSI Z39.48–1992.

For a listing of books published and distributed by Syracuse University Press,
visit www.SyracuseUniversityPress.syr.edu.

ISBN: 978-0-8156-3222-1 (hardcover)   978-0-8156-3515-4 (paperback)   978-0-8156-5095-9 (e-book)

Library of Congress has cataloged the hardcover edition as follows:

Farrin, Raymond.
    Abundance from the desert : classical Arabic poetry / Raymond Farrin. — 1st ed.
      p. cm. — (Middle East literature in translation)
    Includes bibliographical references and index.
    ISBN 978-0-8156-3222-1 (cloth : alk. paper)
    1. Arabic poetry—To 622—History and criticism.   2. Arabic poetry—622–750—
History and criticism.   3. Arabic poetry—750–1258—History and criticism.
    4. Arabic poetry—1258–1800—History and criticism.   I. Title.
    PJ7543.F48 2011
    892.7'109—dc22   2010052104

Manufactured in the United States of America

For

MARIANNE M. FARRIN

and

JAMES S. FARRIN

تِلْكَ آثَارُنَا تَدُلُّ عَلَيْنَا   فَانْظُرُوا بَعْدَنَا إِلَى الآثَارِ

These are our traces, that tell about us.
So those who follow, look at our traces.

—Unattributed
(cited in E. J. W. Gibb Memorial series)

Raymond Farrin received his Ph.D. in Near Eastern
Studies from the University of California, Berkeley.
He is currently assistant professor of Arabic at the
American University of Kuwait.

Contents

x   Contents

Acknowledgments

WORK ON THIS PROJECT has been partially funded by a grant from the Sultan Program of the Center for Middle Eastern Studies, University of California, Berkeley. The university library at Berkeley, meanwhile, has provided me the material for my research. It may be noted here that earlier versions of chapters 8, 10, and 11 have appeared in the *Journal of Arabic Literature* (respectively, no. 34 [2003]: 221–51; no. 34 [2003]: 82–103; no. 35 [2004]: 247–69). I would like to thank Koninklijke Brill NV for the permission to incorporate versions of these articles in the present work.

In addition, I wish to thank the following people for reading chapter drafts and for making helpful suggestions: Dina Aburous, Nicole Bates, Marie-Thérèse Ellis, Robert Greeley, Sara Jurdi Heum, Abbas Kadhim, Nathalie Khankan, Sam Liebhaber, Harry Neale, Simon O'Meara, Mark Pettigrew, and Muhammad Talaat. I would also like to thank my parents and siblings for their moral support.

Professors Maria Mavroudi and Muhammad Siddiq at UC Berkeley read the complete work in an earlier version. Their constructive criticisms and valuable suggestions improved this study in many ways, and I am significantly indebted to them. In some cases, however, I did not adopt their proposed changes, as I sometimes did not adopt those suggestions of other readers in the process of completing this book. The fault for any errors of judgment and oversights herein is entirely mine.

Finally, I wish to thank especially my mentor at UC Berkeley, Professor James Monroe. He inspired me to write on the subject of coherence in classical Arabic poetry, advised me judiciously as I wrote, and then encouraged me to revise and expand my initial study and publish it. His careful readings of all the chapters—including the ones added later, after completion of the initial study—and his insightful remarks on them have greatly contributed to this book.

Introduction

The construction, the frame, so to speak, is the most important guarantee of
the mysterious life of works of the mind.

—CHARLES BAUDELAIRE, "Notes nouvelles sur Edgar Poe"

CLASSICAL ARABIC POETRY, that is, the Arabic poetry dating roughly from
500 to 1250 CE, has, through the ages, been valued by the Arabs as a magnificent
cultural achievement. Critics from the classical period regarded it as proof of the
Arabs' eloquence, a trait by which, in their view, the Arabs were exalted over the
other peoples of the earth. Ancient compilers and anthologists recorded a vast
quantity of this poetry in many large volumes; these works have been carefully
passed down to us. And in the modern period, an Arab scholar may look back
and, expressing a widespread feeling of pride and admiration, say: "The Greeks
are characterized by their philosophy, epic and dramatic compositions. . . . The
Romans by establishing religious, civil, political, and economic laws. . . . The
Indians by making up fictitious fables they placed in the mouths of animals. . . .
The Arabs filled the world with poetry."[1]

Nevertheless, for most of the past century and a half, the classical Arabic
poem has been disparaged in the West, mainly for its alleged incoherence, but
also for its perceived artificiality and monotony. In 1856 German philologist Wilhelm Ahlwardt wrote that the Arabic poem is "never a self-contained whole."
That Arabic poetry had no structural cohesiveness became a commonplace
among Orientalist scholars and led to such formulations as "atomism." "Arab
poetry is essentially atomic," the first edition of the *Encyclopedia of Islam* (1934)
tells us, "a string of isolated statements which might be accumulated but could
not be combined."[2] This judgment was even accepted by a few Arab critics, and
it remained unquestioned into the 1970s. The latest prominent proponent of the

atomism thesis—though he does not fault Arabic poetry for its lack of unity (classical Arabic poems, he claims, were never meant to be unified)—is a professor of Arabic literature at Oxford University, Geert Jan van Gelder. Before we proceed and discuss his critical work, however, it would be useful to back up and refresh our memories on the seminal theoretical discussions of organic unity.

The first exposition of the concept occurs in Plato's *Phaedrus*. In this recorded dialogue between Phaedrus and Socrates, Socrates argues that every discourse must have a definite form, with every part in its proper place. "Every discourse," he says, "should be like a living organism and have a body of its own; it should not be without head or feet, it should have a middle and extremities which should be appropriate to each other and to the whole work." He quotes as an example of a bad work a four-line epitaph that can be read in any order without affecting the meaning, and thus has no clear beginning, middle, and end. Furthermore, all parts of the discourse should relate to the idea of the whole. To these stipulations, Aristotle added that the structural union of the parts should be such that "if any one of them is displaced or removed, the whole will be disjointed and disturbed."[3] These concepts have been elementary to literary criticism ever since.

Yet it may be suggested, by one wishing to ward off the traditional Orientalist criticism, that organic unity is a foreign Western concept that should not be used as a basis to evaluate Arabic poems. In response, I would cite Aristotle. Aristotle writes in *Poetics* that whereas history deals with particulars (what has happened), poetry deals with universals (what may happen). Poetry expresses what a person may feel in a certain situation, according to the law of probability. As long as we understand the poet's particular circumstances, then, we should be able to identify with his or her feelings. In this way, poetry is universal; it articulates likely responses to situations and expresses common human emotions. (Note the observation by eighteenth-century English poet and critic Samuel Johnson: "Poetry has to do rather with the passions of men, which are uniform, than their customs, which are changeable.")[4] So, if we accept the Aristotelian position that poetry is universal—which has never been undermined or seriously challenged—it follows logically that the standard by which poetry is judged should be universal as well. This brings us back to organic unity, the fundamental and encompassing criterion of literary excellence.

Moreover, I would add that it is reckless to assume that this aesthetic principle originated with Western civilization, even if Greek philosophers in the fourth century BCE were the first to put it in writing, as far as we know. More than two thousand years before them, the ancient Egyptians surely had the principle in mind when they built the pyramids. One would be hard-pressed to find in another work of art or architecture a more perfect expression of unity. Each pyramid consists of a base, a middle section, and a top that appear together as one form. And though roughly two and a half million blocks were used to construct the Great Pyramid of Cheops, for example, we could not add to the finished pyramid a block without its being superfluous; likewise, if we took away a single one, the whole structure would be incomplete. It would seem, rather, that the aesthetic principle of structural integrity arises from a basic human desire to create order out of chaos, to assemble a whole from scattered parts. Thus, one must put classical Arabic poetry to the touchstone of organic unity and show that it passes the test, if one wishes to dismiss the familiar Orientalist devaluation.

But van Gelder would have us refrain from rigorously demanding unity in classical Arabic poetry. In *Beyond the Line: Classical Arabic Literary Critics on the Coherence and Unity of the Poem* (1982), he sets out to demonstrate that classical Arabic critics were not at all concerned with structural cohesion in poems. On the basis of many passages from treatises, commentaries, and so on, cited to support his fundamental contention that, almost to a man, critics of poetry restricted their focus to the individual line and did not bother with what lay beyond it, he draws a conclusion that poets themselves were not aware of the desirability of overall unity and so did not think to compose poems that cohere (that throwing lines together might be a slapdash way of composition, we are left to deduce, never occurred to the composers).

Obviously, van Gelder's method of logic—proceeding from a generalization about certain readers' field of view to a conclusion about what the authors originally did not have in mind—is somewhat awkward. What is more, his making much of the ancient critics' failure to go about highlighting organic unity in the poems involves an anachronistic conception of literary criticism. In the premodern era, the literary critic took it upon himself to *judge:* to consider the work at hand and acknowledge the good and censure the bad, such that poets might be chastened and society edified. Entirely consistent with this idea is Wen-chin Ouyang's finding, in *Literary Criticism in Medieval Arabic-Islamic Culture,* that *naqada* (to criticize) corresponds, in its earlier usage in the literary sense, to the English "to pick": "to pick the best poetry, to pick on poetry, and to pick out the forged."[5] In the eighteenth century, literary criticism still meant essentially judgment, as readings in Samuel Johnson readily indicate.[6] It was not until after Samuel Taylor Coleridge argued strongly in 1817 that the legitimate poem "must be one, the parts of which mutually support and explain each other," that critics began to see it as their business actually to reveal just how the component parts of a poem go together and harmonize.[7] Naturally, the revelation of organic unity embarked upon by critics required that they interpret the poem's central meaning and that they clarify the significance of each part in connection to this meaning. Hence, we arrived, over time, at the modern conception of literary criticism: as first and foremost an act of interpretation, in which all parts of the work are taken into account.

Van Gelder ends *Beyond the Line* with a plea that we "let the *qasida* [Arabic ode] disintegrate to some extent," maintaining that it can still be appreciated, despite its incoherence. He elaborates in a 1990 essay, comparing the enjoyment of a disjointed *qasida* to that of a multicourse meal. While taking it (the poem or meal) in, he says, "one is neither contemplating the whole nor comparing present and absent parts, but just relishing every bit piecemeal."[8] We are called, therefore, simply to relax and enjoy what comes our way. Unfortunately, one suspects that those individuals who do not normally consume their poems piecemeal, and who do tend to contemplate the main, underlying point of a work, are not likely to change their habits easily. Furthermore, it seems probable that those who encounter or hear such exhortations, yet are of the type that derives aesthetic pleasure from unity, will be discouraged from reading classical Arabic poetry.

However, as alluded to above, the situation in the field of Arabic literature, as far as classical poetry is concerned, has been changing since the 1970s; van Gelder, though prominent, is one of the few scholars still promulgating the old "atomism" thesis. A number of scholars, including the likes of Raymond Scheindlin, Kamal Abu-Deeb, Adnan Haydar, Andras Hamori, Stefan Sperl, James Montgomery, Julie Scott Meisami, Jaroslav Stetkevych, Suzanne Pinckney Stetkevych, and James T. Monroe, have taken the study of classical Arabic poetry in a new direction. Specifically, they have abandoned the preoccupation with ancient critical and philological writings (which have long engrossed Orientalist scholars, philologists mostly) and have turned to analyzing the poetry itself. Attending to individual poems, they have been discovering, and showing clearly, that the poems are characterized by a high degree of structural and thematic unity.

Probably the major structural pattern occurring in classical Arabic poetry is that of ring composition. Unlike a poem organized rectilinearly, a poem constructed on the basis of ring composition develops, as it were, concentrically (that is, in the manner of A—B—C—B¹—A¹). Examples of ring composition have been found in Homer's *Iliad,* the Old English *Beowulf,* the medieval French *chanson de geste* and medieval German *Nibelungenlieder,* Ezra Pound's *Cantos,* and many other works from both ancient and modern literatures. It has been documented extensively in the Hebrew Bible (in biblical studies, ring composition has been referred to commonly as chiasmus).[9] James T. Monroe has discovered its incidence in Arabic literature and clearly identified the pattern in prose and poetry, particularly in the *zajals* (strophic, colloquial poems) by Ibn Quzman (d. 1160). This study takes Monroe's scholarship as a point of departure and seeks to demonstrate that ring composition is indeed a greatly important structural pattern that occurs repeatedly in classical Arabic poetry—in periods from the sixth century to the thirteenth, in places from the Arabian Peninsula to al-Andalus, and in genres from the panegyric to the satire to the love poem.

Following the more recent trend in scholarship, this study focuses on individual poems and offers interpretations of their meaning. The poems have been chosen for their centrality in the canon as well as for their representation of various time periods, geographical areas, and genres. They are: the *Mu'allaqa* by Imru' al-Qays (d. 542), the *Lamiyyat al-'Arab* by al-Shanfara (d. ca. 575?), the *Mu'allaqa* by Labid (d. ca. 661), three elegies by al-Khansa' (d. ca. 646), a love poem by Jamil (d. 701), a satire by Jarir (d. ca. 730), a wine poem by Abu Nuwas (d. ca. 815), a panegyric by Abu Tammam (d. ca. 846), a panegyric by al-Mutanabbi (d. 965), a love poem by Ibn Zaydun (d. 1071), two *zajals* by Ibn Quzman (d. 1160), a Sufi poem by Ibn al-Farid (d. 1235), and a merchant poem by Baha' al-Din Zuhayr (d. 1258).

Of course, interpretation of poetry is inevitably a subjective performance.[10] Harold Bloom has observed that the strong reader is "placed in the dilemmas of the revisionist, who wishes to find his own individual relation to the truth . . . but also wishes to open received texts to his own sufferings, or what he wants to call the sufferings of history."[11] By no means would I claim that the forthcoming are more than one person's subjective readings. Classics, after all, are open to many possible interpretations. On the other hand, it would seem wise to bear in mind the words of Alexander Pope from "An Essay on Criticism":

> You then whose judgment the right course would steer,
> Know well each ancient's proper character;
> His fable, subject, scope in every page;
> Religion, country, genius of his age:
> Without all these at once before your eyes,
> Cavil you may, but never criticize.

Accordingly, I have tried not to get carried away, with the result that the readings are relevant to only one person, but rather have endeavored, as much as possible, to be aware of the poet's historical and literary context and to read each work in the spirit in which it was composed.

For clarification, I state at the outset that this study aims at three main goals. First, it strives to fill a gap in the present literature on the subject and serve as a comprehensive introduction to classical Arabic poetry. Together, the poems suggest the range and depth of classical Arabic poetic expression; read in sequence, they suggest the gradual evolution of a tradition. Second, it tries, wherever possible, to expand the compass and present the works in a broader comparative light. It is hoped that the reader will view these works not as isolated—notwithstanding their uniqueness and their belonging to a discrete tradition—but rather as part of a great multicultural heritage. Finally, it aims to contribute measurably to recent scholarship and help to put to rest the notion that classical Arabic poetry lacks coherence.

Note on Translation and Transliteration

THE TRANSLATIONS ARE MY OWN, unless otherwise indicated. All the complete poems that are the subjects of individual chapters are presented here in new translations. Nonetheless, I have benefited from excellent previous translations in rendering the poems discussed in four chapters (1–3, 10).[1]

Arabic words have been transliterated without the use of diacritics, excepting the 'ayn and the hamza. Also, in the case of poetry, proverbs, and Qur'anic verses, vowels have been elided and consonants assimilated in order to indicate more closely the sound of the Arabic original.

Abundance from the Desert

1

The Triumph of Imru' al-Qays

The business of life is to go forwards.

—SAMUEL JOHNSON, *The Idler*

THE FIRST POEM WE SHALL READ is the celebrated ode by one of the earliest, and certainly the most eminent, of pre-Islamic poets, Imru' al-Qays (d. 542). The stories told about his life portray an audacious and magnetic personality of mythic proportions. He is said to have been the son of Hujr, the last king of Kinda (an ancient ruling tribe of Yemen that had migrated north and, at the time of the poet's birth around 500, dominated central Arabia). Imru' al-Qays's penchant for composing erotic poetry and for causing scandals with women, though, displeased his father, and the latter eventually banished him from his house. Thereupon, Imru' al-Qays joined a band of fellow outcasts and embraced a rowdy life given to hunting, drinking, and cavorting with such young women as he happened to encounter. When word later reached the prince of his father's assassination by members of a subordinate tribe, he did not let the news affect the backgammon game he was then playing and urged his partner to take his turn. "Wine today, business tomorrow," he is reported to have said.[1] Following a bout of heavy drinking, he embarked on a retaliatory campaign to destroy a hundred of the rebels' tribesmen. In this endeavor he was making progress until his allies abandoned him, at which point he turned to other tribes for support. For a period he wandered among them, recruiting fruitlessly. His desire to avenge his father and restore the throne to himself finally propelled him to visit the court of Emperor Justinian at Constantinople. Justinian sympathized and sent him off with an army, only to dispatch afterward a poisoned robe as a personal gift (the emperor meantime had learned that Imru' al-Qays, during his stay at court, had seduced his daughter).[2] When the poet was nearing Ankara the gift caught up

1

with him, from which he developed ulcerous sores and died. Thus, he is some-times called "Dhu al-Quruh" (the One with Ulcers), as well as "al-Malik al-Dillil" (the Wandering King). "Imru' al-Qays" is itself a byname (his real name being Hunduj), meaning "the Man of Adversity."

Such, in brief, is the legendary biography of Imru' al-Qays. Fortunately, thanks to recent scholarship by Irfan Shahid, we can move beyond legend and speak confidently at least concerning what happened at the end of his life. The detail of the poisoned robe from Justinian, it may be noted, was borrowed from Greek mythology (compare the story of Nessos's robe). But, as Shahid affirms, Imru' al-Qays in all likelihood did head to Constantinople to enlist the emperor's aid. The Byzantines had concluded a treaty with Kinda in 502 and had sent a dip-lomatic mission to the tribe in 530–31 to forge an alliance against the Persians, so it would not have been unreasonable, after all, for the would-be king to turn to Byzantium for assistance against his rivals. Whether he reached Constantinople is uncertain. What seems quite clear, however, is that he was in Ankara when the famous bubonic plague of 541–44, which ravaged the entire Near East during that triennium, hit the city in 542. He was afflicted, and in Ankara he died and was buried.[3]

As a poet, he was often credited during the classical period with introduc-ing many motifs to Arabic poetry, and he has generally been regarded as the first great composer in the tradition. Arab poets before him, in fact, are cloaked in obscurity. Yet it is highly probable that he was working within an established poetic context, developing familiar themes. Furthermore, the technical sophisti-cation evident in the Arabic *qasida,* or ode, at this stage of history points back to a lengthy evolution. One would be more right to consider him, therefore, not as the initiator of a tradition, the first major poet in Arabic literature, but rather as the first major poet of whom we are aware.

The *Mu'allaqa* of his we shall read below, one of seven—by some accounts ten—prized odes (*Mu'allaqat*) from the pre-Islamic era that were supposedly inscribed in gold letters and hung on the walls of the Ka'ba in Mecca, is usu-ally ascribed to the poet's youthful period, before the murder of his father. This ascription seems logical, insofar as there are no references in it to vengeance, a theme that figures in a number of his other poems. At the same time, the poem betrays no callowness in its composer; one may reasonably attribute it to the poet's late youth. Since its first hearing, the *Mu'allaqa* has enjoyed almost universal acclaim and has made an immense impact. "Men treasured jealously the verses that [Imru' al-Qays] had spoken, and transmitted them from mouth to mouth," writes A. J. Arberry. "Many of his phrases acquired the universal currency of proverbs. It is no exaggeration to say that his *Mu'allaqa* is at once the most famous, the most admired and the most influential poem in the whole of Arabic literature."[4]

Nevertheless, in the past century the famous ode has come under suspicion from both Western and Arab critics. In 1913 Salomon Gandz raised doubts over the poem's integrity, seeing in it the patchwork of a transmitter. In his judgment, "the poem must certainly be denied any homogeneous character. It presents itself to us as a compilation of a man whose concern was to select the best from the various *qasida*s of Imru' al-Qays and combine it into one larger whole covered up by a single rhyme."[5] Thirteen years later, in 1926, Taha Husayn rocked the Arab scholarly world by asserting that almost all "pre-Islamic" poetry was actually the work of forgers who came after the Prophet Muhammad.[6] This mass of forged verse included the *Diwan* (Collected Poetry) of Imru' al-Qays, excepting minor portions. Regarding the *Mu'allaqa*, he entertained the possibility of authenticity only for the last two sections. He sensed the poet's personality to be mostly absent from the *qasida* and found that no other Arabic ode exhibited a more labored and strained artifice.[7]

Behind these charges was the perception of disunity, and in the case of the *Mu'allaqa*, no serious attempts were made to alter the perception until the 1970s. At that time, studies appeared by Kamal Abu-Deeb and Adnan Haydar that applied structuralist criteria to the poem and showed that it was indeed put together according to a plan. Suzanne Pinckney Stetkevych followed in 1983 with a critique of the structuralist approach, which led in 1993 to her close reading of the *Mu'allaqa* on the basis of the Van Gennepian rite-of-passage model. Despite their differences, all these readings outline an unbroken, essentially uniform progression in the poem (whether from negative to positive, lack to lack liquidation, or separation to aggregation, respectively) and so confute the allegation of patchwork composition. Our interpretation draws on these readings and highlights an analogous progression, although it derives primary inspiration from a recent analysis by Muhammad Siddiq.[8] Siddiq views the ode as a correlative to the modern bildungsroman, or novel about a character's growth and spiritual development. In fact, like a bildungsroman, the poem provides insight into another's internal struggle, his efforts to digest reality, and enriches our understanding with his experience.

Before analyzing the *qasida,* we may profitably inquire why it was composed in the first place. Indeed, the poem was not apparently meant as a gift to a patron (Imru' al-Qays was later esteemed, notably by the Prophet's cousin 'Ali, for being a poet who did not compose for financial reasons or out of awe for his listener).[9] Clinton Bailey has studied the contemporary context of the Bedouin *qasida,* and he notes that such a poem "is composed either to convey important information or to serve as a release from a deep, personal, emotional experience."[10] If the *Mu'allaqa* was intended to convey specific information, which seems unlikely from the consistent hyperbole and the focus on one individual, the poem would concern principally its first hearers, and perhaps historians afterward. Yet it has resonated among audiences for almost fifteen centuries. Surely they did, and continue to, identify with something personal. One concludes necessarily that the ode was composed out of a desire for personal expression. What, then, is Imru' al-Qays saying about his experience, which others evidently have found so compelling? Let us turn to the poem to find out.

The *Mu'allaqa* may be divided into five sections:

A	lines 1–9
B	lines 10–41
C	line 42
B¹	lines 43–66
A¹	lines 67–78[11]

We will discuss each section individually, and then present a summary of their interrelationship so that the overall unity of the poem is easily perceived.

A

1   Halt, my two friends. Let us weep, recalling a beloved and an abode
     by the edge of the twisted sands, between al-Dakhul and Hawmal

2   And Tudih and al-Miqrat. The encampment traces have not yet been effaced
     for all the weaving by the winds from the north and south.

3   There, in the flat areas and the depressions,
     you may see the dung of gazelles scattered like peppercorn.

4   On the morning of separation, the day they loaded to part,
      it was as if I, standing by the tribe's acacias, were splitting colocynth;[12]

5   There my companions halted their beasts awhile over me,
      saying, "Don't die of grief; show some restraint!"

6   Yet the cure for my sorrow is indeed an outpouring of tears.
      But is there, among disappearing remains, a prop for me?

7   Such is your way; so it was with Umm al-Huwayrith before her
      and her neighbor Umm al-Rabab at Mas'al;

8   When they got up to leave, the aroma of musk emanated from them,
      fragrant as the gentle east wind bearing the scent of cloves.

9   Thus my eyes overflowed with tears of intense longing
      onto my throat, until the tears wetted even my sword harness.

Like many other pre-Islamic poems, this ode begins in medias res at an abandoned campsite. The poet and his two companions have been traveling on camels through the desert. Suddenly, they come upon the traces of a former abode, where the poet once enjoyed happy times with his beloved. At this particular place, located in the desert of central Arabia, the weaving by north and south winds and the intrusion of gazelles have not yet covered the vestiges.[13] The sight of the place abandoned, as it was after the beloved's tribe had departed, brings him back to that sad morning. Then he went off to the acacias to wail, and well-meaning colleagues interposed to arrest his sobbing. He finds himself now filled with the same emotions. Yet contrary to what his friends told him, he knows that his cure is to let the tears flow. Line 7 continues in the introspective vein: it is his habit to vent his feelings in such situations, when he is confronted with loss of the beloved(s). On the occasion when the two mothers, Umm al-Huwayrith and Umm al-Rabab, got up on their camels to leave and their fragrances wafted toward him, he lost control. Line 9 returns again to the present and brings the section to a definitive close. No more remembered showers of grief; this time the shedding is real. From the first line, we are expecting the poet—whether joined by his two friends or not—to comply with the second half of the imperative. Finally, he breaks down completely and drenches himself.

Ancient critics considered the first hemistich of the *Mu'allaqa* the best opening to an Arabic *qasida*, because it concisely evokes the stop on the journey, the place, the beloved, and the nostalgia produced by these elements together.[14] We have seen, in addition, the way it creates suspense that builds up to a climax in line 9. Still, one might expand on the praise and say that the first section as a whole sets exactly the right mood for the poem. Moreover, it orients the listener to take in the overall structure. The section begins with a scene in the present, followed by recollections from the past. In the center, the poet makes a frank statement about his aching heart. Next, he plunges into the past again, only to return to the present at the end, to a resolution of his crisis. Such, we shall see, is the progression of the poem.

Concerning the first section, one must comment as well on the blurred time aspect in lines 5 and 9, which makes them subject to variant readings. Based on the preceding line, it makes sense to interpret that the companions halted their beasts over the poet (5) on the morning of separation, although it is tenable grammatically to argue that this takes place after the stop at the camp remains. Also, contrary to our interpretation, one may assign to the past the overflow of tears (9), as a response to the departure of the two mothers (Umm al-Huwayrith and Umm al-Rabab). However, two considerations militate against this reading. First, it supposes that the poet surrenders to tears earlier in the section (5?), which eases the dramatic tension. Second, it overlooks the logical connection between lines 6 and 9. The poet asks rhetorically if anything remains on which to lean. Surely, he does not see a post or other such object among obliterated traces (one imagines the acacias to be off in the distance). Thus, he stands upright in line 9, and the tears stream down his face, his throat, his chest, and onto his sword harness. Arguments notwithstanding, one cannot deny the momentary temporal confusion that besets the listener upon hearing the first part of the poem. Then again, the effect serves a useful purpose, bringing the listener closer to the poet's psychological experience, in which sad memories blend with depressing reality.

The sensitive listener may also wonder momentarily if he is not involved in the drama. Granted, the poet's persona in the poem (for simplicity, we refer to him as the poet) interacts with two companions. But the reciter, who temporarily adopts the poet's guise, says to the listener, "Let us weep" (*nabki*), "you see" (*tara*), and "such is your way" (*ka-da'bika*). He may further employ gesticulation to show whom he means. Willy-nilly, the listener finds himself a participant, sharing the grief.

The grief, one senses, will not be drowned easily. The poet already cried at the acacias over losing the beloved; here he weeps again. Neither following a prescription formerly nor allowing for the effects of time thereafter has moderated his suffering. If anything, his woe has intensified, because experience has taught him that he has truly lost her. One increasingly appreciates, upon reflection, the profundity of his crisis. The depth of this crisis suggests that emotional recovery will be an arduous process at the very least and may require something extraordinary.

B

10   Ah yes, but many a good day you've had with the ladies,
       and especially I remember a day at Darat Juljul.

11   And the day I hocked for the virgins my riding-beast—
       then how wonderful was the dividing of its laden saddle!

12   Through the day, the virgins tossed onto the fire its meat
       and its fat that looked like the twisted fringes of white silk.

13   And the day I entered the howdah—'Unayza's howdah—
       and she cried, "Woe to you! You'll make me go on foot!"

14   She was saying, after the saddle had listed with us both,
       "You've hamstrung my camel now, Imru' al-Qays; get down!"

15   So I said to her, "Ride on, and slacken the reins,
       and don't keep me from having more of your succulent fruit."

16   Yes, like you, many's the pregnant woman I've night-visited,
       and many the nursing mother also, whom I diverted from her amuleted
             one-year-old;

17   Whenever the babe cried behind her, she rotated her upper half to attend to
             him,
       while her lower half remained firmly in place beneath me.

18   And one day on the back of a sand dune a certain lady refused me,
       and swore a terrible oath never to be broken.

19   O Fatima, easy now, a little less blunt!
       If you really have resolved to cut me off, do it gently.

20   Has it deceived you that my love for you is killing me,
       and that no matter what you order, my heart obeys?

21   If something of my character has hurt you,
       just draw my clothes off from yours; they'll slip away.

22   Those eyes of yours have never shed tears
       but to strike me with their two arrows and pierce the heart.[15]

23   And many a secluded maiden, creamy white like an egg, to whose tent none
             dares aspire,
       I have enjoyed playing with, and not in the slightest hurry either.

24 To reach her I stole past guards and kinsmen
    on the alert for me, eager to announce my death,

25 Doing so when the Pleiades spread out across the sky
    like the jewels in a woman's ornamented sash.[16]

26 I came, and by the tent-flap she had already doffed her clothes for sleep,
    except for a flimsy slip.

27 "By God," she exclaimed, "you're done for now!"
    "I see that your foolishness has not left you."

28 So out I took her, and as we walked she pulled
    over our footprints the train of an embroidered skirt.

29 And when we had crossed the tribe's enclosure
    and reached a low place hidden in the dunes,

30 I drew her locks near, and down to me she bent,
    slender in the waist, plump in the ankles.[17]

31 Taut, white is her belly;
    her upper chest shines like a polished mirror.

32 She turns, revealing a soft cheek,
    and wards me off with the look of a Wajra gazelle protecting its fawn.

33 She shows me the neck of an antelope,
    not ungainly when she raises it, nor unadorned;

34 And thick, jet-black hair decorating her back,
    luxuriant like the large cluster of a date-laden palm,

35 Some tresses twisted upwards and secured on top,
    others straying between the plaited and the loosened strands;

36 And a slight, delicate waist like a camel's nose-rein,
    and now a leg like a tender, well-watered papyrus reed.

37 Particles of musk hang over her bed in the morning;
    she lies sleeping into the forenoon, not rising and girding herself.

38 She gives with fingers soft, long, uncalloused;
    they are like sand-worms of Zabi, or supple, tamarisk tooth-sticks.

39 In the evening, she lights up the darkness
    as if she were the lamp in an anchorite's night-cell.

40 At the likes of her the staid, self-controlled man gazes longingly when she
        stands up,
    revealing her proportions, in a dress between a girl's shift and a matron's gown.

41 She is like the first egg of an ostrich: white mixed with yellow;
    a young lady raised on water pure, unclouded by alighting travelers.

Section B, a continuation of the *nasib*, or amatory prelude (begun in A with the scene at the *atlal*, or traces), reveals the poet's strategy for dealing with his pain. He responds to sadness by remembering previous instances of happiness and of overcoming adversity. He employs the same strategy in other poems (recalling in one after lamenting lost love, "Ah yes, from how many a dark place you've returned to the light!").[18] It is a reasonable approach, since the import of these memories should cheer him. In the *Mu'allaqa*, the memories signify that he has previously enjoyed the company of various women. Therefore, he may logically expect another lady—even several—to take the beloved's place. By the same token, he loved some of these women intensely, and evidently they no longer concern him. Likewise, he may expect to get over his current obsession.

The poet begins this program of mental therapy directly following his breakdown. He first calls to mind two happy days: a day at Darat Juljul and one spent somewhere with virgins. Classical Arab commentators have explained these references with an entertaining story that leads conveniently into the 'Unayza lines (13–15). In brief, the story concerns a day when Imru' al-Qays stole upon maidens who were bathing at a pool named Darat Juljul. Thinking quickly, he gathered up all their clothes into a pile and sat on it, and then announced that each would have to come out if she wished to retrieve her clothes. The maidens remonstrated vociferously, but the poet refused to budge. Hours later, they emerged one by one, until the most reserved, 'Unayza, herself came out. The poet then exuberantly slaughtered his camel for them, and they all feasted. When it was time to leave, the women agreed to divide his saddle load among their camels. Only 'Unayza had nothing extra to carry, so from her Imru' al-Qays solicited a ride.[19]

Indeed, this makes for an excellent story. But it seems a bit too good to be true—especially when other cultures enjoy their own versions and the gist turns up in Stith Thompson's *Motif-Index of Folk-Literature* (see K 1335: "Water-women are powerless when their garments are taken"). At this point, Clinton Bailey helps us understand how such a story attaches itself to the poem and works its way into the commentaries. Every *qasida*, he observes, arises from a narrative context. However, whereas a poem is memorized, the context tends to be forgotten. When it is, the reciter will "construct a new story based as far as possible on indications, which the poem itself provides, of the experiences that initially gave rise to the *qasida*. The reciter will, of course, try to make the story as interesting, and perhaps as edifying, as possible."[20] In this manner, the stories improve. They also proliferate in correspondence to the popularity of the poem and the number of reciters. Semha Alwaya has documented, in the case of a contemporary poem, this latter phenomenon ("Everyone has his own story," one reciter tells her).[21] Over time, though, natural selection occurs, so that when a scholar finally takes interest in a venerable poem, he hears the best story along with it.

Before dismissing the storytelling as an exercise in fantasy, an excursion from the proper business of engaging the text, we may well consider what the reciters are in fact doing. From clues in the poem, they are constructing a background story to explain it. In other words, they are performing the essential function of literary criticism: assigning meaning. Modern critics can only hope that their readings appeal as much to the popular imagination as does the Darat Juljul story. Be this as it may, we are still faced with the task of explaining lines 10–12. Unfortunately, without the original narrative, one cannot know the precise significance. Suffice it to say, from the poetic context, that the memories pertain to the poet's generosity and his ability to please young beauties.

Lines 13–15 deal with another memorable day, one on which the poet brazenly climbed into 'Unayza's howdah while she was riding.[22] Although she protested at this outrageous advance, he would not get down. The memory leads to recollection in lines 16–17 of even more outrageous exploits. These lines, considered among the most licentious in classical Arabic poetry, are an apt private rejoinder to 'Unayza's objections. He recalls that pregnant women and nursing mothers—of all women, the least likely to welcome overtures from a man, particularly one who is not their husband—have surrendered to him. Furthermore, awkward positioning has not posed a problem, as the example of the mother, twisting back to attend to her infant, attests. Reluctant 'Unayza sitting in her carriage would do well to take note. On another level, the sequence of events reflects the poet's purpose to communicate a message to himself. Whatever the timeline of these hypothetical occurrences, in the chain of association, apparent failure is followed by brilliant success. The next set of memories repeats the sequence, such that the poet, after evoking the terrible rebuff from winsome Fatima (18–22), concludes his reveries by recalling yet another fabulous conquest. Thus, he conveys the idea to himself that he recovers from setbacks.

Lines 23–41 constitute the longest and most detailed of the erotic recollections. In them a fair, secluded lady represents the many of her kind with whom the poet has dallied. He compares her in line 23 to an egg, suggesting her creamy complexion and delicacy. Through the comparison he also suggests that she is inviolate. Nevertheless, the determined poet has disregarded danger and made his way at night into her private quarters, where his bravado and desirability overpowered her so that she too risked her life and went with him to a secluded location. Based on close observation that night, he provides a detailed description of her, enlivened with comparisons to desert flora and fauna. By the standards of her society she embodies the ideal woman: dark-haired, shapely, soft, languorous. That she wears jewelry and need not rise early to work betokens affluence; instead of toiling, she spends her time lounging and looking beautiful in her tent.

The poet closes the reverie with striking images that emphasize the lady's luster, purity, and sex appeal. Her face illuminates the night, resembling in its glow the lamp of an anchorite. The next line (40) stands out, in the very large corpus of Arabic poetry pertaining to love, as a singularly powerful expression of a woman's sensuousness. This image of the grave and dignified man gazing longingly at the young body has compelled at least two great poets to imitation.[23] Finally, the poet brings the long subsection to an end with another egg comparison, like that of its beginning (23). The comparison implies once more the lady's color and untainted virtue and creates a sense of closure by bringing the description full circle.

C

42   Let other men find consolation after their youthful follies;
      having known your love, my heart will never be consoled.

Line 42 stands apart from the section that preceded it and, in terms of the overall structure of the *Mu'allaqa*, completes the long *nasib*. The poet snaps out of his spell of reminiscence and makes a declaration about the state of his heart. He still loves the beloved and will never, unlike others, be consoled for her loss. He directs his statement to the beloved, addressing her for the first time by using the second-person pronominal suffix *ki*. One should not construe the line as referring to the guarded, fair damsel of the tent, since she represented a multitude of previous women he knew, not a specific one who continues to dominate his thoughts. After reviewing the past, the poet has come back and here sums up his present and future. Rhetorically, the instances of *jinas* (paronomasia, or employing words of different meanings based on the same root) and a form of *radd al-'ajuz 'ala al-sadr* (repetition of the first word in the last) in *tasallat* (be consoled,

distracted) and *munsali* (consoled, distracted)—both infrequent figures in Imru'
al-Qays's poetry—also set the line off against the preceding section.[24] They call
attention to the line.

The length of this *nasib* and its ending, it may be noted, distinguish the
nasib as highly unusual. In contrast to most pre-Islamic *nasibs*, which are not
more than ten or fifteen lines, the amatory prelude of the *Mu'allaqa* stretches to
forty-two lines, far exceeding the *nasib* length of any other pre-Islamic poem. In
addition, the ending confounds expectation. Nathalie Khankan writes, based on
detailed study of amatory preludes in the *Mufaddaliyyat* anthology, that "there
seems to be a recurrent progression within the *nasib* from sadness to some kind
of relief, from folly and youthful passion to sober maturity." Similarly, Renate
Jacobi remarks in a study of the *nasib* that "statements to the effect that love does
not end are rare and merely made for emphasis."[25] The sentiment expressed in
line 42 thus flies in the face of convention. Indeed, it does not appear elsewhere
in Imru' al-Qays's *Diwan,* and it conflicts with the poet's apparently religiously
practiced libertine philosophy. Surprisingly—especially considering its author—
the sentiment anticipates the 'Udhri stance of lifelong commitment (discussed
in chapter 5). All these factors heighten interest at this point in the poem and
contribute to the *Mu'allaqa*'s exceptionality.

Upon consideration, however, one realizes that this particular *nasib* develops logically from the situation described at the beginning of the poem. At the
outset the poet sinks into the depths of despair, so in order to surface to a happier frame of mind he must exert great and sustained effort. Certainly, doing so
would seem a reasonable conclusion for a person to make. On the other hand,
his response in section A intimates that a straightforward remedy will not be
adequate. Even though before he had wept profusely at the beloved's departure
(its being his cure for grief), we find him in A crying with vehemence again when
the traces stimulate her memory. Not surprisingly, therefore, a basic and direct
approach of extended positive reflection also does no good, and he goes back at
the end of it to the old obsession. This particular beloved (presumably his latest
from the previous year, as she would probably have the strongest hold on his
imagination) he cannot drive from his mind.[26]

Taking psychology into account, we may understand yet more clearly why
his mental efforts were destined to fail. Notably, he imposes pleasant memories forcibly on his consciousness, against the flow of his thoughts. (By way of

comparison, the memories in section A of the separation morning and of the two departing mothers are examples of spontaneous, not forced, recollection.) A number of fine days retrieved by violence are unlikely to withstand and reverse a surge of authentic unhappy feeling. For the grief to be dispelled, his thoughts must tend by their own course toward greener pastures.

Samuel Johnson has said, in this regard, that "the natural flights of the human mind are not from pleasure to pleasure, but from hope to hope."[27] If the poet, then, has resisted nature by going back in the *nasib* section to exquisite pleasures, it is partly because nothing delightful in the immediate future presents itself. His past glories do not necessarily mean that more are on the horizon. At this point, the poet is still hopeless, even after recounting numerous wonderful successes. And given his dogged fidelity to the memory of a lost beloved, consolation would seem impossible.

B[1]

43   Ah, many a stubborn adversary have I driven back concerning my
         attachment to you,
   sincere in his blame of me, unrelenting.

44   And many a night like a wave of the sea has let down its curtains on me,
   thick with various cares, to try me.

45   So I said to it, after it had stretched out its spine,
   raised its buttocks, and heaved forward its ponderous chest,

46   O, you long night, won't you clear yourself off and give way to morning?
   Though morning, when it comes, is no better than you.

47   Oh what a night you are! It is as if the stars,
   by every twisted rope, were fastened to Mount Yadhbul;

48   As if the Pleiades were restrained in midcourse
   by strong flax cables connected to crags of granite.

49   And often have I ridden forth early, while the birds were still in their nests,
   on a steed short-haired, able to shackle wild game, huge.

50   Charging, fleeing, advancing, retreating—all at once;
   he is like a great boulder hurled from on high by the torrent.

51   A chestnut stallion, whose saddle pad slips from his back
   as rainwater cascading slips from the surface of a smooth stone.

52   Full of spirit, despite his leanness—when his ardor rises
   he is as forceful and lively as a boiling cauldron.

53   Gracefully he flows along, while fatigued coursers flounder
      and kick up dust on the trampled trail.

54   The lightweight youth slides off his back;
      the heavy, rough rider, he tosses.

55   Very swift he is, like the boy's button-on-a-string
      after successive twisting of the string from both sides.

56   He has the flanks of a gazelle, the legs of an ostrich,
      the springy trot of a wolf, and the gallop of a fox.

57   Sturdy and well-shaped is his frame. Look at him from behind:
      he bars his leg's gap with a full tail, not crooked, reaching almost to the
             ground.

58   His back, as he stands by the tent, seems the pounding-slab
      for a bride's perfumes, or the flat stone on which colocynth is split.

59   The blood from the herd's leaders spatters his neck
      in the manner of henna juice expressed onto combed white hair.

60   An oryx herd then appeared before us, the females among them
      like the Duwar virgins in trailing skirts.[28]

61   They wheeled around, looking like spaced onyx beads
      on the neck of a youth with many noble uncles in the tribe.

62   He put us in the midst of the leaders,
      while behind him the stragglers herded together, not scattering.

63   Then he attacked, hitting successively a buck and a doe,
      not a drop of sweat on him.

64   Thereafter, through the afternoon, our cooks were busy,
      some roasting meat strips, others preparing a quick stew.

65   We returned in the evening, and as we approached,
      the observer's eye could not take him in: now it looked up, toward his top,
             now down.

66   Then he spent the night saddled and bridled,
      standing where I could see him, not sent off to graze.

Section B¹ exhibits many likenesses to B in terms of structure and theme. As in B, the subsections are marked with opening devices such as *a-la rubba* ("Ah, many a . . .", 43) and the *waw rubba* ("Many a . . ."; 44). A variant of these, *wa-qad* + imperfect ("Often have I . . ."; 49), likewise refers to a frequent or habitual action. The extended description (eleven lines) of an ideal horse corresponds to the long description (twelve lines) of an ideal lady. In B¹, we hear once more of virgins and a feast. The poet also goes back resolutely to memories that boost his ego. These memories demonstrate his fortitude and dominance among men, as opposed to those earlier in the poem that showed his virility and irresistibility vis-à-vis women. The summoning of the past should again be viewed in the context of the lost beloved, as a strategy for dealing with his pain. In another poem, after a *nasib* in which he bemoans the loss of three women, we have these lines:

> Whenever gloom descends on me, I remember
> how many an obscurity that benights the face of a coward I've lifted.
>
> And whenever gloom descends on me, I remember
> how many a raid I've witnessed on the back of a slender, soft-necked horse.[29]

The thematic sequence here of (1) proving his mettle against darkness and (2) riding a horse should look familiar. In fact, next in this poem comes a descriptive passage about the horse that is reminiscent of the description in the *Mu'allaqa*. In both poems, the series of recollections are meant to make the poet feel better.

Line 43 introduces the section from the point where the *nasib* left off. The poet's hopeless obsession with his beloved has earned him the censure of more level-headed thinkers. In a boastful tone, he recalls that he has driven them back one by one. A quibbler might argue here that he mistakes obstinacy for strength. Regardless, he clearly intends self-praise for having endured harassment and proven himself against determined foes. Hence, on a thematic level, while still looking back to the beloved, the line also looks forward. Structurally (by virtue of *a-la rubba*) and tonally, however, line 43 unambiguously marks the beginning of a new section.

In lines 44–48 the poet recalls, by the figurative struggle with night, how many tests of his patience he has been through. The occurrence of the memory at this point in the poem indicates, as might have been expected from his persistent attachment to the beloved, that the poet has reached an emotional and spiritual nadir. The night drowns him in cares. He elaborates on the experience of lengthy tribulation through a famous metaphor. The night, in its slowness to depart, is like a camel that does not want to rise and go away. Or, as the next two similes suggest, its progress is suspended altogether. The Pleiades, known to the Arabs as the "winter star cluster"[30] (and therefore signifying here a long winter's night), appear immobile in the sky, bound by cables to earthen granite. By such vivid images the poet expresses the feeling of interminable despair. His repeat of the cry *a-la* in line 46 (*a-la ayyuha l-laylu t-tawilu a-la -njali . . .*) further signals his despondency.[31]

We see especially clearly in this subsection signs of the poet's strong and valiant personality. He orders the night to clear, even though he knows the morning will be no better for him. Indeed, it is in his nature to strive against adversity, as other examples from his *Diwan* corroborate. In one poem, he responds to a direct challenge to his virility with defiance:

> Oh, Basbasa claimed today that I've grown old,
> that a man of my age does not excel at love-play.
>
> She lied! I may still entice a man's wife,
> and prevent mine from being suspected with a bachelor.[32]

James Montgomery discusses an elegy in which the poet does not surrender to pessimistic feelings. Rather, he concludes on a note of hope and vindication, affirming the possibility of avenging the dead man.[33] Perhaps the most poignant evidence of this indomitable spirit may be found in a poem composed apparently after he had contracted the plague that would kill him. In it he expresses alarm at his affliction, which had so debilitated him that he could no longer put on his clothes. But even this grave condition does not drive him into submission, as the optimistic last line indicates:

> Ah, after lack may well come possession,
> and after old age, long life and new apparel.[34]

Such resistance to the press of difficult circumstances characterizes what Andras Hamori has called the "Poet as Hero." In the *Mu'allaqa*, the poet's heroism manifests itself in his absolute refusal to wallow in sadness despite overhanging grief. Horace writes in *Art of Poetry* that "it is not enough for poems to be beautiful; they must be affecting, and must lead the heart of the hearer as they will."[35] Here, the example of the poet trying repeatedly to pull himself from depression can hardly fail to inspire.

We must now deal with four additional lines—the wolf lines—sometimes included at this juncture in the *Mu'allaqa*.[36] They appear in only one of the two principal recensions, albeit with the caveat that the majority of transmitters reject them as spurious.[37] For numerous reasons, we concur with their majority opinion. First of all, the subsection reflects an attitude of humility and self-pity absent elsewhere in the *qasida* and wholly inappropriate for a proud prince. The composer of these lines does not struggle against hard luck; he accepts it and finds a partner in misery. What is more, when Imru' al-Qays speaks in his *Diwan* of crossing deserts, he speaks of crossing them on fast, sturdy camels. Finally, the wolf passage interrupts the temporal transition from night (48) to early morning (49) that helps connect the night and horse subsections. In short, both ancient authority and poetic evidence come down against the acknowledgment of these lines.

The poet begins the description of his ideal horse with a pair of striking lines. Unlike the quiescent birds in their nests, the vigorous horse, he has us conceive, is out shackling wild game. The horse is so fast, moreover, that it appears to be charging, fleeing, advancing, and retreating all at once. In the second hemistich of line 50, the poet tells us that, in combination with his speed, the horse comes down upon the animals he chases with the force of a boulder hurled by the torrent. The next several lines offer further proof of this horse as the ideal specimen, endowed with characteristics opposite to those traits possessed by the ideal woman in section B. Embodying true masculine features and qualities, the horse is swift, strong, lean, and spirited.

The description in the *Mu'allaqa* in general, and perhaps in this section in particular, has drawn effusive praise from ancient and modern critics. Abdulla el Tayib has recently called the ode "a symphony of descriptive patterns" and counted in it more than seventy descriptive topics. Among the lines that traditionally have been singled out for special praise is 56, detailing the horse's flanks, legs, and manner of trotting and galloping. Qudama ibn Ja'far (d. ca. 932) applauded the virtuoso handling of four comparisons in one line and considered the line one of the best examples of figurative description in the canon. But aside from displaying the poet's technical brilliance, the line may also give indication of an effect the poet was trying to produce in his listeners, one Victor Shklovsky has termed "defamiliarization."[38] We must suppose that his listeners were well-enough acquainted with the Arabian horse that they might easily imagine his steed, however unique. That said, in line 56 the poet seems to be making the act of forming an image as difficult for them as possible. For each body part or type of movement, the listener must call to mind a different desert animal and transpose its respective part or motion to the horse. From these disparate elements, the listener must assemble a composite equine figure. All this effort is required so that perception is not automatic, for, as Shklovsky observes: "Art exists that one may recover the sensation of life; it exists to make one feel things, to make the stone *stony*. The purpose of art is to impart the sensation of things as they are perceived and not as they are known. The technique of art is to make objects 'unfamiliar,' to make forms difficult, to increase the difficulty and length of perception because the process of perception is an aesthetic end in itself and must be prolonged."[39] Through the poet's description of his horse, at times sudden and surprising and at others mentally challenging, the poet forces concentration and so brings us closer to his animal—enabling us really to see his bushy tail, to feel his firm back, to know the thrill of riding him.

Such powers of description of course redound to the poet's credit. The horse passage therefore may be classified as implicit *fakhr,* or self-praise, besides being *wasf* (descriptive poetry).[40] Furthermore, owing to the fact that the poet owns the horse, any glory emanating from it reflects on him. And by extolling his animal for its attractiveness, initiative, and courage, he also indirectly extols himself as possessor of those same qualities. On the whole, though, the poet's persona steadily diminishes in this subsection, while the figure and aura of the horse gradually enlarge. Siddiq has called attention to this important development. As Siddiq points out, when the poet sets out in the early morning (49), he is the agent of action, the one who departs with his horse. But eleven lines later, when we hear of an oryx herd appearing, it appears to both poet and horse (*lana*). The horse then takes control and thrusts the poet among the leaders, before assaulting a buck and doe oryx. Although the poet deserves credit for actively participating in the kill (or so one would assume) and supplying his troop with ample food, the horse is the hero of the hunt. By evening, the horse has grown so much in stature that the eye can hardly take him in. The poet, meanwhile, does not appear in the picture.[41] The shrinkage of the poet to this extent and concomitant expansion of a force from nature marks a significant change from the beginning of B[1], when the poet prominently beat back reproachers and struggled heroically with night. The development reflects the poet's gradual acquisition of perspective on himself and his place in the world, an acquisition that will have major implications for his psychological recovery in the last section of the poem.

Line 66 brings the temporal frame of reference back to night and so signals the end of the section. After a remembered day of hunting, we are back to the time of cares and enforced waiting. Even if a new perspective for the poet suggests incipient change, he is not out of the dark yet.

A¹

67   O Friend! Do you see the lightning? Look, there goes its flash
      reaching down now like two hands from the massed, crowned storm cloud.

68   Brilliantly it shines. It illumines the dark like an anchorite's lamp
      after he has poured oil on the twisted wick.

69   So with my companions I sat watching it between Darij
      and 'Udhayb, far-ranging my gaze.[42]

70   Over Mount Qatan, we guessed, hovered the right of its deluge,
      its left falling on Mount Sitar and further Yadhbul.

71   Then the cloud began releasing its torrent around Kutayfa,
      forcing the lofty Kanahbal trees onto their chins.[43]

72   Its thick spray passed over Mount Qanan,
      sweeping off the white-footed ibex from every ledge.

73   And Tayma'—why, there it left not a palm trunk standing
      nor a fortress, except those built of stone.

74   Mount Thabir, in the first onrush of the deluge,
      looked like a tribal chieftain wrapped in a striped cloak.

75   The topmost peak of Mount Mujaymir, from the accumulation of scum,
      looked in the morning like a spindle's whorl.

76   Through the al-Ghabit expanse it had cast its wares
      like a Yemeni merchant unpacking his loaded saddlebags.

77   It was as if, by morning, the birds all along the valley
      had quaffed strong wine mixed with spices;

78   As if the wild beasts, drowned overnight,
      in the farthest reaches of the watercourse were drawn bulbs of wild onion.

The ode concludes with a storm scene famous for its drama and evocative power. Part of its impact on the imagination comes from a factor of surprise, for the storm motif normally occurs in the *nasib,* not at the end of the poem. However, as Stetkevych lucidly shows, the preceding horse description subliminally prepares us for the storm by repeated association of the animal with water. The horse matches in force a boulder hurled by the torrent, in smoothness a stone over which water runs; the horse flows in its movement and is swift, streaming (*darir*) (50, 51, 53, 55).[44] Also, the last two lines of the horse subsection, by including two references to the observer's eye, provide a transition to "you see" in the first line of A¹. At the other end of the poem, the flood of tears also prepares us for this final rainwater deluge. In fact, our progressive appreciation of ring composition in the poem leads us to expect something of corresponding substance and magnitude to the initial outpouring. In retrospect, the ending is not so surprising as it may seem at first.

Still, to understand fully why the storm scene occurs here, we must analyze its meaning. Let us start close to the surface. At the beginning of the section, the poet returns to current reality and to his companions. He alerts one of them to lightning on the horizon, and so the group takes an elevated position where they command an extensive view and can guess where the rain will fall. The subsequent hyperbole in the description of the storm's effects, as well as in the purported visual acuity of the poet—some of these places are vast distances apart—accords with the hyperbole in the rest of the poem. The poet describes the progression of devastation and detritus and then gives an indication of the storm's results for more local flora and fauna. Yemeni merchants were known for their wares of high-quality, colored clothing (they traded with India). In line 76, the poet suggests that the flood has unloaded on the desert floor variegated patches of cloth, that after the onrush, the desert has bloomed. The last couplet summarizes contrasting effects on the region's wildlife. Songbirds have become ecstatic from drafts of delicious fresh water, whereas ferocious beasts have drowned in it and lie bloated like uprooted wild onions. Thus, the poem ends, for all the violence of the storm, with images suggestive of happiness, security, and prosperity.

In this last section, as elsewhere in the poem, there is an emphasis on visual description. Once the poet tells us that he and his friends have found a place from which to watch the spectacle, he supplies without commentary eight lines depicting the scene. One is left to wonder about the significance of this great storm. In *Poetics,* Aristotle writes regarding tragedy that "incidents should speak for themselves without verbal exposition."[45] The same holds true for literature generally, as this silence encourages an intellectual response from the reader or listener. Unfortunately, for those readers at a considerable remove from the original context, the import may easily remain opaque. We must therefore turn to the literary-historical and anthropological sources available to us in order to understand what the storm would connote for the poet's Bedouin audience and, more important, what the poet is saying through it about his own experience.

Sir Charles Lyall's *Ancient Arabian Poetry* conveniently fills in much of the background. In the introduction Lyall discusses the importance for central Arabia of winter rains, which produce a vigorous growth of herbage. During the period when the Bedouin way of life predominated, the rains allowed the tribes to leave their summer locations next to isolated permanent water supplies and to congregate in the fresh areas of pasture. There, for a few months of winter and spring, until heat and drought forced the tribes to separate and return to their wells, people from neighboring camps might meet and develop relationships. These relationships are the ones we hear of so frequently in Arabic poetry.[46] And from a firsthand account we glean details of what a Bedouin might associate with a plentiful spring—by no means a guaranteed occurrence—brought on by a major storm. Anthropologist Alois Musil relates:

[After a thorough soaking] the whole steppe and even the desert are transformed into a delightful meadow. Every valley and piece of low ground or gentle slope, all the plains composed of fine red sand, as well as the rifts and heights are at once covered with an infinite variety of annuals and perennials. The camels nibble at the greatest dainties only and grow so fat that they can hardly move. The milk often flows or drips from the udders of the she-camels, which are full to overflowing; the mares and foals roll about in the thickest grass and the Bedouins, men, women, old people, and children, have more sweet or sour milk and camel's fat than they know what to do with. . . . In a territory where there is a *rabi'* [abundance] tents can be seen scattered all around. With plenty of good pasture close to their tents the herdsmen do not drive their camels far out. Pure cold rainwater can be found in every low-lying place, rock, crevice, and hole in the river beds. Everyone bathes, the clothes are washed, and parasites of all kinds destroyed. In the afternoons and evenings the young people hasten to the water holes. . . . They bathe separately, the youths in one place, the girls in another. Their shouts of joy and various songs are heard on all sides. In the tents mushrooms and truffles, young bulbs, and fresh vegetables are cooked and enjoyed.[47]

To the poet, such an abundance as produced by this storm would mean, among other things (or perhaps we should say primarily), ample opportunities to meet women. The poem itself suggests as much by the implied connection between the lightning and the ideal woman: both are compared to the glowing lamp of an anchorite (39, 68). The repetition provides a clue as to what the lightning portends. Literary tradition upholds the connection and so gives credence to this interpretation. Consider, for example, lines by the pre-Islamic poet al-Nabigha (d. ca. 604):

Is it a flicker from the lightning flash my eyes see,
or the radiance of Nu'm, or the glow of a fire?

Nay! It is the radiance of Nu'm shining in the murky night
through her robes and curtains.[48]

Based on his record, our poet could surely expect romantic success in the new environment. The excitement expressed in line 67 by his eagerness to point out lightning flashes, and palpable in the charged final description, hence can be attributed, more than to the spontaneous reaction of a sensitive observer to a natural spectacle, to the poet's dawning realization of what now, in all probability, lies ahead: a new beloved. Such an optimistic ending indeed comes as a surprise—notwithstanding all the structural indicators presaging it—after a beginning and a long middle in which gloom reigns. In this light, the *Mu'allaqa* may be read as the poet's triumph over grief; joy, after a terrific struggle, conquers despair. The final triumph is underscored by key movements traceable through the course of the poem: from low in a desert to high on a mountain; from under brackish water to a vantage point looking down on sweet water; from day to night to new day. Mindful of the changes, does one need ask what have become of the previous day's *atlal*, reminders of the lost beloved?

Given all this, it comes as a further surprise that structuralist critics have called the ending "open." Barbara Herrnstein Smith, in *Poetic Closure: A Study of How Poems End,* notes that "the sense of closure is a function of the perception of structure."[49] The last section of the *Mu'allaqa* completes the circle in a multilayered fashion. As we mentioned, in it the poet returns to current reality and the company of his friends. Here also we encounter a profusion of place-names and see evidence of nature's effects on the landscape. In particular, images of weaving in both sections give an idea of nature's unfolding design (2, 75). Even the internal structure of A^1 corresponds to the arrangement of A. Each section begins with a forewarning of precipitation, proceeds to a temporary uncertainty as to where it may happen, and culminates in a tremendous flood.

The ending also highlights an expansion and extension of the poet's vision, coinciding with an implicit adjustment to his view of the beloved. At the abandoned campsite where the ode opens, the poet points out to his friend the dung of gazelles. The focus on a small detail immediately in front of him reflects the great personal importance he attaches to these encampment traces. On the other hand, when he again says "*tara*" to his friend at the sight of lightning, he looks out across a vast distance. A bountiful spring is approaching, and the beloved will go from being his obsession to taking her place among bittersweet memories. He finally sees the big picture.

On a deeper level, the ending bespeaks the poet's acquisition of a healthy perspective on himself and his place in the world, a process begun in B^1. His vaunted capabilities are nothing against nature's awesome power. A relinquishment of control parallels the poet's implicit realization of his relative powerlessness. In the first scene (with the first two words of the poem, in fact), he tries to shape events by ordering his friends to stop and cry. His attempts at control continue through the middle sections by the imposition and maintenance of a rigorous program of mental therapy. But at the end, he can do no more than watch in amazement. The awareness of his own limitations, one infers, enables him to understand that there comes a time for letting go. Joy in the *Mu'allaqa* ultimately is found serendipitously, not achieved by an act of will. However, before he has reached this stage where he may find happiness, he has done what justly could be expected of him: he has chosen receptivity to change despite his heart's reluctance and earnestly sought release from torment. Again, Samuel Johnson: "Of every great and complicated event, part depends on causes out of our power, and part must be effected by vigor and perseverance."[50] If we do our part, the poet seems to be saying, if we struggle to overcome a great loss, the future just might be promising. Sometimes the heavens pour life-giving rain.

SUMMARY: THE *MUʿALLAQA* OF IMRUʾ AL-QAYS

Section	Lines	Structural and Thematic Elements	
A	1–9	*scene with friends* place-names nature changes landscape; weaving *tara* (myopia) forewarning → uncertainty re: location → downpour TEARS	present → past (*sadness*)
B	10–41	*positive reflection:* poet audacious, irresistible to women, resilient after setbacks (Virility) *a-la rubba, waw rubba* virgins, feast long description of ideal woman	past
C	42	*personal statement* poet different from other men: heart will never be consoled for lost beloved	present & future (*hopelessness*)
B¹	43–66	*positive reflection:* poet fends off nagging critics, endures trials, rides a great horse (Fortitude) *a-la rubba, waw rubba, wa-qad* + imperfect virgins, feast long description of ideal horse	past
A¹	67–78	*scene with friends* place-names nature changes landscape; weaving *tara* (farsightedness) forewarning → uncertainty re: location → downpour RAIN	present → future (*joy*)

2

An Outcast Replies

Everywhere the American writer is being dunned to become healthy, to grow
up, to accept the American reality, to integrate himself. . . . Is there nothing
to remind us that the writer does not need to be integrated into his society,
and often works best in opposition to it?

—NORMAN MAILER, 1952 *Partisan Review* symposium,
"Our Country and Our Culture"

OUR SECOND ODE comes to us from the most famous *suʿluk* (brigand) poet of
the pre-Islamic era, al-Shanfara. He is thought to have lived a generation before
the Prophet Muhammad (b. 569/70) and to have been from the tribe of al-Azd,
which occupied the coastal area to the south of Mecca. From his poems, we
understand that at some point he offended his tribe and was forced out into the
desert. This punishment typically followed one of three offenses: disgracing the
tribe by immoral conduct, killing one of its members, or dragging it into insup-
portable conflict with other tribes by repeated provocative acts. Assuming that
he paints an accurate picture of himself, we can at least exclude the first possibility from consideration. The stories of his life indicate that his tribal situation
became untenable when he began a ferocious attack on the related clan of Salaman and attribute his motive variously to resentment at being spurned by one of
their women and to revenge for the murder of his father by one of their men. In
any case, after ostracism he lived perilously as a *suʿluk*. He seems to have gathered
around him a number of fellow outcasts, whom on occasion he led in raids. His
end almost certainly came violently, if not in the manner traditionally described:

His oath was that he would slay a hundred men of Salaman; he slew ninety-
eight, when an ambush of his enemies succeeded in taking him prisoner. In the
struggle one of his hands was hewn off by a sword stroke, and taking it in the
other he flung it in the face of a man of Salaman and killed him, thus making

ninety-nine. Then he was overpowered and slain, with one still wanting to make up his number. As his skull lay bleaching on the ground, a man of his enemies passed by that way and kicked it with his foot: a splinter of bone entered his foot, the wound mortified, and he died, thus completing the hundred.[1]

Though al-Shanfara's biography remains conjectural, based necessarily on clues from the poems rather than on popular stories, there can be no doubt about the exalted position within the canon of his desert ode, which has earned the title *Lamiyyat al-'Arab* (The L-Poem of the Arabs, *L* being the rhyme consonant). Nevertheless, during the past two centuries it has attracted familiar criticism and controversy. Critics have faulted it for alleged disorder. Among them, Francesco Gabrieli has denied that the text constitutes a proper poem and has characterized it instead as an anthology.[2] J. W. Redhouse, who concluded that "the whole poem is shattered into dislocated fragments, entirely void of interdependence," went so far as to rearrange the lines into a supposedly more rational progression. He did so on the assumption that the poem at one time exhibited unity that was later obscured by "the blunderings of successive generations of commentators and translators, blindly following in each other's footsteps."[3] Unhappily for Redhouse's hypothesis, there is no evidence of textual mutilation: early editions conform, with little or no variation, with later ones.

Grave concerns about the poem's authenticity have also been voiced. It had been asserted by an early philologist that Khalaf al-Ahmar (d. 796), a prominent Basran transmitter (and notorious fabricator) of poetry, produced the *Lamiyyat al-'Arab*.[4] Few commentators from the classical period were impressed by this claim—indeed, the vast majority ignored it—yet it has excited considerable interest during the modern period. It would not be worth our while to recount the lengthy debate over authenticity, particularly since 'Abd al-Halim Hifni's cogent rebuttal has made it difficult for us to take the positions of those individuals attributing the poem to Khalaf al-Ahmar seriously.[5] That their case was flimsy to begin with was in fact recognized by Lyall; in 1918 he noted the improbability of the Basran transmitter's having the requisite genius and desert expertise to create the *Lamiyya*.[6] Recent findings have further undermined their argument from a historical standpoint. Alan Jones has discovered allusions to al-Shanfara's poem by both al-Akhtal (d. ca. 710) and Dhu al-Rumma (d. 735) that long precede Khalaf al-Ahmar, and Albert Arazi has shown that at least one other eighth-century transmitter knew the

Lamiyya and attributed it to al-Shanfara.[7] With confidence, we may finally dismiss the claim of Khalaf al-Ahmar's authorship and declare the case closed.

Let us now turn our attention to the ode itself, al-Shanfara's dramatic response to persons who would see him exposed to a ghastly fate. In keeping with the method established in the previous chapter, we will discuss the sections as we proceed through the poem, then supply at the end a structural and thematic summary illustrating its overall unity.

The *Lamiyya* may be divided into eleven sections as follows:

A	1–4
B	5–13
C	14–20
D	21–25
E	26–31
F	32–35
E[1]	36–41
D[1]	42–48
C[1]	49–53
B[1]	54–64
A[1]	65–68[8]

A

1   Raise, O sons of my mother, the chests of your riding mounts,
     for I incline to a tribe other than you.

2   For the night is moonlit and the provisions are at hand,
     and beasts have been saddled and loaded for expeditions.

3   This earth affords a refuge for the noble man,
     for him who dreads contempt, a place to withdraw.

4   By your life, it does not confine a man
     who travels out of hope or fear, if he keeps his wits about him.

B

5   I have closer relatives than you:
     a swift wolf; a sleek, spotted panther, and a shaggy-maned hyena.

6   They are family; none broadcasts an entrusted secret
     or forsakes the offender for what he has done.

7   Each is proud, brave—except that when the first of the prey appear,
     I am braver.

8   And when hands reach out for food, mine is not the fastest,
     for then the greediest clansman is fastest.

9   This only indicates the measure of my superiority to them;
     the most virtuous lets others help themselves.

10   Verily, to make up for the loss of those who hoard favors
     and give no comfort,

11   I have three companions: a brave heart; a shiny, drawn sword;
     and a tawny, long-necked bow,

12   Smooth and taut, resonant,
     complete with a carrying-strap and ornamental ties,

13   And when an arrow slips from it, the bow twangs
     like a woman bereft of her child, moaning and wailing.

The *Lamiyyat al-'Arab* opens with one of the most striking first lines in all of Arabic poetry. With one imperative and explanatory statement al-Shanfara explodes the ethical core of the tribal system. Kinship loyalty holds together the tribe, of course, and the closer the relation between two members of the extended family, the tighter the bond. This ethos is concisely summed up in the saying, "My brother and I against my cousin; My cousin and I against a stranger." But al-Shanfara drives off the very closest of his blood relations—those kin from the same womb—and declares that he opts for a tribe of his own choosing. Moreover, he flips poetic convention on its head. Through the *za'n* (departure) motif a poet normally begins his ode with an expression of pained reluctance. He desperately wants the beloved to stay, even though inevitably she must go with her tribe. Upon seeing the camels moving out, the poet is wont to let down a cascade of tears. Al-A'sha (d. ca. 625) has evoked this emotionally charged moment in the opening line of his *Mu'allaqa:*

Say farewell to Hurayra, for the caravan is getting underway;
But O man, can you stand to say farewell?[9]

Al-Shanfara, on the other hand, evinces no reluctance or sadness. Rather, he orders the riding party to leave and affirms that he will be happier without them. Finally, the line comes across all the more thunderously to one familiar with al-Shanfara's background. (Since al-Shanfara was such a famous *su'luk,* we can assume that most listeners were well acquainted with his circumstances.) In this instance, the abhorred outcast turns the tables on the tribe: he repudiates them. One can only imagine the jolt this line sent through early audiences!

Despite the strong show of defiance at the beginning, al-Shanfara exposes an area of personal vulnerability in lines 3–4. He intimates that opprobrium from his original family does affect him, and he makes clear that he wishes to avoid it. The poet is only human, after all. Tarafa (d. ca. 560), a precocious poet who was seemingly chased away by his family for profligate behavior (he asserts that it was for tremendous generosity), experienced similar injury and complained:

> Injustice from kinsmen is more painful to a man
> than the stroke of an Indian sword.[10]

Yet for the shrewd *su'luk* the earth affords a refuge. In pointing to a safe zone al-Shanfara indicates that obloquy and the possibility of violent retribution are limited to the tribal circle. Society covers just part of the land; beyond the social perimeter, in nature, he may find accommodation.

We learn in section B of his preferred kin. They are nocturnal predators with whom he has an affinity, as we shall see in section B¹. These animals do not abandon a member of the group for the wrongs he has committed. One may play the devil's advocate and note that for this reason they are a convenient match for al-Shanfara and then ask pointedly how he might benefit them. Surely, the tribal members would be asking themselves the same question about the foreigner introducing himself and perhaps wondering uneasily if he would become a burden. Al-Shanfara speaks to this matter and clarifies that he will join the group as a *provider.* Furthermore, he will bring to the group human virtues.[11] After making the risky kill, he will be the one to hold back and let the others consume. Greedy and voracious animals would appreciate such restraint in a clan member.

Al-Shanfara points out that he also has close companions to make up for the loss of selfish and unresponsive ones from among the tribe. The three intimates complement the three animals of his new kin. Even so, the fact that his friends are not creatures tells us that the poet is basically a loner. Given his precarious state, he understandably views as close companions his weapons and the heart that enables him to use them. For close combat, when necessary, he has a sword. But because he is distancing himself from society, he devotes most attention to that friend who allows him to strike from afar.[12] It is almost human in the wailing sound it makes after releasing an arrow. The simile helps us to imagine the deep reverberation of a tightly strung longbow and likewise suggests noises that will be coming from the other direction once the effect of the arrow release is known.

C

14   I am not one quick to thirst, pasturing his herd at night,
      whose young camels get no milk though their mothers' udders are untied.[13]

15   Nor am I a dim-witted coward, cleaving to his wife,
      consulting her about how to proceed in his affairs;

16   Nor a frightened ostrich, whose heart flutters,
      as though in it a sparrow beat up and down;

17   Nor a worthless laggard who stays in his tent, flirting, spending morning
      and evening
      daubing his hair with grease and applying *kohl* to his eyelids;

18   Nor a weak and puny man, more harm than good,
      who leaps up when startled, unarmed.

19   Nor am I baffled by the darkness
      when it descends on a bewildered traveler in a wayless desert.

20   When the hard flintstones come in contact with my camel pads,
      sparks and chips fly.

D

21   I drag out hunger until it dies;
      I turn from the thought and forget.

22   I'd sooner eat dust
      than accept some man's condescending favors.

23   Were it not for my shunning of blame, no comfortable verdant area or
      drinking place
      would be found, without me there.

24   But a proud spirit does not let me remain in blame—
      I must move around.

25   I twist my guts around an empty stomach,
      as a rope maker twists firmly and tightly his strands.

Section C is a continuation of A and B in terms of the rhetorical situation. Factually speaking, the poem was probably first recited among fellow brigands, who committed it to memory and passed it on to other circles. Eventually (or perhaps quite soon), it reached society. In the first part of the poem, however, al-Shanfara is addressing his former tribe. He states what he is not, illuminating his character by negation, and implies that "men" answering to such descriptions may be found in their midst. Unlike these contemptible individuals, he can take the heat, make decisions on his own, help out in a fight. Although he possesses no camel, he manages very well in the trackless wastes without one. Endurance, independence, courage, desert savoir-faire, not to mention generosity (which he has exemplified in B)—these traits are all fundamental virtues in a Bedouin context. So if the tribe does not recognize them in his character, then they must be morally blind. Al-Shanfara reveals his disgust here, which is causing him to go off on his own. Scrofulous society has singled out the truly virtuous for censure. In Mark Twain's novel, the closing words of young Huck Finn, shamed and rebuked by proper white folk for assisting a slave in his bid for freedom, might have a familiar ring: "But I reckon I got to light out for the Territory ahead of the rest, because aunt Sally she's going to adopt me and sivilize me and I can't stand it. I been there before."[14] Notwithstanding circumstantial differences (society still offers Huck the possibility of redeeming himself and becoming an upstanding member, for one), in essence the protagonist's sentiments are those of al-Shanfara.

Al-Shanfara goes on to explain how he deals with the reality he faces as an individual in the desert. After a declamatory first three sections, the tone and subject matter become more personal in D. He suppresses persistent hunger and ultimately suffocates it through willpower and conscious neglect. Thus, he preserves his freedom, acquiring no obligations of gratitude or repayment. His proud spirit also keeps him from settling at any fertile spot. As one would expect of an outcast, he associates blame with places of congregation. Water holes, in particular, seem to connote vulnerability. In another ode, as proof of his fortitude, he reports that many a water hole, as dreadful as a stomach illness or more dreadful, he has approached.[15] Dwelling at a convenient location means he will be joined before too long and persecuted. Therefore, he must move around.

E

26   I set out in the early morning on scanty fare,
      like the gray, narrow-hipped wolf, which the deserts pass from one to another.

27   He sets out at dawn, hungry, nose to the wind, light-footed,
         swooping down into the ravines and hurrying along.

28   He advances toward food, and it eludes him.
         Then he calls out, and rawboned counterparts respond;

29   Slender, white-faced, like arrow shafts
         shuffled in the hands of the *maysir* dealer;[16]

30   Or a swarm of bees roused by sticks
         that a honey gatherer has poked into the hive;

31   Wide-mouthed, as though their jaws were the sides of split wood,
         grimacing, fierce.

F

32   Then he howls and they howl in the open desert,
         like bereaved women lamenting from a high place.

33   He stands blinking and they stand blinking; he takes comfort in them and
            they in him:
         destitutes he consoles and a destitute they console.

34   He complains and they complain, then he desists and they desist—
         for surely when complaint does no good, patience is better.

35   He returns and they return, hastening along,
         each one, despite his hunger, carrying on decently and concealing it.

In section E al-Shanfara begins an extended wolf simile through which he represents his hungry pursuit of food. The wolf travels into the wind so he may smell his prey and not vice versa. When the hunt fails, he calls gaunt mates to the scene. These other wolves are metaphors for the poet's *su'luk* comrades. Their bodies resemble arrows or, one could say, the slender, slightly curved shapes of bees. Both the images of *maysir* arrows being shuffled and honeybees swarming suggest aggregation and agitated collective movement. They also suggest food, but no description of a feast follows. The poet proceeds to describe the wolves' mouths, grim and unfilled.

It may reasonably be argued that lines 32–35 form part of section E, as they contain the conclusion to the extended wolf simile. Here one observes a slight thematic shift, however, from the disappointing hunt to the wolves' collective reaction. In addition, the language becomes highly stylized, and on this basis especially it would appear correct to consider lines 32–35 a discrete unit. The four lines offset each other through a series of repetitions: of one verb in the first hemistichs of the outer lines (32 and 35), and of two verbs in the first hemistichs of the inner lines (33 and 34). Al-Shanfara reproduces this outer-inner symmetry on a smaller scale in the second hemistich of 33, by a variation on the figure *radd al-'ajuz 'ala al-sadr* (repetition of the first word in the last: *maramilu 'azzaha wa-'azzathu murmilu*). In pre-Islamic poetry highly stylized language—that is, more stylized than what the meter and rhyme require—is unusual, and its usage here attracts notice. Upon analysis, we discover in these lines chiastic order of decreasing separation, which finally terminates on the level of a single hemistich (one may represent these repetitions within the section as follows: a b [c d d c] b a). Structurally, this pattern would indicate that we are reaching the center of the poem.

The artful deployment of language in section F invites further consideration. In *Al-'Umda,* rhetorician Ibn Rashiq (d. 1064) notes that repetition, though answerable to a variety of poetic purposes, most befits elegy.[17] In line 33 the verbs for taking comfort and giving consolation (*ittasa* and *'azza*) befit elegy as well, as do the active participles *murmil/maramil* (destitute(s), translatable as "widower(s)"). Preceding this line, in connection to the wolves, al-Shanfara mentions bereaved women, and following it he offers words of wisdom (*hikma*), a familiar recourse of pre-Islamic poets after expressions of lamentation. To the attuned ear, the language has deep elegiac resonance. This emphasis is doubtless intended: the wolves have lost a meal, which hurts as much as the loss of a loved one.

Although in the wild a wolf will cry in the early morning if it has passed the night without finding anything to eat, what concerns us besides verisimilitude is what the scene discloses of al-Shanfara and his fellow outcasts. First, it demonstrates the brigands' solidarity. The other wolves respond immediately to their mate's call, and when assembled they console each other over the joint loss. It also highlights al-Shanfara's leadership position; the first wolf sets an example that the pack follows. Al-Shanfara elsewhere speaks openly of the authority he wields among bounty seekers, referring to the raiding party he spearheads as his "flock of birds."[18] Last, it shows the outcasts' adoption of stoicism, and their brave comportment, in the face of misfortune. To be sure, their lot was not easy. But these wolves, after giving natural vent to grief, see no use in continued complaint when it will not change anything. Containing their intense hunger, they return their separate ways, paragons of seemly behavior.

E[1]

36   The dusky sand grouse drink my dregs,
      after traveling all night to the water, their sides reverberating.

37   We fixed our intention and raced; then their wings sagged while my garment
           was tucked;
      and I got to the water hole first, though I was going at an easy pace.

38   I turned away as they were collapsing at its edge,
      their chins and crops touching the water.

39   Their clamor surrounding the water hole
      was like that of caravans from various tribes stopping there.

40   They converged from all sides and it drew them in,
      as a water hole gathers droves of camels.

41   They gulped hastily, then took off in the morning,
      like a riding party of Uhaza moving out swiftly.[19]

In contrast to the wolf's disappointing hunt, al-Shanfara's race to the water ends in success. The victory over the sand grouse attests to the poet's amazing speed, for which he became proverbial (thus, the hyperbolic expression, *a'da min ash-Shanfara*, "fleeter afoot than al-Shanfara").[20] We infer that for winning the race he gets to enjoy clear, delicious water at the pool. This privilege is a boasting point in classical Arabic poetry. Imru' al-Qays, we recall, indicates of the ideal woman that she has access to unsullied water (*Mu'allaqa*, line 41), and 'Amr ibn Kulthum asserts in praise of his tribe:

When we come to the water we drink it fresh,
   whereas others drink it stirred and muddy.[21]

Hence, al-Shanfara, meritorious for holding back while others reach for food, here emphasizes his superior position by drinking first. We also imagine the poet's dignified, calm manner at the pool, as opposed to the frenzied gulping and noisiness of the sand grouse. The invidious comparison clearly extends to a tribal grouping, who are drawn in by repeated association with the dregs-imbibing birds (39, 41). And from the mention of Uhaza, a branch of al-Azd, one might logically conclude that al-Shanfara has his own tribe in mind.

The uproarious poolside behavior of the sand grouse may seem strange, if effective for satiric application. But it appears to have a basis in reality, judging from a firsthand report by Jibrail Jabbur:

When searching for sources of water, the sand grouse . . . usually flies from its nest in flocks, lands near the water, and then waddles and jostles the rest of the way and drinks its fill. If it gulps the water down it will not be satisfied to drink once, but will stand around the pool and drink several times, or fly and glide around it for awhile, return to gulp a second time, and then fly and return yet again, all the while calling, squawking, and making noise. If it is left undisturbed at the pool for a long period, so many scores of sand grouse will flock around the water and along its banks that the ground will be completely covered with birds—as if a swarm of locusts had arrived or a colorful carpet had been spread over it.[22]

Increasingly, we gain appreciation for al-Shanfara's use of simile and metaphor. As reports such as Jabbur's verify, the descriptions correspond to their originals in precise detail. By the same token, they carry symbolic meanings—at times complimentary, at times belittling—that apply to those individuals concerned and illuminate the poet's situation.

D[1]

42   I am intimate with the earth's face when I take it as my bed,
       lying on a crooked back with dried-out vertebrae pushing through.

43   I rest my head on a forearm, worn to the bone,
       as though its joints, standing out, were dice cast by a gambler.

44   So if Umm Qastal[23] is saddened by al-Shanfara now,
       long was her delight in him before.

45   His crimes follow him.
       They cast lots for the choicest portion of his carcass.

46   Whenever he sleeps, they sleep with eyes open,
       moving in nimbly to do him harm.

47   I am a close friend to anxieties, which revisit me repeatedly
       like a quartan fever, or are more difficult to bear.

48   When they draw near I repel them,
       and then they return, coming at me from above and just below.

C[1]

49   So if you see me, like the daughter of the sand,[24]
       thin and exposed to the sun, barefoot and not putting on sandals,

50   Know that I am the master of endurance:
      I drape its cloth over a desert cat's heart, and wear resolution on my feet.
51   I am sometimes poor, sometimes rich; and riches are attained
      only by him who goes to great lengths and gives generously of himself.
52   I neither become distraught at lack, and expose my destitution,
      nor exult beneath wealth's trappings and strut pompously.
53   Follies do not carry away my self-control,
      nor am I seen chasing conversations and backbiting.

Al-Shanfara returns in section D¹ to the subject of his difficult existence, with its privation and foreboding. Here he graphically outlines the effect on his body of prolonged hunger—or more correctly, given his portrayal, of starvation. He also brings into especially bold relief his close relationship with nature, a relationship that the entire *Lamiyya* celebrates. Literally, nothing comes between him and the earth. The personal tone becomes pronounced in line 44, in which al-Shanfara reflects wistfully on his past, and it remains so through the rest of the section. There was no possibility of his rejoining the tribe; his days of battlefield heroism, of pleasing Umm Qastal, were over. Time was moving inexorably forward, and in his new identity as a *su'luk* he could not expect to live long. From the poet's rueful perception of closure and his ensuing apprehension we sense particularly strongly his humanity. Samuel Johnson has observed that "the termination of any period of life reminds us that life itself has likewise its termination; when we have done anything for the last time, we involuntarily reflect that a part of the days allotted us is past, and that as more is past there is less remaining."[25] Thus, the recollection that his warrior days have come to an end leads, as one might anticipate, to thoughts about his impending doom. He is now like the camel designated for slaughter, over whose flesh eager players draw lots. The only unanswered question is which of those persons seeking his death will get to claim him.

Al-Shanfara has been widely praised for his ability to evoke a scene, and in lines 46–48 he provides a testament to his skill. (One could cite in this regard many exemplary passages in the *Lamiyyat al-'Arab,* starting with the opening lines depicting the tribe's readiness for departure.) While the poet sleeps, specters from his past eye him and close in stealthily. Grave anxieties of similar import presumably come around at night as well. They are like a malarial fever that revisits every fourth night, bringing increased misery and often death in the end. Evidently, the poet, whether asleep or awake, spends many restless nights. Nor can he lessen the mental anguish by willpower. Line 48 conveys this idea vividly through the account of frustration in driving away haunting thoughts. The verb choice *warada* (to go to a water hole, that is, to draw near) and *asdara* (to send away from a water hole, that is, to repel) sets the scene, conjuring the location in which al-Shanfara feels acutely vulnerable. When the worries approach from all sides, he beats them back horizontally. At this stage one imagines the poet on maximum alert, swiveling his head in all directions. But the worries take him by surprise and reattack vertically, from above and just below. Now we envision the poet with a shiver gone down his spine, stomping furiously on his tormentors and frantically swatting them from his hair. In three dimensions we visualize his struggle and perceive that such relentless and enveloping worries cannot be kept at bay.

From quite private reflection al-Shanfara turns outward in section C¹ and addresses himself to a woman (*fa-imma tarayni*, "if you see me"). This petition may be a generic form of address similar to the one used in line 4 to a man (*la-'amruka*, "by your life"). On the other hand, al-Shanfara may well have an individual in mind. Regardless, we can safely assume from the tone and content of this section that the apostrophized woman shares the tribe's disdain for al-Shanfara. He forcefully directs to her words of self-praise and indirect tribal criticism of the kind encountered earlier in the poem, as if in reply to her misplaced censure. He continues in this vein until the end of the ode, enumerating to his implied detractor—and the tribe by extension—his strengths and singular attributes. The beginning of section C¹ therefore marks a significant turning point in the poem, from personal vulnerability back to projected strength. Psychologically, we can interpret the transition as the poet's attempt, by means of affirmation, to pull himself from a gloomy state.

This determination to put on a brave face and to overcome disturbing thoughts, and the extraordinary fortitude he speaks of in lines 50–51, places al-Shanfara in a class with heroes such as Tennyson's Ulysses, men possessed of the will "To strive, to seek, to find, and not to yield."[26] But one need not revisit ancient Greece to locate comparable figures to al-Shanfara. Closer to contemporary experience, the nineteenth-century American Henry David Thoreau would seem to resemble him in numerous respects. Like the poet, Thoreau went into the wild (albeit voluntarily) to get away from society and live a simple life in harmony with nature. "It is life near the bone where it is sweetest," Thoreau writes in *Walden,* the account of his two-year sojourn in the Massachusetts woods by Walden Pond. He strove similarly to exceed conventional bounds, leaving behind an inspiring example and emboldening words that echo line 51: "In the long run men hit only what they aim at. Therefore, though they should fail immediately, they had better aim at something high." And like al-Shanfara, Thoreau was indifferent to material wealth. "Money," Thoreau declared, "is not required to buy one necessary of the soul." Distant from inhabited areas, he recalled with contempt the gossip that passed as news and animated society. Thoreau was above trivial concerns and sought instead authentic, direct contact with the essential facts of life.[27]

However interesting and illuminating it may be to find kindred spirits to al-Shanfara in different times and places, we should not neglect to try to understand him in his own context. Accordingly, it is instructive to juxtapose his *Lamiyya* with the locus classicus of pre-Islamic tribal sentiment, the *Mu'allaqa* of 'Amr ibn Kulthum (fl. ca. 568). In the *Mu'allaqa,* 'Amr ibn Kulthum lauds his tribe for displaying many of the virtues that, here, al-Shanfara highlights in himself: toughness, courage, generosity, independence. The signal difference between the poems, of course, is that one celebrates a tribe, the other an individual. Albert Arazi has pointed to the latter emphasis, as observed in the high number of pronouns and verbs in the first-person singular (more than thirty in the first fifty lines).[28] By contrast, we count in the last fifty lines of 'Amr ibn Kulthum's *Mu'allaqa* more than thirty pronouns or verbs in the first-person plural, through which 'Amr stresses the group. Another important difference between the poems lies in the professed basis for glory. In the case of the *Mu'allaqa,* the tribe's renown stems from its members' illustrious ancestors. 'Amr articulates this idea in the first half of the poem ("We inherited glory") and then returns to it emphatically in the second ("We inherited the glory of [so-and-so]"; "How excellent is the store of [honor of] those [predecessors] who saved it up!"; "from them we acquired the legacy of the noblest"; "by [so-and-so's honor] we are protected"; "So what glory is there except that with which we have been entrusted?!").[29] In these lines, 'Amr is laying emphasis on the second of the two components of nobility for the pre-Islamic Arabs, *nasab* (the other being *hasab*—the two are coupled in the term *hasab wa-nasab*). *Nasab* denotes the collective prestige conferred by outstanding bloodlines. To this distinction the tribe added continuously *hasab,* or nobility gained through meritorious acts, which 'Amr amply testifies to elsewhere in the poem. Unlike *nasab, hasab* could also be acquired by an individual. Al-Shanfara, as an outcast, can claim no ancestral renown; he cannot even claim distinction by relation to an honored father or brother. His glory derives solely from his *hasab,* nobility that he must earn on his own, nobility that he must prove in deed.

Interestingly, in his stress on personal as opposed to tribal virtue, al-Shanfara anticipates a major change in orientation brought about by Islam. The Prophet Muhammad proclaimed a spiritual message of individual responsibility and uttered to his companions, "Whosoever is slowed down [that is, on his path to Paradise] by his actions will not be hastened forward by his lineage" (*nasab*).[30] In behavior, al-Shanfara also conforms closely to models outlined later in the Qur'an. Jacob, when told of the loss of his son Joseph, adopts as his course comely patience (*sabr jamil,* Qur'an 12:18; compare Lamiyya line 34). The Qur'an assures one that all happens according to God's plan and that the righteous shall one day be rewarded, "so that you may not despair over what passes you by, nor exult over what you are given" (Qur'an 57:23; compare *Lamiyya,* line 52). In recognition of al-Shanfara's exemplary behavior as described in this poem, the Prophet purportedly said, "Teach your children the *Lamiyyat al-'Arab,* for it teaches them noble manners."[31] Although this tradition is not included in either of the two authoritative hadith collections (al-Bukhari's and Muslim's) and, therefore, is suspect, the mere fact that someone ascribed the saying to the Prophet suggests a perceived resemblance between al-Shanfara's conduct and the actions promoted by Islam.

Nonetheless, we should be wary of making too much of a few similarities and simply viewing al-Shanfara as a man a generation or so ahead of his time. Essentially, he was a man of his era, though an atypical one. His chief virtues, we have said, were those characteristics prized by his society (in principle, at least, if not always in practice). Furthermore, the pre-Islamic Arabs thought highly of persistence in revenge, as an element of *hamasa* (manly verve and courage), whereas in Islam personal revenge is discouraged: retaliatory punishment becomes the concern of a constituted legal authority, who metes it out in proportion to the crime committed.[32] As we shall soon see, al-Shanfara takes matters into his own hands—at exorbitant cost to his enemies—and certainly feels no remorse about doing so.

B¹

54 On many a cold, foreboding night on which the possessor of the bow
    warms himself by burning it and his arrow wood,

55 I have trodden in the dark and drizzle,
    my companions hunger, cold, fear and trembling,

56 And made women widows and children orphans,
    then returned as I had set out while the night was still dark.

57 In the morning there were two parties sitting at al-Ghumaysaʾ:
    one asking about me, the other being asked.

58 They said, "Our dogs growled in the night."
    We replied, "Was it a wolf prowling or a young hyena?"

59 "But it was only low noise, then they went back to sleep."
    "Was it a sand grouse that was startled or a hawk?"

60 "If it was one of the jinn paying a night visit, then he came bringing
        misfortune."
    "If it was a man—men do not act like that!"

61 Many a dog day on which the air threads rise,
    and the vipers on the scorched earth squirm,

62 I have faced head on, with no veil to protect me
    nor any covering except a tattered cloak,

63 And long, abundant, uncombed hair;
    when the wind gusts, matted clumps fly up from the sides.

64 Long since the touch of grease or a delouser's hand,
    it is caked with dirt, for a year unwashed.

A¹

65 Many a windswept desert like the back of a shield, untrodden,
    I have crossed on two legs,

66 Then, looking from a mountain summit, now squatting, now standing,
    I have joined its beginning to its end.

67 The dust-colored female ibex roam around me,
    like virgins trailing long-trained gowns.

68 They settle down around me in the early evenings,
    as if I were a white-legged male with long horns, heading for the ledge,
        unassailable.

In section B¹, al-Shanfara offers proof of the fortitude and perseverance of which he spoke in the preceding section. Neither of the desert extremes of bitter cold at night and intense heat in the day keeps him from an objective. To give an idea of the extreme temperatures, the poet supplies telling details. The possessor of the bow, in this case al-Shanfara before he sets out on a mission, must sacrifice his weapon to prevent hypothermia. By day, the poet faces the opposite danger. Snakes are cold-blooded; they seek the sun to elevate their body temperatures. But these vipers are writhing. In these conditions, al-Shanfara persists.

To the woe of his enemies, one endeavor he persists in is revenge. The early-morning confusion at al-Ghumaysa' is conveyed through fancied dialogue. In lines 58–59 the survivors—still apparently oblivious to what has befallen their kinsmen—inquire about the strange noise that momentarily woke the guard dogs. The second question, about a startled sand grouse or hawk, would seem to come closer to guessing the nature of the sound. But with our better knowledge of the night's events, we presume that it was probably the half-cry of a man, suddenly and eternally silenced. By line 60 an awareness of the destruction has come over the two parties. Yet futilely they grapple with its mysterious cause. For our part, we know of the agent of destruction only; exactly what happened in the tents is left to our imagination. Did al-Shanfara smite his victims bluntly, or cut their lifelines with surgical precision, or perhaps employ some other method on them too awful for conception? We cannot answer this question. All we can be sure of is that, after he has visited, his enemies lie dead.

It has been cited in objection to the *Lamiyyat al-'Arab*'s authenticity that unlike most pre-Islamic odes, the said ode lacks place-names.[33] It contains none but al-Ghumaysa', designating a place in the Sarat Mountains in the vicinity of Mecca. This argument against the authorship of al-Shanfara is plainly absurd. Why would a fugitive poet report his whereabouts? His poem was going out into a decidedly hostile world. By keeping his locations secret, in fact, he not only protects himself but also adds an element of surprise to his attacks. No one can gauge the proximity of the lurking *su'luk*. In the ode it is the absence of markers besides al-Ghumaysa', no less, that gives us a sense of al-Shanfara's stealthiness. The poet comes out of nowhere, strikes civilization, and then slips back into the obscurity whence he came.

His steadily improving camouflage contributes to his stealthiness. Indeed, in the last two sections, we witness the poet undergoing a physical transformation into a creature of the wild. He begins by shedding the appurtenances of civilization. He burns the bow and evidently puts down the sword, since his companions are now hunger, cold, and fear. We should note that spiritually, however, al-Shanfara remains very much a human. An animal would not persistently seek revenge. Nor in all likelihood would a frightened animal continue forward, whereas our poet overcomes his fear and presses on. To return to al-Shanfara's metamorphosis: throughout his arduous travels, the poet's clothing is disintegrating, and his shaggy, lousy hair is growing. By the time he has climbed the mountain and reached the summit area, al-Shanfara has become, for all practical purposes, an ibex. The most discriminating judges of what constitutes a mountain goat (that is, mountain goats themselves), who by nature are shy of humans, accept him as one of their own.[34]

In addition to suggesting the completed physical transformation, the ending also serves as reply to an implicit question relating to sex. We mentioned that the poet flips convention on its head in the very first line. He furthermore defies expectations at the beginning by not describing a beloved. In early Arabic odes that are not laments, a *nasib* (amatory prelude) is de rigueur; its omission raises eyebrows. Hence, we may say that, from the beginning of the poem, a lady is most conspicuously absent. It cannot be supposed, for that matter, that al-Shanfara was indifferent to women, since he composed what is regarded as one of the most beautiful erotic preludes in the corpus. The description concludes thusly:

She is petite and grand, svelte and shapely;
Could beauty transform a human into a jinni, then a jinni she would be.[35]

Through the course of the poem, al-Shanfara leaves no doubt about his possession of manly virtues—except whether he possesses virility. The symbolism of the conclusion removes any uncertainty on this score. In the wild, pairs of male ibex will face off in strength contests each autumn. As females watch, the males smash heads and lock horns until one surrenders or dies. The winner takes the attendant females—usually between five and fifteen—with him up into the mountains for the winter. Then, in late spring, young are born. Here al-Shanfara, like a victorious male, has the company of a goodly number of prospective mates. They move around him like virgins performing *tawaf*, or circumambulation of a sacred pillar.[36] He is their god.

On another level, the conclusion signifies safety for the poet. He has arrived at a place corresponding to the one alluded to at the beginning, distant from molestation and verbal assault. Mountaintops are choice spots for su'luk poets generally, offering inaccessibility and the benefits of a lookout. For ibex they are home, a fact that recommends the figurative association of a su'luk and his often real-life neighbors at a summit. The qualities of the ibex, we note, further recommend them for poetic usage by a frequent scamperer in the mountains. Like him, they are excellent climbers, wary, intelligent, and uneasy in the presence of humans. Symbolically, as regards a chief concern here of the poet, ibex are identified with isolation from danger. This quality makes them eminently suitable for inclusion at the end of the ode. Alois Musil refers to the security an ibex enjoys in its lofty habitat: "If it descends to the plain, it does not escape the dogs, but in the mountains it cannot be overtaken."[37] So agile and inaccessible are the ibex that they almost elude the claws of death. The pre-Islamic poet Muraqqish the Elder has expressed this idea, speculating:

> If any living thing could escape its fated day, then would escape
> the light-limbed mountain goat, banded with white streaks on its fore-legs.[38]

Even were a hunter able, by luck or great skill, to trap an ibex somewhere up in its domain, he could not consider the hunt over and the quarry taken. Muhammad Ummtayr explains:

> You must be careful handling ibex! The male is especially dangerous. He will first try to pick you up by getting the tips of his horns under your legs or hitting you to knock you off balance. If he gets you down he will crash his forehorns against you until you die. This happened once to a man named Salama. The ibex crushed his head and chest with its horns. He lived for a few hours and his wounds were treated but he soon died. Any male with his horns longer than two hand spans is dangerous like this. If you trap an ibex on a ledge, it will never try to run past you by taking the outside of the ledge. No matter how tightly you hug the wall the ibex will try to wedge himself between you and the wall and try to throw you to your death.[39]

So beware, O reckless fool, of pursuing al-Shanfara the ibex up in his refuge!

Al-Shanfara's worries, should they wish to trouble him now, likewise face a steep challenge and uncertain prospects. The ode ends at nightfall, at the time when the poet's anxieties apparently attack him. Yet here docile ibex settle down around him, evoking an ambience of profound calm. Far below, down by the water holes, we would imagine, the worries would have to begin a long and exhausting trek if they wanted to get at him. It seems that they would have to devise a new plan of attack as well. The poet speaks of heading for the ledge—obviously, he cannot be encircled there. And then there are those solicitous females to work through. Such trouble!

In reality, the poet, as a tribal outcast and renegade *su'luk,* was forever excluded from the company of lovely females. He lived on his own, physically vulnerable. Naturally, he was distracted by worry and haunted by thoughts of his approaching death. Poetically, however, at the end of this ode al-Shanfara is safe and sound at last. He has found a better tribe that accepts him as one of their own. What is more, they treat him with the respect he deserves. Finally, with his mates, he may turn to the pleasurable and life-perpetuating business of integration.

SUMMARY: THE *LAMIYYAT AL-ʿARAB* BY AL-SHANFARA

Section	Lines	Structural and Thematic Elements
A	1–4	[SEPARATION] caravan ready to leave, NO beloved; poet disaffected and disrespected
B	5–13	poet has wild kin (nocturnal predators), human values three companions: heart, sword, bow
C	14–20	*address to tribe* poet lambastes effeminate, excitable tribesmen
D	21–25	disclosure of strategies for suppressing hunger and avoiding blame
E	26–31	wolf's failed pursuit of food; agitation of hungry wolves
F	32–35	wolves grieve and console each other, then pull themselves together smartly and exhibit exemplary patience
E¹	36–41	poet's successful attainment of water; frenzy of thirsty sand grouse
D¹	42–48	description of hunger's effects on body and of unavoidable anxiety attacks
C¹	49–53	*address to woman/tribe* poet praises manly, steady self
B¹	54–64	poet becomes physically wild, remains spiritually human (nocturnal predation) three companions: fear, hunger, cold
A¹	65–68	[INTEGRATION] poet crosses deserts, arrives at refuge; MANY female ibex (preferred kin) circumambulate poet, settle down around him

3

The Price of Glory

The great poet, in writing himself, writes his time.

—T. S. ELIOT, "Shakespeare and the Stoicism of Seneca"

LABID IBN RABIʿA was a late pre-Islamic poet from the tribe of ʿAmir, which occupied territory in the high plateau of Najd to the northeast of Mecca. He was born in the second half of the sixth century and rose to prominence as an eloquent spokesperson for his tribe. During his lifetime, the new religion of Islam brought by the Prophet Muhammad (d. 632) spread across the Arabian Peninsula. Labid embraced Islam and then settled in the garrison town of Kufa, where he died ca. 661. It is said that Labid reached the very old age of 145 or 157 and that toward the end of his life he was visited by people of the younger generations eager to hear pre-Islamic lore. However, it seems that his birth has been pushed much too far back, probably to add authority to some of his reports about the early times. Ihsan ʿAbbas, drawing on accounts of a battle that Labid is supposed to have witnessed as a boy, places his birth close to the year 567.[1] This conjecture seems to be a reasonable approximation. If correct, it would mean that Labid lived into his early nineties—surely a mature age for a man of his era, but still one that is within the realm of possibility.

The ode before us most likely dates from a period around 600, when the poet had already distinguished himself in service of his tribe. That it was included among the Muʿallaqat testifies that Labid's contemporaries—or at least those persons responsible for recording and compiling the celebrated odes one century later—regarded it as a masterpiece. Unlike Imruʾ al-Qays's Muʿallaqa and al-Shanfara's Lamiyyat al-ʿArab, it has come through the modern period unscathed. In 1935 Taha Husayn, a skeptical and severe critic of pre-Islamic poetry generally, identified it as an exceptional poem that exhibits clear thematic unity.[2] More

46

recently, it has been the subject of several excellent studies that have outlined its structure and opened up avenues of interpretation. In particular, we mention the analysis by James T. Monroe, which highlighted the use of ring composition in the poem; the detailed structural analysis by Kamal Abu-Deeb; and the superb close reading according to the rite-of-passage model by Suzanne Pinckney Stetkevych.[3] The foregoing interpretation, though departing in a slightly new direction, clearly owes much to these preceding studies.

In the corpus of pre-Islamic poetry, Labid's *Muʿallaqa* has been seen as a quintessential work. German Orientalist Th. Nöldeke thought it one of the best specimens of Bedouin poetry, and Abu-Deeb has termed it "the key poem."[4] One should not view it as paradigmatic, since it came after most of the early odes, so much as, perhaps, best capturing the spirit of the age. We will read it, then, in attempting to understand and appreciate the poetic expression of one individual, and also to get a better sense for the pre-Islamic Arabian zeitgeist.

The five sections may be divided as follows:

A	1–10
B	11–35
C	36–52
B[1]	53–77
A[1]	78–88[5]

A

1   The campsites at Mina, both for brief stops and for long encampment, are effaced;

left to the wild the low areas and elevations;

2   And the flood channels of al-Rayyan—their trace is laid bare,
preserved like inscriptions carved on rock;

3   Dung-spattered ground over which, since it was peopled, years have passed,
months of war gone by, and months of peace.[6]

4   Mina has been replenished by the rain stars of spring, and struck by the outpouring:

the torrents and the steady drizzle,

5   From every traveling night-cloud and darkener of the morning,
and cloud whose rumble resounds across the evening sky.

6   Sprigs of rocket have shot up, and on both sides of the wadi
      ostriches and gazelles have brought forth their young.
7   And wide-eyed oryx stand peacefully over their newborn young,
      while in the open space yearlings cluster.
8   The torrents have exposed the remains,
      as if they were faded writings, whose texts reed pens have inscribed anew;
9   Or the tracings of a tattoo woman:
      beneath her indigo, sprinkled in spirals, the forms begin to reappear.
10   I stopped to question them. Yet how does one question
      deaf, permanent, inarticulate stones?

Labid begins his ode by describing the setting in which he finds himself. Spring has arrived in Mina, a place in Najd on the pilgrimage route from lower Mesopotamia and northeastern Arabia to Mecca. The campsites of a previous season, both those places for extended stays and those for brief sojourns (the latter used perhaps by travelers to and from Mecca), have been erased and brushed over. It shall be recalled, by way of heightening our awareness of seasonal associations to a Bedouin, that the tribes spent the hot, dry months isolated from each other at their permanent water sources. These locations, at the first signs of autumn, they would leave for the prospect of fresh pasture for their camel herds. "Canopus [appearing in the night sky in early October] has shown himself," Musil records the Rwala Bedouins as saying; "well, then, let us go into the inner desert."[7] There they would roam freely, stopping wherever they encountered an abundance of herbage. It was during the cool and relatively wet months, some of which coincided with the months of peace, that different tribes might camp in the same fertile area and unrelated individuals might be likely to meet. This happy state of affairs lasted until around mid-April, when heat and incipient drought put an end to congregation and drove the tribes back to their dispersed wells and water holes.[8]

With this pattern of experience in his background, the poet has come through, on his camel, to a familiar place. Several years ago, during this season of abundance, he spent time here. But the scene has changed markedly. Gone are the humans with their animals, gone are the black tents that dotted the valley and extended along the flood channels of yonder al-Rayyan. Since that spring, which ended with a gradual spread of barrenness, the valley has come back to life. Rains have fallen recently on Mina, and the place sprouts greenery and hosts varieties of fauna. Offspring are turning up left and right. The effect of this scene, to the lone poet looking on, is one of irony. Mina brims with life, yet at the same time lacks it. The presence of gazelles and oryxes is almost a cruel touch added by nature: these animals are the real antelope prancing around, not their adored figurative counterparts. We perceive from the stark contrast between past and present that human experience remains fixed in time, whereas nature continues in cycles.[9] Through it all, meanwhile, the rocks and landmarks endure. The permanence of geographical features and piles of stones, along with the constancy of celestial bodies, as opposed to man's mutability, is a recurring theme in Labid's poetry. At the beginning of another ode, he observes:

> We wither away, but the rising stars do not,
> and after us the mountains and fortresses remain.[10]

Viewed against solid objects that do not deteriorate, man's transience appears all the more appreciable.

The hearthstones especially are there to remind the poet of his former habitation. The recent rains have cleared them off, so that they look like fresh black ink on parchment, or a spiral tattoo once more vivid on a woman's flesh. Their boldness catches the eye and brings to mind, one supposes, the people who cooked by them and the gatherings that took place around them. Such associations lead (we must assume, along a natural course of thought) to questions about what has become of the other people who used to share the space—and in particular, about the fate of a certain someone. Where might that person be now? Futile questions to be asked, no doubt, of deaf, mute, insensate stones. Even if they could speak, lodged here, they could not provide answers. Regardless, this information is what our poet desires. Alas, he can either be sufficed with memory and speculation or put the matter out of his mind.

B

11   Stripped bare now, what once held all her tribe;
      they departed early in the morning, leaving the rain trench and some thatch.[11]

12   The women stirred longing in you as they loaded their camels,
      and climbed into curtained howdahs, frames creaking.

13   Each litter well appointed and enclosed,
       its poles shaded by brocaded wool and a fine veil.

14   They set out in groups, as if the litters bore oryx does of Tudih,
       and white Wajra gazelles turning their necks to their young.

15   They moved on and faded into the mirage,
       seeming like boulders and tamarisk trees in the winding Bisha wadi.

16   But why recall Nawar when she has gone far away,
       and all strong and weak ties to her have been cut?

17   A Murrite lady who has alighted in Fayd and become neighbor to the people
       of Hejaz—
       how can you desire to reach her?

18   By the eastern slopes of the two Tayyi' mountains, or by Muhajjar she
       lodged;
       or Farda and its nearby Rukham have taken her in;

19   Or Suwa'iq has embraced her. And if she went toward Yemen,
       then I would suppose her to be at Wihaf al-Qahr or at Tilkham.

20   So sever the bond with one you cannot attain;
       the best lover breaks the bond decisively.

21   And give generously to the one who treats you well;
       you can always leave her, if affection sags and its center pole lists,

22   On a jaded she-camel, left a mere remnant by travels,
       with shrunken loins and hump.

23   When her flesh recedes and the joints protrude,
       and at the limits of exhaustion her shoe thongs give way,

24   She is as brisk in the halter
       as a rosy, waterless cloud skimming along on the south wind.

25   Or she is like a swollen-bellied wild ass, impregnated by a white-haunched
       male
       worn thin from chasing, kicking, and biting stallion rivals.

26   Scarred, he takes her up the humpbacked hills,
       vexed by her recalcitrance and cravings.

27   Above the rugged ground of Thalabut he climbs to barren lookouts,
       fearful of hunters crouching behind stone markers.

28   Then, with winter's six months past, having licked dew
       and gone long without water,

29   They bring their matter to a firm resolve;
       and the success of a resolution lies in binding it tightly.

30   The dry grass pricks her pasterns, and the summer winds pick up,
      hot gusts and scorching blasts.
31   The two asses vie in raising dust. Its shadow soars
      like smoke from a blazing fire,
32   Fanned by the north wind, stoked with thistle,
      the smoke of a mighty fire with ardent flames.
33   He pushes on, keeping her ahead,
      for it is his practice, when she threatens to stray, to move her along.
34   Then they break into the middle of a stream,
      and cut through to a brimming spring, thick with reeds,
35   Enclosed by canes that shade it,
      some upright and some beaten down.

Section B comprises the poet's recollection of the departure morning and the first part of the *rahil,* or his resumption of travel away from the abandoned encampment on his she-camel. The thematic progression, so far, matches the frequently discussed tripartite structure of the early Arabic ode. According to the model, the aforementioned ode begins with a poet weeping profusely over some forlorn vestiges, proceeds to a middle part where he cheers up by riding a swift camel, and then concludes with his saying how great he is and/or decorating his tribe or patron. In fact, a multitude of poems follow this general progression. On the other hand, many classic odes—among them, Imru' al-Qays's *Mu'allaqa* and al-Shanfara's *Lamiyyat al-'Arab*—evidently deviate from it. Regarding those poems in the first category, we might pause to recall that, however similarly they may strike us at first, they were composed by unique persons reacting to very specific circumstances. The more closely we look, the more likely we are to notice subtle, individual variations from the archetype. Moreover, patent dangers arise from interpretive overemphasis on the traditional tripartite model. This overemphasis can foster superficial thematic analysis. ("Oh, this is another one of your tripartite odes," one can hear the tyro commenting, thinking he has grasped all the poet has to say.) Besides, the repeated stress on the tripartite nature of the ode necessarily disposes a reader to regard the poem as assembled of discrete components, rather than as composed holistically and as describing a single trajectory of experience. Of course, we will not ever know exactly how the poems came together in the minds of their creators. Yet in the poem before us, at least, we do not find strict thematic segregation. Properly, according to the archetype, the poet's issue with Nawar should be confined to the nostalgic amatory prelude. But this contentious struggle, it shall soon be observed, crosses into the *rahil* and even threatens to go beyond it.

Let us now take a close look at this section. Upon gazing at the desolate stones, the poet thinks back to the departure morn, the last time he saw them this way. Understandably, witnessing the loading of the camels stirred emotion in him, for he knew full well that he would probably never see the beloved again. From Labid's description, we learn that when Nawar travels, she travels comfortably. The woman is most likely a sheikh's daughter, a proud and pampered beauty. In the midst of this evoked atmosphere of loss and melancholy, we encounter an image that may seem comic to us: oryx does and gazelles riding in the camel litters. Comedy, however, was surely not the original intent. The women (gorgeous ones, we are to infer) are glancing back at him in the campsite area like antelope turning to glance at their young. Such looks caused poets to melt.[12]

Labid's recollection ends at the point where Nawar's traveling party faded away. The woman has gone out of sight; recalling her now is a fruitless waste of time and mental energy. Drawing on flawless logic, he asks himself how he can desire to reach her when he has no idea as to her current location. For three lines, nevertheless, he ponders some possibilities. A battle is going on here between reason and emotion. We realize the fixity of this woman's emotional grip on him after remembering that it has been years (!) since her departure from Mina. With admirable manliness, he finally exhorts himself to cut her off once and for all and to give his attention to one in whose tent he may still enjoy warmth and affection. Thus, he affirms, after wrestling with an old nemesis for a while, an eminently practical and self-respecting philosophy: that is, love the one you're with, and only as long as she's good to you.

Lines 16–21 can also be read in a broader context as the poet's struggle to comply with a tribal imperative. Jibrail Jabbur points out that the essence of tribal order consists in the sacrifice of individual interest for the collective welfare. A person must think always in terms of what will benefit the group. Violations of the behavioral code can harm everyone; when an individual commits a crime against an outsider, for example, the whole tribe may be held responsible.[13] With respect to the pertinent concern of sanctioning love unions, the tribal priority is to keep family ties strong. Hence, the first right to marry a woman falls to the paternal cousins. In the case that the woman is divorced or widowed, or no paternal cousins are available or come forward, then she may be married to anyone else, including to a man of a different tribe. (Concerning this last possibility, one must add the caveat that some tribes pride themselves on their noble descent to the degree that they will not permit their daughters to wed outside the tribe.) Nawar, we gather, was at the time young, beautiful, and single. Doubtless, she had caught the eye of a paternal cousin, to say nothing of the impression she had made on the other men in her tribe. Labid, meanwhile, was in all likelihood still an unestablished, random young fellow. (It is entirely possible, furthermore, that aside from being an outsider, he may have belonged to a tribe considered hostile by the Murrites. The accounts tell of a battle occurring around 590–600 between Labid's tribe and the Ghatafan federation that included the Murrites.[14] Nawar's tribe may have decided to camp next to Labid and his kin only because they were arriving during the months of peace.) Therefore, however much he may have grown fond of her during their time together at Mina, and she may have been even of him, his chances of winning her hand were probably less, all factors considered, than the odds of a player today in America of winning the state lottery. Hopeless romances these certainly were, those affairs of the young intertribal couples. Yet they seemed to have happened anyway.

Given the realities of tribal marriage, youths had better get over foolish, transgressive passions. As Labid attests, the best lover overcomes his fondness and breaks the bond decisively. This statement evidently abraded later audiences, to the extent that the standard edition of the *Mu'allaqa* came to read at line 20, in the place of *khayr* (best), the metrically equivalent *sharr* (worst). After further discussion in chapter 5 about philosophies of love, we will be able to surmise when and why people began taking a dim view of firmness such that it would be seen as characterizing the worst lover. For the present, let us note that, at the time when the *Mu'allaqat* were being collected, a Bedouin authority insisted to the Basran transmitter Khalaf al-Ahmar (d. 796) that the correct reading was in fact *khayr*.[15] His testimony correlates with evidence from pre-Islamic poetry. Labid's contemporary Salama ibn al-Khurshub asserts:

> If she comes bringing what she knows I desire, then God be praised!
> Verily, I can give love for love, and can cut the bond if love wanes.[16]

Imru' al-Qays, who could be considered a champion among pre-Islamic lovers, recounts:

> Oh, how many a pretty woman I have cut loose
> and walked away from leisurely.

(Lest we think he is all harshness, he adds later in the poem: "I surely leave the ones who want to part from me / and renew ties with those who crave my company.")[17] It is no surprise, in retrospect, that Imru' al-Qays's clinging hopelessly to the mysterious beloved attracted a crowd of censurers (*Mu'allaqa,* line 43). Not only was such doggedness out of character for him, but it was egregiously out of line with societal expectations. In Labid's *Diwan* also we find evidence that remaining attached to a departed beloved drew blame. In another poem he chides himself:

> I was moved with sadness—would that I had not been—
> disquieted by the memory of one gone afar.

> Foolishly; And had I paid heed to my reprovers,
> minded their words about the shedding of tears,

> I would have cried out to a heart unresponsive to my calls:
> "Following passions to their destination does not win approval!"[18]

Clearly, the poetry documents that, in accordance with pre-Islamic tribal realities, the lovers were expected to put a definite end to whatever personal alliances might begin during the seasons of winter and spring.

So the poet's task, we comprehend, will be to leave Nawar in the past and to complete the trip he has been on and rejoin his tribe. This task will be both physically hazardous—he must cross desert alone—and spiritually arduous. Fortunately, to cover the physical terrain, he has a reddish camel that, like the rain-depleted rosy cloud, has lost weight. She will get him there quickly. The camel likewise resembles Arabian wild asses (now extinct; the African variety is still extant) in her blazing speed and ability to go long without water. The physical aspect, albeit difficult, thereby does not present an overwhelming challenge. The Bedouin poet successfully crosses deserts all the time. Rejoining his tribe in spirit, after experiencing once again a great extratribal yearning, will be much harder.

Concerning this latter challenge, the extended wild ass, or onager, simile has deeper significance. As Jaroslav Stetkevych has illuminated in recent studies, the she-camel in the Arabic ode functions symbolically as an extension of the poet. What she goes through outwardly represents his internal experience. In turn, lengthy similes ostensibly describing the she-camel also trace back to the rider's inner self. In these similes, twice removed from the source of conflict, the poet's spiritual drama plays out; the imagined animals fight his battles. Although it seems fair to assume that the poet knowingly identified with figures he imagined and described, and so was not unaware of a connection between himself and them, we cannot suppose that he was conscious of this psychological process of projection. Accordingly, Stetkevych compares the landscape of experience depicted in the camel similes to Walt Whitman's America, "The wide unconscious scenery of my soul."[19] It is in this landscape that Labid must contend with, and work through, his feelings for Nawar.

Except, as we see in the onager simile, at the first opportunity he declines to do so. He indulges in fantasy instead. Before analyzing the segment, let us first address the question of symbolic identities, since two animals interact here. One can adopt a highly literalist reading and maintain that only the female ass corresponds to the she-camel, as per the comparison in line 25. The problem with this reading is that it separates the male from the dashed line going back to the poet. Given that the stallion plays a major role in the action, one logically concludes that he has a symbolic function. In this case, it stands further to reason that, of the pair, the proactive, controlling male rather than the governable female represents our poet. Having thus identified our protagonist, we may take a more informed look at the sequence of events. The stallion vigorously fights off his rivals, impregnates the female, and has her for himself for the whole winter season. Then, at the critical time when drought forces them to change locations, he guides her—never letting her begin to stray—to an idyllic stream. How might this scenario relate to Nawar? One does not require interpretive keenness to identify her in it and connect the dots. The statement about the binding of resolutions (29), in light of the poet's fantasy, takes on ironic significance. With respect to the onagers, it indicates that pressing forward resolutely will get them to their destination. But presumably subconsciously, once the poet has mentioned in the simile winter's coming to an end, he speaks of binding and tightening rather than of cutting. "Do whatever you can to not let her get away," he seems to be telling himself.

Last, we should note that the poet closes the fantasy with a highly suggestive scene to denizens of the desert. The scene anticipates Paradise as described in the Qur'an, a place of gardens underneath which rivers flow (2:25). More specifically in the context of the poem, it also subtly resembles the howdah Nawar departed in, which was shaded and enclosed. Now the stallion and his mate are shaded and enclosed together. Here the female can give birth to their offspring. Through the simile, the poet arranges a most satisfying resolution to his inner conflict about the female's departure—too bad they are only conjured wild asses! Obviously, he will have to try again if he wants to deal with reality and get over his yearning for Nawar.

C

36   Or is my she-camel like an oryx doe, raided by wolves, who lags behind the
        herd now,
        though a ward of the lead buck?
37   Flat-nosed, bereft of her young, she does not cease circling the dune slopes
        and lowing,
38   For a white fawn, dragged through the dust
        and pulled apart by gray wolves, not about to give up their portion.
39   They chanced upon it while the mother was unaware, and struck;
        the arrows of fate do not miss their mark.
40   She passes the night in sheets of continuous rain
        that drench the scattered shrubs.
41   The raindrops roll consecutively down the line of her back
        on a night the stars are concealed in cloud.
42   She takes shelter in the hollow of an isolated, gnarled tree,
        by the edge of dunes with drifts cresting.
43   In the face of darkness she shines radiantly
        like a diver's pearl slipped from its string.
44   Then, as darkness withdraws and day comes forward,
        she ventures out in the light, her hooves slipping on the clumped, wet sand.
45   She goes forth and back, distraught, among the pools of Su'a'id,
        seven pairs of nights and days.[20]

46   Until, hope depleted, and her full udder dry
      from neither suckling nor weaning,
47   She hearkens to the faint sound of humans lurking
      and takes fright, for man is her bane.
48   And begins to regard both openings—the one in front
      and the one behind—as the source of her fear.
49   The archers eventually give up, and send in
      flop-eared hounds in rawhide collars.
50   They close, and she turns upon them
      with horns like Samhari spears in length and sharpness,
51   To drive them back, knowing full well that if she does not,
      then death is upon her.
52   But Kasab is next smeared in blood, fatally gored,
      and at his attack spot Sakham is left to molder.

This simile also relates ostensibly to the she-camel, although here the comparison applies more to her state while carrying the poet than to her physical attributes. Like the oryx doe, she is separated from the herd, constantly on the move, and exposed to the elements. On another level, we readily perceive, the simile provides graphic entertainment. In fact, these camel similes can be read as short dramas in their own right. Each one offers action, suspense, and a happy ending.[21] To this popular combination, the second simile adds pathos and a measure of violence and gore. Undoubtedly, early audiences left off pondering at some point the similitude proposed and lost themselves in vicarious pleasure.

Symbolically, the section tells of a victorious internal struggle. Our poet, at the second opportunity, does make his hero's journey. Having recognized the oryx doe as an embodiment of the poet's spirit, we see that at the outset she has suffered a wrenching loss. Consequently, she has dropped out of the herd and yearns for her beloved fawn. But fate dictated that it be taken away from her. She searches the terrain futilely. At last, reason prevails and she gives up hope. We sense that here catharsis for the poet has finally taken place. (In her case, biology helps persuade her to abandon the search: her udder, after a naturally determined period, has gone dry.) The animal's own survival has become paramount, which she fights for successfully at the end of the simile.

Before discussing the dramatic conclusion in more detail, let us review the striking image in the middle of the section, the oryx doe under the solitary tree.

That it is set off chiastically (in this instance, by the themes: death, distraught search, tree image, distraught search, death) alerts us to the probability of special significance. Jaroslav Stetkevych has argued convincingly that the icon in classical Arabic poetry of an isolated arboreal shelter for a lone animal represents the tree of life, an ancient Near Eastern symbol.[22] This interpretation pertains to the icon's appearance in Labid's *Mu'allaqa,* as Suzanne Pinckney Stetkevych has pointed out. She also notes that the object of a pearl, to which the ivory-colored oryx doe is likened, occurs in Arabic poetry and the Qur'an as a symbol of immortality.[23] One easily recognizes the basis for the association, inasmuch as the smoothness of a pearl does not roughen or wrinkle, nor does its luster fade. It remains like an eternally young face. In addition, we see that motion stops in the middle of the simile. Between periods of circling and of running to and fro, the oryx pauses for a while and stays perfectly still in her shelter. We get an impression of her stasis and fixity there, which may well remind us of the immobility and permanence of the stones lying in the wadi. Hence, associations stimulated by the tree, the comparison to a pearl, and the sense of holding fast and abiding amid revolving and back and forth movement lead collectively to the idea of eternal life.

The conclusion of the simile drives home the message of survival despite adverse circumstances. Using her two sharp horns, which can grow to two feet in length, the beleaguered oryx impales her would-be destroyers. These dogs symbolize the poet's existential fears, exacerbated when he is alone and more vulnerable. More specifically, they may also bear resemblance in his mind to lions, against which he might have to defend himself with a spear. Al-Jahiz, the prominent Basran litterateur (d. 869), has remarked that the dogs in a scene like this one kill the oryx when the poem is an elegy.[24] In such a poem, the oryx signifies the deceased, and her death is, for the audience, a cathartic representation of that person's demise. But this oryx signifies Labid's inner self, and so she must not die. Her survival demonstrates, rather, that she still possesses a strong will to live. From a period of grief and danger, she emerges battle tested, with sadness behind her. Labid, we realize, has completed his journey. Still alive and having gotten beyond despair, he may now feel a natural urge to exult.

B[1]

53   On such a camel, then, when shimmerings dance in the forenoon's haze
        and dunes are gowned in mirage,

54   I fulfill my yearning, not letting a suspicion grow
     or some harsh critic find fault with a desire.

55   Or did Nawar not know that I am a sure tier of love's knots,
     as well as a cutter?

56   A leaver of places that don't please me—
     except where destiny overtakes the soul.

57   But no, you would have no idea how many nights,
     pleasantly warm, delicious in sport and companionship,

58   I have spent spiritedly talking! How many a tavern-keeper
     I have visited, as soon as his banner is raised, and the wine is choice,

59   And paid a dear price for the vintage in every old, blackened wineskin
     and tar-smeared jar, seal broken.

60   How many a clear morning draft I have enjoyed
     and song of a slave girl, plucking the lute strings with her thumb;

61   Downing my first cup before the rooster's daybreak call,
     that I may take a second when the sleepers are waking.

62   How many a cold, windy morning I have warded off,
     when its reins have been taken up by the north wind,

63   And defended the tribe, my weapons borne by a swift horse,
     whose bridle, at dawn, is about my shoulders.

64   I climbed to a lookout over a windblown gorge,
     the dust rising to the enemy's banners.

65   Until, when the sun's hand dipped into blackness,
     and the mouths of the mountain passes were veiled by the dark,

66   I descended to the plain; and there stood my horse, firm and tall,
     like the bare trunk of a towering date palm that daunts would-be climbers.

67   I got her up to the speed of a chased ostrich
     and then above it, till she warmed up and her bones softened.

68   Her saddle jogged; perspiration flowed from her neck,
     and in frothy sweat her girth strap was soaked.

69   She raises her head and stretches in the bridle, intent
     like a flock of sand grouse aiming for the water hole.

70   How many a royal court I have entered, filled with strangers,
     where bounty was hoped for and rebuke dreaded.

71   There thick-necked men roar threats at each other,
     as if they were the jinn of Badi with feet planted.

72   I denied their falsehoods and upheld their truths;
     no nobleman standing lorded himself over me.

73   How many times I have called for a *maysir* slaughter
      and the gaming arrows, shafts alike;[25]

74   Calling to draw for a barren or nursing she-camel,
      whose meat is distributed to the poor dependents of all.

75   The guest and the client from afar feel as if
      they had come down to the lush valleys of Tabala.

76   Every frail, impoverished woman repairs to my tent ropes,
      weary like a camel left to die, her clothes tattered and shrunk.

77   When the winter winds wail back and forth, the tribesmen pile high
      long troughs of food, and orphans wade into them.

Section B[1] signals the formal end to the poet's *rahil* and implies his arrival in the tribal midst. The mention of a mirage once more and his cutting of ties brings the journey segment of the ode to a structural close. What the poet goes on to say in B[1], all the while addressing himself to Nawar, reflects his desire for psychological closure as well. Truly, the time has come to set the woman straight and to be done with her once and for all (need we remind ourselves, however, that she was the leaver, he the left behind?). One recalls at this juncture the character of Boffin in Charles Dickens's *Our Mutual Friend,* who declares in an argument, "You want the last word. It may not be suitable to let you have it."[26] Before the poet dismisses Nawar mentally, she should know of his present state—how valiant and noble he is, what he has made of himself since the Mina days. In sum, he has a brief message to convey: "It's your loss, dear!"

Accordingly, his first business is to make it clear that, at his end, he has not suffered due to their breakup. On the contrary—life without her has been exquisite fun! His revelry begins before dawn, resumes in the day at the moment a tavern opens for business, and lasts deep into the night. Besides making the important point that he has enjoyed himself immensely in Nawar's absence, these delicious remembrances also speak of his generosity and sophistication. Wine, an import from Syria and Mesopotamia, was expensive in pre-Islamic Arabia, costing about one she-camel per skin.[27] The poet has turned over herds, it seems, so that his boon companions can roister. This action puts him in a class of worthy free spenders including the likes of 'Antara, who avers in his *Mu'allaqa:*

When I drink I dissipate my wealth, but my honor remains
abounding, and untarnished.[28]

For that matter, our poet is no desert rube; he knows how to partake of the luxuries of civilization. When he pulls up at a settlement, he calls for elegant music and goes right for the finest vintages. Such a man delights his friends and impresses those individuals mustered to his service.

In lines 62–69 the poet stresses his valor. Often he has protected his tribe, the horse's bridle skillfully controlled from his shoulders so that his hands are free for his weapons. And when his tribe has required accurate information on the enemy, he has gone to a forward lookout perilously close to their camp. From there, he has sped back to deliver the latest intelligence. By riding this majestic and fast horse he emphasizes his manliness, should Nawar—however implausibly—need a reminder about that quality. Structurally, the description of the horse's speed corresponds to the report of the camel's cloudlike briskness in section B.

He has also spoken out, presumably on behalf of his tribe, at royal councils. This statement is probably a reference to the court of Lakhmid king al-Nu‘man ibn al-Mundhir (r. ca. 580–602) at al-Hira, southeast of present-day Najaf. Labid seems to have visited al-Hira more than once, as part of delegations to answer the tribe's critics and regain al-Nu‘man's favor. In one of his odes he states:

> There is a place for me at the court of al-Nu‘man
> between Fathur Ufaq and al-Dahal.

> ‘Amir called on me to assist it.
> Tongues were joined in battle, and words exchanged like arrows.

> I launched for my tribe target-hitting projectiles,
> neither crooked nor ill-fashioned;

> Pointed ones with eagle feathers attached
> that cause, on that side, incisors and molars to clench.

> We shot at each other while the son of Salma sat looking on
> like a hawk contracting and widening his eyelids.[29]

> The servants stood by holding strainer-necked ewers
> that fill to overflowing when poured from.

Silk garments reveal the forearms of those near the crowned one;
whatever he says they do.

Then the other party turned and walked out listlessly
like laden water-beasts at the river trudging through mud.[30]

It was at the gate of al-Nuʿmanʾs palace, incidentally, that Labid is said to have encountered the poet al-Nabigha. Al-Nabigha won distinction at al-Hira for a series of brilliant panegyrics and "apologies" (more rightly deflections of blame, mixed with praise), which testify to the awe King al-Nuʿman could inspire. Upon seeing Labid, al-Nabigha asked the young man to recite, having recognized in him the eyes of a poet. He heard two odes, becoming increasingly impressed, then, third, this ode. After hearing the last line of the *Muʿallaqa,* he said to Labid, "Go forth; you are the most poetic of the Arabs."[31]

The poet concludes the section with further proof of his generosity. The example of *maysir* slaughters complements the instance of the drinking sessions, showing that he is just as bounteous in the desert among the needy of his tribe as he is in the settlements with his friends. When Labid has charitable gambling on his mind, it makes no difference whether the she-camel brought forth is barren or calf bearing (and therefore more valuable); he will sacrifice her. He thus exemplifies the fundamental Bedouin virtue. It may be pointed out here that Bedouin society is based on the principle of generosity, which enables collective survival in an environment of scarcity. The hoarding of resources, on the other hand, means that members of the group starve. In a social context of extended family and dependents, selfishness of course appears all the more flagrant. The tribe has no tolerance for someone who evinces this quality, as Labidʾs older contemporary Zuhayr indicates:

Whoever has a surplus and keeps it from his tribe
is dispensed with and stigmatized.[32]

In contrast to life in settled areas, where one gains prestige by piling up wealth, among the Bedouins in the desert an individual wins admiration by leveling it.

Reviewing section B¹, we see that the four subsections are linked by the theme of individual sacrifice for the common good. Labid generously gives up his camels for the benefit of others, in times both of hunger and of thirst. In like manner, he bravely exposes himself to danger for the sake of the tribe, whether in proximity to an enemy camp or to a fearsome potentate. This willingness to sacrifice himself is what makes him noble and virtuous. It is also the very quality that he displays in his struggle to terminate his politically unacceptable yearning. As we have said, the essence of the tribal system consists in putting the collective interest above one's own. Labid honorably does his part for the tribe by dissipating his wealth, risking his safety, and subduing his passions.

A¹

78   When the tribal assemblies meet, there is always a man among us
       who seizes the moment and takes on the burden.

79   A divider who gives to the tribe its due,
       and assigns to the others their portions, denying grand claims,

80   Out of preeminence; a bountiful man who helps others to be generous;
       a gracious man; a winner of prizes and a plunderer;

81   From a tribe whose fathers established the norm;
       and every people has its norm and its leader.

82   Their honor is not sullied and their deeds are not inconsequential,
       since their judgment never sways with the winds of desire.

83   So be content with what the Sovereign has allotted.
       He who has divided the qualities among us is most knowing.

84   And when faithfulness was apportioned among the tribes,
       the Apportioner bestowed upon us the largest share.

85   He built for us a house with a lofty roof;
       and the tribe's men and youths rose to it.

86   They are the strivers when the tribe finds itself hard-pressed;
       they are its horsemen, they are its high arbiters.

87   They are a spring abundance to dependents among them,
       and to widows when the mourning year grows long.

88   They are the tribe in which no envier impedes a member,
       and no cur inclines toward the foe.

In the last section Labid turns from self-praise to praise of his tribe. He has taken a place now among his peers and become indistinguishable from them. The time evoked is winter and spring, when plentiful pasturage allows congregation and when tribal assemblies may meet. At a crucial moment during one of these assemblies, a member of the tribe will always step forward and display the same virtues that Labid has frequently exhibited. He speaks the truth loudly, and as a result the tribe gets what it deserves and the others go away with their rightful portions. The man is generous when the occasion calls for generosity, to the extent that those persons near him have plenty to give away themselves. And like the rest of his kinsmen, he possesses *hilm,* or self-control. Passions do not overwhelm his judgment. There can be little doubt that Labid, the man gifted with eloquence, was the one to step forward and shoulder the burden at these meetings. Obviously, a true poet was the exception in a tribe. The emergence of one sparked celebration among the families, for, as Ibn Rashiq writes, "A poet was a defense to the honor of them all, a weapon to ward off insult from their good name, and a means of perpetuating their glorious deeds and of establishing their fame forever. And they used not to wish one another joy but for three things—the birth of a boy, the coming to light of a poet, and the foaling of a noble mare."[33] Labid's point, however, is that any one of his peers could seize the moment and shine. Al-Samaw'al, a Jewish poet and a friend of Imru' al-Qays, has expressed this idea succinctly:

> Whenever a chief among us vacates his place, another rises to fill it:
> a man of words spoken by the noble, a man of acts.[34]

According to Labid, his own remarkable boldness and eloquence characterize all the men of his tribe.

The exceptionality of the tribe, he explains, is owing to divine will. Rhetorically, Labid shifts in line 83 and proceeds to apostrophize the other tribes. What he says should offer consolation and produce an attitude of seemly resignation. "If we happen to be superior to you," he tells them essentially, "then this is what the All-knowing has desired. Accept the matter and deal with it." The references to God also serve as evidence of a religious disposition in Labid. Elsewhere in his *Diwan,* one finds further traces of a religious feeling that apparently preceded Labid's conversion to Islam. For example, in an elegy composed on the occasion of al-Nu'man's death (the potentate had run afoul of the Sasanid king of Persia, who had him jailed and then trampled by elephants), he says:

Alas, all except for God is vanity,
and every happiness inevitably comes to an end.[35]

It is said that Labid only composed one line of poetry after embracing Islam and devoted his efforts instead to memorizing the Qur'an. Although this report is clearly inaccurate (in two poems, for instance, he mentions God's *kitab*, that is, the Qur'an, with notable reverence), it seems perfectly logical that his output decreased after he became a Muslim. Plainly, old subjects like wine drinking and *maysir* playing were no longer appropriate for exuberant treatment, since these activities were newly prohibited. On a deeper level, though, there no longer existed a theoretical basis for poetry of the old sort, which this ode epitomizes. Labid's *Mu'allaqa*, finally and emphatically, celebrates the tribe. But Islam replaced the exclusive idea of tribalism with the broader concept of Islamic unity. Tribal poetry, at least in theory, lost its imperative. And whereas in every tribe the poet had fulfilled the role of eloquent spokesperson, within the single, encompassing Islamic nation that emerged, there was no need for multiple, competing spokespeople; Islam already had its Prophet. Hence, the poet's new role, as a Muslim, was to be a follower and to help in spreading God's word. In this light, we may accept the account of Labid's meeting with the second caliph, 'Umar ibn al-Khattab (r. 634–44), as true in spirit, if not as true in fact. When 'Umar asked the poet to recite for him, Labid responded by reciting Surat al-Baqara from the Qur'an.[36]

As regards the *Mu'allaqa*'s structure, one perceives at the end a completeness and an overall symmetry. In section A the poet highlights the permanence of the valley and the cyclical renewal of life there. In A[1] he stresses the permanence of the tribe and the rise within it of new generations. He does so through the metaphorical description of the tribe as a high-roofed house that God built. Manifestly, a large house built by God is meant to last. In addition, the word *bayt* used in connection with God suggests the venerable Ka'ba in Mecca, referred to in epithets as *al-bayt al-'atiq*, "the ancient house," and *al-bayt al-ma'mur*, "the (continuously) inhabited house."[37] That their abode is lofty also connotes that the men must live up to very high standards of eminence. Successively, they do.

Before discussing the last lines, let us return briefly to the image of the pearl, which we now find occurs almost exactly in the center of the poem. In the context of section C, one interprets the pearl as symbolizing the continuation of life. Like the oryx doe, the poet will survive his loss and carry on. Yet in the context of the poet's spiritual journey that takes place over the course of the ode, the further-reaching association of the pearl not only with life but with eternal life becomes relevant. The poet faithfully rejoins his tribe, and in so doing he integrates with an enduring network. As a committed tribal member once more, he shares in glory that never dies.

Labid closes the *Mu'allaqa* with a recapitulatory rhetorical flourish. He switches to a third-person voice to add an element of objectivity to his statements and repeats *wa-hum* (they are) five times for rhythmic effect. Each and every one of these illustrious men will expose himself to potential harm, both in war and in council, for the sake of the tribe. Each and every one of them will diminish his herd to fortify dependents and to succor widows, who have none to provide for them. In other words, they all meritoriously sacrifice for the common good. In the last line, the poet points to the group's perfect cohesion. Al-Jahiz has noted that envy typically sprouts in families and among close associates.[38] Among the men of Labid's tribe, however, it never has a chance to grow and cause strife.

At the end of the ode, we see that Labid truly is just like the rest of the men in his tribe. We may infer from this point that his experience with Nawar, though personal to be sure, probably resembles experiences that they have all been through. Doubtless, they all had to contend with an unreasonable passion at one time or another. Given what Labid indicates about their willingness to sacrifice of themselves, one rests assured that they, too, proved up to the task. The tribe seems to have been, to use Tennyson's phrase, "One equal temper of heroic hearts."[39] From their midst, Labid speaks finally of the benefits of membership: security, solidarity, participation in lasting glory. Through the course of the ode, though, he intimates the individual human cost.

SUMMARY: THE *MUʿALLAQA* OF LABID

Section	Lines	Structural and Thematic Elements
A	1–10	absence of people wadi, stones are permanent renewal of nature in wadi poet alone
B	11–35	memory of Nawar's departure (sadness) best lover breaks the bond decisively poet rides brisk camel onager simile: stallion will not let mate get away; he guides her to shaded and enclosed spring
C	36–52	oryx simile: loss, grief, acceptance; danger, survival *central image:* oryx taking shelter under solitary tree on a dark and rainy night, shining like a pearl
B¹	53–77	memories of life without Nawar (delight) poet a cutter of love's knots poet rides swift horse import of memories: poet dismisses Nawar; after their separation he has become a valiant and noble man
A¹	78–88	presence of people poet's tribe is permanent rise of new generations in tribe poet surrounded by kin

4

Making the Remembrance Dear

Where care lodges, sleep will never lie.

—WILLIAM SHAKESPEARE, *Romeo and Juliet*

IN THIS CHAPTER we will discuss three shorter works by the preeminent female poet of classical Arabic literature, al-Khansa' (d. ca. 646). Before recounting her biography, let us acquaint ourselves with some general facts about Arabic poetry composed by women during the pre-Islamic period (to which we ascribe the preponderance of al-Khansa''s verse) and take into account the important research that has been done recently on this subject. At the outset, one notes that poetry composed by women constitutes a fraction of what has survived from the pre-Islamic era (and indeed, from the classical era generally). The early scholars who, beginning in the second half of the eighth century, transcribed the old orally preserved Arabic poetry were men, and they got their material from Bedouin male transmitters. Not surprisingly, the poetry they recorded concerns almost exclusively the personal experiences of men and the public affairs of tribes from a male perspective. The relatively small portion of women's poetry that they recorded is furthermore limited quite strictly to one type of expression: the lament for a fallen brother, father, or husband.[1]

Though one may readily accept that the women, who doubtless occupied subordinate positions at assemblies, when they attended them, and did not participate directly in battles, were not suited to be tribal spokespeople (even if they might nevertheless convey public messages in elegies), one must assume, on the other hand, that they had as much to express personally as the men did. Surely, they too were apt to express powerful emotions through poetry. Why, then, did so few of their poetic expressions—besides the elegiac ones—make it into the collections and anthologies? Can we take it on faith that all the scholars and transmitters were simply not interested in the bulk of pre-Islamic women's poetry, however good it might be? Although the scholars and transmitters may have understandably focused their attention on poetry by men, they need not have been oblivious to presumably many great works by women. Specifically, we should wonder about products of those young intertribal romances, those dangerous liaisons that seemed so frequently to have stimulated poetry in the men. Where are the poems by women about getting over lost love (incidentally, how interesting and perhaps moving it would be to hear a poem by Nawar in reference to Labid)? The explanation for their absence most certainly has to do with Bedouin sensitivities to the subject of a woman's amorous passion. What Deborah Wickering notes in "Experience and Expression: Life among Bedouin Women in South Sinai" about the connection between female sexuality and family honor is germane:

> A large part of the family's honor rests in the sexuality of its women. . . . Sexuality is important to honor in two ways. As childbearers, women produce offspring which carry on the agnatic line. Sex outside the bounds of marriage threatens the bloodline, and therefore the honor of the family. Secondly, sexuality is a source of passions and desires which it is necessary to control. Segregation, veiling and mutual avoidance between potential sexual partners minimizes the possibility of threats to honor. A woman's public status demands her propriety. Throughout the woman's life, it is the duty of her father and brothers to protect and defend her honor.[2]

Thus, the Bedouin families, we conclude, could not have wished to hear about whatever attractions their daughters felt to unmarried young men, no less to allow their daughters' inclinations to become public knowledge.

However, as Ahmad Muhammad al-Hufi has indicated, some female expressions of youthful love got through as messages to departed places.[3] Here are a few lines by Asma', a Murrite woman:

> O two mountains of Wadi 'Uray'ira,
> far from the place to which my tribe has safely returned,

> Leave open a path for the south wind;
> perhaps its gentle breeze will treat my sick heart.

—Yet how can the wind treat a lingering passion
and an eye whose tears keep flowing?—

And say to the riders of Tamim, who left in the early morning,
going back with the expectation of depositing their loads,

That a stranger lodges in the folds of the land,
bereft, confounded, given to letting out prolonged moans;

Her insides wrenched by a strong passion,
and torn by a yearning that will not leave her.[4]

Beyond the earshot of brothers and fathers and of other male kin, the romantic messages, we expect, could get more explicit. "I noticed a dramatic difference between how women behaved and acted with each other and how they behaved in mixed company," Wickering writes. In fact, some of the personal stories that the Bedouin women related to her contain bawdy themes. "No Bedouin man listens to this tape," a young lady warns the anthropologist. "No Bedouin man, ever." One supposes that the poetry these Bedouin women recite about themselves and their personal feelings contains, in some instances, bawdy themes as well—for the protectors of their honor are not in the audience (see Lila Abu-Lughod, in *Veiled Sentiments: Honor and Poetry in a Bedouin Society:* "Women recite poems to close kinswomen, women with whom they share a household, or neighbors").[5] Wickering here points to the usefulness of sometimes keeping the males outside the circle: "By maintaining secrecy about their activities, women . . . increase the sense of intimacy among themselves. They also preserve their honor and status by maintaining public behavior and yet allowing outlets for play that challenges taboo and for sentiments, as in their poetry, that fly in the face of public propriety."[6]

Such modern accounts suggest that pre-Islamic Bedouin women likewise sometimes insisted on privacy and give an idea of what must have passed in their circles. The little in the way of poetry that got out of them, or was recited before a different audience in the first place, generally celebrates masculine virtues and upholds tribal values. These poems, excepting the stray lines and coded messages here and there, are the elegies, to which we now turn.

In a recent article about the Arabic elegy (*ritha'*) of the pre-Islamic and early Islamic periods, J. A. Bellamy draws a distinction between the long and the short composition. The long *ritha'*, he concludes, developed from the *qasida*, or ode, which as we have seen consists of multiple thematic sections that together express one main idea or represent a single trajectory of experience. The most famous *ritha'* of this type is Abu Dhu'ayb's sixty-four-line theme-and-variations lament for his five sons, who died of plague ca. 639. Long elegies were the later of the two types to develop and are much less common than short elegies. No long *ritha'* (or at least none that has the characteristic *qasida*-like structure) exists by a female poet. The short *ritha'*, by contrast, developed out of the ancient *niyaha*, or lament for the dead, which constituted part of the funeral rites incumbent on the relatives of the deceased and was originally uttered in *saj'* (rhymed prose). Though the traditional *niyaha* continued to be produced, beginning from an early period poetic meters were introduced to some of these laments and ancient formulas adapted, until gradually an independent poetic genre emerged that was cultivated extensively by both men and women. In the works of al-Khansa', the short elegy form reached its perfection.[7]

A significant number of the pre-Islamic short elegies deal with the theme of revenge. For a tribe in pre-Islamic Arabia, having a reputation for quick and terrible revenge meant increased security: other tribes tended to hesitate before trifling with one of its members. Hence, al-Samaw'al recalls, as a matter for spirited affirmation in his tribe and for serious reflection in others, that "no kinsman of ours ever lay where he was slain, unavenged."[8] (Later, the concept of brotherhood promised security for the Muslims collectively and eliminated the rationale for revenge. Thus, one motive for the composition of laments was eliminated.) In pre-Islamic elegies, the vengeance theme typically occurs either as a statement of intention or as an incitement to action. Traditionally, men made the menacing statements, whereas women incited. Both male and female poets, as Suzanne Pinckney Stetkevych has shown, represented revenge as a means of symbolic purification for the tribe, by which the stain on its honor from a dead kinsman's blood was cleansed with blood.[9]

Al-Khansa' composed individual incitements, or *tahrid* poems, for both her brothers, Mu'awiya and Sakhr, who were killed during the course of a vendetta. In Sakhr's case, one speculates that he may have lain unavenged for a while at least, since al-Khansa' found cause to compose a second *tahrid* in his behalf.

Whether the tribe later retaliated for his death, or perhaps accepted a payment of bloodwit, cannot readily be determined from al-Khansa''s poetry and is not mentioned in the accounts about his death. Regardless, to al-Khansa', the tribe's apparent reluctance to retaliate for Sakhr's loss most likely diminished in importance relative to the loss itself. Moreover, that she continued to weep for Mu'awiya after he was avenged (see, for example, No. 24 and No. 94) shows that her grief did not end once scores had been settled.[10] Her outpouring of laments for Sakhr—subsequent, we can assume, to the two *tahrid* poems in his behalf— originated in all probability from personal feelings for her brother and fond memories of their relationship rather than from any lingering thoughts about the issue of revenge. To understand better these feelings and conceive their relationship, then, and so appreciate better her poetry, we need to familiarize ourselves with al-Khansa''s life.

Al-Khansa' was born ca. 575 into Sulaym, a tribe from the region northeast of Mecca approximately equidistant from Mecca and Medina. Her given name was Tumadir, although she acquired the sobriquet al-Khansa' (the snub-nosed). As this name was also an epithet for the gazelle, we infer that she was exceedingly attractive. An early marriage proposal came from no less a man than Durayd ibn al-Simma, the chief of an allied tribe and a distinguished pre-Islamic poet. Lyall here tells the story, as gleaned from *Kitab al-aghani*:

> Durayd, after divorcing Umm Ma'bad, chanced to pass one day by the tents of Sulaym, where he saw al-Khansa' the daughter of 'Amr son of al-Shurayd, the chief of the tribe. This lady . . . was engaged in the unpoetical occupation of anointing a sick camel of her father's with pitch, and had removed most of her clothing in order to be more at her ease in the work. Durayd watched her, himself unseen, and, although he was then about seventy years of age, fell violently in love with her. He made some verses on her which are excessively comical in their allusions to his passion, the pitch-anointed camel, and al-Khansa''s charms, and next day paid a visit to her father and formally asked her in marriage. 'Amr said to him: "Welcome to you, Abu Qurra: verily you are a noble man, against whose dignity there is no reproach,—a lord not to be turned away from his desire, and a stallion not to be smitten on the nose. But this woman has a spirit like no other of her sex: I will mention you to her, but she must dispose of herself as she pleases." Then he went into the inner tent where his daughter was (separated only by a curtain from the outer, so that Durayd could

hear all that passed), and said—"O Khansa'! there has come to you the Knight of Hawazin, the Lord of the Banu Jusham, Durayd son of al-Simma, asking you in marriage. What manner of man he is you know well." "Father dear," she answered, "do you think I would leave my cousins, who are as bright as spearheads, and marry an old man of the Banu Jusham, who will be an owl today or tomorrow?" [A proverbial way of saying that he was likely to die very soon; the word "owl" was used synonymously with "ghost."] So her father returned to Durayd and said, "Abu Qurra, she refuses you: but perhaps she will consent hereafter." "I heard what you said," answered Durayd, and went on his way. He made another poem on his rejection, in which he censured al-Khansa' for her bad taste. She was urged to reply to it, but refused, saying—"I rejected him, and that is enough: I will not satirize him as well."[11]

Her father afterward arranged her marriage within the tribe to one 'Amr ibn 'Abd al-'Uzza. They had a son, although the marriage was not said to have been happy. 'Amr, it seems, was a wastrel. He twice squandered all their wealth, obliging al-Khansa' to seek assistance from Sakhr. Sakhr responded both times by splitting his herd in two and sending his sister home with the better half. Upon watching Sakhr's second performance, his wife wondered aloud whether he could not be content with giving away a moiety of his camels or if he must also leave himself with the worse half. Sakhr replied:

By God, I will not give her the worse half;
she is a chaste woman who has caused me no shame.

And were I to die, she would rend her veil
and wear a mourning blouse of coarse hair.[12]

It may have come as a relief to Sakhr's wife that al-Khansa''s marriage to the thriftless 'Amr ended sooner rather than later (whether in divorce or in 'Amr's death is unclear). Al-Khansa' was next wed to her kinsman Mirdas, and the union produced four sons and a daughter. We have no reason to suspect that al-Khansa' and Mirdas's relationship was not successful. When Mirdas was killed, she composed an elegy for him. Her matrimonial life concluded with his death.

Thereafter, beginning around 612, misfortune descended upon her brothers. The problems started in 'Ukaz near Mecca, where Mu'awiya mistook a passing

young Murrite woman for a prostitute. He called her over to his side provocatively, arousing her indignation. She happened to be from the household of an
important sheikh. Following the months of peace, hostilities between the families erupted, and Mu'awiya was decisively reckoned with. Sakhr then took it upon
himself to get revenge. He succeeded dramatically, dispatching not only Durayd,
the brother of Mu'awiya's killer, but a quantity of tribesmen as well:

> I killed you singly and in pairs,
> and left Murra a thing of the past, like yesterday.

> I thrust my spear at Durayd, opening a wound
> that squirted like the throat of a slaughter camel.

Elsewhere he adds:

> On that battle-day of Hawza I also killed the two Khalids,
> as well as 'Amr, Bishr, and Bishr's son.

> . . . .

> For we do not undertake tit-for-tat revenge,

> Rather our aim is to obliterate a tribe:
> so we kill the warriors and sell the rest for the pittance that they fetch.[13]

Yet Sakhr himself fell at the hands of the revitalized Murrites three years later.[14]

   In the context of such activity—pervasive in Arabia at the time—the Prophet's example stands out, which we may take a moment here to consider. At the
Battle of Uhud in 625, the Meccans, led by the Prophet's archenemy, Abu Sufyan,
defeated the Muslims of Medina. The Prophet was wounded in the fighting, and
his uncle, Hamza, was killed. For Hamza's death and the reported mutilation of
his corpse, Muhammad initially vowed terrible revenge. Before he had an opportunity to fulfill his vow, however, he received a revelation that proscribed dispro-
portionate punishment for injury and furthermore favored patient endurance
(Qur'an 16:126). Accordingly, when the Prophet triumphantly entered Mecca in

630, rather than harm Abu Sufyan and his followers, he showed mercy to them. The cycle of vengeance had been broken.

In al-Khansa''s life, the death of Sakhr was a watershed. At the time, we recall, she was a widow with six children. Her father, meanwhile, seems to have disappeared from the scene, as he is omitted from accounts of this period (from a line in a poem discussed below, it appears that he was killed also). The loss of Sakhr presumably left no men in the immediate family to protect and support her and the brood. She had become a needy woman—one of those pitiable, ragged creatures who show up in pre-Islamic poetry at the tent ropes of men like Labid, hoping for generosity. Her individual response to this situation was to open the sluices and let out a river of poetry. Some eighty-four elegies for Sakhr poured forth, nearly filling her *Diwan* (the remaining twelve poems commemorate Mu'awiya and other men in her family). Later in life (ca. 629), a conversion to Islam constituted another turning point for al-Khansa'. But traces of the new religion are evident, in pious expressions, in only three of her poems;[15] her language, tone, and imagery in the rest are thoroughly pre-Islamic. (It is plausible that she found at least some consolation from religion toward the end of her life and that she composed most of her poems for Sakhr in the fifteen or so years between his death and her conversion.) Al-Khansa''s works—by which one means first and foremost those laments about Sakhr—represent, as indicated earlier, the culmination and epitome of the pre-Islamic elegy.

*W*e shall read three of her laments for Sakhr. Since the *Diwan* was preserved alphabetically per rhyme consonant, the original chronological order has been lost. Bint al-Shati', in a study of al-Khansa', proposes a chronological order for a number of poems based on theme.[16] We will proceed similarly, conjecturing on the basis of theme a progression in the three elegies. Summary diagrams and concluding remarks will follow our discussion of the poems. The first poem for consideration (No. 56) was composed apparently quite soon after Sakhr's death.[17]

A

1   The crier called out to announce the death of my generous brother—
     a cry that, by my life, was heard.

2   I arose, and from the shock of his demise and from its dreadfulness,
     my afflicted spirit almost went after him.

3   It was as if, in mental disturbance and physical state,
     I was drunk: now getting up, now crashing down.

                                      B

4   Who is there, after you, to honor guests
     when they alight and make themselves heard—
5   As they used to do when you were alive,
     and then enter a place of gifts bestowed, copious watering, and eating to
          satiety?
6   And who is there to handle a crushing matter that descends upon a neighbor,
     and an affair with a person of consequence that has come apart and cannot
          be patched?
7   Who to deal with an uncouth, impetuous conversation partner
     when he strives to overbear on his counterpart?
8   Were you alive, you would have gently smothered his impetuosity with your
          composure,
     for your composure was overspreading.

                                      A¹

9   Whenever I dreaded destitution catching up with me,
     I would draw my veil out of fear.
10   I would call out to Sakhr the generous, and then would find him;
     with him one enjoyed easy circumstances, and all destitution was banished.

At the opening of this poem al-Khansa' registers the shock of Sakhr's death. The crier's call had thunderous personal impact, practically doing her in. In the middle section, she leads us to understand why this news was so overwhelming. Who is there to take Sakhr's place? He was the generous host, the capable mediator, the one to silence an impassioned boor. In the days before piety became a desideratum in a person's character, he was the ideal man. The focus shifts back to al-Khansa' at the end of the poem. She used to call out (a reversal of the situation at the beginning, in which she hears a call) and find Sakhr, who would remove all worries. We sense her current unease through this wistful recollection of the past, and likewise measure the void that has opened in her life. Who will be there for her now?

$\mathcal{T}$he preceding poem, of fairly typical length among those in her *Diwan,* was chosen because it expresses some of her seemingly early sentiments following the loss
of Sakhr. The next one (No. 26) is her longest elegy, and probably her most famous.
We presume this one to be a later work, for reasons that will be enumerated in the
course of the discussion.[18] We shall begin by reading the first three sections.

A

1   Is there a mote in your eye, or some foreign matter,
     or does it drop tears because the abode has been emptied of its inhabitants?

2   It is as if my tears, whenever he comes to mind,
     are an abundance that pours onto my two cheeks.

3   The tearful woman weeps for Sakhr, mad with grief;
     covering him now are layers of dust.

4   Al-Khansa' weeps; as long as she lives
     she will wail and still be terribly remiss.

5   Al-Khansa' weeps for Sakhr, and well she should,
     for fate has dealt her a sudden blow. Truly, fate is most injurious.

6   Inevitably, death comes in some form—let there be warning in this.
     Fate has twists and turns.

B

7   Abu 'Amr Sakhr was the leader among you, the worthy turbaned man,
     the one who rushed to the side of those calling for aid.

8   He was firm-natured, bountiful when others held back,
     bold and head-crushing in battle.

9   O Sakhr, frequenter of a water hole that people warn themselves against
          approaching,
     though going down to it is no disgrace,

10   The black silky one advanced to a momentous engagement,
     with two weapons at his disposal: claws and fangs.

C

11   No, not a bereft she-camel circling a small, stuffed hide,
     uttering two kinds of moaning sounds: loud and soft;

12   Pasturing a short while, then recollecting,
     coming forward a few steps, and turning back;

13   Becoming no fatter when she grazes,
      complaining mournfully and prolonging her groans;
14   Is ever more disconsolate than I was on the day Sakhr left me.
      At times fate renders life sweet, at times bitter.

This poem is the most public lament in our small selection of al-Khansa''s verse, carrying a message to the tribe and to the multitude whom Sakhr helped. Yet, like all her elegies, it issues from the heart. At the opening al-Khansa' finds herself in tears. For the audience's sake, she allows suspense to build momentarily about the cause of her tears before giving the poignant third possibility. We then hear about the tears' abundance. She shifts to a more objective third-person perspective, though, to describe further her manner. One gets the impression that al-Khansa' is standing aside and pointing to herself, drawing attention to the frequency and intensity of her grief. Her repetition of the weeping motif in several lines emphasizes just how often and forcefully she cries. So that the audience grasps the full magnitude of the misfortune, she affirms that crying this way for a whole lifetime—to which she commits herself—will still not do justice to Sakhr's memory. Of course, as important as the crying theme is, she cannot dwell on it indefinitely. One senses that she collects herself, for a period, through reflection on the inevitability of death. A temporary cessation of weeping here will permit her to deliver her message.

Her message, quite simply, is that Sakhr was the best man in the tribe. He was the leader, the bountiful man when others held back. This communication corresponds to what she says about him elsewhere in the *Diwan*. For example, she remembers:

We were like stars with a luminous moon in their midst;
then the moon descended from among us.[19]

Her recognition of Sakhr's superiority, however, contains an implicit disparagement of the other heroes in the tribe. The disparagement can get more explicit, suggesting a degree of incapacity in the lesser kinsmen. In another poem she reports:

When the tribe extended their hands upwards to glory,
he extended his,

And attained that which was above their grasp,
and then reached higher.[20]

Such expressions run counter to the common declarations in pre-Islamic poetry about uniform excellence within a tribe. Labid, we note, does not hint in the eleven elegies on his brother Arbad, who was struck by lightning ca. 629, that the poet's kinsmen were in some way inferior to Arbad. Rather, in one poem he implies that there are many such men among them and that fellow tribesmen could share his, the poet's, sentiments of deepest sadness:

Verily, the misfortune that is beyond compare
is the loss of every brother who was like the light of a star.[21]

Al-Khansa''s statements about Sakhr's preeminence, on the other hand, are close in spirit to typical pronouncements from the courtly panegyric, a genre that came to assume major importance in the literature of the Islamic era.

For all we know, al-Khansa''s claims may have been accurate. Without venturing to form an opinion on this matter, we may nevertheless understand her propensity to cast Sakhr in a uniquely favorable light by recollecting her circumstances. Her best protector and helper was gone. Doubtless, her more distant relations would not have been always inclined to show the same remarkable kindness that he did. On the subject of compensation for a great loss within the tribe, the pre-Islamic poet Hatim al-Ta'i has expressed a familiar theme:

Whenever a chief of ours dies,
an equal to him rises and takes his place.[22]

But such statements must have rung hollow to al-Khansa' at this time in her life, widowed, brotherless, and with six children. In one of her laments she asks:

Who is there to take the place of my mother's son,
now that he has been buried?[23]

There was clearly no one in the tribe who could make up for the absence of Sakhr and fill al-Khansa' with a sense of security. In her eyes, there were no equals around to take his place.

In the latter part of section B, al-Khansa' highlights Sakhr's bravery in conflict by recalling his willingness to approach a dangerous water hole. In spite of
his bravery and fighting skill, on the fated occasion a black panther—death—met
him there. Thus, through metaphors she describes his tendency to charge into
strife and refers to the fated battle. As a woman who perhaps witnessed battle
scenes from the rear, she presumably was not suited to depict fighting in fine
detail. The subsequent lines, section C, she devotes to a touching description of
a she-camel bereft of her calf. According to Bedouin experience, the she-camel
is the animal with the strongest attachment to its young and the one that grieves
most when she loses it. To alleviate a mother's sadness whose calf has been slaughtered, Bedouins fill the calf's skin with dry straw or hay and let the mother sniff
it (al-Khansa''s description, nonetheless, would have us believe that the practice
does not do much good).[24] A grieved she-camel like the one in the tableau has not
mourned ever like al-Khansa' did when she was cut off from Sakhr. We remark,
finally, that in the last line al-Khansa' appears to be looking back on that day. It
seems that some time has passed since the tragedy.

D

15   Sakhr was verily our leader and chief,
      a slaughterer of camels whenever we hungered in winter.

16   Sakhr was out in front when they came to us on their horses,
      a hobbler of beasts when they came starving.

17   Sakhr was the one to whom lead riders directed caravans,
      as if he were a mountain with a fire at the summit.

18   Robust, handsome, complete, self-contained;
      on the morning of fighting a kindler of war's fire.

19   A carrier of standards, a descender into wadis,
      an attester at councils, a dragger of combatants into battle.

20   A slaughterer of grumbling she-camels, an intruder upon tyrants,
      a liberator of captives, a setter of broken bones.

Here, at the center of the poem, we find a description of Sakhr. In it, the
rhetorical tone is heightened through repetition of his name and of lines that are
structured and sound alike. We hear in these lines echoes of the ancient *niyaha*,
which was composed in rhymed prose and featured repetition of the deceased's

name and of introductory words in successive sentences. At the same time, one detects the special artistry of al-Khansa' in the enlivening and counterbalancing of repetition by variation. In lines 15 and 16 she establishes the pattern of *wa-inna Sakhran la . . . wa-inna Sakhran idha. . . .* Then, after beginning again with *wa-inna Sakhran la* in line 17, she coins a simile introduced by *ka-annahu.* Al-Khansa' sets up a pattern, only to follow it with a surprise. In lines 19 and 20, she reproduces six constructs, joining intensive active-participle nouns (five of the *fa''al* form, one of the *mif'al* form) with direct objects. But the first three direct objects, derived from third-weak-radical verbs, are of the type *af'ila,* whereas the second three, similarly derived, are of the type *fa'ila.* Moreover, she ends both lines with a different direct-object type (*fa'l*) coming before, not after, the intensive active-participle noun (*fa''al*). In the original, the effects of such repetition and variation are immediately gratifying to the ear. Study of the lines thereafter adds to one's appreciation for them and contributes to the realization that their composer was a literary artist acutely aware of how to manipulate the language.[25]

In the middle of this section, at the point where the rhythmic pattern discussed above has become established, we encounter probably al-Khansa''s most celebrated line (17). Its many admirers have included, it is said, no less than the Prophet himself.[26] To grasp the line's significance, one must take into consideration the Bedouin context. For the Bedouins, receiving a guest at night is one of the most sacred duties. The night traveler assumedly pulls up hungry and thirsty—and no doubt tense as well, since losing one's way in the desert means death. It is the host's duty to accommodate, revive, and calm him. In the times when the camel was the principal mode of transportation, the generous and hospitable used to pitch tents on heights and light fires to guide and welcome possible travelers in the area. Sakhr, al-Khansa' tells us, is like a mountain with a blazing fire at the summit. His generous light can be seen from all directions across tens of miles. From scattered points around the mountain, caravans are heading inward. Sakhr will host all these caravans, and host them all grandly.

$$C^1$$

21   So I said when I saw that fate heeds no remonstrator,
      and that it alone interweaves the woof and the warp,

22   "A warrior has come to announce the death of him whom I rely on,
      after unconfirmed reports have circulated."

23   Then I spent the night awake, gazing at the stars
       until veils of cloud screened them.

B¹

24   The female neighbor never saw him advancing to her tent
       on a dubious mission when the husband was away.

25   Nor did she see him leaving his abode while victuals were stored therein.
       Instead, he emerged carrying a platter, giving the food away.

26   He was the feeder of fat to the tribe when they craved it,
       the generous one possessing a large herd during drought years.

27   My closest, truest friend among all my relations;
       now he has been struck down, and for me life offers no pleasures.

28   He was always like a Rudayni spear, slender and firm,
       as if his waist, beneath the folds of the striped cloak, were a bracelet.

29   His face illuminated the night, though he cast dark looks at his enemies;
       his forefathers were freeborn men of lofty eminence.

30   He was an inheritor of glory, a man blessed with a pleasing disposition,
       a colossus in the face of adversity, a predator.

31   An upper part of a noble branch not intertwined;
       a man of resolution; at tribal assemblies, a boaster.

A¹

32   Now he resides in the hollow of a tomb;
       rocks and stones have enclosed him.

33   He was open-handed, always finding a way to do good,
       awesome in benevolence, directing good deeds to be done.

34   Let the destitute person weep for him, the person whose spoils fate has
              destroyed
       and to whom wretchedness and poverty cling;

35   And the traveling party whose leader, at a perilous spot, has become confused,
       as if the darkness there were tar.

36   He did not withhold, when the tribe asked for beneficence, the best part of
              his herd,
       and travelers did not pass him in the night.

In section C¹, the tone becomes rather intimate once more as al-Khansa' looks
back on the time when Sakhr died. Again, we sense that some time has passed since

then, especially after comparing this recollection of the death notification with the one in the first poem. In the first poem, al-Khansa' supplies more details about her reaction. Also, in that evoked scene the news seems to her to be more unbelievable. Here, she registers not shock but feelings of distress and sadness regarding the tragedy—the products of months and years, one supposes—through the motif of watching the stars. This scene is nonetheless highly suggestive. Al-Khansa' suggests in it not merely a state of grief and anxiety but also, by mentioning the stars' disappearance behind clouds, her deepening gloom.

Al-Khansa' returns in section B[1] to the subject of Sakhr's distinction within the tribe. Evidently, he did not take after Imru' al-Qays, choosing not to make stealthy nighttime visits to the tents of ladies. He apparently shared common traits with Labid, on the other hand, such as a tendency to speak out vaingloriously at assemblies and a willingness to decimate his herd when circumstances called for it. Thus, as a result of his liberal nature, in winters of drought when no mushrooms, truffles, or other vegetables were available, Sakhr relieved everyone's hunger by slaughtering his beasts. On everyday occasions he was to be seen leaving his tent, giving the food stores away. This latter behavior was probably not always a source of joy to his wife; we suspect that it led to a few discussions inside the tent. Outside the tent, though, it surely made Sakhr popular. As al-Khansa' attests elsewhere, her brother was the place of refuge to the widows of the tribe and the father to its orphans.

From this testimony, and from some of the poetry we have read so far, we begin to detect the existence of an underlying domestic tension between men and women in early Arabia. The men, we have noticed, had their eyes on glory, won through sacrifices made for the tribe and through displays of amazing generosity. The women, by contrast, seemingly had more practical concerns. Who, for example, was going to protect the tent from raiders, if its guardian went off and got himself killed? And how, incidentally, was a mother going to feed her children, if the resident male was always giving the food away? These questions do not seem to have greatly troubled the men. In fact, there are many instances in the poetic record of husbands responding to their wives unambiguously on these issues. The pre-Islamic poet 'Urwa ibn al-Ward was one of those husbands. In one poem he reminds his wife, who has apparently tried to frighten him out of going on a raid, that fate may just as well chance upon the person hanging back as the one plunging into conflict. In another, he upbraids his wife for her stinginess:

Do I hear someone making noise because of an old she-camel
that was given to a poor relation, whose tent ropes cross over ours?

And because of some leftover fat that went his way
—even though he deserved much more?

While eyes have shut, Umm Wahb spends the night
lying among the cushions, mumbling and grumbling.

Truly, storing up fat in our tent is always wrong
when our neighbor has none!

He concludes the poem on a note of self-assurance. Umm Wahb (a.k.a. Sulayma) should know better than to think that he would ever be swayed to see things her way. Furthermore, if he had any doubts about the proper course of action, he would know whom to ask for guidance:

Sulayma has learned that my perspective
and the stingy perspective are vastly different;

And that I don't look at the water container from a miserly standpoint
whether I am thirsty or refreshed;

And that, when flying spears mesh,
I am quick-thinking, clear-eyed, serious;

And that I do just fine with my store of knowledge;
and that I seek answers from those with a clear view of matters when I can't
see.[27]

In the interest of fairness, we should be willing to consider the other side of the story. The fearful and stingy Umm Wahb probably could have provided an unflattering account of her improvident and reckless husband. No doubt, poetic descriptions highlighting these qualities in men were composed and sympathetically received in certain circles. Some poems, surely, included emphatic rejoinders and sections characterized by a tone of self-assurance. 'Urwa lets us hear the opinions of one side, regarding a conflict that was apparently ongoing in countless tents. We must imagine what the women had to say.

Coming to the end of the poem, one notes a recurrence of motifs from the beginning. Again, al-Khansa' mentions her entombed brother (compare line 3). In a figurative sense, al-Khansa' resurrects her brother through the course of the poem by eliciting his memory and now returns him to his resting place. Once more, it is time to cry. In retrospect, one sees that the somewhat theatrical third-person manner of describing her tearfulness in section A had a definite purpose: al-Khansa' was pointing to herself as a model for emulation. All those members in the tribe who would benefit from his generosity, were he alive, should now weep just like her. Similarly, travelers from other tribes who might find themselves in need of hospitality should weep copiously. He was the tribe's best man, the one people turned to for inspiration and succor, and so his loss should be mourned appropriately. One notes also, at the end of the poem, a reference to the striking image from the center. Night has fallen on the bewildered traveling party, which may well represent many groups out there, and the darkness has become the color of tar. Sakhr, the mountain with a blazing fire at the summit, is gone from the landscape.

𝒯he last poem we shall read (No. 52) is one of al-Khansa''s best-known laments.[28] It was presumably composed at a later stage in her life, after long familiarity with grief. The poem deals with her personal experience of ever-present sorrow, from one sundown to the next.

A

1   Recollection keeps me awake at night,
     so that by morning I am worn down from extreme affliction,
2   At the loss of Sakhr; and what brave man is there like Sakhr
     for a day of a sword battle and a horseman's thrusting of the spear?
3   For dealing with the quarrelsome adversary
     when he crosses the line and arrogates a person's right?

4   I have not seen a hardship comparable to that of losing him imposed upon jinn,
      nor have I seen a disaster like it befalling man.

5   Nor have I known of anyone more steadfast in the face of calamities,
      and more discriminating in affairs, who shows no confusion.

6   Many a guest, and person seeking protection, came by night,
      his heart alarmed by every noise.

7   My brother sheltered him and entertained him bountifully,
      so that his mind was free of every care.

B

8   No, by God, I will not forget you
      until I forsake this life and my grave is dug!

9   Sunrise reminds me of Sakhr,
      and I recall him at every sunset.

A¹

10   Were it not for the multitude of people around me
      crying over their brothers, I would have killed myself.

11   Yet I always see a bereft woman crying,
      lamenting the fatal day.

12   I see her dejected and weeping for her brother,
      the evening following his great misfortune or the day after.

13   They do not weep for the likes of my brother;
      nevertheless, I bear his loss by constraining myself to patience.

14   On the day of separation from Abu Hassan Sakhr,
      I bade farewell to my delights and my cheer.

15   Oh, my sorrow for him! Oh, the sorrow of my mother!
      Does he really spend the morning in the tomb, and the evening too?[29]

In section A we see that al-Khansa''s grief for Sakhr is beginning to take its toll. She greets each new day wretched, having suffered through the night. The contrast could not be more plain between the calming influence of Sakhr on his guest and the unsettling effect of his absence on al-Khansa'. The one arrives completely unnerved from a dangerous journey and proceeds to settle in comfortably and sleep soundly; the other retires to the familiar surroundings of her own tent and lies unhappily awake. The cause of her unhappiness she explains in lines 2–7. Sakhr was the brave warrior on the day of fighting (early morning was probably understood here, being the usual time for raids and battles). He was the outspoken and principled advocate on the occasion of council. And, as we have just noted, he was the kind and liberal host on the night of social obligation—which in his case occurred with extreme frequency. A loss like this one, borne by al-Khansa', has not been suffered either by the jinn or by man.

At the center of the poem, al-Khansa' vows never to forget Sakhr and then indicates in a famous line why doing so would be impossible anyway. Both sunrise and sunset remind her of him: the former because of his valiant fighting around that time, the latter because of its associations with his gracious hospitality. With these two daily reminders of Sakhr, how could she ever forget him?

In section A^1 al-Khansa' turns her attention to the immediate scene. Tribal hostilities are continuing to produce lamentation in the camp. The sight of other women in tears, signifying to her that she is not the only person afflicted with disaster, enables al-Khansa' to endure her suffering. Nevertheless, their weeping, unlike hers, is visible for only a brief period. Her identification with some of her tribeswomen therefore has limits. Indeed, one senses in these lines that al-Khansa' has come to feel a certain degree of alienation from her tribe. Grief for Sakhr, at this time, seems merely to be her own concern and her mother's. Life has apparently gone on for the rest of her kin: they now have their own fallen brothers to cry over.

By the end of the poem, we notice a clear structural correspondence between the first section and the last. Whereas the first highlights Sakhr's distinction among the men, the last underscores al-Khansa''s unique place among the women. He was the best man, and now she is the most faithful grieving woman; he bore up against calamities, and now she patiently endures suffering (excellence, we gather, ran in the family). The last line points back identifiably to the first through the reference to morning and night, here as they pertain to Sakhr. Despite the passage of time since Sakhr's demise, al-Khansa' has difficulty believing that he resides permanently underground. He is so regularly present in her mind that his removal from the camp seems impossible.[30]

The summary diagrams below illustrate the organization of these poems according to the principles of ring composition.

NO. 56

Section	Lines	Structural and Thematic Elements
A	1–3	crier announces generous brother's death; al-Khansa' almost follows her brother
B	4–8	*who can take Sakhr's place* (he was the gracious host, the capable helper, the composed interlocutor)?
A¹	9–10	destitution used to follow al-Khansa'; she would call to her generous brother and find him

NO. 26

Section	Lines	Structural and Thematic Elements
A	1–6	Sakhr now covered by dust; al-Khansa' weeps demonstratively
B	7–10	Sakhr was superior man in tribe: worthy, generous, fearless
C	11–14	comparison to bereft she-camel: on day of separation from Sakhr, al-Khansa' was sadder
D	15–20	description of Sakhr, *the mountain with a fire at the summit;* heightened rhetorical tone
C¹	21–23	recollection of al-Khansa''s night spent in deep despair after hearing of Sakhr's death
B¹	24–31	Sakhr was tribe's illustrious son: noble, public-spirited, predatory
A¹	32–36	Sakhr now entombed; let the destitute and the imperiled night travelers all weep for him

NO. 52

Section	Lines	Structural and Thematic Elements
A	1–7	Al-Khansa' recalls Sakhr from evening to morning; Sakhr was uniquely excellent among the men in: defense of weak persons (during morning) accommodation of guests (during night) endurance of afflictions
B	8–9	Al-Khansa' will not forget Sakhr; *sunrise and sunset bring him to mind*
A¹	10–15	disbelief that Sakhr spends morning and evening in the grave among the women crying for their brothers: al-Khansa' cries longest al-Khansa' endures her affliction

Reviewing our selection of al-Khansa''s works, we notice that a mood of nostalgia pervades the three poems. Al-Khansa' recalls Sakhr in them very fondly, and so, naturally, she also expresses great sadness over losing him. Suzanne Pinckney Stetkevych and other scholars have observed that the early elegiac poem shares a mood of nostalgia, and much thematic content, with the *nasib*, or amatory prelude of the Arabic ode. From our reading of Imru' al-Qays's *Mu'allaqa* and the *Mu'allaqa* of Labid, we are familiar with some of the characteristic themes of the *nasib*: separation from the beloved, recognition of the person's excellence, weeping, and sleeplessness.[31] Al-Khansa' invokes all of these themes in the poems we have read. Of course, there are signal differences as well between the early elegy, epitomized by the works of al-Khansa', and the *nasib*. The elegy concerns usually a familial relationship, whereas the *nasib* concerns a romantic one. Another difference, we see, has to do with the continuance of the poet's love. In theory at least, the *nasib* represents the final tribute to a dear departed friend: after recalling a beloved and bemoaning her loss, the poet must leave her in the past and get on with his life. Al-Khansa', on the other hand, continues to cry for Sakhr through one poem into the next.

Her desire to remain in a state of mourning surely has its origin in the deep love she felt for Sakhr and from the negative changes she suffered as a result of his loss. However, we presume that it was encouraged to a certain extent by her social environment. The expectations of women, in this regard, seem to have differed from the expectations of men. Certainly, the men cried when their loved ones died, as many elegies composed by men attest. Yet there was evidently an expectation that they get quick revenge if necessary and so make up for the loss, or else come to terms with it through philosophical reflection (Labid's elegies for his lightning-struck brother, Arbad, and Abu Dhu'ayb's elegy for his five sons who died from plague, for example, represent poetic attempts to put death in perspective). Continued displays of weeping, as al-Khansa''s contemporary Mutammim ibn Nuwayra found, were liable to draw blame. He reports here in reference to his dead brother, Malik:

My companion reproached me for crying at gravesites,
for releasing a steady stream of tears.

"Do you cry at every mound you see," he asked,
"at every one that lies between al-Liwa and al-Dakadik?"

"Grief stirs up grief," I replied,
"so let me be. Every grave is the grave of Malik."[32]

The women, we suppose, were not subject to similar criticism for extended weeping. Rather, society probably looked on it favorably as an enduring tribute from them to some of its illustrious members. The designation of a full mourning year for widows implies that public grief by women was meant to last. Al-Khansa''s propensity to weep long and profusely for a great man of the tribe was most likely nurtured in an atmosphere of approval.

In this social environment, there doubtless emerged a number of women given to wailing for their departed heroes, and one imagines that a spirit of competition arose among them. For her part, al-Khansa' apparently came to feel quite competitive vis-à-vis her bereft kinswomen, since she adverts to the shortness of their weeping in No. 52 and, so often in her poetry, affirms the supremacy of Sakhr. In fact, she is said to have considered herself the most afflicted of all the Arabs. At 'Ukaz, Hind bint 'Utba, wife of the Prophet's archenemy from Mecca, Abu Sufyan (and mother of the future fifth caliph of Islam, Mu'awiya ibn Abi Sufyan [r. 661–80]), reportedly challenged al-Khansa' for this title. Hind had lost her father, 'Utba, her uncle Shayba, and her brother Walid at the Battle of Badr (624) fought against the Muslims. She approached al-Khansa' and informed her that she herself was actually the most afflicted of all the Arabs. When al-Khansa' asked for substantiation, Hind recited:

I cry for the chief of the two basin-shaped valleys,[33]
their protector from every would-be transgressor.

For my father 'Utba of the many blessings, and Shayba,
and Walid the guardian of honor—know that this is my woe!

They are the family of glory, from the family of Ghalib,
of whom many noble sons are praised.

Al-Khansa' replied in the same meter and rhyme:

I cry for my father 'Amr with an eye abounding in tears,
which shuts only briefly while the carefree soul sleeps.[34]

And for my two brothers: I shall never forget Mu'awiya,
who was visited by noble delegations from the two stony tracts.

Nor Sakhr—and was there ever a man like Sakhr,
when stalwart fighters approach in the morning, led by a chief?

So know, O Hind, that their loss is my calamity
when the fires of war blaze around me![35]

Perhaps from these lines in the *Diwan,* and from such signs in her poetry as we have noted, the later reciters detected a competitive streak in al-Khansa' and could not resist the urge to tell stories that dramatized her character. It may have been the case concerning her supposed recitation of the long poem (No. 26, discussed above) at 'Ukaz to the Prophet's poet, Hassan ibn Thabit. When al-Khansa' reached the end of the poem, Hassan is said to have exclaimed, "By God, there is no one equipped with a womb more poetic than you!" Al-Khansa' added, "Nor anyone equipped with two testicles."[36] With even more confidence we may assume, on the belief that al-Khansa' possessed a heart, that the story told about her daughter's wedding day is a fabrication. While preparing her daughter for the occasion, al-Khansa' is said to have let out a series of observations about her own greater beauty previously as a bride, the higher quality of her own wedding attire, and so on.[37] Obviously, the stories about her life cross over from biography into the realm of legend. As regards al-Khansa''s grief, and especially her grief for a favorite brother, suffice it to say that she truly felt her superiority to the clusters of bereft women around her.

Let us finally attempt to consider her person as reflected in the three elegies and ponder her overall poetic achievement. Unfortunately, we see only one side of al-Khansa', so it is difficult to imagine her various aspects. We may say, at least, that she remembered her brother's kindness and was the most faithful and loving of sisters. We sense, moreover, that she was strongly competitive. Last, we infer that she was steadfast. God knows that she suffered in her later life, being widowed, brotherless, and impoverished. But she chose to abide patiently, rather than to self-destruct or seek numbness, and to make her grief the source of poetry. From such raw material she went about fashioning some of the most eloquent poems in the language. Listeners and readers have been attuned to her sad tones ever since.

5

Martyr to Love

The heart wants what it wants, or else it does not care.

—EMILY DICKINSON, 1862 letter

IN THIS CHAPTER we shall read a poem by Jamil (ca. 660–701), our first poet to have lived entirely during the Islamic era (begun 622). The era dawned with a series of stunning military conquests that further confirmed to Muslims, after the miracle of the Qur'an, the truth of the new religion and the reality of divine intervention in human affairs. It seemed manifest that God had intended Islam to spread and God's community to prosper. What had begun as a small religious community, comprising the town of Medina and, later, also the town of Mecca (where the Prophet had first proclaimed God's message to a hostile audience), expanded rapidly into a vast empire. By the time of the Prophet's death in 632 all of Arabia had submitted to Islam. Under the four rightly guided caliphs (Abu Bakr [r. 632–34], 'Umar [r. 634–44], 'Uthman [r. 644–56], and 'Ali [r. 656–61]), rebellious parts of Arabia were first pacified, and then the entire Near East was brought under Muslim rule as Byzantine and Sasanian armies were routed successively. Mu'awiya, the son of Abu Sufyan and Hind bint 'Utba (Hind was al-Khansa''s rival in affliction, as we recall), had himself pronounced the next caliph in the holy city of Jerusalem and thereafter made strategically located Damascus his capital. In Damascus he founded the mighty Umayyad dynasty, which was to last until 750 and witness the expansion of the empire to its greatest extent. By 732, a mere 110 years since the Prophet had governed one town, and only a century after his death, the lands ruled by the caliph in Damascus stretched from the Atlantic Ocean and the Pyrenees in the West to the Indus and the confines of China in the East—an expanse significantly greater than the territory of the Roman Empire at the height of its glory.

Coinciding with such heady changes in the religious and political life of the Arabs was the emergence, in the field of poetry, of a new genre. Among the generation of poets who arose ca. 670, the *ghazal,* or independent love poem, came into being. To be sure, the *ghazal* was not an entirely new creation. Rather, it was derived to a certain extent from the traditional ode, a poem with which we are familiar from our readings in chapters 1–3. Motifs of the *nasib* were retained in the *ghazal,* often in slightly altered form. Subsequent sections of the traditional ode, in the case of the love poem, were either dropped or modified and incorporated. These changes reflected new circumstances in the Islamic era. In the rapidly growing towns of Mecca and Medina, where one form of *ghazal* took shape, poets were no longer faced so often with the arduous task of getting over a lost beloved; they might frequently continue to dally with the particular lady if it suited their fancy. Among the Bedouins, meanwhile, passionately devoted lovers could now permit themselves to adore the lady from afar and cultivate a lifelong obsession (on their rationale for this novel allowance we shall say more below). The urban and desert *ghazal* forms are, therefore, in one important way similar: both involve a romantic relationship situated in the present that might carry into the future. Both represent a thematic departure from the traditional ode, which speaks of a romantic relationship that should remain in the past. Yet the two types of *ghazal* are distinct inasmuch as they express different philosophies of love arising from different contexts. In Mecca and Medina, 'Umar ibn Abi Rabi'a and his school of bons vivants gave voice to a mostly lighthearted, fulfilled type of love. The Bedouin 'Udhri lovers, on the other hand (of whom Jamil was the principal figure), composed poems of deep, unfulfilled longing. Before we get to Jamil's life and poetry, though, let us further consider the 'Umari brand of *ghazal* and its social context.

When Mu'awiya took control in 661, he provoked resentment among large numbers of Muslims. After all, he belonged to the family of Meccan aristocrats who had initially opposed Islam violently; his father had been the Prophet's staunchest enemy. The rancor was especially concentrated in Medina and Mecca, where many of the Prophet's earliest followers and their descendants resided. Logically, Mu'awiya decided to exclude these malcontents from positions of power. Yet they had to be treated delicately because of their well-known ties to the Prophet. In order to soften their antagonism and simultaneously to distract them from politics, Mu'awiya conferred on these people enormous stipends.[1] As conquest followed conquest, wealth was poured into Mecca and Medina in quantities that would have been unimaginable one generation before. Individuals of formerly modest means were transformed into multimillionaires (we are told, for instance, that the Prophet's companion al-Zubayr ibn al-'Awwam became possessor, by the end of his life, of a fortune of some fifty million dirhams).[2] Slaves were sent down constantly, especially pretty songstresses from Syria, Palestine, and Persia. Many residents of the two towns, as a result of Mu'awiya's policy, were effectively neutralized. They erected private palaces and gave themselves over to enjoyment of the good life.

It was in this milieu that the 'Umari *ghazal* took shape. Stylistically, the 'Umari *ghazal* tends to be much simpler than the pre-Islamic ode, almost conversational. Lighter and shorter meters are used more often, probably to meet the needs of singing by the newly arrived performers. In the poems, the author usually recounts an amorous adventure with a lady he knows or has just met. Typically, he portrays himself as the bold, conquering hero who gets through difficulties and overcomes the lady's objections. Here, for example, Waddah al-Yaman describes an encounter with quite a reluctant woman:

She said: "Do not come to our house:
our father is a jealous man.

"Do you not see the gate barred between us?"
I said: "But I can spring over it."

She said: "But the castle stands between us;"
I said: "I shall climb in from the roof."

She said: "But the lion is up there;"
I said: "My sword is sharp and cutting."

She said: "But the sea is between us;"
I said: "I am a good swimmer."

She said: "But God is above us;"
I said: "Yes! but He is Merciful."

She said: "You always have an answer.
Come when people are asleep,

"And light on us like dewdrops, by night,
when there is no one to blame or forbid us."[3]

As is evident in these lines, the individual who tries to discourage Waddah from visiting is a free woman. In fact, despite the plenitude of concubines in Mecca and Medina, the 'Umari poets devoted their attention to wellborn Arab ladies, composing almost exclusively about them. We may suppose that they were inspired by the chase, the pursuit of difficult conquests, rather than by the easy catch. For his part, 'Umar ibn Abi Rabi'a of Mecca, the leader of the school, seems to have been addicted to the chase. Although he owned scores of slaves, in his *Diwan* he details love affairs with noble Arab women—more than forty of them. He was apparently in his peak form during the Hajj season, when strangers came to town, and rued that the season did not last the entire year. The ladies, meanwhile, were evidently often enamored of 'Umar; in the events described in one poem, four of them cleverly plot to get him alone and succeed in spending a night with him. Many of his adventures are reminiscent of the escapades of Imru' al-Qays. In a famous *ghazal* he tells of surprising the Bedouin Nu'm (who figures in a number of his *ghazals*) by slipping past hostile male relations and entering her tent at night. They spend blissful time together and then face the quandary of how to get the poet out of the campground alive after darkness has lifted. Fortunately, Nu'm is able to enlist the support of her two kind sisters, and the three of them close ranks around him. The group exits as a unit, Nu'm and her sisters concealing the poet within their silken wraps:

And so, shielding me from my enemies,
were two swollen-breasted girls and a nubile third.[4]

From reports like this one, we can assume that 'Umar and the poets of this school consciously modeled themselves after Imru' al-Qays. Like the pre-Islamic bard, they embarked on daring sexual exploits and prided themselves on their frequent successes. Nevertheless, they were sometimes thwarted. We conclude our brief consideration of 'Umari *ghazal* poetry with two lines by 'Umar, attesting to the tantalizing coyness of Hind. Thusly he begins and ends a *ghazal* about her:

Would that Hind made good on her promises,
and cured my spirit of its ailment.

. . . .

Whenever I ask, "When shall be our tryst?"
Hind laughs and replies, "After tomorrow!"[5]

In contrast to the poets of the 'Umari school, the 'Udhri poets fell desperately in love with a single lady and remained attached to her exclusively all their lives, even though she was chaste and forbidden to them in marriage. They got their name from the Banu 'Udhra, a Bedouin tribe from the Wadi al-Qura area in northwest Arabia, lying approximately halfway between Medina and the crossing point into Sinai. Jamil belonged to this tribe (as did the first 'Udhri poet, 'Urwa ibn Hizam [d. ca. 650]), and, as indicated above, he best represents the 'Udhri school. In the following discussion, we shall first go over Jamil's biography (insofar as it can be inferred from his poetry) and highlight noteworthy aspects about his experience and philosophy as a lover, next analyze his most famous *ghazal,* and finally comment on the significance of his life and poetry to Umayyad and later audiences.

In his youth, Jamil became infatuated with Buthayna, a young woman of his tribe. She responded favorably to his overtures, and the two began to meet—privately. Far from the eyes of watchful guardians and of ever-ready gossips, they got to know each other better. Whether Jamil had honorable intentions at this early stage by his tribeswoman, and inclined to matrimony, cannot be determined. However, we should probably give him the benefit of the doubt, based on the earnestness with which he loved her afterward. Accordingly, we may take it on faith that this rather short and direct attempt at persuasion—had it succeeded—would not have affected his commitment to her:

"Come, Buthayna, let us trade our religion for the pleasures of this world,
for next year we may repent."

"Suppose we do trade our religion, as you say, Jamil,
and then our Appointed Time comes?"[6]

Clearly, Jamil was attracted to the corporeal Buthayna, presumably as well as to the spiritual one. On magical occasions, she did satisfy his cravings somewhat. He gratefully recollects in one poem their memorable night alone:

> She showed her generosity in speaking,
> and sometimes in offering me the saliva of her mouth.[7]

On the whole, though, it seems that Buthayna was tantalizing, just like Hind. Not only did she usually refrain from granting small favors, she often did not show up at their rendezvous. Jamil says:

> I look to you, thinking of what you promised,
> as the poor man looks to the rich man.

> This debtor of ours, hardly a destitute, promises to fulfill obligations,
> yet he defaults on each one.

> What is your promise,
> but like the lightning flash from a cloud that pours no rain.[8]

From Jamil's testimony, we may say that Buthayna was essentially a miser with her favors and her time. Her miserliness may well bring to mind the character of pre-Islamic wives. Those women in most cases did not know the meaning of generosity—at least as they were portrayed by their poet-husbands. Then again, their concern for preserving food stocks, we recall, was rational in light of the family's requirement to eat. From a domestic point of view, the women were being prudent. Likewise, Buthayna seems to have demonstrated good sense in her dealings with Jamil. If, as a rule, she prevented him from enjoying the objects of his desire, it was for a sound reason: compromising herself could turn out disastrously if the indiscretion were exposed. Furthermore, discouragement of a hot-blooded youth in these situations was most befitting of a Bedouin Muslim woman. And, if she frequently failed to meet him as promised, perhaps she was concerned about their being seen and talked about. Upon further consideration of the poet's criticism of her, we may say that Buthayna was indeed an intelligent and virtuous young lady!

Before long, Jamil asked for Buthayna's hand in marriage. His request was denied. We ascertain from his poetry that slanderers were active behind the scenes, speaking ill of him to her family. It may be that her family, in any event, had already decided upon a closer match for Buthayna within the tribe. The slanderers approached her also with news, and apparently she believed some of their reports and cooled to Jamil. He went away to Syria, although he could not forget her and kept coming back periodically to visit. Life without her was impossible, and he clung to the hope that she would show him more kindness. He says, perhaps exaggerating his condition slightly:

> Were it not for what I hope to receive,
> the crier would have called out to her, announcing my death.

> O Buthayna! Be generous and requite a lover who is seriously ill,
> and cure him of his pain and sickness!

> A little from you is a lot; it benefits me greatly,
> whereas a lot from anyone else does me no good.[9]

We surmise that her feelings for him were not constant through this period, that her affection ebbed and flowed. Buthayna was probably not averse, generally speaking, to having a devoted admirer, and she probably allowed herself most times to be generous—with a few kind words, if with nothing else—when he came to visit. In due course, she was married to a Nubayh ibn al-Aswad, one of her close relatives. The thought of her marriage, understandably, appalled Jamil; in a poem he urges her to flee if the man's perspiration ever drops on her.[10] Yet he continued to love her, even in her new state. Alteration did not affect his feelings:

> I loved single women when Buthayna was single,
> and when she married, she made me love wives.[11]

At this point, we note that Jamil has broken fundamentally from his pre-Islamic forebears and violated what was, for them, a principal (if not *the* principal) rule of love. "Sever the bond with one you cannot attain," Labid told himself famously, when it became obvious to him that Nawar was lost and could not be regained (*Mu'allaqa*, line 20). Jamil now cannot attain Buthayna, yet he refuses to sever the bond. Predictably, censurers rushed in and had their say.[12] Jamil stubbornly resisted them. Slanderers tried changing his opinion of her, but he would hear none of their malicious talk.[13] Reportedly, his father eventually took him aside and tried talking some sense into him, apprising his son in effect of the multiplicity of fish in the sea. Jamil replied that God had decreed that he should love Buthayna and asked rhetorically if it was possible for a person to change his fate.[14] Ah, here was a forceful response, abstracted logically from the new worldview. Well versed in the Qur'an and mindful of the Islamic conquests, Muslims during this period were, no doubt, acutely aware of the existence of a divine plan and of the utter futility of opposing it. It is reported further about the man-to-man discussion that the father, upon hearing Jamil's response, broke down in tears.[15] What could he say?

We should not, however, suppose that Jamil was consigning himself to endless torture by preserving the bond with married Buthayna. A. Kh. Kinany observes perceptively that "no one would stand suffering without hope, and no one would agree to suffer willingly in the present, if he did not expect a magnificent reward in the future."[16] Significantly, Jamil now knew, as a Muslim, that awaiting him was an afterlife. In similar circumstances, his 'Udhri predecessor 'Urwa avers:

> I look forward to the Day of Judgment,
> since I am told that then I will meet 'Afra'.[17]

The Day of Judgment has distinctly positive associations for Jamil also.[18] After his suffering, therefore, would come blessed relief. He loved Buthayna truly—more so, certainly, than anyone else did—and by celestial law one day he would be reunited with her, eternally.

In Jamil's *Diwan*, expressions of love frequently take on a religious aspect. It seems reasonable to assume that these declarations were mostly the product of the later stage of their relationship, when Jamil was far from the everyday Buthayna and left to ponder a mental image of the lady. We have encountered in pre-Islamic poetry religious associations for the beloved; Imru' al-Qays compares the ideal woman's shining beauty to a monk's lamp (*Mu'allaqa*, line 39). Yet such associations become conspicuous in the *ghazal*, especially in the 'Udhri *ghazal*. References are now made to the Qur'an and to the practice of Islam. For instance, Jamil says of his beloved:

> She was favored in terms of beauty over other women
> just as the Night of Power and Excellence was favored over a thousand months.[19]

And Jamil admits that when he performs his daily prayers, he thinks of Buthayna.[20] In the Islamic era, miracles from the beloved are even possible. Were Buthayna's spittle put to the lips of the dead, we are told, the dead would come back to life.[21] These examples and others suggest that the 'Udhri poet came to regard his love metaphorically as a religion, with the beloved as its deity. Islam, as Monroe has remarked, provided the 'Udhri poet with a new model attitude to assume before the beloved.[22] A Muslim submits and bows down before God. Increasingly, it seems that Jamil prostrated himself, setting the prime example for the 'Udhris, before Buthayna.

As has already been intimated, Jamil's continued fixation on Buthayna did not exactly please the members of his tribe. Stubbornly, he was contravening established tribal principles, acting independently. A further brief consideration of Islam's influence on the Arabian zeitgeist sheds additional light on this behavior. The tribe had always promoted, among its members, conformity to the norm of illustrious predecessors. Islam, by contrast, fostered a spirit of individualism. The Muslim was aware that a person would be judged one day individually according to his or her own actions, irrespective of whatever tribal affiliation that person might boast on earth. The seeming contradiction that arises between individualism and fatalism can be reconciled (or merged) in a philosophy of, shall we say, willful fatalism. Kinany points out, along these lines, that "'Udhri lovers hid a remarkably free and powerful will behind their so-called fatalism."[23] Regarding Buthayna, we may remark that Jamil wanted to stay attached—or, perhaps more correctly, he did not want to undergo the excruciating experience of cutting the bond—and that fatalism as well as the hope for an eventual reunion gave him a rationale for following his heart. Of course, this entirely reasonable personal desire conflicted with the tribal obligation to accept reality and settle down with, and start producing children with—well, with a closer relative than Buthayna! Arguably, nowhere is Jamil's independence more outstanding than when he affirms that even if his family were at war with Buthayna's family, he would still be at peace with her.[24] The maverick lover has obviously lost complete sight of tribal priorities. A striking juxtaposition can be made, in this connection, between the allegiances of Jamil and Labid. As the *Mu'allaqa* shows, Labid is willing to sacrifice his feelings for Nawar so that he may wholeheartedly rejoin his tribe. On the other hand, Jamil would not sacrifice his feelings, not even in the event of intratribal warfare. His loyalties remain firmly with Buthayna, no matter how it conflicts with the interests of his kin.

We can conclude confidently that, with such an attitude, there was no place for Jamil in his tribe. He persisted in making short visits, though, to the now married Buthayna. Late in his life, he emigrated to Egypt, where he lived a short while. He died there at the approximate age of forty-one.

We will turn next to his most celebrated *ghazal* (No. 45).[25] Since evidently there have been many apocryphal lines attributed to Jamil (a matter on which we will comment later), we must first attempt to establish the authenticity of the whole poem before us. Although Jamil's *Diwan* existed in classical times, it has been lost to posterity. All that has come down to us of his verse is what is contained in various anthologies. (In the modern era, the scholar Husayn Nassar has reassembled Jamil's *Diwan* out of poems and fragments gleaned from the anthologies.) We find Jamil's *ghazal* as a complete poem, then, in three anthologies: in *Kitab al-amali* (The Book of Dictations) by al-Qali (d. 967), in *Muntaha al-talab* (The Goal of Desire) by Ibn Maymun (d. 1193), and in *Tazyin al-aswaq* (Decoration of the Markets) by al-Antaki (d. 1599). Each version differs slightly with respect to the individual lines, the line order, and the overall length (for example, the length ranges from thirty-five lines in al-Qali's version to thirty-seven in al-Antaki's). Though the possibility exists that one of the later versions was transcribed from a copy of the *Diwan,* in the absence of such evidence it makes sense to suppose that the later versions contain a few corruptions and to regard the oldest version as the one most likely to be authentic. This oldest recension is the one translated below.[26] Our anthologist, al-Qali, however, acknowledges that, by his time, two versions already existed: one transmitted to him by Ibn Durayd (d. 933) and another by al-Anbari (d. 940; al-Anbari, we may recollect, was the editor and commentator for the most comprehensive early edition of the *Mu'allaqat*). According to al-Qali, the two versions differ in their line order and in their wording in certain places.[27] He does not indicate which version he chooses to record, although we must assume that he passed on what he thought was the correct version. Incidentally, al-Qali was not without at least one critic. Geographer and philologist Abu 'Ubayd al-Bakri (d. 1094) was sufficiently alarmed at the mistakes he saw al-Qali making in *Kitab al-amali* that he wrote a whole book dedicated to pointing them out.[28] Notably, about al-Qali's transmission of Jamil's *ghazal* he has nothing to say.

Having identified our source text and deduced that it was considered faithful to the original by tenth- and eleventh-century authorities, we proceed to argue for the poem's authenticity on the basis of three observations. In the first place, the *ghazal* can be traced plausibly to a period of Jamil's life. It seems clear that Jamil went finally to Egypt: he addresses one poem to ʻAbd al-ʻAziz ibn Marwan, the Umayyad governor of Egypt under the caliph ʻAbd al-Malik (r. 685–705), and he contemplates in another poem the prospect of dying there.[29] This *ghazal*, we shall see, was apparently composed in Egypt during a late period in the poet's life. Second, its length suggests that it was not fabricated in a subsequent era in order to accompany music. The thirty-four songs of Jamil's poetry included in *Kitab al-aghani* (ca. 950) average four lines in length and do not exceed thirteen lines. Hence, although there may have been a strong demand for music on the theme of Jamil and Buthayna (as the number of songs indicates), there was evidently no demand among music lovers of the period for a long *ghazal*. Perhaps a clever composer might have found it convenient to forge a few touching lines about Buthayna to go with a tune, but it is improbable that such a character would have had reason to work up thirty-five. Finally, we observe that the poem is structurally and thematically a coherent whole. It betrays no signs of a transmitter's patchwork; rather, it holds together organically according to the principles of ring composition. This poem appears to be the work of a single artist reflecting on his state and his beloved.

So, on the assumption that this *ghazal* is indeed the authentic expression of Jamil near the end of his life, let us read what he wishes to express.

A

1   Alas, would that the days of carefree pleasure were new,
and that a bygone time, O Buthayna, would return.

2   Then we would be completely satisfied, as we once were,
when you were a true friend, and what you gave generously was a trifle.

3   Whatever I forget, I shall never forget her words to me
after my travel-worn camel had drawn near: "Is Egypt your destination?"

4   Nor her communication: "Were it not for the watchful eyes,
I would come to you. Don't blame me; I would ransom my forefathers for you."

B

5   O my two friends, the passion that I keep from view is apparent:
      my tears this morning bear witness to that which I conceal.

6   By God, I have found that many a tear will flow
      when the abode is distant.

C

7   If I protest to her, "What I feel inside, Buthayna, is killing me!"
      she says to me, "It is fixed there, and growing."

8   And if I implore her, "Give me some of my sanity back, so I can live happily
      with other people," she replies, "For you, that is a remote possibility."

D

9   Thus I am sent back, denied in my request,
      and my love, unlike what perishes in this world, endures.

10   You will be requited with blame, Buthayna,
      for allowing a dear friend who is praiseworthy to depart.

E

11   I told her, "Know that between you and me
      there are oaths and a divine pact."

12   My love for you was both long-standing and newly acquired,
      and what is love but a wealth of feeling acquired early and late?

F

13   The path to a love union, whether or not she smooths it
      by promising what I desire, is truly steep.

G

14   I have destroyed my life waiting for her favors;
      and she wore out that time when it was new.

With our background in pre-Islamic poetry, we notice, by way of contrast to the style of the traditional odes, the lyrical character of this poem. The *ghazal* features plain statements about Jamil's relationship with Buthayna and straightforward expressions of emotion. The thematic shifts, within the bounds of a single subject, are frequent, reflecting the mental agitation of the poet. The themes themselves are perhaps more immediately accessible than the ones encountered in pre-Islamic poetry, which are conveyed often through desert imagery and less in need of explication.

At the same time, we recognize an initial progression comparable to that seen in the odes. The *ghazal* begins with nostalgic remembrance of times of happy love, as well as evocation of departure (here, though, the poet must depart with his companions—as presumably was the situation in reality—rather than the beloved with her tribe). The outpouring of tears comes next per the traditional sequence of experience. Novel, however, is the poem's subsequent development— or, perhaps we should say, its lack of development. Our poet does not step back from the emotional crisis, recognize his folly in continuing to think about the unattainable woman, and then manfully cut ties and move forward. He dwells on the topic of his beloved, offering testament to the fact that she owns his heart and retains full control of his sanity. During their last meeting, we suppose, Jamil reminded her of their solemn oaths taken together. These oaths probably pertained to their being true to one another and to treating each other with love and respect. But clearly much has changed in Buthayna's life since they were sworn. As for Jamil, the unrequited lover, little has changed but the scenery around him; inside, the love endures and continues to grow. Tragically, he realizes the toll that this love for Buthayna is taking on his life, yet he can do nothing about it. He has committed himself irrevocably, no matter how unforthcoming or unavailable she may be and no matter how far away she may reside.

F¹

15   Would that the slanderers who came between us had poison mixed for them
      by black foreigners speaking unintelligible Arabic;
16   And that every sunrise and sunset
      found them constrained in additional shackles and fetters.

E¹

17   Some women suppose, ignorantly, that when I approach,
      I approach in order to woo them.
18   I divide my glances equally so that none thinks I am interested;
      while in my heart, they and I are widely separated.

D¹

19 Oh, would that I knew whether I will again spend a night in Wadi al-Qura—
  if I passed a night there, I would be full of joy!

20 Whether I will ever descend into a valley,
  down through narrow passes where the wind whistles;

21 And whether, in the rest of my life, I will ever encounter a good day,
  when the frayed rope of happiness is new again.

22 For after despair, objects of desire may yet be attained,
  and necessities may still be sought though they are far.

23 And would that I knew whether I will ever urge on, through a wind-swept
   desert,
  a tall, brisk she-camel, a match for slender, strong-necked mounts;

24 On a dreadful route along which vultures,
  at places where travelers become confused, arrive in delegations.

C¹

25 She captivated me with eyes of an oryx fawn in a herd,
  a neck elegant and comely, and a bosom shiny like a silver tray.

26 She walks with a lofty, swinging gait,
  just as one who is proud of the fold of her sash struts to her sisters-in-law.

27 If I should visit her,
  an ungenerous obstructor steps in my way.

28 He repulses me, disregarding my love for her and falsely charging me with
   offenses;
  the man is most obstinate!

29 So I turn away as if I have made up my mind to avoid her,
  until he stops paying attention, and then I return.

30 Whoever is granted someone like her for a companion,
  is rightly guided in this world.

31 My passion dies when we meet,
  and revives when we part.

B¹

32 They say to me, "Jamil, go off, wage jihad!"
  Yet what jihad except the one for the ladies would interest me?

33 Every hadith they utter brings a smile,
  and every glance they direct fells a martyr.

A[1]

34   Whoever has doubts about my love for Buthayna,
      can consider Barqa' Dhi Dal my witness.
35   O Umm Dhi al-Wad' Buthayna, don't you know
      that I laugh and smile at the thought of our times together—when you were
      stingy?

The second half (or part) of the poem, according to our view, is slightly longer than the first. Jamil devotes more attention to an imagined return and arrival (D[1] and C[1]) than to a corresponding previous visit and departure. This evident inclination to dream is understandable, as happy visions may offer the poet psychic comfort. Whether he will actually undertake another visit, now that he has grown old and gone so far away, is unclear, although the recurrent "Would that I knew" suggests that he has made no firm plans to go back. Interestingly, the hopes expressed of attaining objects of desire after despair and of seeking remote necessities (line 22) echo the sentiments voiced by Imru' al-Qays at the end of his life: "After lack may well come possession; and after old age, long life and new apparel."[30] But the similar hopeful statements come from two different men, and one would suppose that, of the two, Jamil would be the less likely to strive in order to turn his hopes into reality. Imru' al-Qays, we have seen, struggles against fate; Jamil submits to it.

By this stage in the relationship with Buthayna, Jamil's love has become, practically speaking, a spiritual affair. The ungenerous obstructor—presumably Buthayna's husband—does not realize this fact and imputes base motives to the returning visitor. Jamil is harmless in Buthayna's presence, judging by what he says about his passion in line 31. Line 31 has been called the most amatory in Arabic poetry.[31] Surely, 'Umar would disagree, being of the "out of sight, out of mind" way of thinking. About one of his mistresses, Shanba', and the matter of distance and proximity's effects, 'Umar remarks:

The heart had almost been consoled;
and whoever remains for long, at a distance, forgets—

Except that, if you meet the beloved after a period of absence,
you find that the malady returns.[32]

Absence makes our poet's heart grow fonder, however, whereas being together with the beloved extinguishes his desire. For Jamil, it's all about the yearning.

To Jamil's friends in Egypt, the yearning doubtless had a sad appearance. Line 32 reports their well-meaning, if ignored, advice. Samuel Johnson has said that "the safe and general antidote against sorrow, is employment."[33] The pre-Islamic solution to sorrow, we have seen, was to ride off on a swift she-camel—in other words, activity and exposure to new surroundings. Here in the Islamic age, the obvious solution is to go off and fight a holy war, which Jamil's friends propose to him. Yet Jamil indicates that he prefers another kind of holy war. In justifying his preference, he points to the pleasing effect of the ladies' every hadith ("a bit of conversation," although Jamil is punning here, since the word also means "a legally applicable saying of the Prophet") and to the ultimate distinction of martyrdom. To their specifically Islamic suggestion, he wittily formulates a specifically Islamic response. The man will not yield. Nothing can divert him into pursuits unrelated to Buthayna or distract him from his pining.

At the end of the poem, Jamil cites Barqa' Dhi Dal in reference to his love and apostrophizes Buthayna. We are told that at Barqa' Dhi Dal Jamil waited for three days and three nights and without food or water to meet Buthayna alone, so he could say good-bye. He was heading off to Egypt.[34] Though the story may not be true in fact, we accept it as true in spirit, for Jamil evokes what happened at Barqa' Dhi Dal as proof of his devotion. He concludes by reminding Buthayna that the recollection of their good times together brings him great pleasure. By mentioning the beloved's memory, her *dhikra,* he alludes to the most famous motif in all classical Arabic poetry: weeping at the thought of the beloved. The locus classicus for this motif is the drenching opening of the *Mu'allaqa* of Imru' al-Qays, which remains always, we can assume, in the back of listeners' minds. Jamil says that he laughs when he thinks back to the happy times with Buthayna. Perhaps he does. But surely he also must cry.

The following summary diagram illustrates the structural completeness of Jamil's *ghazal.* Unlike most of the poems we have read so far, this one does not exhibit significant thematic progression. Here, the returns to themes from the first part, while evoking the earlier sections, do not mark at the same time some key interim development. Nor would we expect to observe a significant overall progression in a poem by Jamil. It seems that, no matter what happened as life went on, he was constantly returning mentally to Buthayna.

NO. 45

Section							Lines	Structural and Thematic Elements
A							1–4	poet remembers happy times when Buthayna was stingy; departure for Egypt
	B						5–6	poet weeps in front of friends
		C					7–8	poet imagines conversation; Buthayna has taken poet's sanity
			D				9–10	poet leaves Buthayna
				E			11–12	poet reminds Buthayna of their oaths and pacts (probably re: fidelity); his love is long-term
					F		13	path to love union is difficult
						G	14	poet has destroyed his life waiting for favors (Buthayna is stingy); she wore out his youth (she did not satisfy his desires even then)
					F¹		15–16	poet wishes that ill befall slanderers (who came between him and Buthayna)
				E¹			17–18	evidence that poet is faithful: he takes no interest in other women
			D¹				19–24	poet imagines going back to Wadi al-Qura
		C¹					25–31	Buthayna captivated poet; he imagines visit to her
	B¹						32–33	friends recommend jihad as cure for sorrow; poet will not follow recommendation
A¹							34–35	citation of Barqa' Dhi Dal; poet remembers happy times when Buthayna was stingy

One cannot conclude a discussion of Jamil and his poetry without addressing the subject of the public's fascination with him in the early Islamic era and their enthusiastic reception of his work. As a devoted lover Jamil became legendary. Stories evidently proliferated about him, as can be perceived from reading the long chapter on Jamil in *Kitab al-aghani*.[35] His transmitter, Kuthayyir (d. 723), emulated him, becoming an esteemed 'Udhri poet-lover himself. The legendary figure Majnun Layla, "Crazy about Layla," was patterned after Jamil, probably by the Arabs of the North Arabian Peninsula (to whom Majnun is linked) around the time of Jamil's death to show that they, too, had been distinguished with an 'Udhri-style poet-lover (the Banu 'Udhra, it will be noted, hailed originally from the South, that is, from Yemen).[36]

The stories about Jamil often feature an adventurous, stealthy visit to the beloved and invariably emphasize what become hallmark 'Udhri traits—fidelity and chastity. A story about the early part of his life demonstrates that he was completely chaste even then. In this story Jamil meets Buthayna at a discrete location under the cover of darkness. Unbeknownst to them, however, Buthayna's father and brother arrive and take up a position nearby to eavesdrop. The suspense builds, since Jamil asks Buthayna to cool his burning desire. When a surprised Buthayna queries him about what exactly he has in mind, he tells her that he seeks the kind of special comfort that one lover may give to another. Buthayna recoils and exclaims that such a request from Jamil is totally out of character and informs him that he will never see her face again if he should petition her in this way again. Jamil laughs, thoroughly amused. Of course, he had not actually wanted this kind of special comfort: the request had been only a test. Had she consented, he would have known she might have consented in a similar situation with another man, which would have signaled to him to end the relationship forever (he is chaste and faithful, we understand, and expects Buthayna to be so as well at this stage of their relationship). Having heard this exchange, the father gets up and leaves with his son. Jamil, the father explains, can safely be left alone with Buthayna.[37]

From the stories, Jamil emerges as a new archetype for a Bedouin lover: gallant, devoted, pure. These qualities, we presume, were appealing qualities in a man to listeners of a newly spiritual, monotheistic era. In passing, we may now surmise that it was during the period of 700–750, when stories about Jamil most likely began circulating widely, that Labid's famous line about the best lover breaking the bond decisively began to ring false to listeners, such that it was changed by some reciter—to popular approval—into a statement about the worst lover.

Verse attributed to Jamil appears to have contributed to his legendary status and idealization as a lover. Though one cannot be absolutely certain about which poetry is genuine and which fabricated, it seems sensible to view skeptically those isolated lines that highlight his severe asceticism or extreme chastity. For example, we might doubt that Jamil, even as a devoted admirer grown accustomed to scantiness from Buthayna, could affirm the following:

> I am content with the small things Buthayna accords me; they are so insignificant
> that if the suspicious man who spies on us knew of them, he would be reassured.

> I am content to hear her say "No" and "I cannot,"
> to hope for favors that are always denied.

> I am content to receive from her just a quick glance
> and go the whole year without a rendezvous, from beginning to end.[38]

Likewise, we might question whether Jamil ever made this oath, taking into account the manifold expressions in his *Diwan* of craving for Buthayna:

> By the one before whom men bow down in worship,
> I swear that I have no knowledge of what lies under her dress;

> Nor of what is inside her mouth, and that I have never desired such knowledge;
> our meetings involved solely conversation and looking at each other.[39]

This example would appear to make too much of the chastity of Jamil's youth, whereas the previous one would appear to exaggerate the asceticism of his later life. That both examples turn up in the *Diwan* as detached statements, and not as part of longer poems, renders them yet more dubious. Such lines could have been slipped somewhat easily into the *Diwan* by a crafty transmitter to enhance the Jamil legend. This last consideration aside, it is hard to imagine such pronouncements being made by a real man.

Why, we may ask ourselves, was 'Udhri Jamil so popular in the Umayyad era and beyond, to the degree that he was transformed into a legend? Clearly, his poetry, the basis for his popularity, struck a chord. Yet what specifically resonated to the early audiences? In order to propose an answer to this particular question, let us reconsider for a moment his most famous *ghazal*. In it we find expressions of longing for a bygone time when the poet was happy with a mere trifle and wistful speculation about whether he might ever return to Wadi al-Qura, the place where he experienced this happiness. With this thought in mind, we might recollect the historical circumstances at the time of composition. During this period the Muslim Arabs were sweeping through Syria, Iraq, Persia, Palestine, Egypt, North Africa, and the Iberian Peninsula (al-Andalus). Bedouins in the late seventh and early eighth centuries were migrating and settling down in the new cities of Basra, Kufa, and Fustat (Old Cairo), as well as the established ones of Damascus, Jerusalem, and Alexandria (to name just a few of their destinations). In far-flung locations, a process of settlement and urbanization was under way. We suppose, therefore, that the communities of former Bedouins, suddenly surrounded by city walls and the trappings of wealth, identified closely with Jamil's nostalgic sentiments about the past. Their spartan desert existence, in memory, surely had been simpler and happier. One can imagine them thinking back to the days of carefree pleasure and wishing, too, that the old days were new. Similarly, one can envision them wondering whether they would ever return, on the backs of swift she-camels, to their native wadis. Alas, would that they might go back and be happy there again as they once were!

Such nostalgic thoughts, in essence, are pastoral longings. Paul Fussell, in "On the Persistence of the Pastoral," has astutely observed that "the pastoral impulse—that is, the hankering after an easier form of the world—is never destroyed. Founded as it is on the bedrock of universal human wishes, it merely changes its external shape from age to age, incarnating itself now in this form, now in that, but never vanishing."[40] Indeed, we see it manifest itself in the bucolic poetry of Theocritus (d. ca. 260 BCE), which first appealed to the urbanized Greeks in Alexandria. We recognize it in these lines voiced by a displaced shepherd to his colleague, from *The Eclogues* by Roman poet Virgil (d. 19 BCE):

O! must the wretched Exiles ever mourn,
Nor after length of rolling years return?

Are we condemn'd by Fate's unjust Decree,
No more our Houses and our Homes to see?
Or shall we mount again the Rural Throne,
And rule the Country Kingdoms, once our own!
(trans. John Dryden)

In English literature, we recognize the pastoral impulse perhaps most notably in Milton's classic poem *Paradise Lost.* Furthermore, pastoral longing, as a universal feeling, not only finds expression in high literary forms. We detect the same wish to return to a simpler way of life in this reminiscence by a contemporary Bedouin woman, who has moved to a coastal town of Sinai:

We were far, far away in the mountains where there is a valley with palms. We stayed there, and ate dates and figs and we were happy; we were happier than anyone in the world.
    After that we gathered everything and left, and we came here to Nuwayba.[41]

In the period that concerns us, pastoral longing takes shape primarily in poetry about the Arabian Peninsula. As the Bedouins distanced themselves from their homeland, increasingly it seems, they looked back. Jaroslav Stetkevych writes: "The Bedouin poet thus began possessing Tihamah, the Hejaz, and, above all, Najd when he stepped out of them; and when he had lost these regions in the dispersions of the empire, these places, these names, then possessed him."[42] The longing is also evident in the construction of numerous winter palaces by the Umayyads on the edge of the Syrian Desert. There, during the temperate and rainy months, they could witness the desert bloom, as all the tribes used to do in the season of congregation, and enjoy the pastime of hunting. And presumably from within the court, from the harem, we hear the sound of nostalgia for the old life. Here are lines attributed to Maysun, wife of the caliph Mu'awiya:

Truly, a tent cooled by rustling breezes
is dearer to me than a high palace;

And more than the sound of a tambourine,
I love the sound of the wind in a ravine;

I prefer the watchdog's bark
to the purr of a friendly cat;

And I would rather wear a wool cloak
than be dressed in finery;

And I would take an honorable, lean cousin
over some heavyset, courtly man.[43]

One might contend that the pastoral longings of the period are most pronounced in the *Diwan* of Jamil. Life in the Hejaz that he remembers is always idyllic. He forgets (or does not wish to remember) the harsh realties of desert life, the long months of drought. Here, for instance, he recalls an oasis atmosphere:

Alas, would that I knew whether I will ever spend a night
by a wide torrent bed that issues into an area thick with palms;

At a place where the air is redolent with musk—or rather,
with the musky scent diffused by Buthayna, trailing her skirt in the sand.[44]

The place, cool probably at this time, fertile, and fragrant, suggests Paradise on earth. There, as we would expect, is Buthayna. In fact, throughout the *Diwan,* Buthayna is closely associated with the setting of the poet's youth. She never leaves the Hejaz. One realizes that she symbolizes to the poet an inextricable and essential part of his lost Paradise. Yet he could return to the Hejaz for brief visits through much of his life, it seems, and later in his imagination. There, always, was Buthayna, fresh and beautiful. One real or imagined visit prompts him to remark:

You are like the pearl in a Persian king's crown,
luminous in your youth, still under twenty.

We were neighbors; our springtime abode was always the same;
how have I grown old, while you have not changed?[45]

What, in Paradise, we might ask, does change?

In summary, we conclude that Jamil's poetry gave poignant expression to the pastoral longings of his time, and frequently satisfied vicariously the desire to go back to the scene of former happiness.

Finally, we note that the collective remembrance of a golden age and the vicarious return to it imply a disaffection to a certain extent with current reality. Renate Jacobi has found that 'Udhri love is consistently identified with the Bedouin as contrasted with urban love and that 'Udhri stories as a phenomenon reflect a yearning for a society where the segregation of the sexes is not so strictly observed.[46] Truly, one supposes, it became more difficult for the sexes to intermingle freely in the walled and subdivided cities, where segregation might more easily be enforced, than it had been in the open desert. Furthermore, new doctrine was formulated that established strict guidelines regarding visual contact among nonhousehold and nonfamily members. This principle is the doctrine of the licit and the illicit looks. According to the doctrine, the first look is permitted, since it may occur inadvertently, whereas the second, being intentional, is forbidden. Al-Jahiz took issue with this doctrine in his "Epistle on the Singing Girls" (written probably between 800 and 850) and affirmed that "Looking is licit provided that there is no admixture of forbidden behavior." He cites the example of Jamil and Buthayna, among other 'Udhri couples, as proof that men and women could enjoy innumerable glances without being stimulated to lustful activity.[47] In his response, we sense a dissatisfaction with the conservative turn that society had taken, and from it we appreciate the mental relief that stories of Jamil and Buthayna and stories of the other 'Udhris must have afforded to urbanites. These lovers of old had ample opportunities to visit each other and were able to nurture a relationship. In addition, the gallant hero, once exiled, could find his way back to the beloved repeatedly, since, as a rule, the two protagonists were from the same tribe. Yet for all their private meetings, the lovers remain virtuous; Jamil and Buthayna look at each other innocently. Jamil, the paragon of chastity, defies the logic of social restriction. This discussion leads us from our proper subject and leaves a fictionalized impression, however. The idealized representation of Jamil ultimately tells us more about the freedom-loving character of people in a conservative urban society than it does about the Bedouin poet. Jamil the great poet, we discern from his works, was recognizably human.

6

Flyting

The poem's message should slaughter.

—ʿANAYZ ABU SALIM AL-ʿURDI, quoted in
Clinton Bailey, *Bedouin Poetry from Sinai and the Negev*

OUR NEXT POET, Jarir, was born ca. 653 in Yamama, the desert region of central-northeastern Arabia. He belonged to Kulayb ibn Yarbuʿ of the very large Tamim tribal group. Around 690 he moved to Basra, where he made a name for himself. His specialty was satire; over the next several decades he abused scores of fellow poets. Likewise, they satirized him. After several decades of activity in Basra, and in the cities of Syria and Palestine during periodical visits, he retired to his native Yamama. He died there ca. 730.

Though satire was not discussed in the opening chapters of this study, it indeed was a major mode of early Arabic poetry. Yet it was becoming even more prominent in the Umayyad period and taking on a new aspect. Pre-Islamic satire, it may be said, was predominantly tribal. Even when one smeared an individual, one could expect that his or her kin would feel insulted, and harsh lines might come back from any poet in the concerned tribe. With the advent of Islam, there was initially an effort to suppress satire due to the Qur'anic emphasis on brotherhood (49:10, and many places elsewhere). The second caliph, ʿUmar, for example, warned against vilifying (which meant to him essentially, "That you compare people and say: 'So-and-so is better than so-and-so, or: the clan of so-and-so is better than so-and-so'"),[1] and governor of Basra Ibn ʿAbbas (d. 689) later reportedly declared: "Hija' [satire] is not proper, for you cannot avoid making *hija'* on other persons from his clan, so that you would wrong those who did not wrong you and abuse those who did not abuse you. . . . You know the virtue that lies in forgiving."[2] Nevertheless, satire gained in popularity, especially in the form of scornful exchanges

115

between rival poets. No fewer than ten pairs of poets during the Umayyad period were largely absorbed in the enterprise of humiliating one another. It was, as Salma K. Jayyusi has pointed out, an Age of Satire.[3] And notably, in contrast with what unkind words were earlier launched from one side to the other and vice versa, the satire was more personal, aimed particularly at an individual.

It perhaps may be useful here to clarify the nature of satire in classical Arabic poetry. As a rule, it is invective. The formal exchange of invective that became so popular, furthermore, is best described as flyting. This term originally referred to a form in the Scottish poetic tradition (as in the fifteenth-century "The Flyting of Dunbar and Kennedie"), but close analogues to the Scottish form existed previously—besides in classical Arabic poetry—in Greek and Roman and also in medieval French traditions. Generally speaking, the form is related to the poetic contests that are found in many literatures. Invective, the substance of these classical Arabic duels, is of course ancient, as old as verse itself. We might recall that satire, though manifold in expression, has for much of history been associated specifically with this kind of personal poetic abuse. So it was, one notes, in sixteenth-century England and France. Compare, for instance, Joseph Hall:

The *Satyre* should be like the *Porcupine,*
That shoots sharpe quils out in each angry line,
And wounds the blushing cheeke, and fiery eye,
Of him that heares, and readeth guiltily.

It may be of further interest to note, in this regard, that satire qua invective was condemned widely by western Europeans in the eighteenth century on moral grounds and had lost much of its popularity among them by the mid-nineteenth century. Similarly, we may add, invective has declined in popularity in the Arab world during the modern period, with the major exception of the bold poetry by Muzaffar al-Nawwab (about contemporary Arab rulers).

In this chapter we shall read a poem (No. 50) from the most famous flyting in Arabic literature, between Jarir and al-Farazdaq.[4] Before we get to the poem, however, let us first acquaint ourselves with Jarir's opponent and with the provenance of their dispute.

Al-Farazdaq was born in Yamama a few years before Jarir. He belonged to Mujashi' ibn Darim, also of the Tamim group. His father, Ghalib, was a man of very high standing in Mujashiʿ. As a youth al-Farazdaq showed an aptitude for poetry and an inclination for vaunting himself and for belittling others; he soon developed into a fearsome satirist. He was introduced by his father, it is said, at Basra (the family had settled there) to the fourth caliph, ʿAli. "Teach him the Qurʾan," the caliph told Ghalib, after hearing some of the young man's poetry.[5] Probably Ghalib did teach him some of the Holy Revelation. A number of years later, while performing the Hajj, al-Farazdaq vowed to compose no more poetry until he had memorized the Qurʾan completely. He went so far as to attach chains to himself to symbolize his commitment. He was in this state, back in Basra, when Jarir's name came to his attention.

Jarir, meanwhile, had been involved for numerous years in disputes with other poets of Yamama. Eventually, al-Baʿith, a kinsman of al-Farazdaq, weighed in on the side of one of the poets Jarir had been criticizing. Jarir responded with a lampoon on al-Baʿith and the tribe of Mujashiʿ. Al-Baʿith sent word to al-Farazdaq, and the latter found himself compelled to make a reply. He said in a poem:

> News from al-Baʿith reached me,
> and between us lay Zarud and the dark-colored sands.
>
> So I said, "Does that son of a wicked woman suppose
> that I have become distracted from taking arrows from my quiver?"
>
> And if I have made a vow, to which these chains attest,
> that does not mean I have become distracted from matters of tribal repute.
>
> I am the one accountable for my tribe, their protector,
> and it is up to me, or someone of my stature, to defend their honor.[6]

Hardly deterred, Jarir composed a poem filled with ridicule of al-Farazdaq and further insults of his kin. Again al-Farazdaq made an answer. Thus began a poetic dialogue that was to last more than forty years and ended only with al-Farazdaq's death (ca. 730). During the course of the long flyting, a number of poets joined al-Farazdaq's side, including al-Akhtal, court poet of the Umayyads. Jarir took to abusing these poets, too. Naturally, concerns beside the flyting, such as Jarir's concern to address his other opponents also, arose for the two men during this period. For each man, however, satirizing the other remained his chief business.

The poem below cannot be dated precisely. But it apparently belongs to the earlier part of their interaction rather than to the later, since Jarir alludes in it to al-Farazdaq's wife, Nawar, in such a way that suggests the couple were still married at the time (ultimately, they were divorced).[7] There also exists a disagreement over whether this poem was recited first or second in the round of flyting. (Al-Farazdaq's accompanying poem, in the same meter and rhyme, is not closely connected thematically to this one; it seems probable that both were composed individually before being recited together.) If the exact situation that gave rise to the poem therefore remains obscure, the place of its first recital can at least be confidently identified: Mirbad, the large meeting area on the outskirts of Basra. Mirbad functioned as 'Ukaz had during pre-Islamic times, as an entrepôt for goods and information and as a forum for new poetry. There, Jarir and al-Farazdaq fought their fiercest battles. There, in all likelihood, Jarir, flanked by supporters and loosely enclosed by a crowd, recited his poem to al-Farazdaq, al-Ba'ith, and a cohort of Mujashi' men.

We shall read the work as a sample of Jarir's invective. Then, after summarizing the work's structural and thematic elements, we shall conclude with a few observations about poetry and society in the Umayyad period, based on our reading of the poem.

A

1   What is it about encampment traces, by the curved sands of 'Unayyiq
     or by the hard ground of Matar, that stirred your longing?

2   There strong winds spared
     the tent stays and the hitching posts for colts.

3   Is it something like the separation you faced that day at 'Unayza,
     like the passion you experienced at Shaqa'iq al-Ahfar?

4   Yes, I saw your fire that season when it was burning brightly,[8]
     and I saw the most comely faces around it.

5   As for al-Ba'ith, it became apparent that he is a slave;[9]
     and perhaps, as pertains to him, you shall have more to say.

6   Baseness has muzzled al-Ba'ith;
     and al-Farazdaq's mother has groaned loudly at the worst little camel that
         came forth.

7   Truly al-Farazdaq and al-Baʿith and al-Baʿith's mother and father
     are the very worst foursome!

8   Al-Farazdaq tripped and fell in the contest, and then quick wit covered him
     on a racecourse where truth prevails.

9   You wish to be among the front-runners, O Farazdaq,
     after you extinguished your fire and approached mine.

10   Indeed my fire burns whomever I seek out for his insolence;
     its heat reaches those who go astray.

11   Woe to you for your errant boasting,
     while your father's inner and outer garments are sullied with shame!

12   What do you have to say for yourself, now that I have triumphed over you,
     and the Muslims acknowledge what I say?

13   When you ask an opinion, the judges rule against you;
     when you boast, my boasting rises above you.

14   Lo, I am the day whose light spreads over you,
     and the night that takes your vision.

Jarir opens the poem with a short *nasib*. One is apt to wonder about the purport of this prelude, occurring as it does in a satire. Its brevity suggests that, in the context of the poem, the memories themselves are not so important. More important, one gathers, is how they reflect on the poet—that is, how they help to form in our minds an image of him, which we can then compare to the subsequent representation of al-Farazdaq and the others. What might Jarir wish to communicate about himself through the *nasib*? From these few lines we understand that he is a Bedouin who has known beloveds in various seasons and that one of them was quite beautiful and moreover often surrounded by lovely friends. Imru' al-Qays immediately comes to mind. Yet Jarir's *Diwan* indicates that we are not to think here of another Don Juan. His poetry leads us to believe that he grew up chaste, albeit against his will. Experience, he states, taught him a hard lesson:

> I have found that the promised rendezvous
> moves like the shadow of a cloud.[10]

In another poem he reports of a beloved:

> I fell for a jinni who withholds her favors,
> one beautified alternately by coquetry and shyness.[11]

Even when he was in dire need, evidently the young women he loved were not inclined to succor him. In a poem recited before 'Abd al-Malik (r. 685–705),[12] he says:

> From the water hole you drove a man raving with thirst;
> and had you wished, you could have let him drink.[13]

Consistently, Jarir represents himself as a man who was attracted to beauty yet barred from attaining his goal. He loved honorable women, in other words, and did not commit any great transgressions. Looking back, he summarizes nostalgically:

> Gone is a praiseworthy youth.
> Would that that time might return, or could be purchased.[14]

Taking Jarir's *Diwan* into consideration, we can be assured that he evokes at the beginning of this satire his own praiseworthy romantic history.

The transition to al-Ba'ith in line 5 requires comment, as the connecting idea from line 4 is probably somewhat obscure. It is clear enough that mention of the fire and the lovely faces in 4 logically precedes a statement of what al-Ba'ith looks like. Yet implied in the transition is a contrast between the nobility of the beloved and her companions—associates of the poet—and the ignominy of al-Ba'ith. Among the Arabs, clear and bright, good-looking faces were associated with, and taken to symbolize, nobility, as well as honor. On the other hand, darkness of visage, ugliness, and so forth connoted baseness.[15] That al-Ba'ith is a slave, therefore, can be discerned by looking at him. (And hence Jarir quips elsewhere, at the expense of a tribe: "When you encounter Taym together with its slaves, you say: / 'Who are the slaves?'")[16] The outward appearance of those individuals the poet loves—his own kind, we infer—and the ones he disdains tells much about them.

Thereafter, Jarir begins to satirize al-Farazdaq, who concerns him for the rest of the section. He stresses that al-Farazdaq loses badly in their poetic contests. This fact can be verified, he remarks significantly, by asking the Muslims.

B

15   We charge on our horses, and you see the cloud of dust;
    we strike with the shining swords of the mighty;

16   While Mujashi' does not guard jealously its womenfolk,
    and does not give those who solicit protection their due.

17   Our warriors wait to attack your tribe
       as our horsemen did by the mountain on the morning of Mujazzal al-Amrar.[17]

18   My tribe: those whose frequent mention sharpens my hearing,
       by whose light I see;

19   Those who bring their full-grown camels to water despite the threatening
            spears;
       who color their stallions' bridles with the enemy's blood.

20   Are you thankful, then, for those who drive from you captives,
       and take from you women on swaying camel saddles?

21   My horsemen are known at the narrow passes,
       and they spread dust at every brown place.

22   We are the builders of columns and the raisers of horsemen
       that tower above all other columns and horsemen.

23   Rabi'a calls, and our coat of mail is ample,
       secured at the waist under a sword-suspensory.[18]

                                    C

24   Truly al-Ba'ith and that slave of the Maqa'is family[19]
       do not read a sura of the learned.

                                    B[1]

25   Send word to the Banu Waqban that their women are loose,
       daughters of the weak man marked for servitude.[20]

26   You are the sons of a slave woman,
       so the door of nobility has been closed before you, you sons of al-Nikhwar.

27   O Banu Qufayra! On the day when qualities were apportioned,
       you were allotted the lowliness of Nizar.[21]

28   Indeed the lowborn—the sons of the lowborn—are Mujashi';
       and they are the most impure in the area of the loincloth.

29   The army struck at the daughters of Mujashi'
       until the daughters had had enough, and they were no longer virgins.

30   Verily the wanton daughters of Mujashi'
       are refuges for thieves and playfields for profligates.

31   The Mujashi' daughter whose husband is away
       weeps despondently whenever she hears a donkey bray.

32   The daughters of Mujashi' do not crave what is small;
       they want something like a fuller's mallet.

Sections B and B¹ serve as evidence of the persistence of pre-Islamic values, beside the new Islamic values, in Jarir's time. The satire in these sections is purely tribal, based on a stark contrast between two sets of kin. Jarir's tribe consists of brave, respected warriors who respond to appeals for aid. Al-Farazdaq's kinsmen, meanwhile, do not protect their charges. Worse, their womenfolk have a licentious streak. In its obscenity, however, Jarir's satire is rather distinctly of the Umayyad period. Unlike pre-Islamic invective, which tends to be somewhat restrained in terms of sexual content, scabrous language, and the like, the work of the Umayyad satirists can be really quite harsh and explicit. (Note Joseph Hall: "It is not for euery one to rellish a true and naturall Satyre.")[22] Evidently, the audiences for this poetry, in places such as the garrison city of Basra and its northerly counterpart Kufa, enjoyed it that way.

A¹

33   O little son, born of hairy pubes! What do you think, your training period over,
    now that our warfare has inflicted upon you serious injury?[23]

34   The *qasidas* have traveled and have destroyed Mujashiʿ
    in what lies between Egypt and south Wabar.[24]

35   Are you angry at me that the son resembled Qufayra
    in the vicinity of the collar and the cheek?[25]

36   When al-Khatafa built our abode,[26] I was pleased with what he built,
    while al-Farazdaq's father was busy pumping a blacksmith's bellows.

37   They reprove others after a blacksmith has allowed access to their women
    and settled the tribe in the abode of perdition.

38   Do not boast when you hear Mujashiʿ men around you
    bellowing like bulls!

39   He said, once word of his wife reached him:
    "Nawar of Mujashiʿ is not *nawar*!"[27]

40   She called out, in a drunken fit, to her cousin Daris:
    "Help me find my bracelet! Woe!"[28]

41   Al-Farazdaq slept away from Nawar
    as he slept away from Jiʿthin on the night of betrayal.[29]

42   Indeed the *qasidas* will continue roaming the land with the particulars of
        Jiʿthin
    as long as night-travelers sing.

43   You spend the nights drinking
       with those of clipped forelocks and wet fingers, who operate wine-presses.
44   Do not boast, for the religion of Mujashi' is the religion of Magians:
       you circumambulate idols.

In the last section Jarir returns to addressing al-Farazdaq personally. He alleges that his opponent has descended from a line of slaves, including great-grandmother Qufayra, the woman al-Nikhwar, and the man Waqban. Al-Nikhwar, judging from her name, is most likely fictitious.[30] Waqban, though, was one of several slaves owned by al-Farazdaq's grandfather Sa'sa'a who were made to work as blacksmiths. Jarir insinuates that Waqban actually is al-Farazdaq's grandfather and that his son—al-Farazdaq's father—was likewise tasked with ironwork (that Qufayra could not be al-Farazdaq's great-grandmother, if it were true, does not seem to have been of particular concern to Jarir). Hence, slave blood runs thick in al-Farazdaq.

The allegation about blacksmithing merits some further discussion on its own. The Arabs during this period, and similarly earlier, disparaged people who performed manual labor, whether by compulsion or as a means of support. Men in the desert region traditionally raised camels, trained a few select horses, and, most important, fought. The settled artisan did none of the above, and the slave participated in these activities only when his master called him away from menial tasks. Blacksmiths, then, performed contemptible work and had no opportunities commonly to win glory. They merely served the noble caste, a point that Jarir emphasizes in this line:

You are blacksmiths;
you fashion the swords we wield on battle days.[31]

Through our above discussion of Waqban and the Farazdaq family connection to ironwork, we have seen how Jarir seizes on a half-truth, and then exploits it to create a damaging, false impression. It may be added that Jarir reinforces this false impression in the public imagination by playing on the same theme in virtually all his other satires on that individual. This technique he uses, one readily finds, with respect to what unfortunately befell al-Farazdaq's sister Ji'thin. She was once touched on the shoulder, it so happened, by a man of another tribe in return for al-Farazdaq's incivility. Jarir made use of this unpleasant encounter for some forty years, referring to it constantly and bringing many new details to light about the orgy that supposedly took place. The scandal of Ji'thin became notorious.

Jarir ends the poem by adverting to al-Farazdaq's debauched behavior and his impiety. He spends nights away from home, drinking and (as may be assumed from many references in the *Diwan* to his nocturnal behavior) fornicating. And he has evidently infected his wife, Nawar, with his habits, except for spending nights abroad. As for al-Farazdaq's spiritual convictions, they should not be construed as strict Magian. Elsewhere Jarir says:

> Christians love you on their holy day,
> and on the Sabbath your coreligionists are the Jews.[32]

Whatever al-Farazdaq is, he is not Muslim. The adjective *pagan* perhaps fits him best. Truly, such a man has no reason to boast.

NO. 50

Section			Lines	Structural and Thematic Elements
A			1–14	in youth, Jarir loved noble women Al-Ba'ith is clearly a slave address to al-Farazdaq: Muslims verify that Jarir defeats him
	B		15–23	Jarir's tribe are glorious fighters; they respond to calls for aid the tribe waits to attack Mujashi'
		C	24	Al-Ba'ith and al-Farazdaq do not read the Qur'an
	B¹		25–32	Mujashi' men are lowborn; they do not protect their charges Mujashi' women are licentious
A¹			33–44	Al-Farazdaq sleeps away from wife and drinks Al-Farazdaq is a slave of blacksmith ancestry address to al-Farazdaq: Jarir harms him; a pagan like al-Farazdaq should not boast

Now that we have read from Jarir, let us consider for a moment his opponent's brand of satire. The satiric poems by al-Farazdaq are also based on the principle of contrast. One part of them, invariably, consists of reminders to his adversary of his own forebears' distinction. For example, he tells Jarir:

> My father is the sheikh with the copious and steady stream of urine, a
>   Mujashi' man.
> He raised me, and my paternal uncles are 'Abd Allah and Nahshal.
>
> Three predecessors. So come forward, O son of the wallowing place,[33]
> with ones comparable; each is superior in nobility and honor.[34]

The other part invariably features scornful statements about his rival's family and relatives. Jarir's father, for instance, receives relentless abuse. He is typically identified as a mule driver, or simply as a mule (the "wallowing place" in the line above signifies a mule's dirty wallowing place; it is an epithet for Jarir's mother). Moreover, time and again, he is singled out as destitute. For example:

> Your father's life was always hard:
> he subsisted on scraps like the dogs.[35]

We find the same pattern in the satire by al-Farazdaq paired with Jarir's poem in the flyting series (No. 49). Lest Jarir forget whom he is dealing with, he emphasizes:

> What a line of fathers I have, O Jarir,
> each one like the moon or the sun!
>
> Each inherits noble qualities from his illustrious predecessor,
> and looms large on the day of boasting.

And from his position of grandeur, he asks:

> O son of the wallowing place, how do you seek to impugn Darim,
> when your father takes his place between a female and a male ass?[36]

Such a style, based solely on invidious comparisons of lineage and not based also on comparisons of individual merit, is traditional, characteristic of pre-Islamic satires. In terms of subject matter, therefore, Jarir's may be described as a newer style. Other differences as well distinguish the two men's poetry. In keeping with tradition, al-Farazdaq's satires tend to be relatively short; many of them are epigrammatic. The satires by Jarir, on the other hand, often run long ("People never tire of hearing wickedness," he explained).[37] Also, Jarir's verse is noticeably more graceful and flowing. "Jarir scoops poetry from the sea," it was frequently said in this regard, "whereas al-Farazdaq cuts it from rock."[38] Thus, clear distinctions separate the work of these two men. It might be added that a debate raged throughout the Umayyad period, and for a long time after, over whose poetry was superior. On the whole, the elite and the learned favored al-Farazdaq's poems, whereas the general public preferred those by Jarir.

We can well imagine the pleasure that the flyting of Jarir and al-Farazdaq afforded crowds at Mirbad and at other places, how good lines were greeted with throaty calls and laughter. Indeed, the flyting in this period was a prime form of competitive public entertainment. The contest resembled horse racing, as the poets repeatedly suggest. Each vied for precedence and glory, to the cheers of supporters. The winner was hailed as a champion; the loser, as Jarir liked to point out, ended up with dust on his face.[39]

Clearly, the phenomenon of flyting reflects the partisanship that still existed in the Umayyad period. Society was in transition, shifting from one Bedouin-tribal in character, to one urban-Islamic, and old loyalties continued to hold even as tribally diverse cities grew.

References in the poems to social inferiors indicate that changes, meanwhile, were occurring in the composition of the individual tribes. On the tribe's historic composition, we recall what pre-Islamic poets claimed: that it was one of brothers, equal in all respects. Yet the tribes in fact comprised multiple classes, as Adel Sulaiman Gamal explains:

> The tribal body embraced three main classes. The first of these in the scale of social status was the freeborn man of pure blood, i.e., the male descendant from a common ancestor who gave the tribe its name. They represented the elite of the tribe and attached great importance to the purity of their blood. The second class consisted of the clients (*mawali*). The clients were either free men who joined a certain tribe seeking its protection (after expulsion from their own tribes), or manumitted slaves who remained within the structure of the tribe

through the bond of *wala'*. The third class was the slaves. Some of these slaves were of Arab stock who had been captured in battles or bought; it was the practice of some Arab tribes to sell their captives. In addition, there was a regular slave trade in some parts of Arabia which provided non-Arab slaves brought from nearby countries. Sons born to tribesmen of slave mothers were considered slaves and were looked upon as inferior members of the tribe even if they possessed high qualities that exceeded that of the free men.[40]

The development in the Umayyad era was the incorporation by each tribe of large numbers of slaves and clients. (The newcomers to Islam, Persians for the most part, were required to affiliate themselves as clients to an Arab tribe; more will be said about this group in the next chapter.) Here Jarir registers what has been happening in society, speaking of the gravely altered Banu Hanifa:

Hanifa has divided in three:
one third are now slaves, and another third are clients.[41]

For satiric purposes, however, the clients were usually ignored, comparisons typically being drawn to the more lowly slaves.

The flyting specifically between Jarir and al-Farazdaq reflects a conflict also within the top level of society (distinct from the lateral conflict between tribes), between men of different stations with perceptibly different value systems. Al-Farazdaq represents the man at the top of the tribal hierarchy, for whom inherited glory is essentially everything. What can the son of a donkey driver say to him? He ridicules Jarir as an upstart, a saucy pretender to nobility from humble parentage.

Interestingly, Jarir does not seem to have been affected by al-Farazdaq's ridicule. It is said that he listened to his poems with patience and equanimity. (By contrast, al-Farazdaq would reportedly wince, fidget, and so forth when Jarir recited.)[42] In his poetry, Jarir is dismissive of al-Farazdaq's capacity to injure, such as in this line concerning one of Jarir's transmitters:

Al-Farazdaq has declared that he shall kill Mirba'—
Rejoice, O Mirba', at the prospect of a long life![43]

In fact, Jarir is dismissive of the threat from his opponents collectively. Here he describes them, having just come forward toward him:

The poets yelped to one another,
stricken by my retaliation,

As if they were a pack of foxes
that had entered the den of a lion with a tremendous roar.[44]

Jarir was apparently confident in his ability to respond devastatingly, as this last example implies. The following story in *Kitab al-aghani* about his long and brutal retort to Ra'i al-Ibil suggests that he soon found—or was inspired with—the right words to say:

There was a poet of repute, well known by the name of Ra'i al-Ibil, who loudly published his opinion that al-Farazdaq was superior to Jarir, although the latter had lauded his tribe, the Banu Numayr, whereas al-Farazdaq had made verses against them. One day Jarir met him and expostulated with him but got no reply. Ra'i was riding a mule and was accompanied by his son, Jandal, who said to his father: "Why do you halt before this dog of the Banu Kulayb, as though you had anything to hope or fear from him?" At the same time he gave the mule a lash with his whip. The animal started violently and kicked Jarir, who was standing by, so that his cap fell to the ground. Ra'i took no heed and went on his way. Jarir picked up the cap, brushed it, and replaced it on his head. Then he exclaimed in verse:

O Jandal, what do Banu Numayr say
when the male organ disappears into your father's buttocks?

He returned home full of indignation, and after the evening prayer, having called for a jar of date-wine and a lamp, he set about his work. An old woman in the house heard him muttering, and mounted the stairs to see what ailed him. She found him crawling naked on his bed, by reason of that which was within him; so she ran down, crying "He is mad," and described what she had seen to the people of the house. "Go away," they said, "we know what he is at." By daybreak Jarir had composed a satire of some eighty lines against the Banu Numayr. When he finished the poem, he shouted triumphantly, "Allahu Akbar!" and rode to Mirbad where he expected to find Ra'i al-Ibil and al-Farazdaq and their friends. He did not salute Ra'i but immediately began to recite. While he was speaking al-Farazdaq and Ra'i bowed their heads, and the rest of the company sat listening in silent mortification. When Jarir had uttered the line—

> Lower your eyes in shame, for you are of Numayr—
> no peer of Ka'b not yet Kilab—

Ra'i rose and hastened to his lodging as fast as his mule could carry him. "Saddle! Saddle!" he cried to his comrades; "you cannot stay here longer, Jarir has disgraced you all." They left Basra without delay to rejoin their tribe, who bitterly reproached Ra'i for the ignominy which he had brought upon Numayr; and hundreds of years afterwards his name was still a byword among his people.[45]

While we presume, hence, that Jarir was confident in his ability to destroy all manner of enemies, we also suppose that he felt secure, not vulnerable to serious charges. Though he may indeed have come from an ordinary, even rather poor, family, he was still of pure Bedouin stock. Moreover, he was chaste. And if he did sip date wine on occasion, as the above story would indicate, he was not by reputation a drinker. Proud al-Farazdaq, by contrast, opened himself up to criticism by his un-Islamic behavior.[46] Here Jarir observes pointedly (the second example concerns us in particular):

> Verily al-Farazdaq is disgraced by his vices;
> he is a slave by day, a creeping fornicator by night.[47]

John Dryden has said, "A satirical poet is the check of the laymen on bad priests."[48] With some validity, one may regard al-Farazdaq as representative of the old, reactionary priests in a newly Islamic age. For them, blood—by which standard they were eminent—was of singular, paramount importance. Jarir, in his sustained satire of al-Farazdaq, affirms as one of the more commonly born Arabs that now, in the new age, individual virtue also matters.

7

Pleasure in Transgression

There are more things in heaven and earth, Horatio,
Than are dreamt of in your philosophy.

—WILLIAM SHAKESPEARE, *Hamlet*

IN THIS CHAPTER we shall study a wine poem (*khamriyya*) by the most famous libertine poet in Arabic literature, Abu Nuwas (d. ca. 815). Before giving our attention to Abu Nuwas, however, it would be useful to consider the immediate historical and literary backdrop behind him.

In the last two chapters we have been discussing poets of the Umayyad period. A noteworthy poet of this period, as yet unmentioned, an important forerunner to Abu Nuwas with respect to wine poetry, is no less than an Umayyad caliph. This caliph, al-Walid II (al-Walid ibn Yazid), is not remembered for his political accomplishments: he spent two decades reveling as heir apparent and then one year reveling as caliph before he was assassinated in 744. Yet he did leave a few palaces and hunting lodges in the Syrian Desert and a *Diwan* of 115 poems. The art from the palaces speaks of a proud man devoted to pleasure: frescoes at one show a hunt, a pool scene with an almost naked young woman, and a prominent regal figure (shades of Imru' al-Qays?); a mosaic in the private quarters of another depicts a lion preying on a gazelle.[1] From his poetry, we know that al-Walid II did not care a fig for orthodox religious sensitivities. In one poem he invokes the pious people, and God and the angels also, to bear witness:

That my pleasures are listening to music, drinking wine,
and biting ripe cheeks.[2]

Al-Walid II stands out in Arabic literature, besides as the subject of accounts relating to prodigious wine consumption, as the poet who established the *khamriyya*

130

as an independent genre. The following *khamriyya,* which contains themes Abu Nuwas was later to develop, is al-Walid II's most famous:

Cut through the whisper of cares with music,
and rejoice, in Time's despite, with the daughter of the grape.

And welcome the easy life in its abundance;
do not follow regretfully the traces of what's past.

With a pale wine embellished by antiquity,
an old lady that gets more desirable with age.

More delicious to drinkers at her wedding party
than the young woman of noble lineage.

She revealed herself, and then was rarefied
until she appeared in an extraordinary light!

Prior to the mixing, she was fire itself,[3]
and after it, she was liquid gold.

As if the glass containing her was a torch,
blazing before the observer's eye,

Before noble youths of Banu Umayya:
the family of glory, illustrious action, and honor.

They have no peers among men; and I am unique among them.
None traces his origin to such as my father.[4]

Al-Walid II was one of the last Umayyads, and his rule only briefly preceded a major political transformation in the Near East. These excerpts from a sermon by Abu Hamza, preached in the Hejaz of the Arabian Peninsula ca. 747, suggest what bitter anti-Umayyad feelings were being harbored among Muslims around the time of al-Walid II:

Then the sinner al-Walid b. Yazid [al-Walid II] took charge. He drank openly and he deliberately made manifest what is abominable. Then Yazid b. al-Walid [Yazid III; son of al-Walid I, r. 705–15] rose against him and killed him. . . . These Banu Umayya are parties of waywardness. Their might is self-magnification. They arrest on suspicion, make decrees capriciously, kill in anger, and judge by passing over crimes without punishment. . . . These people have acted as unbelievers, by God, in the most barefaced manner. So curse them, may God curse them![5]

Yet it was not from the Hejaz to the south that grave trouble came for the Umayyads. In the East—in Iraq, in Persia, and especially in the northeastern province of Khurasan—disaffection was spreading. The 'Abbasids (descendants of al-'Abbas, uncle of the Prophet) had been denouncing the Umayyads vehemently in mosques and other public places and soon emerged as leaders of a revolt. In 750 their army swept into Syria and overwhelmed the military force of the Umayyads. A general massacre of the Umayyad family ensued (only one male escaped with his life; he is discussed briefly in chapter 10). The 'Abbasids then established a new Islamic state, with Iraq its new center.

For our purposes, we might take notice here of just two new aspects of the 'Abbasid Islamic state. First, the rulers and their high officials, on the whole, were outwardly religious, whether they were actually devout or not. The poem below, from the senior vizier Yahya ibn Khalid (who served long under Caliph Harun al-Rashid [r. 786–809]) to his son al-Fadl, who apparently had been throwing caution to the wind in his extracurricular activities, indicates how one of the leading 'Abbasid figures was to comport himself:

Devote yourself by day to worthy endeavor,
and grimly endure your beloved's absence.

Until night comes along,
drawing its veil over the faces of vice.

Then defy the gloom with all you delight in;
for night is rather day to the artful.

How many a young man, an ascetic you would suppose,
ushers in night with something unexpected!

No sooner does night lower its curtains on him
than he turns to fine comforts and most splendid entertainment!

A fool, on the other hand, lets his pleasure be seen;
then every watchful enemy runs off to describe it.[6]

The other new aspect of the ʿAbbasid state of which we might take notice was the increased integration into government of Persian converts. These converts, from the eastern territories of Islam, had broadly supported the ʿAbbasid revolution and, in the new state, many more of them were able to rise to positions of influence. Most conspicuous at court were the Barmakids, a Persian family that held a succession of very high posts from the 750s until their downfall in 803 (Yahya ibn Khalid, quoted above, was of this family). Whereas in the Umayyad era the ruling class had been essentially Arabs, it now included Muslims of other ethnicities, especially Persians.

In the multiethnic environment of ʿAbbasid Iraq, a movement called the Shuʿubiyya emerged, whose effects may be discerned in Abu Nuwas's poetry. We recall from the previous chapter that the Arabs of the Umayyad period had been in the habit of looking down upon the non-Arab Muslims, who were required to affiliate themselves to an Arab tribe as clients (mawali). The attitude expressed by al-Mughira ibn Habnaʾ, in the course of a flyting with Ziyad al-Aʿjam, is characteristic:

Go back to where you came from, Ziyad,
and don't aspire to what, as a Persian, is beyond you.

. . . .

You satirize the noble while you are the most ignominious of men
and the foreigner in speech.[7]

But the Qurʾan states, with total clarity, that God made mankind into "peoples [shuʿub, whence Shuʿubiyya] and tribes [qabaʾil] so that you may get to know one another" and that "the noblest among you in God's view are the most pious" (49:13). Some Muslims in the 'Abbasid period, the Ahl al-Taswiyya (Proponents of Equalization), took this verse as proof that Arab Muslims were not innately superior to their non-Arab counterparts. Going further than them, the Persian Shu'ubi respondents asserted their own superiority to the Arabs. Of the Shu'ubiyya representatives in Arabic literature, most important is the great poet Bashshar ibn Burd (d. 783). This poem by Bashshar, composed in a shortened *rajaz* meter, gives us an idea of their view of the Arabs and of some of their talking points:

Is there anyone who will inform the Arabs for me—

Those alive and those dead and buried—

That my honor exceeds any of theirs?

Chosroes is my grandfather; he exalts me. And Sasan is my father,[8]

And Caesar my maternal uncle, should I reckon my genealogy.

How many—how many a father I have who wore a crown,

Ruled haughtily, and caused stubborn knees to bend!

He conducted his morning audience decked in jewels,

Robed in ermine, and curtained from common view.

Behind the veil servants hastened to him with vessels of gold.

⁂

No, he was not given camel milk from wrinkly skins;

Nor did he ever drive scabby beasts with song;

Nor pierce colocynth out of aching hunger;

Nor strike mimosa with a stave, to get its bitter fruit.

We never roasted a skink, with squirming tail;

Nor did I ever dig for a lizard, in stony ground, to eat it.

My father did not warm himself standing astride a small fire;

Nor drive away a prophet, nor prostrate himself before idols.

No, certainly not! Nor did he once ride a laden hump-back.

⁂

Verily, in the bygone ages we were always kings.

⁂

We brought our horses from Balkh[9]—this no lie—

And gave them to drink from Aleppo's two rivers,[10]

And had them trample over Syria's hard terrain.

We proceeded to Egypt as a clamorous army,

And took for ourselves what realm had been snatched by others.

Thus we continued, riding all the way to marvelous Tangier,

Restoring sovereignty to the family of the Arabian Prophet.

Congratulations, O Abu Fadl al-'Abbas, most worthy of the Quraysh
    to carry the Prophet's standard![11]

Who is there who has opposed right guidance and religion,
    that has not been plundered?

Who, O who has resisted it or tried to encroach on its domain,
   that has not been overrun?

We are stirred on behalf of God and Islam to the most violent anger!

⁂

I am descended from two lines of Persia, and Persia's staunch defender.

We are the ones with crowns, with sovereignty;
   the most honorable, the victorious.[12]

Abu Nuwas's mother, Gullaban, was Persian. Though he was not a Shuʻubi, as Albert Arazi has conclusively shown, he shares the Shuʻubi sentiment insofar as he depreciates the Bedouins. Yet he diminishes them and belittles their way of life to promote the Iraqi civilized life by contrast. Unlike the Shuʻubis, who reflect proudly on Persia, he reflects swellingly on pre-Islamic Yemen and finds there the existence of an authentic Arab urban civilization.[13] But we should not go further into the meanings of his poetry, it seems, without first acquainting ourselves with the poet.

Abu Nuwas was born ca. 756 in Ahwaz, a city located in southwest Persia. His father, an Arab from Damascus, died when he was a few years old, and soon after the mother took the children to Basra. In Basra, Abu Nuwas received a thorough education from numerous learned men and eventually began to compose poetry. When he was in his twenties or thereabouts, he met in Basra supposedly the only woman he ever loved: a woman by the name of Jinan. Here he describes the sight of her, the day of a sad event in her household:

O fawn brought out of her covert by a funeral,
   wailing amongst those of her kind!

She weeps, dropping little pearls from narcissi,
   and strikes two roses with jujube.[14]

Don't weep for one who rests in his grave—
   weep for one who lies slain at your door!

The funeral today brought her outdoors
despite guards' and maids' previous efforts to hide her.

Death, as ever, befalls her admirer when she turns . . .
yet still I keep looking her way.[15]

They began to correspond, and he composed many tender poems about her, a number in the form of love letters. Still, the relationship never progressed; the household did not see fit that it should do so, and Jinan, for her part, was unwilling to risk her situation for a love affair. He noted once wistfully:

Jinan's face is a lovely garden
containing all varieties of color.

Its splendor is offered freely to the eyes
but barred from the fingers.

And I may only look upon it
just like all the other people.[16]

In 786, when he was about thirty, Abu Nuwas left Basra for Baghdad, where it seems he got over Jinan soon enough. Truly, he would have had much to divert him there. The capital, founded only in 762 by al-Mansur (r. 754–75) and given the title Madinat al-Salam (City of Peace), was prospering incredibly and growing at an astounding rate. Consider, for example, that the annual inflow to the treasury during the time of Harun al-Rashid (r. 786–809) was some 150 million gold dinars (the equivalent of some 3 billion silver dirhams). What had started as a building site was being transformed, in less than one lifetime, into the world's largest metropolis by far. By 800 the population had reached roughly 2 million people (for comparison note that Paris, the largest city of Western Christendom, had, in the fourteenth century, about one-tenth this population). In terms of area, Baghdad had grown by 800 to the approximate size of Paris in 1900.[17] Small wonder then, taking into account what had emerged there, that a dialogue such as this one might afterward take place:

"O Yunis, have you ever been to Baghdad?"

"No."

"Then you haven't seen the world."[18]

In Baghdad Abu Nuwas, supported by patronage from the Barmakids, threw himself into a life of pleasure. He was asked one time if he would perform a pilgrimage to Mecca, and he replied that he would perform one only when Baghdad's delights were exhausted.[19] He did travel in Iraq, however, on getaways with friends, to try local vintages. One of his favorite destinations was Dayr Hanna (Hanna Monastery) near Kufa, about which he sang famously:

> O Dayr Hanna, namely the place with the little monk cells:
> others may sober up from you, but I never will.[20]

The rural monasteries typically sold their own wines; the profits helped to cover monastic expenses. The monasteries usually afforded a pleasant garden to drink in and rooms for retirement. Abu Nuwas also greatly enjoyed staying a night or two with his friends (sometimes more nights) at rural taverns, which were often enhanced by gardens and singing girls. Judging from the descriptions, nothing was lacking at these places that might contribute to the guests' comfort. Indeed, in a poem not unlike many others, discussed by James Montgomery, Abu Nuwas depicts an earthly symposium he attends in terms of the Qur'anic Paradise.[21]

While Abu Nuwas, on the one hand, was evoking in his poetry features of a new reality, on the other hand, he was very aware of the traditional desert lifestyle as it had been evoked in Arabic verse. He often refers to it, in fact, in comparisons. For example:

> Better than an abode at Dhu Qar
> is a tavern in al-Anbar.

> And being surrounded by sweet basil and fragrant narcissus
> is better than being amongst loaded she-camels.

> And conversing easily with the singing girls,
> now with a fawn adjusting her non-Muslim's sash,

Is more delicious than toiling through a desert
and chasing after a mirage.

And hearing the sound of a lute close by
from the fingertips of a perfumed young woman,

Is better than recalling
Umm Najiya, Umm 'Amr, and Umm 'Ammar.[22]

The theme of rebellion, one readily discovers, figures prominently in Abu Nuwas. He derides classic stances and makes light of time-proven occasions for melancholy. For example:

Stop by the encampment where the ladies departed
and weep if it makes you sad.[23]

Similarly:

Tell the tearful one standing over the encampment traces
that there's no harm in sitting down.[24]

And:

The poor wretch turned aside on his journey to interrogate a former abode;
I turned aside to get directions to the local tavern.[25]

Clearly enough, Abu Nuwas marks a major break from the ancient poets. Aspects of civilized life, not of desert experience, are his concern. For this radical shift in emphasis, and for the noticeably increased use of rhetorical figures in his poetry (which coincided with the increased philological study of old Arabic poetry, especially at Basra and Kufa)—we will study one example of our poet's pronounced use of rhetorical figures below—Abu Nuwas came to be regarded as pivotal in the poetic tradition.[26] "What Imru' al-Qays was for the ancients, Abu Nuwas is for the moderns," Abu 'Ubayda (d. 824) said.[27] Scores of poets were influenced by his style and his choice of subject matter.

This is not to say that literary authorities necessarily approved of the moderns' ways. "Whatever is good came from their predecessors," quoted the philologist al-Asma'i (d. 831) from his teacher Abu 'Amr ibn al-'Ala', "and whatever is ugly is theirs."[28]

Before proceeding, we may pause to consider a contemporary poet with whom Abu Nuwas is frequently contrasted. In this man's work we detect a reaction to the sensual excesses often associated with Abu Nuwas, excesses that our poet lovingly described. The other poet is the Kufa-born Abu al-'Atahiya (d. 826). Abu al-'Atahiya, incidentally, composed in his early career love poetry and drinking songs. Around 796, though, he executed an about-face and went off composing ascetic verse. M. A. A. El Kafrawy and J. D. Latham, in "Perspective of Abu al-'Atahiya," plausibly connect this reversal to a loss of favor with the Barmakids.[29] Certainly, he does not come across as a disinterested ascetic. One of his favorite themes is the speedy transformation of kings to bones; likewise, he is fond of juxtaposing palaces and graves. He repeatedly confronts the great with death and warns them to prepare for the world to come. One can well suppose, therefore, that he was aroused by a rejection from a powerful family. From another standpoint, however, it is apparent that he seeks to address not only the ruling class; all who are complacent and living a good life may find themselves beset by his dire warnings. In one poem he says:

> Man flees death—
> but does flight do him any good?

> Every person some time will undergo the traumas of death,
> and death surely brings manifold traumas!

> O people! What has come over you?
> Your unmindfulness is incredible!

> Sickness and death are coming your way,
> then burial, a descent, and an uproar of voices;

> And an inscribed scroll, and scales, and a final reckoning,
> and a fire with leaping flames![30]

Such preoccupation with other people's death as the fixation evinced by Abu al-'Atahiya is unprecedented in Arabic literature. His *Diwan* serves as a useful reminder to us that not all the poets of this period were involved in celebrating an abundant life and otherwise depicting favorably the new conditions.

In 803 the Barmakids fell dramatically. It appears that Ja'far, another son of Yahya ibn Khalid, got romantically involved with 'Abbasa, sister of the caliph Harun al-Rashid.[31] For this association he was put to death, and the other Barmakids were cashiered. Thereafter, Abu Nuwas went to Egypt and spent time at the court of al-Khasib. But he returned to Baghdad in 806, attracted once more to the 'Abbasid capital. The next seven years were, it turned out, the most brilliant of his career. He became boon companion to al-Amin, the young heir apparent (nineteen years old in 806) who before long took over as caliph (r. 809–13). As a caliphal boon companion, Abu Nuwas would have been expected to recite poetry, provide witty conversation, and—especially in the case of a pleasure-loving personage such as al-Amin—take part in drinking parties. Nevertheless, the seven years were not, in their entirety, ones of wine and roses. Harun al-Rashid had Abu Nuwas put in prison for three months (where he passed the time, it is said, playing backgammon and chess),[32] and even al-Amin once imprisoned him for a short while. Evidently, it was politically expedient at times to punish the profligate poet.

Abu Nuwas is best known for his erotic and bacchic poems, and we shall first speak generally of the former before discussing the latter in some detail. His erotic poems may be divided into ones about women and ones about boys. Some of his poems about women, we have seen, are expressions of unsatisfied longing; others—presumably later ones, in the main—feature descriptions of sensual enjoyment and of attainment of the beloved, often through cunning. Whereas he may have been, in the case of Jinan, wary of approaching his love object, it seems that in other cases he was bolder. Of one voluptuous woman he has noticed outdoors, he says, having caught up:

> I walk beside her, crowding her intentionally,
> though the street is wide.[33]

When he could coax a woman to have a seat close by, such as at an evening party, he had no qualms about putting alcohol before her:

So I spent the night in pleasure,
now pouring her wine, now kissing her;

And gathering her delectable fruit,
and indulging my spirit with what it desired.[34]

If things did not go his way, he might even take the step of invoking a supernatural power. He reports:

When my beloved began to treat me coldly
and the letters and news stopped coming,

My passion intensified, till my distress over her
was on the verge of killing me.

So I called the Devil, and said to him,
as tears streamed down my cheeks:

"Don't you see how I've wasted away,
and how my eyelids have ulcerated from crying and lack of sleep?

If you don't cast love for me in my beloved's breast—
and this you can do—

I won't compose poetry, nor listen to music,
and inebriation won't course through my veins;

I'll lean over the Qur'an in study,
morning and night;

I'll strictly observe the fast, and pray five times a day,
and contrive ways to do good as long as I live."

I had hardly finished, when my beloved came to me,
saying: "I'm sorry!"[35]

On the whole, though, Abu Nuwas's love poetry is more concerned with boys than with women. These boys are always prepubescent youths, who are described as creatures delicate like the women. Many of the boys he encounters in taverns, as servants. For instance:

> He's a singer and cupbearer in one,
> and by my father, what a dear companion![36]

Monasteries also are likely places where he might grow enamored of one of the beardless youths. As a rule, the youths do not return his affection.[37] This rejection does not seem to have deterred him. Many of his poems detail a guileful, facilitated predation—or, to use Philip Kennedy's phrase, "stolen physical love through the instrument of wine."[38]

Abu Nuwas, it may be noted, established a fashion with these poems, since homoerotic Arabic poetry largely did not exist before his generation and it occurs throughout the classical tradition thereafter. Whether in actuality pederasty became more common around this time is unclear, although it stands to reason that it did, and, furthermore, that a phenomenon of pederasty was connected to the increased prevalence of slaves during the 'Abbasid period.[39]

It goes without saying that these poems strike the modern reader as outré, if not as plain abhorrent. We should recall, however, that in Arabic culture during the 'Abbasid period, as in Greek culture earlier, boys were regarded as natural sexual partners for a man. In popular imagination the Arab man, who wore a beard to signify his virility, was idealized as a dominating Penetrator, and so any from the category of beardless nonmen—women and boys—were physically suitable for him. Of course, from the religious angle penetrating a boy was sinful, however physically normal it might seem. On this tension, and further on the ambiguous position of boys between femininity and manliness, the comments of Everett K. Rowson in "The Categorization of Gender and Sexual Irregularity in Medieval Arabic Vice Lists" are illuminating:

> Official morality restricted a man's penetrative options to his wives and female slaves, but if he chose to become a "profligate," he could expand these options and seek penetrative satisfaction with other women or boys. Such a course made him a sinner, but did not imperil the status and honor due him as a man. . . .

Boys, being not yet men, could be penetrated without losing their potential manliness, so long as they did not register pleasure in the act, which would suggest a pathology liable to continue into adulthood; the quasi-femininity of their appearance, a condition for their desirability as penetratees, was a natural but temporary condition whose end marked their entry into the world of the dominant adult male.[40]

Apropos of boys, one need mention a special Baghdad phenomenon of this time that began because of al-Amin's strong liking for them. Zubayda, al-Amin's mother, was aware of her son's particular fondness and evidently became concerned about the matter of succession. So she devised the ruse of sending the empire's most beautiful slave girls to his private quarters at night, dressed as boys. (He eventually did father a son, Musa, but not a successor.) Word spread of their novel appearance, and then many girls were copying the style. The so-called *ghulamiyyat* (from *ghulam*, "slave boy") were recognizable by their cropped hair, buttoned shirts, and rolled sleeves.[41] Abu Nuwas, we take it, was charmed by the *ghulamiyyat*. "Boyish in public, girlish in private," he describes one of them.[42] Here he writes of another, a certain Ma'shuq:

A lad, or just like one,
a sweet aroma, a delight to the one who embraces her.

A union of form and fashion, if you will;
but no description suffices her.[43]

Leaving now women and boys for wine, we come to the main part of Abu Nuwas's oeuvre. Several hundred wine songs exist in his *Diwan*. For these works Abu Nuwas earned recognition as the master of the *khamriyya*, as the poet who defined the genre.[44] Usually, the poems involve a reported trip to a tavern or monastery with some worthy companions. In the brief poetic narrative, once at the drinking location, Abu Nuwas shows disregard for his money (he pulls out eighty dinars in one instance) and purchases a wine of excellent quality. The wine is remarkably old; not too infrequently it dates, according to Abu Nuwas, to the time of Noah.[45] Sometimes his friends buy jars of it as well. Wine served, the revelry commences, and it ends only when a good time has been had by all the friends.[46] (Commonly, Abu Nuwas also makes mention of the young cupbearer—be this individual a male or female—who may or may not assume importance in the story.)

In the center of an Abu Nuwas *khamriyya,* one can expect to find a detailed description of the wine. Most often, the wine's appearance is what captures his attention. For example, he says about one white wine:

> When a fellow drinker quaffs it
> you would think he is kissing a star.[47]

The bubbles especially stimulate wonderment.[48] He likens the bubbles to ascending *waws* (*waw* being an Arabic letter: و); at the surface they call to mind locusts jumping in the afternoon sun.[49] On hearing the effervescence, to mention here an aural association, a quite rare occurrence, he thinks of a priest whispering verses before a cross.[50]

Consistent and very noticeable in the *khamriyyat* is the evocation of the wine personally in terms of the beloved. She is the long-preserved virgin of noble lineage whom the poet craves. In these poems, he pays the guardian a bride-price for her. True to his imagining, after her seal is broken, she brings him intense satisfaction.[51] She cures his ill. She also kills, leaving the poet flat on his back—or, as the case may be, facedown.

Below we shall read Abu Nuwas's most famous wine poem: "The Qasida Ibrahimiyya," named after its addressee, Ibrahim al-Nazzam (d. ca. 836). Al-Nazzam was one of the foremost theologians of the early ninth century. He belonged to a group of rationalists, the Mu'tazilites, that had originated in Basra during the latter part of the Umayyad period. These Mu'tazilites were profoundly concerned with the question of free will versus predestination (a question open to debate, since the Qur'an is not definitive on it; see 41:46 and 74:31). The Mu'tazilites held that God is always just, that God does not preordain evil only to punish for it thereafter.[52] In their view, man thus creates his own actions, and so he bears responsibility for them. God ultimately rewards and punishes, they maintained, by fair principles and never by whim. Going further than the others, however, al-Nazzam put a limit on divine omnipotence, insisting that God actually was incapable of evil; He must do in the hereafter what is right for men. Al-Nazzam is the person who, having been attracted also to Baghdad (ca. 800 the city was replacing

Basra as the intellectual center of the Islamic world), had a brush with the poet, or, if not, at least heard of his activity.[53] The position of Islam was clear: fornication, sodomy, and alcohol consumption were all *kaba'ir*, that is, major sins. Al-Nazzam evidently reproved the poet and informed him that he was going to hell unless he repented and changed his ways. Abu Nuwas composed this poem in response, which we shall consider first thematically and then, according to our practice, in terms of structure:

A

1   Spare me your blame, for blame is enticement,
     and medicate me with the illness itself.

2   A golden manifestation, at whose abode no sorrows alight—
     were a stone to touch it that stone would be touched by joy.[54]

3   From the hand of a maiden, dressed as a lad,
     gazed at yearningly by fornicator and sodomite.

4   She rose with its ewer while the night was pitch-black,
     and from her face, in the house, was a luminous glow.

B

5   Then out of the ewer's mouth she poured liquid
     so clear and bright that one almost could not behold it;

6   Thinned next with water until it was delicate,
     and the water had mixed in agreeably.

7   Were you to marry it with light, the light and liquid would intermingle,
     producing glistenings and sparkles.

A¹

8   She came around to men granted a loan by Time;
     and they were afflicted, but only with what they desired.

9   For such a heart's longing, then, I weep,
     and not for a former abode occupied by Hind or Asma'.

10   God forbid that a tent be erected for such a pearl,
     and that camels and goats pass over it!

11   So say to whoever claims philosophical knowledge:
     you grasped one or two things and missed the rest.

12   Do not deny God's forgiveness to another, if you are pious,
     for doing so is blasphemy.

Abu Nuwas opens his *qasida* with a dramatic imperative, suggestive of John Donne's, "For God's sake hold your tongue, and let me love," at the beginning of "The Canonization." What is also striking about the poem's opening, besides the strong expression of sentiment, is the unflattering framing of the addressee. Though al-Nazzam was a pioneering rationalist, a man at the forefront of the day's intellectual debate, Abu Nuwas casts him here as the familiar censurer. Like so many a captious person before him, al-Nazzam is chiding a poet for his love.

The rhetorical figures are noteworthy in this first line (as we have observed, the pronounced use of figures is characteristic of the moderns). In the first hemistich there is an instance of antithesis (*tibaq*), by the mention of blame and enticement. Abu Nuwas brazenly equates these two in a paradox. Of course, in a normal sense, reproach does not equal encouragement. Yet for one such as Abu Nuwas, it does (compare this remark of another dissolute person: "How can one compare the chilly tepidity of the permitted with the heat of the forbidden?").[55] In the second hemistich there is an instance of antithesis, by the mention of medication and illness (at the same time as an occurrence of *jinas,* the articulation of different meanings by words derived, or seemingly derived, from the same literal root).[56] Abu Nuwas is making a second paradox here. What a doctor diagnoses as the malady cannot, positively, be itself the cure. To the habitual drinker, however, it is.

Through these two paradoxes, Abu Nuwas first reduces his critic to blank expression and silence—blame being enticement, al-Nazzam should not wish to goad the poet to more sinning by his frowns and reproofs—and then provocatively instructs him to render himself useful. In the next line he implies a straightforward explanation for his addiction. Why should he give up this beloved? She is a source of *joy,* not sadness. He should have, instead of condemnation, more of her. The glowing description of the wine in the center of the poem emphasizes her worthiness. As for the allusion to fornication and pederasty, though evocative of what transpires probably in an establishment where such a wine flows, it is included, we find, primarily to annoy al-Nazzam.

As he does so often, Abu Nuwas in this poem discredits the culture of the Bedouins. His beloved is vastly superior, vastly more *civilized,* than those beloveds of his literary forebears. And in keeping with his heightened cultural status vis-à-vis the Bedouins, he treats the traditional censurer less respectfully.

He does not accept the censurer's logic, as a canonical poet such as Labid might; nor, for that matter, does he ignore him practically while parrying the reproofs with wit, as an 'Udhri poet such as Jamil might. Rather, he confronts the censurer openly and refutes him.

At the end of the poem, Abu Nuwas directs attention to the other's arrogance. Obviously, the knowing critic does not know everything, since this splendid embodiment of qualities should be loved devotedly. The poem takes on a religious and social significance in the last line. God, as the Qur'an states (4:48), may forgive all sins but polytheism. Moreover, God is identified countless times in the Holy Revelation as the Merciful, the Compassionate. So who is al-Nazzam to deny God's forgiveness to the poet? Abu Nuwas implies forcefully that a modicum of humility would befit his critic. It would improve his interaction with people around him, assuredly, to say nothing of the consideration of him by Almighty God. Ultimately, the poet, albeit by means of a provocative response, calls for tolerance on the part of the critic for one such as himself, who does not share exactly the critic's worldview.

Recent studies by James Montgomery have illuminated the pattern of ring composition in poems by Abu Nuwas.[57] "The Qasida Ibrahimiyya" also has a circular arrangement, as Philip Kennedy has indicated.[58] The summary diagram below shows the precise ring structure of this poem:

Section	Lines	Structural and Thematic Elements
A	1–4	*Al-Nazzam apprised:* poet exasperated with blame, wants medication this beloved extraordinary: no sorrows visit her abode cupbearer described
B	5–7	*description of wine:* wine is exceedingly bright, admits quantity of clear water, combines with light to wonderful effect
A¹	8–12	cupbearer serves wine superiority of this beloved to those of Bedouins *Al-Nazzam apprised:* he does not know all, might prudently keep in mind that God forgives whom He will

By 813 Abu Nuwas's best years had come to an end. At the conclusion of a two-year civil war, Caliph al-Amin was captured and killed by the forces of his half-brother, al-Ma'mun (r. 813–33).[59] Abu Nuwas composed numerous elegies for the slain caliph. Ca. 815 the poet became ill and died. He was buried in the western outskirts of Baghdad. A source who knew him, cited by Abu Hiffan (d. ca. 869), indicates that he repented within a week or so of death.[60] Indeed, in two poems in which he alludes to a serious illness, he confesses being a great sinner and asks God's forgiveness.[61] By all appearances, his repentance came at the eleventh hour, following a history of major transgression. According to al-Nazzam's reasoning, we suspect, he would not be admitted to Paradise. Then again, al-Nazzam would not be the One judging him.

Since Abu Nuwas lived a large portion of his life, the record would have us believe, avidly pursuing illicit pleasure, it does not seem fitting to close this chapter by pondering a late repentance by him. Abu Nuwas, after all, is the icon of debauchery in Arabic literature. What follows, therefore, is a twelfth-century representation of a literary character—a representation that perhaps evokes, minus a few friends in the scene, the way our poet liked to live—and two lines of poetry: "So I went by night to the tavern . . . and there was the old man in a gay-colored dress amid sealed jars and a wine press; and about him were cupbearers surpassing in beauty, and lights that glittered, and the myrtle and the jasmine, and the pipe and the lute. And at one time he bade broach the jars, and at another he called the lutes to give utterance; and now he inhaled the perfumes, and now he courted the gazelles."[62] Last, we quote flagrant Abu Nuwas:

Pour me a cup, and announce that it's wine;
don't refresh me quietly when you can do it out loud.

For what is the good life but consecutive bingeing?
Time is short when drunkenness is long.[63]

8

The Poetics of Persuasion

Forego making apologies, for most of them are false.
—Quoted in AL-JAHIZ, *Kitab al-bayan wa-al-tabyin*
(The Book of Eloquence and Exposition)

WE TURN NOW TO AN ODE composed by one of the major poets of the 'Abbasid era (750–1258), Abu Tammam (ca. 804–46). Abu Tammam was born near Damascus, where his father, a Christian by the name of Thadhus, kept a wine shop. At some point Abu Tammam changed his patronymic to Aws al-Ta'i, claiming descent from the tribe of Tayyi', and converted to Islam. He spent his youth as a weaver's assistant in Damascus. Subsequently, he traveled to Egypt and earned a living there as a water seller. He also studied poetry while in Egypt, and by the time of his return to Syria in 830 he had chosen for himself the life of a poet. In the following period Abu Tammam emerged as the greatest panegyrist of his day. He also distinguished himself as an anthologist, compiling of mostly pre-Islamic poetry the extremely popular *Hamasa*, which remains a standard anthology up to the present. He died and was buried in the Iraqi city of Mosul.

It goes without saying that during the years of Abu Tammam's life, which roughly coincided with the apex of 'Abbasid power and glory, there was great wealth to be found at court. One example suffices to give us an idea of the extent of this wealth. For the 825 wedding of Caliph al-Ma'mun (aged thirty-nine years) to the eighteen-year-old Buran, the bride's father, a provincial governor—doubtlessly no richer than the regular figures at court—was able to host the caliph and his entire retinue for seventeen days of feasting. Ambergris candles were set out in such number in the hall that they turned night into day (their smoke bothered the caliph, though, so they were replaced with tallow ones). At the final ceremony, the bride and groom were seated on a gold-embroidered mat and showered with a thousand pearls of unusual size. The guests, for their part, were shown considerable regard by the host:

> Indeed, he distributed among the members of the family of Hashim [that is, the relatives of the caliph] and, similarly, to the generals, secretaries and other outstanding personages, balls of musk the size of filberts with a note hidden inside of each giving the name of an estate, or a slave girl, the description of a horse, etc. Each one opened the ball which had fallen to his lot, read the note and found in it a better or less good prize, depending on whether fortune had favored him more or less. He then showed the note to an officer entrusted with handing out the prizes and claimed an estate in such-and-such a district of such-and-such a province, or a certain slave girl named such-and-such, or else a horse described in a particular way. In addition to all this, gold and silver pieces, bladders filled with musk and eggs of ambergris were tossed to the rest of the people.[1]

Coming from outside the court, a poet like Abu Tammam, by skill, might get his hands on some of that wealth. Truly, he did. He eulogized so successfully, in fact, that the other poets were reportedly unable to get a single dirham for their verse; Abu Tammam was always claiming the rewards.[2] Before we continue with the subject of Abu Tammam's poetry and look closely at one of his poems, however, let us recall the panegyric tradition that he was working within and briefly discuss the nature of the genre.

During the pre-Islamic period—which was characterized, as we have seen, by a tribal ethos—encomiasts were exceptional. The poet typically praised himself and his fellow kinsmen, not a potentate. Al-Nabigha (d. ca. 604) of the tribe of Dhubyan went against the grain and earned a place for himself in literary history as the first major Arab panegyrist. He did so by heaping tributes on al-Nu'man, the king of al-Hira. For these poems he was remunerated handsomely. Yet his career seems to have ended abruptly when the patron was removed from power and cast at the feet of riled elephants.[3] Al-Nabigha returned thereafter to his tribe, and from within this circle he was not heard from again. One suspects that, having neglected his brothers and taken to lauding a petty king, he was not finally held aloft as a hero. In any case, al-Nabigha's brilliant odes won him lasting fame, and his success at court was paradigmatic for future poets. Poets in the Umayyad era similarly gravitated to court and earned an excellent living by praising royalty. But better working conditions (that is, the existence of an apparently stable dynasty and the concentration at court of incredible riches) meant that many poets clustered there. The ones who glorified rulers were no longer exceptional. From this crowd we single out for mention the Christian poet al-Akhtal (d. ca. 710), poet laureate of the Umayyads. The conditions for praise poetry during the 'Abbasid period, as indicated above, were likewise excellent. Abu Tammam followed the example of his predecessors and made a name—and a profit—for himself by exalting others.

In fairness to the poets composing in this tradition, we may accept that often they were motivated, at least partially, by admiration. Naturally, the possession of vast authority and wealth stimulated wonder and instilled a certain degree of respect. Moreover, each poet surely had among the elite his favorite, whom he celebrated more out of esteem than desire to flatter. He may also, in some cases, have sought to bring out the best in the patron by motivating him to greater heights and by reminding him of social values. At the same time, we recognize nonetheless that the panegyrical poem constitutes, in essence, part of a transaction. Even admiring and excellence-promoting poets, one must assume, expected kind treatment in exchange for kind words. Usually, a poet would indicate that he wanted a prize, dropping hints about gifts and complimenting the patron on his generosity. In doing so, he was throwing down the gauntlet, challenging the other to prove himself a ready benefactor. Suzanne Pinckney Stetkevych has summarized the panegyric ritual, highlighting the requirement for the patron to fulfill expectations: "We can reduce the qasida ceremony to the simplest case or pattern: a poet comes before a patron offering him a poem praising his generosity and requesting a gift. The patron, if he denies the request, at the same time denies the claim of the poem, that he is generous, and in doing so undermines his own moral authority. . . . To legitimize himself, that is, to confirm the veracity of the virtues enunciated in the panegyric, the patron must accede to the poet's request or demand."[4]

But patrons did not always legitimize themselves, be it out of anomalous incapacity, parsimony, or animosity. The Mu'tazilite judge Ahmad ibn Abi Du'ad (d. 854) failed to show himself as generous on one occasion before Abu Tammam, because he suspected the poet of having defamed him. What was a poet to do then? If the patron was his sole source of income, he might express profound regret for the offense (stressing that it was certainly unintentional) and ask submissively to be restored to favor. But there were many patrons among the 'Abbasids and their governors, so this humble response was not necessary. Alternatively, as long as he did not fear the man, he might satirize him. This response at least would assuage the poet's wounded pride and serve as a warning to anyone who might think of treating him stingily. Perhaps, however, the poet did not want to write off the patron just yet and still regarded him as a potential source of bounty. In such a case, he might try to win him back and obtain a prize through persuasion. Abu Tammam adopted this middle course and composed the poem (No. 37) we shall read below.[5]

Since the ode deals with a personal matter between these two men, it behooves us first to take into account their interaction up to the time of the poem's composition. Ibn Abi Du'ad, the patron, rose to prominence as a judge in Baghdad under Caliph al-Ma'mun, and after the accession of al-Mu'tasim (833), he was made chief *qadi*. He became acquainted with Abu Tammam early in the poet's career, and by sending him to recite before al-Mu'tasim in Samarra after the capture of Amorium (838), he helped propel him to stardom.[6] Yet their relationship seems to have been problematic; before the incident that inspired this ode, Abu Tammam had once censured Ibn Abi Du'ad, for which affront the poet later apologized.[7] On this occasion, though, Abu Tammam clearly did not mean to speak negatively about the judge. The judge, it will be perceived, was not even on his mind. As the following account indicates, he meant only—in response to provocation—to clarify a few points about tribal affiliation:

'Awn ibn Muhammad reported to me that Muhammad ibn al-Warraq said: "I was sitting with a group of men at the edge of Samarra's al-Hayr section, looking at the horses, when Abu Tammam passed by and sat next to us. One of us said to him: 'O Abu Tammam, what origin would you wish for yourself if you were not from Yemen?' Abu Tammam replied: 'I would not wish for myself any other origin than that which God chose for me. Why, from whom would you have me descend?' 'From Mudar,' he said.[8] At this Abu Tammam conceded that Mudar had been honored with the Prophet, and invoked God's blessing upon the Prophet. But he immediately asserted that otherwise the progeny of Mudar could not compare with the kings of Yemen; from Yemen came so and so, this eminent person and that. He went on boasting in this fashion and began casting aspersions on the honor of Mudar. The news was relayed to Ibn Abi Du'ad [who was affiliated with Mudar], and more was added to what had been said, prompting the latter to declare, 'I do not want Abu Tammam to enter into my presence; keep him from me.'"[9]

Abu Tammam addressed the situation by composing a fifty-one-line poem for the judge, in which he praises him profusely and attributes their estrangement to slander. He closes the poem with a warning:

> Whosoever inclines to slanderers
> shall have his ears lashed by sharp tongues.[10]

Yet Ibn Abi Du'ad had apparently lent an ear to slanderers and was not mollified by this ode. What is worse, the following two lines in the *Diwan*—composed in the same meter and rhyme—strongly suggest that the judge refused to pay for the poem:

> Does my master deprive me of wealth—
> do I seek it from a dry palm?!

> If this be so, then I assert that generosity
> now has for its lord someone other than Ibn Abi Du'ad![11]

We note here, incidentally, that Abu Tammam associates dryness with lack, and also with stinginess. These associations are common in Arabic poetry; conversely, clouds, rain, wetness, and spring all connote plenitude, as well as generosity. After being deprived, then, Abu Tammam went away in dudgeon, only to come back a year later with a fresh ode for the *qadi* and an appeal from the poet's advocate, the governor of Armenia, Khalid ibn Yazid al-Shaybani. Even after the passage of a year, though, Ibn Abi Du'ad was evidently still annoyed with Abu Tammam and delayed granting him a hearing. Eventually, the poet seems to have grown impatient and dispatched these additional lines:

> O Ahmad, the enviers are legion,
> and the rain cloud pours where you choose.

> Do not be distant when I am near, for how often
> have you been sought after and were not distant, though you were far!

Listen and you will hear the purest of lines.
They are stars portending good fortune.

Do not let the texture of these lines wear out;
donning the striped garment pleases when the garment is new.[12]

Upon receiving this message the *qadi* relented, and Abu Tammam was admitted to offer his new composition. We shall now discuss No. 37, explaining how the poet progressively builds his argument for the judge. In keeping with our method, we shall conclude with a summary diagram that illustrates the overall unity of the poem.

A

1   Have you seen what fair necks and cheeks showed themselves to us
     between al-Liwa and Zarud?

2   Companions of the woman, heedless of the nights,
     who tied knots of love into bracelets and necklaces.

3   Fair-skinned; ardent desire lays her low
     as the east wind at eventide bends the tender willow bough;

4   An oryx doe whose large, dark eyes shoot arrows into men's hearts
     when it departs in the morning; a languid, deep sleeper who hunts none
          but the proud and mighty.

5   He who has experienced loving her is without resolve;
     the mighty chieftain in her presence is pliable.

6   Nothing at a familiar springtime abode of theirs pertains to me,
          except feelings of overwhelming sorrow
     and the determination of a man forcing himself to be patient.

7   If Mas'ud watered the encampment traces with the rain of tear ducts,
     well, I am not Mas'ud.

8   They departed; then I cried for a year after them
     and stopped, observing Labid's rule.

9   How appropriate for an ember of passion that is extinguished by tears
     in this case to go on burning its fuel the longer.

10   I do not drive a young she-camel with singing,
     nor am I seen saddling up alongside a ladies' man.

11   My yearning is something I have removed like a floating impurity from my drink,
     stripped like a piece of bark from my wood.

Abu Tammam begins the ode with a *nasib,* evoking the scene of morning departure from pre-Islamic poetry. The pretty ladies are riding off in their howdahs, turning back as they go and affording the poet a last view of their profiles. These women are companions of the poet's beloved. The beloved, like the many women before her who captivated poets, is oryxlike in appearance, irresistible, capable of subduing even the most powerful of men. After a joyful period of falling in love with her, the poet has lost her. Spring has ended, and now come the tears. Though Abu Tammam is not a pre-Islamic poet, he has experienced the profound sadness felt by one on the morning of separation. We realize that Abu Tammam is drawing an analogy here between loss of the beloved and loss of his patron.[13] When the rift occurred, Abu Tammam wept copiously. Therefore, the judge should understand, the poet cared deeply for him and could not have intended any insult. His grief-stricken reaction belies what the slanderers presumably said about him. How could he have thought so little of the patron as to trivialize his ancestral prestige, when he so clearly loved the man?

Once he has established his emotional affinity with the pre-Islamic poets, Abu Tammam goes on to differentiate himself from them. He was an urban panegyrist, after all, not a Bedouin poet or a Mas'ud who used to weep over abandoned campsites.[14] Furthermore, those lovers, at least in theory, wept for the beloved only for a short time and then rode off on a camel and were done with the matter. When the rains returned six or seven months later and the tribes congregated again, they were out looking for new women. In contrast, Abu Tammam has been crying nonstop for his beloved for a whole year. How appropriate it is, considering the exceptional intensity of his passion!

Crying for a whole year not only reveals the extent of his affection but also fulfills a prerequisite for reconciliation. If we consider the poet's rhetorical situation, we perceive that some sort of statement of regret is required to placate the judge. However, pride does not allow him to acknowledge wrongdoing. At a rhetorical impasse, Abu Tammam manages to produce a saving poetic reference. Regarding his sadness, he refers in line 8 to a ruling by Labid, namely, "Whoever weeps for an entire year has apologized."[15] Conveniently, the year's worth of weeping qualifies as an apology, as enunciated by Labid, and also obviates the necessity of saying anything. Tacitly, Abu Tammam gives the judge what he wants, though he does not accept blame. In fact, by invoking the departure motif in this section, he even undercuts the tacit message, implying that it was the judge who went away and left him. Contrary to the import of the poetic reference, the image suggests that Abu Tammam cried over being forsaken, not over doing something wrong.

As he makes clear by the end of this section, Abu Tammam has completed the grieving process. After a year of weeping, the time has come for making amends; the ball is now in the judge's court. Abu Tammam stresses that he has gotten over his yearning for the beloved, intimating to Ibn Abi Du'ad that no more conciliatory odes will be forthcoming.

B

12   My year and the year of the fine camels was spent
      between scorching heat and a rock-solid desert.

13   Every day in the great expanse I left for the birds a feast:
      the daughters of al-'Id.[16]

14   How far from them was a praiseworthy garden
      until they were brought to a halt before Ahmad the praised!

15   At the halting place of the Arabs, where they found security for the
              frightened
      and succor for the afflicted.

16   In it the sons of Ishmael and the sons of Hud
      untied their baggage and put down their worries.[17]

17   Thereafter, hopes of generous treatment brought to these men delegations,
      since they left his place well equipped to be hosts themselves.

18   He initiated generosity and renewed it towards them,
      and how many an initiator of benefaction does not repeat it!

Abu Tammam follows the *nasib* with a short *rahil* (camel journey) and numerous lines describing the destination and the hospitality of the host. Because Abu Tammam does not always find occasion to incorporate a *rahil*—or, for that matter, a *nasib*[18]—one may reasonably inquire after its purpose. Suzanne Pinckney Stetkevych, in her seminal study *Abu Tammam and the Poetics of the 'Abbasid Age,* analyzes several courtly panegyrics in which the poet revitalizes traditional *qasida* motifs by deploying them metaphorically. We have seen him do so in section A, where he suggests, through the figure of the beloved, Ibn Abi Du'ad. In section B, the poet conjures a year spent in the desert as a metaphor for the privation he endured away from this man. After conveying his grief and apologizing through the metaphor of weeping for the beloved, he tries to win some sympathy through the figurative *rahil*. The conditions were so harsh that daily he left she-camels as food for vultures. While the pathetic image of camels dying sets this part against the typical poetic *rahil* (which exemplifies the strength of the mount), its brevity and lack of progression distinguish it as well. Evidently, Abu Tammam did not share the attachment to the animal that many of his predecessors had, and so is not wont to wax prolix on the subject. (Besides, listening to a jeremiad might get tiresome for the judge. The detail about the vultures, he probably concluded, sufficiently dramatizes his plight.) Nor does Abu Tammam, by means of the *rahil*, move on and get over his fixation, as these predecessors did. In a pre-Islamic *qasida*, the typical *rahil* enables the poet to leave the beloved behind; it carries him forward into the fold of his tribe. But in this *qasida* the *rahil* brings Abu Tammam back to the same old beloved, because the two have unfinished business to settle. Hence, the poet next speaks highly of his destination and host, which should further dispose the judge to forgive him and recompense him. In line 14 he derives flattering adjectives from the root of the patron's name (*h-m-d* in Ahmad → *mahmuda, al-mahmud*: "to praise" → "praiseworthy, the praised"), a signature feature of his style. Abu Tammam then refers to the security that the patron provides and his generous treatment of his guests. He bestows gifts with such exuberance that afterward his guests have enough property at their disposal to accommodate whole delegations themselves. Last, in noting the recurring aspect of Ibn Abi Du'ad's giving, he drops a hint that he, too, would like to be the recipient of renewed benefaction—a tangible indicator from the patron of forgiveness.

To effect the change of heart, Abu Tammam also offers the judge a framework through which he might see beyond tribal distinctions and recognize the poet as his brother. He does so by specifying Ishmael (son of Abraham), a North Arabian prophet and ancestor to 'Adnan, and Hud, a South Arabian prophet and admonisher to the people of 'Ad. The offspring of both men were eventually united by their acceptance of Islam. The example demonstrates that under Islam, tribal rivalries and geographic antagonisms are tempered; "A Muslim is the brother of a Muslim," the hadith says.[19] Abu Tammam promotes a broader and more inclusive concept of Arab unity through reference to these descendants and implies that tribalism has been superseded.[20] Ibn Abi Du'ad might therefore regard all the northerners and the southerners who gather under his tent as his coreligionists and treat them all as his brothers.

Transition

19   O Ahmad ibn Abi Du'ad, you surrounded me with the protection I needed
      and treated me by administering medicine to the corner of my mouth.

20   And bestowed upon me affection which I have safeguarded like a sacred trust
      from separation and estrangement.

21   And truly how many an enemy has said to me sententiously:
      "How many's the devoted one who is not loved in return!"

These three lines provide a brief transition from the *rahil* and description of the halting place to the subsequent formal argument. They also mark the beginning of a *madih* (praise segment) that continues to the end of the poem. Here for the first time Abu Tammam addresses his patron directly, reminding him that the latter was once his protector. As a result of this kindness Abu Tammam has remained faithful, he asserts, and has not questioned the judge's sincere love.

C

22   The descendents of Iyad have proliferated and today constitute the bulk of Ma'add;
      they are the support of its great edifice.[21]

23   Within Iyad, Zuhr raises you to the heights of noble deeds and grandeur,
      unto the shining eminence of fathers and grandfathers.[22]

24   If the Iyad men are the roots of the Ma'add tree
      and a major section of the Ma'add rock,

25   And share with the rest of Ma'add a common lineage,
      you share with us a reputation for liberality.

26   From our two tribes came Ka'b and Hatim,
      who divided the lands of nobility both newly acquired and inherited.

27   This one took the place of the clouds and died in glory
      the death of a generous hero.[23]

28   If he were not martyr in this act, then his kinsmen would not be willing,
      by the thousand, to follow his example.

29   Nonetheless, the two of them did not endure as much hardship in the cause
          of glory
       as you have in the cause of Unity and Justice.

In this section Abu Tammam begins his formal argument before the judge. The lines make up the first half of the poet's case, which includes a preface of ample praise for Ibn Abi Du'ad's lineage, a comparison between the patron's and the poet's kin, and a substantiation for the comparison containing a directly relevant precedent. Once he has salved old wounds by lauding the judge's tribe and clan, he draws a parallel between Iyad's reputation for liberality and the standing of al-Tayyi'. From the two tribes came the Bedouin heroes Ka'b and Hatim. Significantly, these men shared the noble quality of generosity. Since they shared this virtue, Abu Tammam suggests to the judge, then surely we can share the honor of noble ancestry. Such logic accords with the concept of brotherhood introduced in B: under Islam, solidarity and mutual respect replace competition; a Muslim transcends feelings of rivalry toward his brother.

In line 29 he reinforces the idea that the judge might live up to the example of these legendary figures. Indeed, he has already surpassed them in suffering. Though this notion is certainly an exaggeration (Ka'b died in the cause of glory, and Hatim, while pursuing glory, was abandoned by his father), it is probably true that the judge experienced discomfort while upholding the Mu'tazilite principles of unity and justice. During this period the Mu'tazilites, despite their enjoying caliphal approval, faced hostility from the orthodox masses.[24] So if the judge has undergone hardship as the heroes did—more hardship, even, according to the statement here—it should be easy for him similarly to share glory. Furthermore, he might well follow their example in a concrete sense and give away his possessions. Abu Tammam cites Ka'b and Hatim to suggest sharing glory, and also to suggest sharing material items. Once again, we find him dropping a hint in the poem of what he wants besides reconciliation.

Rhetorically, Abu Tammam holds his ground in this section after the preface of tribal praise. Through the dual example of Ka'b and Hatim, he justifies his pride in the Tayyi' affiliation while also providing a basis for joint recognition. The alleged insult of Mudar (and Iyad by association) arose from boasts he was making about his Yemenite ancestry, and he does not back down from his boasts here. Rather, he cites an example that illustrates that each man can be justifiably proud and at the same time still respect the other's lineage.

D

30   Hear, then, the speech of a visitor
       who never doubted his opinions in the vast and featureless desert;
31   Who bargains for some words from you with his whole work,
       and for the benefit of your approval with his exertion.

Here we find the core of the ode: two lines that indicate what Abu Tammam's performance is all about. He begins the couplet with an imperative verb, demanding his listener's attention. He then indicates that during the year in the desert he never became confused and disillusioned. He always believed that Ibn Abi Du'ad would forgive him and now has come back. The next line sums up the transactional nature of the panegyric delivery. With the poem Abu Tammam is bargaining for a few conciliatory words from the patron—just enough so he knows the other no longer harbors any hard feelings toward him. The judge should realize that the poet is offering a lot in return for a little: a *whole* work for only *some* (or *a portion of*) words. It is an advantageous exchange. In addition, the line itself should please the judge, due to its cleverness. Abu Tammam makes a pun with the word *kamalan* (whole). The ode, it may be mentioned, is composed in the *kamil* meter. So when Abu Tammam says he is bargaining for a few words with his whole work, he means at the same time, literally, that he is bargaining with his *kamil*-metered work.[25] As for the specific kind of approval he seeks in return for his exertion, it probably can be guessed. Shall we just say that a mere pat on the back or a simple "Good job, my friend" is surely not what he has in mind.

This part of the ode also marks an equilibrium stage in the power struggle between the poet and his patron. Abu Tammam starts out in a defensive posture, apologizing and repairing previous damage through copious praise. He steadily becomes more assertive in section C by pointing to his own glorious lineage. Here, buyer and seller are in the midst of negotiations, and neither one has the advantage (even if one party is being told that he is getting an excellent deal). In the remaining lines, however, the power balance tips in Abu Tammam's favor, and the judge finds himself increasingly on the defensive.

C¹

32   He left by night and was forced into exile, due to shame at what they alleged,
      not due to fear of your punishment.

33   Coming back, you were the spring season in front of him,
      and behind him was the moon of the tribes, Khalid ibn Yazid;[26]

34   The abundant rain from Zuhr is a cloud of mercy,
      and the support from Shayban a towering mountain of iron.

35   Tomorrow my innocence will become evident,
      if you explore then my coastal plains and interior highlands.

36   This al-Walid saw the proof after they said:
      "Yazid ibn al-Muhallab is perishing."[27]

37   The falsehood set forth in his presence was removed,
      for its building was not solidly constructed.

38   Then Ibn Abi Saʿid [that is, Yazid ibn al-Muhallab] was able to take
          possession
      of a happy king's mind through the gratitude of the al-Muhallab family.[28]

39   Khalid, as advocate, is no less than Ayyub or ʿAbd al-ʿAziz,
      nor are you, as arbiter, less than al-Walid.[29]

This section, which includes a reference to Khalid ibn Yazid al-Shaybani's intercession on behalf of the poet and a citation of historical precedent for pardon, constitutes the second half of Abu Tammam's formal case before the judge. After recalling his flight from court, where his reputation had been tarnished, Abu Tammam describes his return. In front of him was the hope of spring rain, or benefaction, while behind him, lighting the way forward, the shining honor of Khalid ibn Yazid. He wishes for mercy from the judge yet feels secure with the strong backing of Khalid. In line 35, he proclaims his innocence and represents his physical exterior and interior as coastal plains and inland heights. The poet is referring here to outlying and central parts of the Arabian Peninsula.[30] Should the judge bother to do some exploring, he will find the poet to be pure through and through.

Abu Tammam locates his precedent for official pardon in the annals of Umayyad history, in the file of Yazid ibn Muhallab. In 705 the ruthless governor of Iraq, al-Hajjaj ibn Yusuf, turned on his brother-in-law, Yazid, and had him thrown into prison. There Yazid languished and his health declined, until he managed to escape and flee to Ramla in Palestine, residence of the caliph's brother, Sulayman ibn 'Abd al-Malik. Sulayman sympathized with Yazid and sent his son Ayyub with him to Damascus to intercede before the caliph. In Damascus the caliph's son 'Abd al-'Aziz joined the case to argue in Yazid's behalf. When al-Walid, who had permitted Yazid's imprisonment by al-Hajjaj, saw Yazid enter his chamber flanked by his nephew Ayyub and his son 'Abd al-'Aziz as advocates, he granted a pardon. According to the traditional interpretation offered for line 38, Yazid's relatives afterward thanked the caliph's brother Sulayman profusely for his efforts, thus securing his favorable disposition.[31] By the reference to profuse thanks, then, the poet suggests the effusive praise that might follow a Sulayman-like demonstration of sympathy from the judge. More logically, though, Abu Tammam indicates in line 38 the gratitude of Yazid's family to Caliph al-Walid. Based on this reading, the poet here suggests his ebullient reaction to an al-Walid-like pardon.

With the second explicit comparison to Ibn Abi Du'ad in line 39, Abu Tammam rests his case. He concludes very persuasively, considering that the listener was an 'Abbasid judge, an official for the dynasty that regarded itself superior to the Umayyads in all virtuous qualities. If this Umayyad al-Walid had been clement, Ibn Abi Du'ad could not be less so. On the subtextual level of the power struggle, one here detects Abu Tammam gaining leverage on the judge. Abu Tammam has offered what he can in the way of regret and eulogy, and now it is his patron's turn to yield and show flexibility.

Transition

40   I would ransom you with my soul from any dungeon of misfortune
       into which the key was not thrown!

41   Thrown to one who is not near to the slanderer,
       and from the member of a distant clan not far.

These two lines, along with 19–21, frame Abu Tammam's formal defense, although thematically they bear an inverse relation to the first transition. Now the patron is in danger—he might not live up to the Umayyad standard of mercy—and so requires support and protection. Abu Tammam gallantly offers his soul for the *qadi* at risk. Likewise, here it is the judge who is said to be devoted to the other, despite the distance separating them, and unreceptive to insinuation. Tonally, however, the two sections are consistent: in both of them the poet addresses his patron in an intimate voice, one that he does not employ elsewhere in the poem.

B¹

42   When your cloud shaded me, those witnesses turned against me—
       and they had been on my side—

43   Suspecting that I would have a day according to their wish
       like the day of 'Abid.[32]

44   It was a desire whose wicked realization they did not attain
       by means of a demon or an evil spirit.

45   They pulled out an arrow of dissension by which the feather of refractoriness
              takes flight,
       but it did not hit the mark.

46   And if God willed to unfold a concealed virtue,
       then He preordained for it the tongue of an envier.

47   Were it not for the enveloping fire,
       the pleasing aroma of aloes-wood would not be known.

48   Were it not for the dread of the consequences,
       the envier would enjoy advantage over the envied.

Section B¹ treats the subject of enviers and highlights the poet's immunity from their attacks. When his supporters saw the judge earlier favoring him, they turned against him, hoping he would have a fateful day like 'Abid ibn al-Abras. Contrary to their wishes, the machinations did not meet with success. They backfired, lines 46–48 would have us conclude. The conceit in these lines is readily explained. Enviers bring attention to a neglected side of the envied individual's personality. Once their lies are refuted, hidden virtue in that person emerges. Hence, the jealous witnesses have, over time, enhanced Abu Tammam's reputation. What is more, since enviers live in dread, those attacking the poet could not have relished any temporary gains they might have achieved.

Like section B, B¹ also articulates an Islamic worldview. God's authority in exposing virtue is acknowledged, and God's fiery wrath is alluded to. The references to fire and wrath in particular evoke Qur'an 4:54–56, which describes the burning in hell of disbelievers who had apparently rankled with jealousy at God's bounty to mankind. In her study of Abu Tammam, Stetkevych discusses a poem for which the pre-Islamic age "plays the 'Old Testament' to an Islamic

'New Testament' that both abrogates and fulfills it."[33] Similarly, we find in two sections of the present ode the pre-Islamic age abrogated (though not fulfilled) by contemporary religious reality. Just as in section B pre-Islamic tribalism gives way to a broader concept of Islamic brotherhood, so in B¹ the hideous pre-Islamic punishment envisioned for Abu Tammam is superseded by a just Islamic retribution awaiting the enviers.

As regards argumentation, the poet backs off further in this section from admission of wrongdoing. The fault lies entirely with ill-wishers who tried to incite the judge against him. But in a panegyric, this last clarification poses a hazard. If Abu Tammam was unquestionably blameless, then the patron must have been in the wrong for believing slanderers. How exactly can the poet say so? Deftly, he gets out of the predicament by rewriting history: the break between the two men never occurred. Though the slanderers' arrow *did* hit the mark, and Abu Tammam spent a year suffering as a result, he relates events as if the judge, from the beginning, cleverly saw through their base designs. In this way, he also short-circuits his patron's decision-making process and relieves him of a mental burden. Abu Tammam was forgiven all along—there is no concession to make. The poet then adds lines that have the ring of Qur'anic truth (46 and 48) and inherited wisdom (47) to make his lie sound like scripture, acknowledged fact. He does it so that the patron cannot possibly question his simple thesis: the poet is innocent, the enviers are guilty, and the judge was sapient throughout.[34] He only stops short of recording that the judge has already ordered punishment to be visited on their heads. Therefore, should that worthy official now wish to add to what awaits them in the hereafter for refractoriness and attempting to involve him in unseemly business, he might justly do so. In fact, it would be high time.

A¹

49   Take it, the consistently rhyming work
      by one not ungrateful for ample beneficences.
50   Fast-traveling rhymes these are that fill every ear with wisdom and
          eloquence,
      and cause the blood to rush in every jugular vein.
51   The ode is like the piercing spear-thrust from a man avenging his brother;
      like the cleaving sword-stroke;

52   Like the necklace of pearls and coral-stones separated by gold beads
       on the neck of the tender young woman;
53   Like the long, striped cloak
       made in the land of Mahra or the country of Tazid,[35]
54   Presented to the noble man at the large gathering and donned,
       that signifies glad tidings—
55   The glad tidings brought to the rich man, the father of consecutive daughters,
       who has been blessed with a newborn horseman;
56   Like the charms for black snakes and speckled vipers,
       that have long extracted the venoms of resentments and rancor.

In the last section Abu Tammam presents his carefully wrought ode to the patron. Through the similes describing his poem, he again evokes the pre-Islamic period. Some of the motifs in this section, moreover, correspond to motifs in A. This return to the time period evoked at the beginning and to some of the themes from the first lines brings the ode to a fitting close.

Abu Tammam begins the last section by offering his work to Ibn Abi Du'ad and then launches into his string of similes that continues to the end of the poem. Let us first consider the opening part of A¹. One hears in 49–50, in addition to assuring words that the poet will be grateful, a prideful tone that anticipates the tone of swaggering self-assurance of al-Mutanabbi (d. 965). Furthermore, one senses the commanding presence of the poet. By contrast, he is completely absent in a caliphal panegyric such as the Amorium poem, where the triumphant caliph occupies the entire stage. Here, the poet stands man-to-man with the patron; he is not awed or frightened by him. Rather, he speaks out loudly and takes credit for his skill. His rhymes not only edify the listener, he affirms; they also stimulate the flow of adrenaline. The ensuing two similes likening the poem to instruments of combat follow from this last reference. The mortal effect of his poem, whether as a spear or a sword, corresponds to the impact of the beloved's arrows (line 4) on her lovers. In this section, however, the poet recalls specifically the pre-Islamic motif of *tha'r* (revenge), not the idea from amatory poetry of a beloved's deadly glances. He implies that, through the poem, he is delivering a deathblow to the people who slandered him.

On a deeper level, lines 49–51, along with the remainder of the ode, represent a return to the reality of the situation between these two men. Despite the cozy illusion offered in B¹, a deep rift separated them. Reconciliation required a conscious decision from the judge and a willingness to open wide his purse. Given these facts, lines 49–51 concern the possibility that the judge might decide not to forgive the poet and adumbrate Abu Tammam's probable response. One may recall at this juncture al-Nabigha's famous line to King al-Nu'man, also concerning the possibility of stubbornness. Al-Nabigha composed his 'Ayniyya presumably when he was in Syria, at a great remove from the court of al-Hira near the Euphrates. Nevertheless, he finally acknowledges that, should his poem not placate the king, then the man's wrath will inevitably overtake him:

> For you are like the night that catches up with me,
> even if I suppose the distant place from you to be wide.[36]

Abu Tammam comes up with a strikingly different response, reflecting an opposite power imbalance with his patron. Instead of submitting to a dark and miserable fate, he steps forward with a thinly veiled threat. He boasts in these lines of his poetic prowess, which can just as easily be employed for satire as for panegyric. One year earlier, the sharp tongues of slanderers posed the danger to the judge. Now, after the judge has refused to pay for an ode, the sharpened weaponry of the poet is the threat. Abu Tammam can easily retire, as he makes clear, to the protection of Khalid ibn Yazid, whence he might unload a barrage of invective that would render Ibn Abi Du'ad the mockery of 'Abbasid circles. These piercing thrusts and cleaving strokes might soon descend on the judge if he does not react appropriately. On the psychological plane, then, we see toward the end of the poem Abu Tammam having gotten the better of his foe, ready to finish him off should the man not openly surrender.

From violence Abu Tammam turns to beauty and gift giving, more fitting themes for the conclusion to an ostensible panegyric. He compares the ode to a precious necklace worn by a delicate young woman, evoking the lady of the *nasib*. The comparison to a necklace, a commonplace in Arabic poetry, reinforces the analogy made in section A between the beloved and the patron. She was associated with jewelry, and now he has this poem. The poet next proposes a masculine simile in lines 53–55. The ode resembles a striped cloak brought from Yemen—an apt present from Abu Tammam—whose recipient is a noble and rich man. At a large gathering the man is presented with this gift, which carries the news of a long-awaited son. After a succession of daughters, or poems composed by lesser encomiasts, he finally has a son. Abu Tammam's gift tells him that his name will now be passed down through generations; he will be remembered. Such a valuable and enduring contribution, symbolized by the cloak, naturally produces extreme joy in the patron, contrasting with the deep despair of the poet at the beginning of the ode.

Before we consider the last line, we might take a moment to ponder what the ostentatious presentation of the Yemeni garment discloses at this stage about the expectations on the judge and the relative advantage held by the poet. In a contemporary panegyric to Khalid ibn Yazid, the situation is reversed. In it Abu Tammam does not praise his own poetry. He recognizes the support Khalid provided him during hard times and then exemplifies Khalid's generosity:

> I came to him as a visitor, and he gave to me of his possessions
> not the old clothes but the new.[37]

Significantly, the patron clothes Abu Tammam, for which the poet expresses his appreciation. A request for further recompense is merely understood at the end of the poem, not underscored. One might describe this technique as the polite approach. On the other hand, at the end of the present ode Abu Tammam clothes the patron, and in front of an assembly no less. The patron would not want to show himself incapable of magnanimity before his peers. To do himself honor, he must forget petty grievances, embrace the poet, and thank him generously for his beautiful gift. The weight of obligation is upon him.

The last line of the ode again brings to mind the distant past, before the 'Abbasid era of doctors, medical advances, and translations of Galen from the Greek. Just as the charms of former years once extracted real poisons, Abu Tammam's poem removes the venoms of slanderers. In its mysterious potency, it retains the *sihr* (magic) of pre-Islamic poetry despite adaptation to suit modern circumstances.[38] And like the confident sorcerer who has recited his incantations, Abu Tammam projects a spirit of optimism at the end of the ode. Of course, the attribution to magic is another fiction—the potency of the poem derives from its controlled mixture of flattery, argument, and intimidation. This mixture ultimately proved efficacious: the judge submitted and signaled forgiveness, and Abu Tammam got his reward.

SUMMARY: NO. 37

Section				Lines	Structural and Thematic Elements
A				1–11	*nasib;* pre-Islamic setting; beloved shoots arrows at admirers; poet must apologize (*poet at disadvantage*)
	B			12–18	*rahil;* pre-Islamic tribalism replaced by Islamic brotherhood
		Transition		19–21	*madih* (continues to end of poem); patron protects poet
			C	22–29	precedent for sharing glory
			D	30–31	poet bargains with patron (*balance of power*)
			C¹	32–39	precedent for pardon
		Transition		40–41	poet rescues patron
	B¹			42–48	pagan sacrifice of poet superseded by Islamic punishment for enviers
A¹				49–56	presentation of gift; pre-Islamic setting; poet threatens to use weapons against patron; patron must forgive (*patron at disadvantage*)

9

The Would-Be Prophet

Horses, night, and the desert know me;
so do swords, spears, the paper and pen.

—AL-MUTANABBI, No. 194

IN THIS CHAPTER we shall consider the last of the three great 'Abbasid pan-
egyrists, al-Mutanabbi (d. 965), widely thought of as the greatest Arab poet (the
Mu'allaqa of Imru' al-Qays, as we have indicated, is generally regarded individually
as the greatest Arabic poem). Before proceeding, however, we will briefly discuss the
second major 'Abbasid panegyrist, Abu Tammam's successor, al-Buhturi (d. 897).

Al-Buhturi was born in 821 at the town of Manbij in northern Syria. He
emerged as a gifted poet and dedicated his early poetic efforts, as a teenager, to
the praise of his tribe. Thereafter, he went off in search of patronage. He met Abu
Tammam, who recommended him to various grandees. After Abu Tammam's
death ca. 846, he was granted an audience with Caliph al-Mutawakkil (r. 847–61),
an opportunity that marked the beginning of a long and illustrious court career.
Over the next half century, roughly, he praised six 'Abbasid caliphs and a large
number of their viziers and governors. He retired finally to his birthplace, where
he had acquired substantial land, and died there.

Al-Buhturi is most famous for his descriptive poetry. What follows is one
of his most admired descriptions, of the Ja'fari Lake made by al-Mutawakkil (or
Abu al-Fadl Ja'far; the former is a byname, short for "al-Mutawakkil 'ala Allah,"
"the One Who Trusts in God") within the walls of his grand Ja'fari Palace, a few
miles north of Samarra:

Whoever gazes upon the beautiful lake,
with its peripheral abodes of lovely maidens,

170

Reckons it superior to the sea;
the latter he ranks second.

What has come over the Tigris lately, like the jealous one,
vying now and then with the lake in beauty?

Has she not seen that the guardian of Islam guards it from blame,
that the builder of glory has built it?

It is as if Solomon's jinn had charge of its creation
and attended to every detail.[1]

Were the Queen of Sheba to pass by, she would say:
"It is the floor of the palace exactly."[2]

Delegations of water pour into it hurriedly
like horses on the loose.

It is as if the white silver of ingots
flows in its tributaries.

When a breeze passes over it, the breeze makes ripples
that reflect like chainmail.

The brow of the sun, some mornings, sports with it;
the welling sky, some mornings, cries on it.

At night, when stars appear in the lake's edges,
you would think a firmament had been built into it.

The enclosed fish do not reach its limit
due to the space between this end and that.

They swim in it with winged bodies
like birds flapping through air.

When they go down, they come to a great basin;
when they go up, a vast plain.

They veer often to the engraved dolphin
that, by the side, flirts with the lake.

The lake's distant flower beds, looking on, dispense with the clouds—
no need for those water skins.

When it swells and overflows, when its wadi is full,
it is like the palm of the Caliph.

On the day of the lake's naming, its standing was increased—
to a point even above where it was—when it was named after him.

The lake is surrounded by luxuriant gardens; at their near boundaries,
you see always peacock feathers, conversing with the water.

And the lake is bordered by two flat-topped hills, like Sirius and Procynon[3]
in early morning, each trying to rise above the other.

Once the efforts of the Commander of the Faithful are manifest to describers,
however, no description comes close to the achievement.[4]

On the subject of al-Buhturi, we might also speak of his famous poem that features a description of the Sasanian Ctesiphon ruins and the impressive battle wall painting he saw there.[5] The *qasida* is striking not only for its vivid description, the length of which—at thirty-seven lines—does not conveniently permit a rendering here, but also for its themes and structure.[6] Though presumably al-Buhturi often composed, at least partially, for gain, he was clearly moved to compose this poem by a sense of indignation. Pridefully, he declares in line 1:

I have preserved my soul from what pollutes it
and not taken gifts from any coward.

It soon becomes apparent that the cause of his indignation is mistreatment from a patron. It is not in his nature to stand for such abuse. As he says:

If ever I'm ill-treated, I'm apt
not to be seen at dawn where I was at dusk.

Next he mentions a camel journey, which ends at the ruins of Ctesiphon. There he grows absorbed in historical contemplation and increasingly becomes aware and appreciative of the former splendor of the once royal city. As a whole, the poem marks a familiar emotional progression: from unhappiness (in this case, anger) to a certain solace. The philosophy it articulates resembles that of Labid, as expressed in his *Mu'allaqa* (line 21): that is, love the one you're with, and only as long as she's good to you. Yet the beloved is now the patron, and the measure of affection, it seems, is not kisses but currency. Structurally, however, the poem defies expectation completely. It begins by evoking the milieu of a patron and ends by calling to mind a desolate city. It is the reverse of the traditional movement from abandoned encampment to hospitable patron (or welcoming tribe). Al-Buhturi travels from the present to the past and finds there a valuable lesson—that others besides Arabs may possess greatness and splendor. He says in the last line:

Now I see myself loving noblemen generally,
of every origin and stock.

Now, as a result of his experience, he may well seek out other patrons, too.

After al-Buhturi's appearance in Iraq, and until about the middle of the tenth century, the most contentious critical debate of Arabic literature concerned the assignation of precedence between Abu Tammam and al-Buhturi. Al-Buhturi was seen as more traditional in figurative expression, Abu Tammam as more experimental; al-Buhturi had a simple style, Abu Tammam a learned one characterized by an abundance of rhetorical devices (*badi'*). Each poet's work attracted numerous partisans. Then al-Mutanabbi came on the scene, the poet who, in the words of Ibn Rashiq (d. 1064), "filled the world and engaged its people."[7] Eventually, everyone was talking about him. Before reading one of al-Mutanabbi's many outstanding poems, we will follow the course of his adventurous life, which indeed contributed to his extraordinary renown.

Al-Mutanabbi was born in 915 at Kufa, the son of a water carrier. Despite the family's poverty, he received a thorough early education in Kufa's schools.

Beginning in 923 the town was subjected to a series of attacks by Qarmati rebels.[8] He fled at some point along with his kin and lived for a number of years in the desert among Bedouins. His study and composition of poetry, begun at Kufa, continued in the desert. Later he returned to Kufa, and then went to Baghdad, carrying just a handful of dirhams. He earned some money in the capital by praising a fellow Kufan (someone who had distinguished himself fighting on the town's outskirts) but left for Syria when he was seventeen. There he apparently started calling for a revolution and soon found himself in prison.

From the poetry of his youth, we know that al-Mutanabbi was warlike. He says:

Unless you die an honorable death beneath swords
you will die in dishonor, taxed by ignominy.

So rise up, trusting in God, in the way of the glorious warrior
who sees death in battle like honey brought to the mouth.[9]

He was acutely aware of his talent. That he thought very highly of himself is an understatement, and his coming from a humble background meant simply that he excelled independently. People closest to him were distinguished by association:

I am not ennobled by my tribe; they are ennobled by me.
And I boast of myself, not of those who preceded me.[10]

Moreover, he was incredibly ambitious. These lines are famous:

What tall height to reach?
What great man to fear?

When everything God has created,
and what He has not,

Is as negligible in my aspiration
as a single hair in my part.[11]

It is this young man, then, who seems to have gotten it into his head to lead an insurrection. He was evidently with the tribe of Banu Kalb near Baʿlabakk in present-day Lebanon. Unfortunately, the tribespeople, it appears, did not heed his call. Word of his activity, however, reached the governor of Hims, and he was arrested.

When he got out of prison two years later, he had been dubbed "al-Mutanabbi," "the Would-Be Prophet" (Abu al-Tayyib Ahmad ibn al-Husayn being his formal name). Ibn Jinni (d. 1002), who became a reciter of his poetry about fifteen years thence, said he received the nickname because of this line, the last from a poem on his experience presumably with the Banu Kalb:

> I'm treated by these people—God bring what they deserve—
> as Salih was by Thamud.[12]

Al-Tha'alibi (d. 1038) records it was said, though, that previous to his incarceration he had actually claimed prophethood.[13] Al-Mutanabbi, we understand from a conversation that occurred toward the end of his life, was rather embarrassed at the events of this time and did not wish to shed much light on his nickname. Al-Tanukhi (d. 994) reports saying to him in the Persian city of Ahwaz:

> "I want to ask you about something I have had in mind for years. I was always too ashamed to talk to you about it because of the many people who were present with you at Baghdad. But now we are in solitude and I simply must ask you about it."—There happened to be in front of me a partial copy of his poetry on which was written "The Poetry of Abu l-Tayyib al-Mutanabbi." He said: "You want to ask me about the reason for that?"—And he put his finger to the writing where it said "al-Mutanabbi." So I said: "Yes." He said: "That was something that happened in my youth which a certain childishness had brought about." . . . I saw that this was difficult for him, so I considered it bad to go any further and force him to tell the story in clear detail and so I abstained from it.[14]

Clearly, the issue of his byname's provenance cannot be definitively resolved. Yet we have good reason to prefer the first explanation. As Ibrahim 'Awad has noted, a number of considerations put an actual claim to prophecy in doubt. First of all, the poet was young—only a teenager (the Prophet Muhammad, by contrast, did not hear the angel Gabriel's voice until he was forty). Prophets typically received enlightenment and came forth at an older age. Second, the punishment of two years' imprisonment would not appear to correspond with an egregious religious challenge. Had he really made a claim so offensive to orthodox Islam—Muhammad is the seal (that is, the last) of the prophets—one would expect the governor to have treated him more harshly, to have killed him probably. And third, the poetic evidence for a prophethood claim does not exist. In fact, this line from a prison poem, addressed to the governor, suggests that our poet, looking back, saw the violation he was charged with as merely wanting to start something (what it was he chooses not to remind the man), not as making a plainly shocking religious claim:

> Be discriminating: between the allegation I did something
> and I wished to is a large divide.[15]

One may add that, in pre-Islamic times, it had been quite common to name a poet after an especially striking line in the poet's work.[16] We are disposed to conclude that this tendency is also what happened in the case of al-Mutanabbi.

He spent the next dozen or so years as an itinerant panegyrist, visiting the courts of Damascus, Antioch, and Ladhiqiyya (Laodicea) in Syria; Tiberias and Ramla in Palestine; and Tripoli in present-day Lebanon; among others in the region. The period, we note, was witnessing a proliferation of provincial courts, concomitant with an erosion of 'Abbasid authority. (By 945 the debilitated 'Abbasids could not resist a challenge posed by the army of the Persian-speaking Buwayhids. Baghdad was taken, power was transferred east to Shiraz, and until 1055 Iraq was governed as a province by the Buwayhids. The 'Abbasid caliphate continued as a religious edifice, though the person in the throne room in Baghdad was manipulated from Persia.) Poets toured lesser courts in search of a good opportunity. Al-Mutanabbi, during this phase of his life, praised thirty-two men—governors and minor princes—through forty-four poems.[17] All the while, as he sought a better situation, he was honing his skills, developing his art.

Common themes emerge from these poems. A salient one is his contempt for society. He says:

> I criticize this age for its little people:
> the most learned is an idiot, the most resolute a scoundrel.[18]

The high and mighty, or those persons commonly deemed so, are not respected by him. He describes a prominent group thusly:

Rabbits—except that they are kings—
sleeping with their eyes open.[19]

On the other hand, he professes the highest regard for the local patron. For example, he says to one:

I marvel that you were able to grow
given that you were made perfect at birth.[20]

There is a spirit of "us versus the world" that runs through these poems. Compare this line, in which al-Mutanabbi and the patron are equated in terms of excellence:

You are the poet of glory and I am the poet of words;
both of us are masters of the precise meaning.[21]

Yet it will be readily observed in these works that the identity of the patron is always changing; the only consistent praise is for the poet himself.

Within depraved society, al-Mutanabbi singles out the clustering poets for especial criticism. At one court he calls them "flies."[22] Besides being devoid of talent, they, unlike himself, are greedy and utilitarian:

I came to you seeking illustrious qualities;
others came seeking good wages.[23]

Overall, we sense that this period for al-Mutanabbi, though artistically beneficial, was personally frustrating. These lines perhaps best express the predominating sentiment of his twenties and early thirties:

How long this waiting and delay,
how long this plodding and dull perseverance?

And being distracted from the pursuit of glory
by the sale of poetry in a stagnant market?[24]

In 948, when he was thirty-three, his fortunes changed. His fame had been gradually spreading, and that year he was offered a plum position of court poet to Sayf al-Dawla (Sword of the State). This patron was no minor player. Having recently become ruler of northern Syria, Sayf al-Dawla had then taken on, according to the treaty he had signed with his Ikhshidid rival in Egypt, the responsibility for defending the abode of Islam against resurgent Byzantium. Energetic at thirty-two years and courageous, he was eager now to take the fight to the enemy. And at his court in Aleppo he was gathering many of the day's finest scholars, philosophers, litterateurs, and poets. On top of it all, he had a reputation for breathtaking generosity.

The position was offered to al-Mutanabbi at the salary of three thousand dinars per annum, plus bonuses. As resident poet, he would be expected to compose three poems per year (he might earn bonuses for supererogatory contributions). Al-Mutanabbi responded with a condition: he would not kiss the ground before Sayf and then recite standing, as was the custom at Sayf's court, after the practice in Baghdad;[25] he would be seated to the right of Sayf's throne (a place normally reserved for princes) and recite there. Sayf al-Dawla accepted this condition.

The handsome salary and special privileges accorded him started al-Mutanabbi on the wrong foot with some members of the court. This line from his first poem to Sayf surely made matters worse:

> I got angry for him when I saw his qualities and no one to describe them,
> while his poets were stammering nonsense.[26]

At some point, Abu Firas al-Hamdani, Sayf's cousin and a highly respected poet himself, conveyed this thought to Sayf's ear: "That fluent talker is awfully bold and familiar with you, and you give him three thousand dinars a year for three *qasidas*; you could distribute two hundred dinars among twenty poets, and each would come forward with better poetry than he does."[27] Nevertheless, the principal poet was retained.

Annually, Sayf conducted military campaigns against the Byzantines. Al-Mutanabbi accompanied him and composed about them a series of masterpieces. By this time, we appreciate, our poet had thoroughly developed his amazing talent, and here he had found in Sayf a patron whom he truly admired. Notably, the admiration translated into expressions of love (al-Mutanabbi, incidentally, innovated by addressing his patron explicitly in terms of the beloved).[28] Considering the quality of the poems, one supposes that feelings of love went both ways.

The nine years al-Mutanabbi spent with Sayf al-Dawla, until he was forty-two, were the brightest of his career. Finally, however, the poet's enviers conspired successfully and alienated Sayf al-Dawla from him. Al-Mutanabbi departed and went to Damascus.[29]

He was not there long before the Ikhshidid ruler Kafur recruited him. From his capital of Fustat (Old Cairo; the Fatimids, who reigned until 1171, founded the current city in 969), Kafur controlled not only Egypt but the Hejaz of Arabia, Palestine, and southern Syria as well. Al-Mutanabbi traveled to Egypt and praised Kafur, yet he was nostalgic. He begins one *qasida* revealing, "I struggle with my passion for you, but the passion is just too strong."[30] Kafur set the poet up in a fine house and paid him well, though the patron fell short of expectations: al-Mutanabbi had been led to believe that, in return for his praise, he would receive a governorship south of Beirut. We suspect that Kafur, reflecting on the poet, became distrustful. He supposedly remarked to him after a while: "When you were poor and friendless you exalted yourself to the level of prophethood. If you got a governorship and acquired a following, who would be able to tolerate you?"[31] Over time, Kafur heard fewer and fewer panegyrics. In the last to Kafur, al-Mutanabbi says:

Does it do me any good that the curtains between us are raised,
when between me and what I hope for there is still a curtain?[32]

I make few my salutations so as not to disturb you
and maintain a silence so you are not troubled to respond.

But in my soul are needs, and you are sensitive;
my silence to you is discourse and clarity.[33]

The governorship was never conferred, and in 962 al-Mutanabbi fled Egypt. He posted a scathing satire to Kafur, and would later nullify all his eulogy of the Ikhshidid:

That was not praise of him;
it was satire of mankind.[34]

He reached Kufa, and then went to Baghdad. There he established residence and gave lectures to literary assemblies on his poetry.

Probably the most noteworthy occurrence during his time in Baghdad involved an encounter with a critic. Soon after al-Mutanabbi's arrival in Baghdad, the 'Abbasid vizier al-Muhallabi had made inquiries as to whether al-Mutanabbi might praise him. Al-Mutanabbi replied that he only praised rulers. So al-Muhallabi instructed a number of his courtiers to cut the poet down to size. One who responded immediately was al-Hatimi, an eminent philologist who evidently had known al-Mutanabbi in Aleppo. He showed up on an evening when al-Mutanabbi was lecturing to a "rabble" and proceeded, according to his account, to shame the poet before the crowd. "I bore down upon him like a torrent rushing down towards the bottom of the valley," he tells us in *Al-Risala al-mudiha fi dhikr sariqat Abi al-Tayyib al-Mutanabbi wa-saqit shi'rihi* (The Illustrative Treatise on the Plagiarisms of Abu al-Tayyib al-Mutanabbi and the Mistakes in His Poetry).[35] The accomplished poet becomes the student as the philologist identifies in his work plagiarisms, grammatical errors, and stylistic shortcomings (in reality, we assume al-Mutanabbi was dismissive of the criticisms and somewhat amused by the man).[36] Al-Hatimi, in fact, did not let him go at that, but later wrote a second treatise charging the poet with stealing ideas from Aristotle.

In early 965 al-Mutanabbi was invited to Shiraz, the court of the Buwayhid 'Adud al-Dawla (Arm of the State), who ruled Iraq, Persia, and the Islamic lands to the east. As far as Arabic literature is concerned, 'Adud al-Dawla was the most educated of the Buwayhids; he even composed some Arabic poetry. The appreciation of Arabic poetry at Shiraz during his reign is suggested by this reported conversation dating prior to 965, initiated by one of 'Adud's attendants: "The court of our ruler is not lacking anything except one of the two Ta'i's [Abu Tammam and al-Buhturi, of the Tayyi' tribe]." Adud al-Dawla replied, "Were al-Mutanabbi to join us, he would replace them."[37] Al-Mutanabbi came in late spring, and he composed for 'Adud al-Dawla several brilliant panegyrics. After a few months' stay, during which he received two hundred thousand dirhams, he got permission to leave to take care of some personal business in Baghdad. He made it to a point about sixty miles southeast of his destination, along the Tigris. There his caravan was attacked by brigands. Al-Mutanabbi and his son, Muhassad,[38] were killed, and the treasure he was bringing back was stolen.

As is clear from the foregoing narrative, al-Mutanabbi stepped on a quantity of toes during his lifetime, especially those belonging to literary fellows. For about a generation thereafter, smarting opponents (and others who came to their side) sought to turn public opinion against him. We may add to the example of al-Hatimi, the critic mentioned above, the mention of al-Sahib ibn 'Abbad (d. 995). Al-Sahib, the son of a vizier, had invited al-Mutanabbi in 965 to Isfahan, Persia, offering to share his fortune with al-Mutanabbi if the latter would praise him. Al-Mutanabbi never bothered to respond. Doubtless resentful, al-Sahib later wrote *Al-Kashf 'an masawi al-Mutanabbi* (The Disclosure of al-Mutanabbi's Shortcomings), dealing with the defects in al-Mutanabbi's poetry. But in the eleventh century, opponents of al-Mutanabbi became harder and harder to find. We will conclude this part of our discussion by quoting a story that evokes, for the period following his death, the steady expansion of al-Mutanabbi's popularity.

> It is said that there was a man from Baghdad who loathed al-Mutanabbi, so much so that he swore to himself not to live in a town where al-Mutanabbi was mentioned and his poetry recited. So he went east, and whenever he heard al-Mutanabbi mentioned in a place he would continue his travels. Finally he reached the eastern end of the Islamic world. He asked the people there if they knew of al-Mutanabbi. They said "no," and he settled there. The next Friday, however, having gone to the mosque to pray, he heard the preacher declare, after reciting God's blessed ninety-nine names:
>
> > Speaking these has not added to His knowledge,
> > yet for pleasure we recited them.[39]
>
> So he went back to Baghdad.[40]

As al-Mutanabbi's *Diwan* is filled with magnificent poems, any of a large number of works could have been chosen for a detailed analysis. We have chosen the poem below only because its composition seems to have presented an especially difficult rhetorical challenge—making the patron, Sayf al-Dawla, feel powerful and encouraged after a disastrous military campaign. In advance of reading the poem, however, we will familiarize ourselves with the Byzantine-Muslim conflict and then with the enterprise of 950.

By the early 900s the Muslims and Byzantines had been fighting each other for more than two and a half centuries. The goal for the Muslims was Constantinople, but they had not taken it. The Taurus Mountains in southern Anatolia formed a natural boundary between Islam and Byzantium, albeit one that had been crossed on many occasions. In the tenth century (specifically after 926) the Byzantines, formerly on the defensive, were gaining the upper hand.[41] They were growing stronger in Anatolia and were able to make incursions into northern Syria. For a while Sayf al-Dawla, Islam's champion, was successful in holding them back. He also conducted some audacious raids into Anatolia. Yet in terms of waging the war against Byzantium, he was alone; the other Islamic rulers, morally supportive, were not giving him matériel.

In 948 and 949 the Byzantines had come over the Taurus Mountains and had taken the fortifications of Mar'ash and Hadath, about a hundred miles north of Aleppo. Sayf al-Dawla rallied forces for the response. In August and September 950, he led an expedition of thirty thousand men northward. It was the first large offensive since he had become ruler at Aleppo and the first expedition to include al-Mutanabbi among its participants.[42]

They crossed into Anatolia and proceeded northwest to the city of Kharshana, fording the River Alis (Kizil Irmak in modern Turkey) en route. The Byzantines' commander in chief, or "domesticus" (that is, the emperor's field deputy), the elder Bardas Phocas, had delegated authority in this part of Anatolia to his son Leon. Leon kept a distance to the north of the large Muslim army, evidently preferring to wait for an ambush opportunity. Sayf did not take Kharshana in front of him, but he ravaged the countryside. From Kharshana he went east, passing through an area called Marj, and reached the town of Sarikha. He pillaged Sarikha and razed its churches, putting up *minbars* (pulpits) in their stead, which were used for a Friday service. Then he returned west and forded the Alis once more.

He must have learned that the Byzantines were assembling to the north of Kharshana, and so, leaving baggage at a base camp, he crossed the Alis again and headed north with his crack troops. At al-Luqan, Leon Phocas, seeing Sayf's vanguard and considering it a detachment, welcomed combat. Sayf won the battle, killing many men and taking some eighty high-value prisoners for future ransom (Leon himself escaped). Next Sayf returned to his camp and, seeing that the fall season was already quite advanced, decided to repair with his booty and captives to Aleppo.

The army was in the Taurus Mountains region when it found the way obstructed with tree trunks. Suddenly, from above, the enemy started hurling rocks, and then Leon Phocas came and attacked from behind.[43] Sayf fought at the rear while the rest of his army struggled to go forward. Eventually, the front troops got through to the next valley, and Sayf followed. The weakened Arab army found the next pass filled by enemy warriors, and so expedience dictated a detour to the east. Along the eastern route, however, the army was again attacked from behind. As darkness approached, fighters began peeling off and slipping forward to the baggage. Sayf was practically alone against the Byzantines at the end of the day. That night, at a camp near Hadath, he tried to rally the troops for a morning counterattack. Yet many were too exhausted and dispirited to answer his call. So, making a fierce resolution, he ordered the tired ones to destroy the baggage and slaughter the prisoners, lest they encumber him or be of use to the Byzantines against him. Meanwhile, he would fight his way forward, past Hadath, and lead the army back to Aleppo. The fatigued elements were overtaken by the Byzantines late the next morning; Sayf, for his part, reached Aleppo after considerable effort.

All in all, Sayf al-Dawla lost five thousand men in this campaign and the entire booty he had acquired; additionally, three thousand of his men were taken prisoner. Following a debacle of these proportions, what was a panegyrist to say? Al-Mutanabbi was on salary—it was expected that he come up with something. Moreover, silence from him would emphasize the failed outcome. Let us read, then, what the poet said in this situation.[44]

A

1   Others than myself are deceived by the majority of men:
     when they fight they are fearful, when they talk they are brave.

2   Zealous warriors they, until tested—
     and in experience lies what checks deception.

3   How to characterize life? By my soul, I have learnt:
     life is dirtiness, what you do not covet.

4   Beauty does not consist in an attractive visage;
     an admired man by the loss of honor is defaced.

5   Do I cast glory from my shoulder, and seek it elsewhere,[45]
     and leave spring abundance in my sheath, and search for pasturage?

6   While the Yemeni swords—may they still confer distinction—
     are the remedy to every noble man, and the blight to his foe;

7   And the bravest rider is he who, when horses rear
     in a mountain pass, blood on their sides, settles them.

8   And who, when riders abandon him, feels totally at ease;
      and who, when they anger him, utters no profanity.
9   Rulers all remain inaccessible behind their armies.
      But in this case, the army remains inaccessible behind its mighty warrior.

Clearly, al-Mutanabbi cannot open the poem with praise of Sayf (as he does, for example, in the case of No. 226, his poem celebrating the reconquest of Hadath in 954).[46] He therefore avoids the subject of his patron at the outset, instead expressing his disgust at those men who deserted from combat and would not fight when Sayf tried to rally them. These men are mere talkers. Stepping back from the particular, he finds their disgraceful battlefield reticence not surprising, for life has taught him to expect ugliness and disappointment. What seems appealing initially often turns out decidedly unpleasant. We note here that Sayf would share these feelings after his calamitous expedition. The poet is speaking for himself and also for the patron.

The negative thoughts in the first four lines lead the poet to a grim question: should he abandon his patron? Certainly, the man's military project did not end in success. He goes about answering it for himself by extolling Sayf (a felicitous way to handle the question, considering that Sayf probably was sitting next to him). The patron is still the hero, the generous man at court and the strong and bold leader in the field. He has not been tarnished. And, as the poet's shaping of events will make clear, his recent project, including the horrendous depletion of fighters at the end, augurs well for future campaigns.

B

10   He led the troops on bridled mounts,
      their slowest speed, quickness, their first watering place, the last.
11   No intervening country detained him;
      he advanced like death: his thirst never slaked, his hunger never sated.
12   Until he pulled up at the outskirts of Kharshana,
      bringing misery for the Byzantines, and for their crosses and churches—
13   Taking prisoner their wives and children, and killing their adolescents;
      plundering their wealth, and burning their fields;
14   Marj was left to him, and in Sarikha he had *minbars* erected
      and performed with the troops the Friday prayers.

15   Vultures became habituated to Byzantine bodies,
      to the extent that they almost started descending on them alive.

16   Had the Disciples watched Sayf,
      they would have made loving him a pillar of their faith.

C

17   The Domesticus blamed his eyes when gloom covered the horizon,
      after he had thought it was only a scattering of clouds,

18   Comprising iron-clad warriors of whom the newly weaned is already a man,
      on bulky coursers whose yearling is the size of a two-year-old;

19   The dust of al-Luqan fills their nostrils
      while drafts of Alis are still in their throats.

20   When the horses encounter the foe, they do so as if to go through them.
      Spears open in abdomens wide enough passage.

21   Their eyes find the way in the darkness of battle,
      the spears being candles, lit at the ends.

22   Before arrows impact, and before enemy soldiers think to flee,
      the steeds are upon them bounding and trampling.

23   Whenever a distressed infidel calls for aid,
      a tawny lance interposes, separating two of his ribs.

24   If Phocas's son got away—well, those greater than him were shackled,
      and those more resolute in fighting were slain.

25   But none really escaped the shiny edges of swords:
      he who made off carried fear in his gut.

26   He stops distant from the scene, a crack-brained man,
      and drinks wine for a year, yellow in the face.

27   How many a Byzantine general's last breath was kept for the swords
      by a faithful guard not imbued with piety.[47]

28   The guard halts the general when he would wander,
      and drives from him sleep when he reclines.

29   Death leaves in the morning—but still is in view
      when Sayf says: "Come back!" Then it pounces.

B¹

30   Say to the Domesticus: the Muslims you came upon are yours;
      they betrayed the emir and he requited them.

31   You found them lying in the blood of your dead
      as if they had empathized with the ones killed.

32   Weaklings such as them, among the enemy, the hand refrains from
          touching;
      even when it moves to strike, it desists.

33   Don't consider those you captured to have any life in them;
      the hyena only eats what is dead.

34   Have you not reached now the upper end of the valley
      where individual lions are roaming?

35   Each long-bodied horse splits your ranks with its fighter,
      and every sword-stroke takes from you more than it leaves.

36   God therefore put the soldiers at your disposal
      so the troops would be without cowards when they return.

37   Now subsequent raids will all go Sayf's way;
      and every raider will be behind him.

Al-Mutanabbi switches to a third-person voice at the beginning of section B
for his chronicle of the campaign,[48] adding an element of objectivity to his statements. The poet bolsters Sayf by recounting his swift arrival at the destination
and his early devastation of the Byzantine heartland. We note here the poet's
technique of subdividing the sections of his poem (which correspond on a larger
scale, we apprehend, according to the principles of ring composition) into segments of two to four lines, and of closing each section with an emphatic final line.
In B, for example, lines 10–11 evoke Sayf's race into central Anatolia, lines 12–15
detail the destruction he wrought there, and line 16 delivers a remarkable opinion based on the witness of Sayf's performance.[49] The poet, one readily appreciates, has composed his work with great care.

Section C, the second part of the chronicle, treats the clash of forces north
of Kharshana. The Muslim army is represented as a gathering storm to the eye
of the domesticus (his next in command, if one wishes to be completely factual).
We have become familiar, so far in this study, with positive associations for rain
clouds (for example, of fertility and of generosity; warfare, meanwhile, is commonly signified by fire). Yet in passing we mention that poets may also suggest
conflict through inclement-weather figures, if perhaps less frequently: the thun-
der sound of an approaching army, for instance, the lightning flash of swords,
and the rainlike spilling of blood. Differently considered, lines 17–18 mark a shift

from the distant focus to the close-up on the part of the domesticus, from a realization of the Muslim forces' number to an awareness of their size. Viewing the approach from his perspective heightens the drama, for it conveys surprise and a dawning realization of doom. We are then with the Muslims in line 19, getting a sense of their speed just before impact.

At the exact center of the poem (line 25) we discover an allusion, by the mention of shining swords, to Sayf. The central subsection (24–26) deals with a crucial point: the domesticus got away. But really he did not—he is debilitated by fear at what he saw, and *he knows Sayf will be back.* Let what happened to the generals be a lesson to him: Sayf controls Death. He reined it in for the generals, and he will rein it in for the domesticus, too.

Naturally, the events of the return are not suitable for this chronicle. So the poet makes the army's succumbing to the domesticus the basis of an invective, one that takes away the other's victory. Agency for what happened in the pass belonged to Sayf—he gave the cowards what they deserved. Moreover, killing such feeble creatures signaled the Byzantines' lack of honor. And their liquidation, not to mention his ending up in the mountainous region, now bodes ill for the domesticus. He should soon expect Sayf, leading an army trimmed of its cowards.

A¹

38   The noble follow in their forefathers' footsteps,
     but you create what comes next, you innovate.

39   Does one occasion mar you, when you were the hero,
     and others than yourself the weak and impotent?

40   —He whose place is above the sun,
     so that nothing could lower or raise him.

41   Re-engaging the enemy from the rear of his army did not betray his soul,
     though his commanders and followers had betrayed it.

42   Would that kings rewarded according to abilities,
     so that base poets would not greedily gather.

43   You have approved that they observe while you visit war,
     and listen while you knock at iron helmets.

44   They broadcast your deeds through fraudulent transactions,
     though you were the one who knowingly profited.

45   Now Fate is apologetic and the Sword is waiting,
     and their land to you is spring and summer terrain.

46   Mountains do not afford refuge to a Christian;

       they would not to a vigorous, white-footed ibex were he to become one.

47   I have not praised you for standing firm in a dreadful situation

       while others escaped, except after I saw you there myself;

48   For the brave may be thought of as lightheaded,

       and the fearful may be thought of as steady.

49   Indeed, every man carries a weapon,

       but not every clawed creature is a lion.

In the last section al-Mutanabbi addresses Sayf al-Dawla directly. He reassures him in lines 38–41 that he was not at all shamed by the debacle, as he previously reassured himself in lines 5–8 of A. Al-Mutanabbi next speaks disdainfully about the other poets. Implicitly, they are linked to the spineless men referred to at the beginning—mere talkers, these fellows. Yet the poet is in a tight spot here, for Sayf has employed them. Sayf knew they were frauds, of course, and he let them sing his praises anyway. Also, this activity went on, we ascertain, before our poet's arrival in Aleppo. Sayf may now expel those frauds and keep the poet who, accompanying him to the battle scene, can faithfully describe his heroism.

Having gotten thus far, we notice a main theme running through the poem, that is, appearances differing from reality. In A the poet recalls the eager and boastful campaigners who then exited when the fighting got intense; in C he affirms that the one who got away really did not, the man being plagued by dread; B^1 concerns a large depletion of the Muslim army that was actually a boon; and A^1 raises the issue of fraudulent poets. The theme of appearances differing from reality is absent only from section B, which describes the early part of the campaign, an obvious success. Both Sayf and the poet can discern the reality despite deceptive appearances. Evidently, the overall lesson to be drawn from the expedition, having reconsidered it through al-Mutanabbi's poem, is that what appears to have been disastrous has been, in actuality, beneficial (the poem, we are reminded, represents an effort to encourage Sayf).

Al-Mutanabbi concludes his work with a peroration, consisting of two segments (45–46 and 47–48) and a final line. The first segment contains two striking lines of encouragement. The second links Sayf and the poet: al-Mutanabbi's praise comes from another rare hero, one who stands beside him in the ferocious heat of battle. And the last line closes the poem resoundingly. On poetic conclusions (and openings) Ibn Rashiq has remarked: "If the beginning of a poem is its key, the end must be its lock."[50] Al-Mutanabbi ends his poem with a clinching statement that distinguishes the likes of Sayf and himself from others—reinforcing once more the main theme of appearances differing from reality—and, at the same time, points directly back to the opening line. So now, given that Sayf has heard this poem, has recently purged his army, and has gained al-Mutanabbi as his fearless companion, who will go out with him at the vanguard . . . Woe to the Byzantines!

SUMMARY: NO. 188

Section	Lines	Structural and Thematic Elements
A	1–9	*poet addresses self* disgust at cowards; appearance versus reality disappointment at recent outcome Sayf still hero; poet would not leave him
B	10–16	*beginning of campaign* race into central Anatolia destruction of Kharshana area and Sarikha
C	17–29	clash of armies *central statement:* none escaped shiny swords (appearance versus reality); fear plagues him who got away killing of captured generals
B¹	30–37	*end of campaign* Sayf gave cowards what they deserved Sayf soon will be back, leading charge
A¹	38–49	*poet addresses Sayf* disgust at other poets; appearance versus reality expectation of success in near future Sayf still hero; poet next to him

10

Letter to a Princess

Would that the night were always bright moonlight, and the depression
always freshly green.

—RWALA BEDOUIN

IBN ZAYDUN, the most illustrious poet from the nearly eight-hundred–year
period of Arab-Islamic civilization in al-Andalus (711–1492), was born to a prominent Córdoban family in 1003. He received an excellent education in his childhood and early youth at the hands of numerous scholars. During the 1020s, as
the Umayyad dynasty that ruled al-Andalus was struggling to persist, young Ibn
Zaydun took a leading part in fomenting unrest. When the Umayyad house finally
collapsed in 1031, he was on the scene backing the local Córdoban figure, Ibn
Jahwar. Subsequently, he was appointed minister of the Jahwarid petty state and
its ambassador-at-large. He was dispatched frequently on missions to the various
parts of al-Andalus, which had become politically fragmented upon the dissolu-
tion of Umayyad rule. One of his outstanding diplomatic successes occurred at
Granada, where he negotiated a treaty of mutual defense against the Banu 'Abbad
of Seville. While in his midthirties he entered a tempestuous romantic relationship with the cultured and sophisticated Wallada, daughter of the Umayyad caliph
al-Mustakfi. This experience probably was the major development of the middle
period of his life and certainly inspired his greatest verse. A notorious incident
connected to this love affair (discussed below) led to a turn in his fortunes—soon
after the incident he lost the confidence of Ibn Jahwar completely. Following a stay
in prison, Ibn Zaydun escaped Córdoba, and he spent most of his later life as senior
minister and principal poet in Seville. He died and was buried there in 1071.

Before discussing the relationship with Wallada and reading his chief work,
let us briefly review the political and cultural history of al-Andalus prior to Ibn

190

Zaydun, so that we may consider his most remarkable poem in its Andalusi context. The Arabs entered the Iberian Peninsula in 711, as previously indicated, and within five years conquered practically all of it. Al-Andalus became a province of the vast Umayyad Empire, of which we recall Damascus was the capital. Soon the victorious immigrants, however, were riven by dissent; North Arabians disputed with South Arabians, and between 732 and 755 numerous conflicts broke out. It was not until the fugitive Umayyad prince ʿAbd al-Rahman I appeared on the peninsula, and was championed by the South Arabians, that the infighting came to an end. He pacified the peninsula and established an enduring independent dynasty there, with Córdoba as its capital.[1]

Gradually, the Arabic culture brought by the immigrants pervaded the region. By the mid-ninth century, native Christians had grown intimately familiar with it, as this complaint by Álvaro of Córdoba reveals:

> My fellow-Christians delight in the poems and romances of the Arabs; they study the works of Muslim theologians and philosophers, not in order to refute them, but to acquire a correct and elegant Arabic style. Where today can a layman be found who reads the Latin Commentaries on the Holy Scriptures? Who is there that studies the Gospels, the Prophets, the Apostles? Alas! the young Christians who are most conspicuous for their talents have no knowledge of any literature or language save the Arabic; they read and study with avidity Arabian books; they amass whole libraries of them at a vast cost, and they everywhere sing the praises of Arabian lore. On the other hand, at the mention of Christian books they disdainfully protest that such works are unworthy of their notice. The pity of it! Christians have forgotten their own tongue, and scarce one in a thousand can be found able to compose in fair Latin a letter to a friend! But when it comes to writing Arabic, how many there are who can express themselves in that language with the greatest elegance, and even compose verses which surpass in formal correctness those of the Arabs themselves![2]

Significant for cultural development in al-Andalus was the magnificent long reign (912–61) of ʿAbd al-Rahman III, great-great-grandfather of our poet's beloved. Under his bold leadership the state, which in the decades preceding his accession had been weakened by civil wars, was made stronger and richer than it had ever been before. His nonmilitary interests included architecture. He allocated state resources to impressive projects, including the enhancement of the Great Mosque of Córdoba (founded by 'Abd al-Rahman I) and the construction of a splendid royal suburb of palaces and gardens three miles northwest of the city, in an area overlooking the Guadalquivir River. He named the suburb Madinat al-Zahra' (City of the Bright-Faced), after a favorite concubine. To his son, al-Hakam II (r. 961–76), 'Abd al-Rahman bequeathed a restored, prosperous empire. A lover of books and learning, the son went about establishing twenty-seven free schools in Córdoba, endowing chairs at the college (part of the Great Mosque) and filling them with top professors from the East, and swelling the college library's holdings to several hundred thousand volumes. In addition, he obtained for the royal collection many prized manuscripts, including, at the cost of a thousand dinars, the first copy from Aleppo of al-Isfahani's *Kitab al-aghani*. Smaller libraries in the capital also flourished during his rule, increasing in number to no fewer than seventy.[3] Thus, through intensive investment in learning, investment made possible by prosperity, was the soil prepared for the cultural efflorescence that later took place.

To be sure, culture in al-Andalus, and specifically literature, had never been neglected. The first ruler, 'Abd al-Rahman I, for instance, himself composed poetry. And in the ninth century, poets who were abreast of the literary movements in Baghdad enjoyed favor. But it may be said that, on the whole, the forms and styles popular in al-Andalus in the early period were replicas of the types of the East. A truly distinctive Andalusi literature began to emerge only in the tenth century. We note that, in 929, 'Abd al-Rahman III proclaimed himself caliph, rival to the caliph in Iraq. As the glory of al-Andalus reached unprecedented heights, a similar spirit of confidence and self-awareness to the one demonstrated by 'Abd al-Rahman entered the literature. Through their works literary artists such as al-Sharif al-Taliq (d. 1009), Ibn Shuhayd (d. 1035), Ibn Hazm (who was also a philosopher [d. 1064]), and, of course, Ibn Zaydun affirmed that an authentic Andalusi literature might, in terms of excellence, take its place beside—and even surpass—the literature of the East. This new, authentic Andalusi literature flourished especially during the period of political decentralization, that is, 1031–91. In this era numerous courts existed in various attractive locales, and each court patronized the arts. If one wished to be yet more specific and indicate precedence among the eleventh-century courts, one would point to the one in Seville under the Banu 'Abbad, for it was the most glittering.

Ibn Zaydun, then, lived in an environment and a historical moment conducive to the composition of poetry. Culturally, al-Andalus had caught up with the East, and its poets were making fresh, startling contributions to Arabic literature. They were no doubt keenly aware, meanwhile (particularly because so many tomes had recently been brought into al-Andalus), that a long, rich tradition preceded them. Five hundred years, indeed, had passed since Imru' al-Qays—and so many poets had left their marks subsequent to him! How did one show respect for such a venerable tradition, while at the same time producing something new? In "Tradition and the Individual Talent," T. S. Eliot considers essentially the same question as a modern English poet reflecting on his own rich heritage. Eliot insists that the poet, in the course of his training, procure a consciousness of the past. "He can neither take the past as a lump, an indiscriminate bolus," Eliot details, "nor can he form himself wholly on one or two private admirations, nor can he form himself wholly upon one preferred period. . . . The poet must be very conscious of the main current." Only then can he contribute meaningfully to the tradition, adding a work that asserts its relation to the old masterpieces. "The existing monuments," he says, "form an ideal order among themselves, which is modified by the introduction of the new (the really new) work of art among them."[4] In reading Ibn Zaydun's *Nuniyya* (poem in *nun;* No. 1), we will observe the way in which the poet demonstrates his familiarity with tradition and, at the same time, introduces to it something unmistakably new.[5] Before we get to his poem, though, we would do well to acquaint ourselves with his beloved Wallada and to learn of some of the details of their relationship.

Wallada was born in 1011, an Umayyad princess. Her father, al-Mustakfi, succeeded as caliph when she was twelve; he was killed when she was fourteen. In Wallada's twentieth year the Umayyad dynasty fell. Later, as a single, independent young woman, she set herself up in an elegant Córdoban residence. There she hosted a literary salon that became the talk of Córdoba's elites. Suitors gathered around her hopefully. We hear that she was fair—the beauty of her day. That she was proud as well may be deduced from these lines:

I am—though mankind may stare at my dazzling beauty—
like the gazelles of Mecca, forbidden to hunters.

One supposes these creatures immoral on account of their easy conversation,
but Islam averts them from indecency.[6]

When she was about twenty-seven, she took an interest in the suave and
eloquent ambassador-at-large attending her salon. She had this message placed
in his hands:

Wait for darkness, and then visit me,
for I believe that night keeps the secret best.

What I feel for you is such that, were they to feel this way,
the moon would not glow, the night would not spread, and the stars would not
    travel.[7]

He waited, and then took her out to a lush and secluded garden. One guesses that
it was outside the city in Madinat al-Zahra', which doubtless featured romantic
settings. After they drank the wine he had brought, they took turns confessing
their affections. As Ibn Zaydun later wrote, the rest of the night was spent ten-
derly conversing and "picking flowers from lips."[8] In the morning, at their place
of parting, he recited these lines:

The lover who bids you farewell, having confided his secret,
bids farewell to patience.

He repents that he did not take more steps
in seeing you off.

O sibling of the full moon in splendor and eminence,
may God preserve the time that has caused you to rise!

Though I may afterward complain of long nights without you,
how much do I now complain of this night's shortness with you![9]

There followed a blissful, dreamlike period of private encounters and
increasing closeness. Euphoria permeated and uplifted them both. Nevertheless,
they had to do their best to contain feelings of giddiness, since disclosure that a

change had come over them would expose the princess to gossip. We may well imagine that this restraint was difficult. Also difficult, certainly, was enduring separation—the more so when being apart did not end quickly. Here are some lines Wallada sent to Ibn Zaydun when he was away, presumably on a diplomatic mission, after they had been in love for some time:

> Alas! Is there a path for us after this separation,
> now that each lover complains of what he confronts?
>
> I used to, during the times of our winter trysts,
> spend the nights on burning coals of passion.
>
> How is it that now, by evening, I have become as one cut off?
> Fate has made what I dreaded catch up to me.
>
> Nights pass, and I do not see our separation coming to an end,
> nor patience liberating me from the slavery of desire.
>
> May God water whatever land has become, in the morning, your abode,
> with the discharge of every driving, long-lasting rain.

He replied, in the same meter and rhyme:

> May God curse whatever day on which I do not encounter your face,
> due to absence and separation.
>
> How can life be sweet without a cause of joy—
> and what joy is there to one sleepless and depressed?[10]

Below this reply, he added some comments about her last line (she had asked him to help her with her poetry). It sounded more like an imprecation than a benediction, he remarked delicately; he cited an example of how the thought might be more aptly expressed. One wonders how Wallada took this criticism. We do know, though, that at some point she was offended by a grave breach of etiquette. At one of her salons, it so happened, Ibn Zaydun forgot himself upon hearing her slave girl ʿUtba sing and spontaneously called for an encore without first consulting the hostess. When he later took 'Utba's side after Wallada had hit her, he erred further. Wallada registered her disapproval and dismay in these lines:

> If you had been just toward the love we share,
> you would not have taken an interest in my slave girl, and preferred her.
>
> You left aside a branch laden with beauty,
> and turned to the one that holds no fruit.
>
> You know very well that I am the full moon in the heavens,
> yet, to my distress, you have been smitten by Jupiter.[11]

The poet offered an apology, pointing out that a steed might stumble on occasion.[12] When she refused to be placated, he protested at her hard treatment of him and entreated:

> If I committed a sin unintentionally, you have punished me unjustly
> with punishment more severe than that imposed on a deliberate sinner.
>
> Come back to giving me the love you gave at the beginning,
> for I will not return to doing what you hate.
>
> And remove the mask of anger from the face of contentment,
> so that I may be the first to bow down and worship.[13]

But it seems that Wallada was already slipping away. Around this time, she happened, in the course of one of her strolls, to pass by the mansion of Ibn 'Abdus. Ibn 'Abdus was a highly placed government minister, in his fortieth year or thereabouts. Recent rains had caused a large puddle to form in front of his mansion, and he was standing outside by the entrance looking at it. She recited:

> You are the Nile, and this area is Egypt;
> your water has overflowed, and now both of you are a sea.[14]

The recitation by the princess nonplussed him, and he was silent as she resumed her stroll. However, he began to attend her salon. We presume that his presence there aroused Ibn Zaydun's suspicions immediately. The poet took the step of trying to make Wallada jealous, writing as if he had important matters for disclosure:

Who will convey my message to the moon that has appeared full and
    gorgeous,
to the young branch that has grown straight and true,

That for the time when she gave me her affection—that for what she did—
I owe her my thanks.

As for the other beloved, the one who has turned harsh and indifferent,
we do not consider her hostility a major event.

We could not take in any more—Jupiter filled our eyes.
We stopped gazing at Saturn.

My comely one, you, then, are the beloved whom I continually shade with
    fondness,
to whom I give drinks of satisfaction repeatedly.

This is the truth; I do not speak in deceit:
were you to say, "Die," I would not reply, "No."[15]

We would concur with ʿAli ʿAbd al-ʿAzim's judgment that Ibn Zaydun fooled no one with these lines except perhaps himself. In them, moreover, as ʿAbd al-ʿAzim observes, the poet makes the serious mistake of denigrating the lady (by means of the unfavorable planetary comparison).[16] Not surprisingly, this short poem did not bring Wallada back to his side. He wrote again, this time composing a longer piece in which he tries to pull at the heartstrings through melodrama. Toward the end he declares:

I say farewell to you—a final farewell—
and adieu to a love that died before its time.

It was not of my own volition that I went about consoling myself,
but rather I was compelled to do so; I'm no hero.

My heart did not know how to pull away
until it saw yours setting the example; then it did likewise.[17]

He composed also a poem for Ibn 'Abdus, though opposite in thrust. He
tells the man that Wallada is a mirage, that she is water elusive to the grasp. In
case this information does not give Ibn 'Abdus pause, Ibn Zaydun notifies him,
al-Shanfara-like:

How many a fool whom pride has moved against me
have I left with no heartbeat inside of him!

He adds a message for the lady:

And warn your friend of someone who, when exercised,
is a master of the art of diabolical fury![18]

Nonetheless, the two poems apparently did not put the brakes on what was
then in motion. We have evidence that some people taunted Ibn Zaydun about
the developments. He affected disregard:

They said: "Abu 'Amir ibn 'Abdus has begun to frequent her house."
"The moth is attracted to the fire," I replied.

You have tried to shame me because he has taken my place with the one that I
    love,
yet there is no cause for shame in that.

She is a tasty meal. I picked and sampled, and ate the best parts,
and left the rest for the mouse.[19]

One may wonder here, given the tartness of the lines, whether Ibn Zaydun
allowed them to go into general circulation. If he did, if he actually went public with such sentiments, it would have been an impetuous and consequential
move indeed. His fellow Córdoban Ibn Hazm analyzed behavior of this sort,
whereby the disgruntled former lover seeks to destroy the lady's reputation. Ibn
Hazm concluded that it "is the strongest possible proof that the one so behaving

is entirely bereft of reason, and no more in his right mind."[20] Be that as it may, we can infer that Wallada was at least generally aware of what Ibn Zaydun was saying about her. She wrote:

> Ibn Zaydun, in his ignorance, backbites me wrongfully,
> while I have done nothing wrong.

> When I approach his house he looks at me askance,
> as if I have come to castrate his servant 'Ali.[21]

At this point, Ibn Zaydun took a drastic step. It appears he had decided that if he could not enjoy Wallada's affection, he would make sure that his rival could not either. He had learned that Ibn 'Abdus, pursuing his courtship, had sent a female friend to Wallada to speak highly of the man and act as his go-between. So Ibn Zaydun interposed and wrote a letter of response to Ibn 'Abdus, signed in Wallada's name. It became known to readers of Arabic literature as "The Satiric Letter" and was long studied—with pleasure, one suspects—as a model of lacerating prose. In the first half, he mocks the minister's pretensions. The Great Ibn 'Abdus, we read, was there commanding Alexander to go into battle against the Persians; he employed Caesar to tend his livestock. Plato was his student, and Aristotle studied his teachings through Plato's transmission of them. After thus raising him up ridiculously in the first part of the letter, he cuts him down to size in the second. In this part he proceeds to describe him: Ibn 'Abdus is distinguished by a small head and a long neck; bad breath; a hurried, shuffling gait; and a stuttering, mumbling elocution. How, then, the affronted Wallada asks, would a woman such as herself be attracted to him? Things seek their likenesses; East and West do not meet. Age is also a factor in their incompatibility: he is a weakened, decaying old man. Is she so desperate that she would favor him? (The letter, it must be said, is not altogether complimentary of Wallada, who comes across as candidly sexual [for example, "I would not want to ride an ox after having ridden a stallion"]).[22] There follows a warning that the crude, presumptuous suitor will be driven away abusively to graze in the field where he belongs should he attempt to return to her house. The letter ends with a satiric line from al-Mutanabbi, to the effect that though one might not be cognizant of one's lowliness and insignificance, others certainly are.

Needless to say, the letter was not appreciated by certain parties. The Córdoban public, however, which received a copy, found the missive highly amusing. In response to what he had done, Wallada sought to tar the poet:

They call you "the Sixer,"
and it is an epithet that will stick to you always:

A sodomite's plaything you are, and a buggerer;
an adulterer, cuckold, pimp, and thief.[23]

Ibn ʿAbdus chose to work behind the scenes to get his revenge (literary repartee does not seem to have been his forte). In confidential meetings with Ibn Jahwar he raised questions about Ibn Zaydun's loyalty. Before long, the poet was tossed in prison. He dwelled there for what must have seemed an eternity. He composed several long conciliatory poems to Ibn Jahwar, but none hit the mark. In addition, he penned during this period another classic of Arabic prose, "The Earnest Letter." In it he lays out his case fully before the ruler. The letter is remarkable not the least for its erudition; one has difficulty believing it was written in a jail cell and not in a large college library, where the great many works it draws upon could be consulted. Meanwhile, he seems to have experienced a change—or, perhaps more accurately, a softening—of heart toward Wallada. He would have had plenty of time as a prisoner to recall their happy moments and to forget what had recently passed between them. These lines, from a poem composed probably from prison, indicate a more tender disposition to her:

Toward you, among all creatures did my joy travel at dawn,
and you, despite time, remain the goal of my originality.[24]

. . . .

I have a hope, and were the slanderers to desist,
its tree would bring forth the fruit of success.

It astonishes me how an enemy gets the better of me;
yet he wields your approval, and that is more cutting than my sword.

. . . .

Were I able, I would fly to you yearningly.
But how does one fly with wings that are clipped?[25]

After almost a year and a half of incarceration, Ibn Zaydun despaired of being released. The letter had failed to mollify Ibn Jahwar. So, presumably assisted by his childhood friend, the ruler's son, he escaped.[26] He fled southwest along the Guadalquivir River approximately eighty miles to Seville. There he composed for Wallada his emotive *Nuniyya*. Since its composition, the poem has attracted special attention. It was said that whoever memorized it would die far from home, so strangely powerful and affecting did it seem. On the other hand, it was also said that a person's polite education was not complete until he was able to recite it.[27] The *Nuniyya* has taken a prominent place in the canon; it is the most famous love poem in Arabic literature. Let us now turn to it.

A

1   Day has revealed the wide gap opened between us;
      the pain of withdrawal has substituted for encounter's delight.

2   Alas! The morning of separation came. Death greeted us,
      and the crier of our passing rose, and sent us off.

3   Who will tell those who, by their leaving, attired us in a robe of sadness
      that does not wear out with the seasons, though it wears us out,

4   That Time, which used to make us laugh convivially because of their
            presence,
      has come around to making us weep?

5   Our enemies seethed because we were refreshing each other from the cup of
            love.
      They called for us to choke, and Fate said: "Let it be."

6   Thus the knot our souls had tied came undone,
      and what our hands had joined was broken.

7   We used to have no fear of being separated;
      now we have no hope of coming together again.

The poem begins on a nostalgic note, evoking the grievous difference between past and present. We soon recognize in the section, from opening sections of Arabic odes, the theme of morning departure and the mood of melancholy. Yet the *Nuniyya*, though it includes familiar elements, has a music all its own that resonates very personally. We can notice this immediately. Rhetorician Ibn Rashiq has said that the poet must take care to make the opening line excellent, since it is the first to hit the ears of the listener and sets the tone for the whole poem.[28] Ibn Zaydun, we find, has taken care to sound *na* in the first line five times.[29] (*Na* denotes variously, when it occurs as the pronominal suffix and not as part of the root, the subjective "we," the objective "us," and the possessive "our.") The repetition literally sets the tone for the rest of the poem, for the poet repeats *na* therein more than a hundred times. He furthermore has arranged that *na* be accorded special emphasis, being the rhyme syllable. One senses gradually that he has some idea he wishes to stress by it. What he stresses—or softly suggests more than a hundred times, if one prefers—is the idea of mutuality. Ibn Zaydun reinforces this idea yet further both by the repeated use of reciprocal verb forms (there are three in the first line and many in the rest of the poem) and by the studious avoidance of the grammatical first person (of which an idiomatic first-person expression in B is the only instance). The *Nuniyya,* shall we say, is all about "us."[30] Though the poet cannot know how Wallada feels about him after the passage of a year and a half, he implies in this section, beginning in the first line, and then in many places in subsequent sections, that his feelings are hers, that mutually they suffer from separation.

In line 6 Ibn Zaydun indicates that the love he and Wallada once enjoyed was both a knot of the souls and a link of the hands, both spiritual and physical. To understand the significance of this indication, we must first recollect the division that had existed in Arabic love poetry since the Umayyad era and consider contemporary philosophical ideas on the nature of love. Poets of the 'Udhri tradition, starting mainly with the Bedouin Jamil and continuing in the 'Abbasid period notably with the courtly poet al-'Abbas ibn al-Ahnaf (d. 813), greatly admired their beloveds ethereally for the most part (or entirely, depending on the poet) and subsisted without physical contact. Per contra, poets of the 'Umari school, of whom 'Umar ibn Abi Rabi'a is the founder and Abu Nuwas a star student, were primarily (or wholly) concerned with the pleasures of the flesh. In general, therefore, spiritual love in the form of a fruitless, abiding attachment and physical love in the form of a transient, usually satisfied lust were expressed by different poets composing in two distinct traditions. We might add that the 'Udhri-style love attracted more adherents among poets in the ninth and tenth centuries and was the one that suited conservative urban society and seemingly found favor with the critics. "Whoever aspires to the status of a refined lover, let him first be chaste," says Ibn Dawud (d. 910) in his famous anthology of love poetry, *Kitab al-zahra* (The Book of the Flower).[31]

Yet in the early eleventh century, some philosophers were bridging the divide between spiritual and physical love. Although Ibn Hazm viewed true love as a spiritual process, a fusion of the souls, he thought that bodies played a part in bringing the souls together. "When a spiritual concord is once established," he writes, "love is immediately engendered. Physical contact completes the circuit and thus enables the current of love to flow freely into the soul."[32] Ibn Sina (d. 1037) brings us even closer to our poet's expression. Prior to Ibn Sina, the Brethren of Purity (ca. 960) had elaborated a Neoplatonic division of the soul into (1) nutritive-appetitive, (2) emotional-animal, and (3) rational parts. According to the Brethren, spiritual love, emanating from the rational soul, was good and worthy of man, whereas physical love, emanating from the appetitive soul, was bad and to be eschewed. Ibn Sina adopted a new attitude, derived from Aristotle and affirming the possibility of a mixed love. In his *Treatise on Love,* he differentiates between (1) physical love from the animal soul, (2) mixed love from both the animal and the rational souls, and (3) pure, spiritual love from the rational soul exclusively. Of these three kinds of love, the first is blameworthy in man, whereas the second and third are good. The innovation in his philosophy is that physical love is considered good if it is blended with the pure, spiritual love of the rational soul.[33] Ibn Zaydun seems to be drawing freely on these recent philosophical ideas, for he articulates in line 6 a love that perfectly harmonizes spiritual and physical aspects. By apparently taking in new philosophical notions and regarding his love in a new way, he reconciles the two poetic traditions.

At the end of the section, Ibn Zaydun expresses resignation that he will not be reunited with Wallada. Despite its obvious continuation, his love for her would appear now, after the grim morning of separation has come, to be hopeless.

B

8   O would that I knew, seeing that we have not satisfied your enemies,
     whether our enemies have obtained a share of satisfaction from you.

9   In your absence, we have believed only in keeping the faith;
     devotion to you has been our religion.

10   We do not deserve that you should gladden our envier
      or cheer someone who loathes us.

11   We used to think that despair would finally bring us consolation;
      now we have despaired truly—so what is there about it that increases our
         yearning?

12   You left, and we went our way, and since then our heart has not ceased to ache,
      nor have our tear ducts dried up.

13   When intimate thoughts whisper of you, sorrow almost finishes us off;
      we would be done for, were it not for our resorting at last to patience.

14   Losing you has transformed our day and night:
      mornings have turned black; nights are no longer white,

15   As they were when life's side was unrestrained due to our intimacy,
      and pleasure's springtime habitation was undisturbed due to our mutual
         consideration;

16   And as they were when we pulled down the branches of our love union,
      from which fruit hung invitingly, and plucked whatever we desired.

17   May your days always be watered with spring rains,
      for you were nothing else than the scent of sweet basil to our spirits.

18   Do not suppose that distance alters us
      as it has altered so many lovers!

19   By God, our passions have not demanded a substitute,
      nor have our hopes turned elsewhere.

Whereas through most of section A the poet speaks for both himself and Wallada, here he addresses her from his own perspective. Noticeably, he employs the formal royal "you" (*kum*) form of address. She is a princess, after all. He attests emphatically to his devotion, an attribute of an 'Udhri lover. But he also speaks more of both spiritual and physical love (15–17). And he ventures to blame her gently in line 10 for giving comfort to the enemy. Ibn Hazm, for the most part traditional in his views on submissive, courtly love, has affirmed that "the duty of fidelity is incumbent upon the lover more than upon the beloved, and applies to him far more strictly."[34] In this section, however, Ibn Zaydun implies that it applies to himself and to Wallada equally. Throughout the poem, he calls for equal treatment, reciprocity, mutuality, not gracious leave to adore the lady.

Line 14, in which the poet implicitly compares Wallada's face to the bright and beautiful full moon, is perhaps the most striking and memorable line in the

Nuniyya. A lunar metaphor, invoked to suggest an attractive face, is itself commonplace: such a figure occurs throughout classical Arabic poetry. Yet Ibn Zaydun stretches the familiar by describing the whiteout effect caused by Wallada's visage, bringing to mind only the very shiniest of moons. To the image of white nights spent with Wallada, he arrestingly juxtaposes the notion of black mornings now spent without her. This latter image conveys the true darkness of his current disposition. Although the line is striking in its imagery, thematically and rhetorically it accords with the rest of the poem. Again, the poet associates the morning with the beloved's absence; this association remains consistent through the entire *Nuniyya.* Rhetorically, he evokes the difference between past and present using the figure of *tibaq,* or antithesis, juxtaposing day-night, black-white. Tibaq is the most frequently used rhetorical figure in the *Nuniyya*—small wonder, since the poem emphasizes the extreme contrast between past times of joy and present sorrow.[35] Line 14, because it presents this abysmal and depressing contrast probably in the most vivid terms possible, can be viewed as emblematic of the whole poem.

C

20 O night-traveling lightning, go in the early morning to the palace,
    and offer a drink to one who used to pour for us pure love and affection.

21 And ask there: do frequent thoughts of us distress a dear friend,
    of whom frequent thoughts have come to distress us?

22 And O gentle east wind, carry our greetings to one who,
    despite the distance, would revive us were she to send her greetings;

23 One whom Fate is not helping us to reach,
    however frequently we petition it.

24 A descendant of royalty, as if God created her from musk
    and mankind from clay;

25 Or fashioned her from unalloyed silver,
    and then crowned her with native gold by way of innovation and
        embellishment.

26 When she inclines, necklace pearls weigh her down;
    when she walks, anklets cut her soft skin.

27 The sun was a nursemaid to her within her veils,
    though it touched her barely.

28 It is as if the brightest star was fixed on her cheek
    as amulet and ornament.[36]

29   No harm, though, in our not being her peer,
      for as lovers we were a perfect match.
30   O what a garden, where our gazes once gathered rose and eglantine,[37]
      displayed so fresh by youth!
31   And O what a life, in whose splendor we enjoyed
      diverse favors, and delights of all kinds!
32   And O what times of ease and pleasure,
      during which we strutted in silken robes of happiness, extending their
      trains!
33   We do not name you out of veneration and respect,
      moreover your exalted status makes this unnecessary:
34   You are unique, and not associated with anyone in an attribute;
      so the description suffices to clarify whom we mean.

The center of the poem deals with themes of royalty and identity. Ibn Zaydun begins the section by tasking natural phenomena, dispatching them on important personal missions to the palace. Although poetically he makes use of common motifs here, he does so in such a way as to suit his own purposes. As a motif, the lightning stimulates in the poem thoughts of a beloved, through its connection to rain and the spring season of aggregation. It flashes to the poet, typically, from her direction.[38] Likewise, the literary east wind, bringing the scent of perfume, summons for the poet a beloved of the past-present, or one of the future.[39] Yet Ibn Zaydun directs the lightning bolt and east wind to visit Wallada on his behalf, because she is the one who might need a gentle reminder of the other party. Viewed another way, his calling on natural phenomena to help him may be seen as indicative of a feeling of closeness to nature, a feeling that characterizes Andalusi poets generally.

In lines 24–28, the very center of the poem, we find a flattering description of the beloved. She is a privileged woman unaccustomed to going outside or to lifting a finger. As such, she shares with her predecessors described in poems certain physical aspects, namely, paleness, softness, and weakness (not to mention muskiness). Exemplifying one of these aspects, Imru' al-Qays says about a beloved:

She is a retiring maiden; were a young, small ant to crawl over her skin,
it would leave a track.[40]

Exemplifying another, al-Aʿsha reports of Hurayra in his *Muʿallaqa:*

> When she gets up to visit her neighbors, languor almost fells her,
> but, bracing herself, she is able to stand and walk.[41]

Nevertheless, in appearance this beloved stands out. To visualize how, we recall Imruʾ al-Qays's ideal woman, representative of the Arabian women who were apt to captivate poets. Her hair was jet black. Our poet's beloved, in contrast, is an Andalusi blonde. And this aspect, locally, makes her more appealing, for blondes were preferred in the Iberian Peninsula ("Look for freckles," advises the Andalusi proverb).[42] Wallada, surely, would not have found anything to object to in this description of herself. Nor would she, certainly, have disapproved of being given pride of place in the poem. Overall, the description bespeaks an awareness, on the part of the poet, that at the heart of a love poem to a lady belongs praise.

After lauding Wallada, Ibn Zaydun makes the brash claim that as lovers they were equals. Even if she were not royal, this assertion would be considered bold (compare Ibn Hazm, "The beloved is not to be regarded as a match or an equal to the lover").[43] Still, it is consistent with sentiments expressed elsewhere in the *Nuniyya*. In this section, furthermore, the poet clarifies the basis for equality. We have noted that Ibn Zaydun articulates in the poem a love consisting of spiritual and sensual elements. Here he leaves no doubt that physical compatibility, not spiritual love or a harmonious combination of spiritual love and bodily attraction, has been the great equalizer between him and Wallada. The subsequent reverie about the garden, the favors enjoyed, and the days of ease and pleasure makes this point clear. Their physical chemistry rendered the difference in station irrelevant.

Once he has highlighted the basis for parity, Ibn Zaydun takes the liberty in line 33 of addressing Wallada using the intimate *ki* form. He is being coy here, saying he does not name her out of veneration and respect, while using a familiar form of address. At the same time, he is complying with an imperative of Arabic love poetry, that is, to avoid naming the beloved. This rule seems to have come about, we observe, as a result of the urbanization that began in the Arab world in the late seventh century.[44] Urban love affairs of the kind spoken of in poetry were typically ongoing ones, not seasonal affairs between intertribal couples that ended decisively at the termination of spring, such as were remembered by

Bedouin poets. Hence, the urban poet-lover, if he wished to keep seeing the lady, did not want to expose her. Doing so would invite problems for her and doom the relationship. Also, he had his personal security to worry about: the lady might live just around the corner, and her family could easily track him down if he named her and started describing her fine points, rhapsodizing of love unions, and so forth. Innocent relationships, too, could be harmed by a revelation of the name, as afterward clouds of suspicion tended to gather. Avoiding mention of this detail became de rigueur, if the subject itself was often referred to. Thus, courtly al-'Abbas ibn al-Ahnaf:

> As for her name, it is suppressed;
> I will not, God willing, divulge it to you.[45]

Avoiding mention of the name even became, according a spurious hadith first recorded by Ibn Dawud, part of a way to achieve martyrdom. "He who loves and remains chaste and conceals the secret and dies, dies a martyr," we read in *Kitab al-zahra*.[46] Returning to the last two lines of this section in the *Nuniyya*, we see that Ibn Zaydun complies in a tongue-in-cheek manner with this imperative. He does not name her, yet through his description the reader—presumably only one person, initially—knows exactly whom he means, for, in her beauty and glory, she was unique.

B¹

35   O what a garden of immortality—for whose Sidra and fresh flowing Kawthar
       we have been given Zaqqum and Ghislin![47]
36   It is as if we never spent a night together, with love in our midst,
       whilst good fortune had lowered the talebearer's eyelids:
37   Two secrets preserved in the mind of darkness
       until morning's tongue was about to give us away.
38   No wonder we remembered sadness when reasoning men proscribed it,
       and forgot patience, heading off without it.
39   Indeed, on the day of separation we read sorrow as graven suras,
       and took patience as a lesson to be memorized by rote.
40   As for your love, it is a watering hole we have not compared to any other,
       though our drinking there has increased our thirst.

41   We have not turned from the horizon of beauty where your star shines,
      seeking consolation, nor have we emigrated from it with bad feelings;
42   And not by choice have we traveled on a parallel route,
      but rather, frustratingly, vicissitudes have kept us from approaching.

In section B¹ we notice a return to themes from B. The poet again uses religious metaphors and again evokes the stark contrast between past happiness with Wallada and current misery without her. In line 37 he once more associates morning with the beloved's absence, albeit implicitly in this case. Here also he conveys the opposition between sorrow and patience. And in the last five lines of B¹ he develops the travel theme, which he introduced in B (12). Incidentally, in these last five lines one hears faint echoes of the pre-Islamic *nasib-rahil* sequence: in the allusion to rational observers scolding the poet for being sad over a departed beloved and in the description of his journey. Ibn Zaydun, it may be pointed out, richly exploits the metaphorical possibilities of the travel theme, indicating that he has left patience behind, that he has bypassed desert watering holes, and that, though he has moved forward, he has moved no farther away.

Although this section, therefore, bears a resemblance to B, at the same time it differs from B in two key respects. First, there is no reference here to spiritual love; the poet suggests the sensual aspect only (we shall comment on his focusing of attention on the sensual aspect after reading the last section). Second, he addresses Wallada using the intimate *ki* form solely (and continues to do so for the rest of the poem). Upon consideration, we would not expect him to revert to the *kum* form. He has highlighted their equality as lovers, so addressing the lady now in an intimate way is appropriate.

A¹

43   We grieve for you when a new vintage, mixed with water, is put into our
           hands;
      we lament when our singing girls sing—
44   Cups of wine do not elicit from our inner selves a trace of mirth,
      and lute strings do not amuse us.
45   Be true to our vow, as we are,
      for the noble person treats another fairly, as treated.

46   We have not sought a companion to detain us from you,
      nor have we had another lover turn us her way.

47   Even if the wondrous full moon declined in our direction from her apogee,
      she would not—pardon the thought—titillate us.

48   Show your faithfulness, and if you do not generously accord us a tryst,
      then your dream image will satisfy, memory will suffice.

49   And, in the reply there would be gratification,
      if you enclose the favors that you have always brought near.

50   May God's peace be upon you, as long as our love for you still burns,
      the love we conceal, the love that reveals us.

In the last section of the poem, Ibn Zaydun stresses the theme of loyalty and implores Wallada to send a response. That he cannot be diverted by wine or music or titillated by a wondrous belle indicates that Wallada is always on his mind. The assertions about his loyalty may be interpreted, taking into account Ibn Hazm's words, as placing final emphasis on a theme that runs implicitly through the whole poem, for, according to the philosopher, "to yearn affectionately for the past, and not to forget the times that are finished and done with, is the surest proof of true fidelity."[48] Meanwhile, throughout the poem, he has subtly tried to stir her memories as well, to stimulate in her fond recollection of their past. Here he explicitly asks her to be true and to show her faithfulness by sending a reply to his poem. Again, we find that he calls for reciprocity between them, mutuality.

To encourage her to respond, he adopts at the end a highly personal tone—twice issuing gentle imperatives—and makes a series of erotic references. In order to understand better what he is trying to do here by, figuratively speaking, getting very close to Wallada, we might pause to reflect briefly on an essential difference between spiritual and sensual love. As we have seen, Ibn Zaydun articulates a love consisting of a harmonious blend of spiritual and sensual elements and in the course of the poem progressively stresses the latter element. Spiritual love, we find, might continue without physical contact between two lovers. Truly, spiritual love requires no reciprocation and can abide in the heart of the lover even if the beloved ceases to feel anything for him.[49] Were the poet to emphasize, therefore, how much his soul yearns for her, even how much he adores her as a goddess, he would not necessarily prompt a response. By contrast, sensual love flourishes only as long as each side desires the other; it must be preserved through contact and shared passion. By getting intimate with Wallada in this poem, especially right at the end, he is trying to relight her fire. It is hoped that, newly motivated, she will act and send him a response.

In his series of erotic references, Ibn Zaydun mentions the lady's *tayf*, or dream image. This image is a motif from the pre-Islamic *nasib*, like the morning departure of the beloved (*za'n*) motif and the poet's halt at an abandoned campsite (*atlal*) motif. In the early poetry the dream image of the departed beloved— or her phantom, to be precise—is usually represented as visiting the poet while his companions slumber. The phantom disquiets him and reminds him of his loss, and the poem is, then, his way, artistically, to deal with the loss and to transcend it. But, as Renate Jacobi has shown, the motif underwent development in the early Islamic and Umayyad periods. Gradually, coinciding with the process of urbanization and the tendency for the relationships reported in poetry to be ongoing as opposed to past affairs, the phantom evolved into a welcome dream image that offered the poet an ersatz union with his absent beloved.[50] This notion is certainly the kind of visitation that Wallada's dream image offers Ibn Zaydun. We can infer as much, should there be any doubt about the matter, from this line in one of his poems:

> There is no harm in your begrudging us greetings,
> since your dream image is generous with embraces.[51]

Noteworthy, however, is how the idea of ersatz nighttime contentment combines with ideas expressed elsewhere in the *Nuniyya,* such that the poem as a whole suggests a novel concept. Consistently, Ibn Zaydun has associated mornings with dismal sorrow. But in Arabic poetry, night is typically the time when a distraught poet suffers the worst torment. This concept, that night brings the most profound gloom, goes all the way back to Imru' al Qays and the poet's classic evoked long night of despair, slow to rise and move on like a ponderous camel, seemingly interminable, as if its stars were immobile, tethered to terrestrial granite. Yet Ibn Zaydun has said that his mornings have turned dark and does not complain in the poem of his nights. Thus, he suggests that, for him, mornings are more difficult to bear. During the nights, as he indicates here, at least he may obtain some relief in his dream world.

In line 49 Ibn Zaydun entertains the possibility that Wallada may send him a reply. In fact, that he presumes to come close to her in this section shows he still clings to a strand of hope. He does not think, evidently, that she will be offended by gentle imperatives from him and his sexual references. Moreover, it remains conceivable that she has been, or, through encouragement, once more will be, faithful to him. Their relationship might still be revived.

Ibn Zaydun concludes the *Nuniyya* with an extension of God's *salam*, a fitting end to his love letter of a poem. He implies by the last words that, try as he may in accordance with decorum and prudent discretion, he cannot hide his feelings. It must have been obvious to people around him in Seville, one imagines, that he had left his heart in Córdoba. In the *Diwan* we find detached these two lines:

O one whom in the morning I have made known,
on your account my heart suffers affliction and distress.

When you are absent, I do not encounter anyone who sets me at ease;
when you are present, everyone, to me, is present.[52]

These lines, thematically linked to the ending of the *Nuniyya*, further illuminate how the poet must have been feeling at this time in Seville and help us more fully understand his closing message. In short, by admitting that he cannot hide his emotions in spite of himself, Ibn Zaydun is telling Wallada how much he loves her.

Finally, we offer an observation based on the poem's ring structure, exposed previously by James T. Monroe. As Monroe points out, the last word, *tukhfina*, completes the circle, taking us into the semantic field of the very first word, *adha*. Both signify that their hidden love affair has now come out into the light.[53] After drawing near to Wallada, conjuring darkness by mentioning a tryst and the beloved's dream image, and contemplating a hopeful possibility, Ibn Zaydun thus closes his poem by pointing to the time of separation, exposure, and hopelessness. It is as if, by recalling finally the poem's sorrowful beginning about the apparent established fact of their separation, he anticipates that Wallada's reply will never come. And indeed, it never did.

SUMMARY: THE *NUNIYYA* OF IBN ZAYDUN

Section	Lines	Structural and Thematic Elements
A	1–7	we, us, our (*na*) morning, separation spiritual and sensual love hopelessness
B	8–19	formal address (*kum*) religious metaphors white nights with Wallada black mornings without her departure sorrow; patience
C	20–34	poet dispatches lightning and east wind to palace beloved referred to indirectly (she) center of poem: *description of Wallada* poet and beloved equals as lovers poet does not name beloved out of respect, yet addresses her familiarly
B¹	35–42	intimate address (*ki*) religious metaphors nights of love sorrow in morning departure patience a lesson learned by rote
A¹	43–50	intimate address (*ki*) associations with night: tryst, dream image gentle imperatives, sexual references: sensual love hope (reply from Wallada?) → exposure

11

Season's Greetings

A man is legally reckoned a Muslim on the basis of his overt behavior.

—AL-JAHIZ, *Epistle on Singing-Girls* (trans. A. F. L. Beeston)

OUR NEXT POET, Ibn Quzman, was born in Córdoba ca. 1078, and died and was buried there in 1160. Very little else is known about his life. Yet he is a major figure in the Arabic poetic tradition, recognized as the supreme master of the *zajal*, a vernacular, strophic genre native to al-Andalus. He distinguished himself as poet, moreover, by relentlessly parodying hallowed conventions.

Among his works, which include an abundance of *zajal* wine songs, love poems (typically bawdy in the extreme), and mock panegyrics, several *zajals* stand out. These poems are the occasional pieces presented on the advent of 'Id al-Adha (Feast of the Sacrifice), in which he reminds a patron of the upcoming celebration and requests from him a ram to slaughter. Seasonal greetings of this specific type are not found in *qasidas* or *muwashshahat* (that is, other strophic poems native to al-Andalus; these poems were composed in classical Arabic) and, as far as we know, were quite new to the *zajal*. To be sure, there existed a tradition of congratulatory poems addressed to rulers on feast occasions, and these poems may be viewed as a development within this tradition. The 'Id, in fact, presented an annual opportunity for the poet to express his allegiance and for the ruler to recognize it and confer benefaction. In this regard Suzanne Pinckney Stetkevych points out, concerning the poet's offering, that "the ritual presentation of gifts or poems to rulers or liege lords on holidays . . . served as a means of reaffirmation of the societal contract, which is perceived as lapsing, or being in danger of lapsing, with the end of the seasonal or ritual cycle."[1] Yet 'Id poems primarily about the poet's need for a ram—and not about congratulations and the patron's continued fitness to rule—were, we have indicated, to all appearances quite new.

214

Two of these particular *zajals* (No. 8 and No. 48) have been selected for perusal;[2] they will be analyzed below in terms of theme, structure, and import. On the basis of James T. Monroe's interpretations of numerous *zajals* by Ibn Quzman, one would expect to find in these works more than shocking entertainment.[3] Indeed, as we shall see, the humor and iconoclasm of Nos. 8 and 48 furnish evidence of brilliant literary innovation necessitated by a stagnant market for poetry and furthermore convey, at a level below the surface, trenchant social criticism.

Before reading the poems, let us first recall the context. By all accounts, Ibn Quzman lived during a difficult period for poets. The Berber-speaking Almoravids (al-Murabitun) from North Africa had defeated all the "Party Kings" (Muluk al-Tawa'if) by 1091 except for the Banu Hud of Saragossa and had settled in al-Andalus. Not surprisingly, given their linguistic background, they showed scant appreciation for classical Arabic poetry. On the other hand, they took extreme interest in jurisprudence; under the Almoravids, Malikite religious scholars enjoyed a golden age. Historian al-Marrakushi (b. 1185) tells us that no one met with favor from the ruler 'Ali (r. 1106–1142) unless he was an expert in canon law and that 'Ali would huddle with at least four jurists (*fuqaha'*, singular *faqih*) before issuing a decree, no matter how trifling.[4] The jurists quickly climbed into all the positions of power and influence. There they did not hesitate to enrich themselves, while in most cases reserving for traditionally secular poets only their censure. Ibn al-Banni expresses the resentment felt by the latter for the arriviste religious scholars:

> O men of hypocrisy, you have donned your mantle of knowledge,
> and set out like wolves on a dark night,
>
> And possessed the world with your Malikite doctrine,
> and divided up its property by means of Ibn al-Qasim.[5]

Hence, the court, filled with Almoravids and jurists, ceased to promise reward for literary craftsmen. Their resultant disaffection found vent in a new "hatred of Seville" (the Almoravid capital until their fall in 1145) topos. In some instances, this motif expanded to a "hatred of al-Andalus" theme overall. Ibn Baqi (d. ca. 1150) had this to say:

I remained in your midst despite want and destitution,
and would not have done so had I been wellborn and self-respecting.

Your gardens yield no fruit;
your skies pour no rain.

Yet I have merit, and if al-Andalus turns me out,
Iraq will embrace me.

Prospering here by one's intellectual abilities has become a base practice,
a craft entrusted to miserly upstarts.[6]

Nevertheless, Ibn Quzman chose to stay in al-Andalus and continue in the trade. It meant eking out a living by composing for the not-so-notable in return for modest sums. At times, it also meant trying to wring compensation from stone-faced jurists, as they were proliferating and gaining control over limited resources. Let us now turn to a *zajal* composed for a member of this second audience, the Córdoban *faqih* Ibn Mughith, and then to another *zajal* addressed, in all likelihood, to one of his colleagues.

No. 8

0 *O one whom I rejoice upon seeing,*
   I must have my ram to sacrifice!
1 I won't be disappointed in my request;
   The matter, no doubt, is inscribed on your mind—
   May God and your exaltedness save me
   Should it be erasing my name!
2 Were he strong, were he stubborn,
   I still wouldn't fear slaughtering him, by God.
   I would slit his throat faster than any butcher;
   But my chance to slaughter hasn't come yet.
3 I must have broiled meat to tear off,
   And a dish of roasted lungs to swallow,
   And ram's head soup to make,
   And meat strips to dry on my terrace.
4 What do you think—isn't it pleasing to the taste?
   I string the pearls, and you get the necklace.

Am I not giving thanks for your favor with praise?

When are people going to find something like my praise?

5   Does anyone else know what I know?

Is this jewel not one of my jewels?

Only my praise has salt.

So cast the flour and I'll throw on the salt.

6   Ibn Mughith, O lord of lords,

You are my country estate, you are my property.

And if Time wants to fight me,

Then you are my sword, you are my spear.

7   How lucky I am! I rejoice and clap my hands.

I'm not afraid of worries coming my way,

Nor of the times wronging me;

I've made my peace with misfortune.

In the *matla'*, or refrain of the poem, Ibn Quzman gets right to the point: he needs a ram to sacrifice for 'Id al-Adha, as prescribed for every free Muslim who can obtain a ram. In strophe 1, he projects optimism that the patron will supply one, although he acknowledges the possibility that the patron may have forgotten his name. This prospect would not be so troubling were it not that he congratulates Ibn Mughith elsewhere for having memorized Ibn al-Qasim's *Al-Mudawwana al-kubra* (The Great Body of Laws), which fills some sixteen volumes in a modern edition. If we suppose the possibility raised here to be a reality, then either this man is drawing a blank on the name despite prodigious powers of recollection, or he is purposely trying to purge it from his memory— neither of which speaks well of their relationship. Though the poet stops short of next giving his name (doing so would reveal a lack of faith and might annoy the patron in the event that he does remember it), he follows with two strophes that should at least bring a clear image of the poet to mind. Irrepressible Ibn Quzman has come before the jurist again, and now he wants a ram so he can consume it voraciously.

At the center of the poem, Ibn Quzman pauses to ask his patron what he thinks, so far, of the performance. One imagines that Ibn Mughith felt at least slightly uncomfortable at being buttonholed for a sheep, especially from the likes of Ibn Quzman. Refusal, however, would be awkward, since the poet was ostentatiously presenting a *zajal* to him. According to the principles of gift giving, he faced subordination to the initiator if he did not respond in kind.[7] Although Ibn Quzman refers to the composition as an expression of thanks, he has not yet received anything. It is the patron's turn, in keeping with protocol, to hand over what he has been thanked for and thereby complete the exchange.

Ibn Quzman devotes the next strophe to self-praise and follows these words with terse vocative praise for the patron ("O lord of lords"). The remainder of strophe 6 is less complimentary and less generic. Specifically, it prompts ironic associations with al-Mutanabbi's 954 'Id al-Adha poem to Sayf al-Dawla. In that famous panegyric, the poet represents himself as a Samhari spear in the hand of the ruler; in this *zajal*, Ibn Mughith appears in the hand of the poet, both as a sword and as a spear wielded against Time. Likewise, the patron stands for wealth. In other words, Ibn Quzman wants to use him. The slight mockery of the patron does not seem to dim the poet's hopes for success—not after he has stated his need and proclaimed the value of his gift. He closes the *zajal* as he opened it, optimistic about his prospects.

No. 48

0   *The time for Feast preparation has arrived, it must be pointed out.*
     Monday's the procession, so give me the reward.

1   The burden of the Feast entails carrying rams and baskets,
     Pots and bowls, jars and wine containers.
     In anticipation of brisk business the perfume vendors all sit in their stalls.
     And, for the roasting of sheep's heads, a crowd gathers in every quarter.

2   For the enjoined sacrifice, every wretch buys a ram:
     In appearance for God, in reality for the children's enjoyment.
     How one suffers from heat during the Feasts!
     But in going out to the *musalla* the heat is dissipated.[8]

3   On the eve of the Feast, every adorned face is outdoors.
     At the cemeteries, meanwhile, people weep over departed loved ones.
     A commemoration of sorrows, a celebration of joys;
     As tears of condolence fall on knavery's clothes.

4   I'll be concise, for long-windedness doesn't please me.
     Why ask about the fine points, if you've got a handle on the fundamentals?
     What I've come for, I must say:
     The whole story is that I want something; you've understood the allusion.

5 Give me my ram for the Feast, to dye with safflower and to swallow,

  To slaughter, slice, jerk and preserve,

  To skewer, so I can eat broiled meat until I'm stuffed.

  Then I'll put on my festive clothes and pay you a visit.

6 Whoever has me at his side, wherever he goes,

  Sees me going about playing tricks, deceiving, and slandering.

  No matter where his feet go, nothing tears his clothes;

  He could even ride on my back, were it not for my cloak.

7 Don't doubt my affection—be sure that I love you.

  You are as you are in your glory; what more can I say?

  Would it be right to carry on, while you're busy with your Feast?

  I've never seen a prince to enjoy verbosity.

Zajal No. 48 also deals with an incipient 'Id al-Adha celebration. Here, the poet announces, in the *matla'*, the feast's arrival, then demands of his unnamed sponsor the reward for bringing good news. He proceeds in strophes 1–3 to describe the outward signs of the feast: people buying and selling, carrying supplies, going to the *musalla* for community prayers, paying respects to the dead. As for tears falling on knavery's clothes, the image intimates the atmosphere of iniquity that used to hang over the cemeteries of Córdoba during Ibn Quzman's day and implies that rogues attempted to draw close to mourners by showing sympathy and offering their condolences. Warm embraces with sensuous mourners, we suppose, were sometimes attained. Incidentally, it seems that the visitors to the tombs (not the dissembling sympathizers), for their part, were often willing participants in debauchery. Based on knowledge of what transpired at the cemeteries of Baghdad, Ibn 'Aqil (d. 1119) had the following to say:

O Visitor of these tombs! Think of your visit and the big difference there is between it and the purpose originally prescribed for it. The Prophet said, "[Visit the tombs], they will remind you of the Hereafter." How engrossed you are in glancing at the radiant faces in those gatherings, with sowing the seeds of sensual delight in your heart, and of carnal appetite in your soul, distracted from looking at the decaying bones and, reflecting on them, calling to mind the Hereafter! On the contrary, you set out only in search of your own pleasure;

and you return only as a sinner. To your mind, there is no difference between visiting the graves, and visiting the gardens for a joyful event. You could at least commit your sins between your own walls! . . .

How it does distress me that some let slip away Feast days during which people acquire all kinds of spiritual gains! Would to God they emerged from them in idleness, one like the other! They are not content until they make them, year after year, occasions for seizing the opportunity to extract fully the sensual delights, and harvest the forbidden venereal lusts.[9]

Writing in the nineteenth century, Edward W. Lane records that the Cairo cemeteries at feast time could serve as a theater for similar wantonness; he adds that some women brazenly elected to spend the nights there in tents.[10] Through the inclusion of unsavory details such as this one about knavery in the public domain, Ibn Quzman imparts to his description an element of what Mikhail Bakhtin has called "grotesque realism" and evokes the earthy side of the feast.[11]

In strophe 4 Ibn Quzman sums up his point succinctly—he wants something—and affirms that the specific meaning has not been lost on his patron. On the first pass such reassurance would seem to compliment the patron, as it brings to mind the proverb *inna l-labiba min al-isharati yafhamu* (The wise man understands from a mere sign).[12] Upon slight consideration, one realizes that the poet is actually imputing to him extreme denseness. It is already clear from the imperative in the refrain that Ibn Quzman wants a reward. Given that the refrain was repeated during a performance after each strophe, the patron, so far, has heard this information four times; he will hear it four more times as well. The poet belabors his point by making an allusion. Moreover, that he desires a ram should be apparent from the seasonal context and from the repeated mention of rams in the first two strophes. Yet the poet leaves nothing to chance, beginning strophe 5 with an unambiguous order: "Give me my ram for the Feast." Evidently, Ibn Quzman views repetitiousness and painful clarity on this point together as a fair price to pay for ensuring that the presumable dolt understands.

This forceful manner of exposition leads one to believe that the patron, like Ibn Mughith, was a Malikite *faqih*. From the poetic record, we may surmise that when the jurists and poet met, they spoke a language of imperatives and blunt replies. For example, in No. 71 a white-bearded man crisply directs Ibn Quzman to repent, as does the meddlesome jurist in No. 148, whom Ibn Quzman calls an "idiot."[13] Though each side perhaps had many things to say about the other in private, in public encounters it seems there was little dialogue. Two more pieces of evidence also indicate that the *zajal* was directed at a *faqih*. One is the word *muluki* (prince) in strophe 8, which echoes the term *muluk al-din* (kings of religion) from No. 15, referring to the likes of Abu Bakr ibn Faraj, a jurist.[14] The other consists in the references in strophe 4 to the *usul* (sources, or fundamentals) and *furu'* (ramifications, or fine points) of law. Though ostensibly the poet asks here about his own speech, by implication he raises a question about the jurists' predilection, indulged conspicuously during the Almoravid period, for formulating religious law and extending it into all aspects of life. If one has mastered, Ibn Quzman implies, the sources of the religion—primarily the Qur'an, and secondarily the sayings and doings of the Prophet—then why should one trouble with legal minutiae? The question would unsettle a *faqih*, since it gives cause to wonder about his raison d'être.

In strophe 5 Ibn Quzman's true intention becomes clear. He wants a ram, once again, so he can gorge himself with its meat. The images of the poet eagerly preparing the meal and gormandizing do not remind one of traditional Arab models of deportment. In his study *Of Dishes and Discourse,* Geert Jan van Gelder points out that "the bedouin poet-hero should disdain food, neither partaking of it nor depicting it lovingly."[15] We might find al-Shanfara the paragon of this sort of restraint. In his *Lamiyyat al-'Arab,* he prides himself on subduing hunger and declares, "When men reach out for food, I am not the quickest of them, for the greediest men are the quickest" (line 8). In contrast, Ibn Quzman surrenders to his appetite, and by the rapid succession of verbs in the strophe he suggests his eagerness and voracity.

His zeal and immoderation in the consumption of food also show disregard for religious precepts. The Qur'an frequently counsels patience and urges man to gain mastery over the spirit that incites him to evil (*an-nafsu l-ammaratu bi-s-su'i*). From accounts of hadith we learn that the Prophet himself never ate to the point that he was sated.[16] Later religious treatises and encyclopedic works are explicit about the connection between satiety and sin. The Brethren of Purity (ca. 960), for instance, devote a section of their *Epistles* to the subject, and al-Tawhidi (d. 1023) provides authoritative opinions on the precise boundary of moderation, over which a Muslim should avoid trespass.[17] A religious listener would surely note the discrepancy between Ibn Quzman's approach to food and the Islamic one.

The poet concludes the *zajal* with two strophes in which he describes part of a projected holiday visit to the patron and eulogizes the man. Normally, a holiday visit to such a personage would be taken as a sign of abiding respect and admiration, a reaffirmation of allegiance. True to form, however, when Ibn Quzman displays fealty and bestows praise, he undercuts the performances with irony. We cannot imagine that a rigid *faqih* would enjoy hearing that the poet was apt to engage in horseplay around him. (Nor, for that matter, can we suppose that he would be pleased to hear about the vibrant underside of the 'Id celebration.) The poet's readiness to clear a path in front of him does not impress us, since at a difficult patch he would not take the man on his back because of the inconvenience to his cloak. In the last strophe, the praise comes through—after one filters out the noise of love assurances—as decidedly faint. "You are as you are in your glory, what more can I say?" can mean a lot of things, including that the patron possesses no glory of which to speak. Ibn Quzman here does not even pull out his pro forma lines about stellar ancestry, cloudlike generosity, and so forth. Rather, he ends the poem without them, apparently convinced that his patron has already had enough. Like the Almoravid rulers, to one of whom Ibn Quzman dedicated a miniature four-strophe panegyric, this patron does not seem to take pleasure in verbosity.

*I*t should come as no surprise to those readers familiar with modern scholarship on Ibn Quzman that these two poems are organized according to the principles of ring composition. Monroe has already identified the method of ring composition in twelve Ibn Quzman *zajals*; at this stage, one would expect to discover chiastic order in most, if not all, of his *zajals*. We merely note, additionally, that in both poems vicarious meals precede visits for praise. The poet needs to be paid for present services before he will exert more effort in the patrons' behalf.

The thematic summaries below reveal the concentric organization of each poem. The summaries are followed by a discussion of the import of these poems.

NO. 8

0   Refrain: Demand for ram

   1   poet confident about request
      Refrain

     2   poet battles with ram
        Refrain

       3   poet wants food (ram)
          Refrain

         4   poet implies that patron owes him ram for poem
            Refrain

       5   poet wants food (flour)
          Refrain

     6   poet battles with Time
        Refrain

   7   poet confident about future

0   Refrain: Demand for ram

NO. 48

0   Refrain: Demand for reward

   1   people busy preparing for feast
      Refrain

     2   people walking to *musalla*
        Refrain

       3   faces adorned; visits to cemeteries
          Refrain

         4   poet says he wants something
            Refrain

       5   ram dyed; visit to patron
          Refrain

     6   poet walking with patron
        Refrain

   7   patron busy preparing for feast

0   Refrain: Demand for reward

In his introduction to the *Diwan,* Ibn Quzman says that he has made the *zajal* "easy, but difficultly easy; both popular and learned, hard yet obvious, obscure and clear."[18] The statement implies that his poems, however entertaining and accessible, contain much below the surface, and it invites us to search in them for deeper meanings. These 'Id poems, we realize, satisfy inquiry; like fine art generally, they can be appreciated on multiple levels.

On one level, we may regard them as documentation of the sorry state of literary patronage during Ibn Quzman's lifetime and of his innovative response to the situation. That he would have to ask for food tells most of the story. Do we need to be reminded of the days when al-Nabigha (d. ca. 604) got one hundred fine camels for delivering a short apologetic poem to the king, when the Christian poet al-Akhtal (d. ca. 710) earned thousands of dirhams for occasional panegyrical services to the caliph 'Abd al-Malik, when al-Mutanabbi (d. 965) received an estate, a horse, and a slave girl just for showing his cleverness in a single line?[19] This poet—with a talent that so far has won him nine centuries of fame—is only hoping for a medium-size animal, and he has no guarantees that he will get it. As mentioned above, the wretched conditions for poetry meant seeking a new audience and essaying a popular form. But the response from modestly endowed aristocrats was not sufficient, one infers, to provide meat at feast time, so the poet had to go out and petition potentially hostile jurists. In the face of such hardship, Ibn Quzman manages to develop a new type of *zajal* (itself a fresh genre to serious poets) and add to the vast treasure of Arabic poetry more unique and glittering pieces.

As James T. Monroe and Mark Pettigrew have recently argued, one has grounds to suspect that Ibn Quzman's *zajal* poetry came to be influenced by the *maqama,* a picaresque genre invented by Badi' al-Zaman al-Hamadhani (d. 1008) during a similar patronage crisis when Persian-speaking Buwayhids controlled Iraq.[20] Al-Hamadhani's protagonist Abu al-Fath al-Iskandari is a veritable chameleon ("Cleave not to one character," he says, "but, as the nights change, do thou change too").[21] Similarly, we find Ibn Quzman appearing in various guises depending on the occasion: in some poems he turns up as the seducer, in others the lady's fool; he plays the passionate lover of wine, but also poses as the local imam. In Nos. 8 and 48, he adopts the persona of a *tufayli,* or uninvited guest. One recalls the notable *tufayli* performance of Abu al-Fath, in which his hand wandered over a banquet table "playing the role of ambassador between the viands of various hues, seizing the choicest of the cakes and plucking out the centers of the dishes, pasturing on his neighbor's territory . . . stuffing his mouth with morsel after morsel and chasing mouthful with mouthful."[22] Ibn Quzman's anticipated attack on the meat strips and dish of roasted lungs comes from the same school of manners.

Fedwa Malti-Douglas has made a careful study of the principal source book on *tufaylis*, *Al-Tatfil* by al-Khatib al-Baghdadi (d. 1071), and identifies the character type's distinguishing features. By definition he is any uninvited guest, but the anecdotes narrow this category. Almost invariably, they also represent him as someone with an attachment to food. In addition, the anecdotal *tufayli* lives by his wits. In fact, cunning would seem an essential attribute for the *tufayli* who wishes to carry on in this lifestyle, as Malti-Douglas discerns a "relationship between cleverness and the delivery of the goods."[23]

Returning to these 'Id poems, we see that Ibn Quzman's persona, if we make exception for his showing up a day or so before the roast, conforms to the *tufayli* paradigm elaborated by Malti-Douglas. He came uninvited and had a tangible goal in mind. Furthermore, he relied on trickery to win the day. "Be with people like the chess player," advises the venerable Abu al-Fath, and "take all they have and keep all thou hast."[24] Part of Ibn Quzman's trickery, we have seen, consists in his not giving anything. His eulogy of the two patrons is so ironic and sparse that it should be called scorn. On the other hand, he leverages the encounter so he may take what they have—at least from it one ram. It could not be gainsaid that he sought to fulfill a religious duty; on paper, they would have to find his demand legitimate. Granted, he might be told to go away and come back after the sacrifice and so receive, according to the charitable custom, a portion of meat. But Ibn Quzman wants more than a modest share. For this reason, in order to discourage a parsimonious response, he puts each patron on the spot. Here, the poet was coming forward with a *zajal*—they were obliged to present a valuable gift in return or accept symbolic subordination. Because of the legitimacy of his request and the factor of social pressure brought to bear on his audience, and since he composed six 'Id al-Adha poems, we may assume that Ibn Quzman's seasonal ploys usually worked.

Therefore, on another level one appreciates the poet's cleverness, his judicious following in the footsteps of literary forebears and timely adoption of a *tufayli* profile to get what he wants. Yet a *tufayli*'s buffoonery could also be used to raise a very serious issue, as it does at the banquet crashed by Abu al-Fath.[25] Regarding the performance of Hajj duties on the days preceding the sacrifice, S. A. Hussain observes that "ritual is meaningless unless there is sincerity and understanding."[26] Ibn Quzman, by his avidity to consume, does not inspire confidence that he either contemplates or understands the significance of the 'Id. He seems particularly far off the mark when, in No. 48, he speaks of the ram as being "in appearance for God, in reality for the children's enjoyment." Perhaps so that people do not develop faulty notions of the sacrifice, through which they commemorate Abraham's obedience to God such that he was willing to take his son Ishmael's life,[27] and through which they recognize the example of God's mercy in accepting an animal substitute, the Qur'an states, "It is not their meat nor their blood that reaches God: it is your piety that reaches Him" (22:37). Clearly, what matters to God, in enjoining the rite, is that it be carried out with pious intentions.

Would this issue of the inner dimension to religion have any special relevance for Ibn Quzman's audience? In the East around this time, it certainly had relevance. The great Islamic theologian al-Ghazali had made the inner dimension to religion his life's purpose after giving up a prestigious teaching post at Baghdad's Nizamiyya College in 1095. To al-Ghazali, the enormous emphasis placed on religion's exterior aspects had gone a long way toward killing its spirit. In his monumental *Ihya' 'ulum al-din* (The Revival of the Religious Sciences) he launched a frontal assault on the jurists, who were filling the land with their fatwas. But for all their vigilance, they were incapable of judging whether the religion was being practiced in earnest. He cites the example of the zealot who had killed a man because he was not a true Muslim, to whom the Prophet asked, "Did you open his heart?" One may earn the approval of a *faqih* at prayer time, notes al-Ghazali, by dutifully mouthing the words and going through the motions, while one ponders financial dealings in the market.[28] He also took exception to the jurists' worldliness. They had become vile by their association with the rulers and now looked for ways to help the latter achieve personal ends by means of legal ruses.[29] Al-Ghazali recognized the importance of abiding by religious law as a protection for the individual, but affirmed that doing so was not sufficient to gain Paradise.[30] Consistently, he called on Muslims to be sincere in their practice and so endeavored to return to orthodoxy its spirituality.

Needless to say, the ideas of al-Ghazali were not popular in al-Andalus. Later, the Almohads (al-Muwahhidun [r. 1145–1230]) embraced his ideas and made them the basis for their sweeping reforms. But during the early Almoravid period, the Córdoban *faqih* Ibn Hamdin (d. 1115) declared that anyone who read *The Revival* was an infidel and circulated among his friends a fatwa condemning it. They all signed the fatwa, and it went to the ruler, 'Ali, who put it into effect. Across al-Andalus, copies of al-Ghazali's book were collected and burned. Until the end of Almoravid rule, possession of al-Ghazali's writings remained a crime punishable by confiscation of property and death.

Significantly, Ibn Quzman's persona in these *zajals* shows respect for the jurists' obsession with legality. He scrupulously wants to perform his religious duty and slaughter a ram. His project is in strict conformity with the letter of the law. Nevertheless, if his persona appears ridiculous because of his eagerness to devour meat on a solemn occasion, therein lies a message. At this point, we become aware of the poet's serious underlying criticism of the religious formalism of the day. Correct behavior, we perceive, must be motivated by sincere spirituality, lest it seem absurd. Ultimately, what al-Ghazali communicates through *The Revival of the Religious Sciences,* Ibn Quzman demonstrates by negative example through these 'Id poems—that piety is in the heart.

12

Ecstasy

Provide me one telling detail of her,
so it's as if you're giving me her first name, last name, and nickname.

—BAHA' AL-DIN ZUHAYR, No. 21

IN THIS CHAPTER we shall read poetry by Ibn al-Farid (d. 1235), the greatest
Sufi poet in the Arabic literary tradition. To comprehend more fully his verse and
consider it in context, however, we must first inform ourselves about Sufism and
review the historical development thereof.

Sufism, or Islamic mysticism, has its basis in the human spirit's yearning
for communion with God; it answers the needs of those individuals who want to
experience God *personally.* The well-known hadith, spoken by God through the
angel Gabriel, apprises man: "My servant draws nigh with nothing more dear to
Me than such obligations as I have imposed upon him, and still he approaches
Me with supererogatory works, so that I may love him. For if I love him, I am the
Ear by which he hears, the Eye by which he sees, the Hand by which he takes,
and the Leg by which he walks."[1] Sufism, then, essentially is about drawing near
to God through piety, and experiencing God's love. God—while also being awesome and fear-inspiring, of course—is after all the Loving One (Qur'an 85:14).

The word *Sufi* is thought to be derived from *suf,* or "wool": the first Sufis
typically wore coarse woolen clothing. They were ascetics, and asceticism has
remained always fundamental to Sufism (it being understood that a person who
occupies himself with physical indulgence cannot progress spiritually toward
God). They emerged in the early eighth century, in strong contrast to persons of
the Islamic Empire given to luxurious habits and worldliness. Al-Hasan al-Basri
(d. 728) was the first major Sufi figure. His teaching has come down to us in the
form of sayings; here are some of his utterances:

"God has made fasting a hippodrome for His servants, that they may race towards obedience to Him. Some come in first and win the prize, while others are left behind and return disappointed.

"You meet one of them with white skin and delicate complexion, speeding along the path of vanity: he shakes his hips and claps his sides and says, 'Here am I, recognize me!' Yes, we recognize you, and you are hateful to God and hateful to good men.

"Cleanse your hearts (by meditation and remembrance of God), for they are quick to rust; and restrain your souls, for they desire eagerly, and if you do not restrain them, they will drag you to an evil end."[2]

Al-Hasan al-Basri was said to have been extremely fearful of God; his face suggested to all that he had just witnessed a terrible calamity. In his outlook, he was characteristic of the early Sufis, who were reputed to have been acutely aware of God's wrath. Their fear of hellfire and their corresponding hope of heavenly reward were reputedly the motivating factors in their asceticism.

The next major Sufi, Rabi'a al-'Adawiyya (d. 801), also of Basra, was contrastingly motivated by a desire of intimacy foremost; she is widely regarded as the person who introduced the element of love to Sufism. What follows is a transcribed Rabi'a prayer: "O God, if I have worshipped You out of fear, then burn me in Hell; and if I have worshipped You out of desire, then exclude me from Paradise; but if I have worshipped You out of love, then deprive me not the contemplation of Your Eternal Beauty."[3] She reportedly received multiple marriage offers, but accepted none. She rebuffed one suitor with these words: "O sensual one, seek another sensual like yourself. Have you seen any sign of desire in me?" To another she said: "My existence is in Him, and I am altogether His. I am in the shadow of His command. The marriage contract must be asked for from Him, not from me."[4] About loving God she has a few short poems to her name, of which this one is famous:

I love You with two loves:
with longing and a love because You are worthy of it.

As for the longing,
it involves my remembering You and none else.

As for the love of which You are worthy,
it involves Your lifting of the curtain, and my adoring gaze.

But I have no praise in the one or the other;
the praise for them both belongs wholly to You.[5]

Rabi'a was buried at Basra, and her tomb became an object of pilgrimage. The Persian mystic 'Attar (d. 1230), indicating her standing among later Muslims, wrote of her in *Tadhkirat al-awliya'* (Memoirs of the Saints) as "that one set apart in the seclusion of holiness, that woman veiled with the veil of religious sincerity, that one on fire with love and longing, that one enamored of the desire to approach her Lord and be consumed in His glory, that woman who lost herself in union with the Divine, that one accepted by men as a second spotless Mary— Rabi'a al-'Adawiyya, may God have mercy upon her."[6]

After Rabi'a, Dhu al-Nun al-Misri (d. 859 in Egypt, following a return from Iraq) developed Sufism further. He reacted to the prevailing rationalism of his time and differentiated, from the purported wisdom of intellectuals, the mystic's *ma'rifa,* or gnosis. "Real knowledge is God's illumination of the heart with the pure radiance of knowledge," he says. "True knowledge of God," he states elsewhere, "is not the knowledge that God is One, which is possessed by all believers; nor the knowledge of Him derived from proof and demonstration, which belongs to philosophers, rhetoricians, and theologians; but it is the knowledge of the attributes of Divine Unity, which belongs to the Saints of God, those who behold God with their hearts in such wise that He reveals unto them what He reveals not unto anyone else in the world."[7] With his identification of mystical gnosis as a kind of insight distinct from, and superior to, the insight of the mind, Dhu al-Nun made an important contribution to Sufi doctrine.

Moving ahead, we need mention the important contributions of al-Junayd of Baghdad (d. 910), the "Sheikh of the Order." Among his key works are the *Kitab al-tawhid* (Book of Union) and the *Kitab al-fana'* (Book on Annihilation), in which he treats the mystical experience of passing away from oneself and abiding in God (discussed below in connection with Ibn al-Farid). His imprudent pupil, al-Hallaj (d. 922), marks the culmination of early Sufism. Al-Hallaj spoke in brazen terms about his union with God, provoking the ire of religious authorities (he also passionately advocated social justice). He is chiefly remembered in Islamic history for having declared once, "Ana al-Haqq" (I am the Truth). In addition, these lines of his are often cited:

> I am the Beloved, and the Beloved is I—
> we are two spirits in one body.
>
> When you see me, you see Him,
> and when you see Him, you see us.[8]

He was accused of promoting *hulul* (the incarnation of the divine and the human in one body, a profoundly objectionable notion in Islam). After enduring an extended incarceration, he was put to death. On the necessity of this final punishment, we have the following, ultimately persuasive, communication by the vizier Hamid Ibn al-'Abbas to Caliph al-Muqtadir (r. 908–32): "The *fuqaha'* have agreed by *fatwa* on his execution. His heresy, his blasphemy . . . his claims to divine power have been revealed and made public. If the Commander of the Faithful does not carry out what the *fuqaha'* have ruled on, there will be people who will rise up and be emboldened to rebel against God and His prophets."[9]

In the tenth and eleventh centuries, Sufism continued to appeal to those Muslims who wanted an intimate relationship with God. The aggregate of Sufis came to comprise twelve religious orders, we are told.[10] The increasing formalism of religious practice during this period steadily drove many Muslims into the Sufi ranks. Yet on the whole, Sufism was a marginal phenomenon within Islam. And it remained so until the Sufi conversion of al-Ghazali.

Al-Ghazali (d. 1111), introduced in the previous chapter, distinguished himself early as a brilliant jurist. But no sooner had he attained prominence in the role of professor at Baghdad and his fame begun to spread than he reconsidered his life's course and his faith. Momentously, he abandoned his academic position and took up Sufism. In his autobiographical *Al-Munqidh min al-dalal* (The Deliverer from Error), he recalls the process that led to this break:

> Then I turned my attention to the Way of the Sufis. I knew that it could not be traversed to the end without both doctrine and practice, and that the gist of the doctrine lies in overcoming the appetites of the flesh and getting rid of its evil dispositions and vile qualities, so that the heart may be cleared of all but

God; and the means of clearing it is *dhikr Allah,* i.e. commemoration of God and concentration of every thought upon Him. Now, the doctrine was easier to me than the practice, so I began by learning their doctrine from the books and sayings of their Shaykhs, until I acquired as much of their Way as it is possible to acquire by learning and hearing, and saw plainly that what is most peculiar to them cannot be learned, but can only be reached by immediate experience and ecstasy and inward transformation. I became convinced that I had now acquired all the knowledge of Sufism that could possibly be obtained by means of study; as for the rest, there was no way of coming to it except by leading the mystical life. I looked on myself as I then was. Worldly interests encompassed me on every side. Even my work as a teacher—the best thing I was engaged in— seemed unimportant and useless in view of the life hereafter. When I considered the intention of my teaching, I perceived that instead of doing it for God's sake alone I had no motive but the desire for glory and reputation. I realized that I stood on the edge of a precipice and would fall into Hellfire unless I set about to mend my ways. . . . Conscious of my helplessness and having surrendered my will entirely, I took refuge with God as a man in sore trouble who has no resource left. God answered my prayer and made it easy for me to turn my back on reputation and wealth and wife and children and friends.[11]

Al-Ghazali's great achievement, accomplished primarily through his *Ihya',* was to reconcile Sufi doctrine with orthodox practice, spirit with letter, and so bring Sufism into the mainstream. During the twelfth century Sufi orders proliferated in the Islamic world. They were manifestly individual: each formed around a sheikh and had its own rituals (novices learned these customs and then strove to reach the states of ecstasy and illumination attained by the sheikh). But collectively, their appearance and popularity were owing, in large part, to the influence of al-Ghazali.

To conservatives, however, Sufism remained a heresy. For example, Ibn al-Jawzi (d. 1200) featured it in his book entitled *Talbis Iblis* (The Devil's Delusion). About the famous Sufi convert and author of the *Ihya',* one might be curious to know, he had the following to say: "How cheaply has al-Ghazali traded theology for Sufism! . . . Glory be to Him Who withdrew Abu Hamid from the orbit of theology by the authorship of the *Ihya'.* Would that he had not related therein such unlawful things. It is amazing that he should both relate them and express his approval of them and should call the possessors of states [that is, the Sufis] his friends: and what state is more vile and disastrous than that of one who opposes the Shari'a and approves what is opposed to it?"[12]

Concluding our rapid overview of Sufism during the classical period, we must discuss, however briefly, its magnificently illustrious theorist Ibn 'Arabi, "al-Shaykh al-Akbar" (Supreme Sheikh). Ibn 'Arabi was an Andalusi, born in Murcia and educated at Córdoba and Seville. He left al-Andalus at the age of thirty-five and traveled to Cairo; from there he went to Mecca; he settled down finally in Damascus, where he died in 1240.[13] He contributed to Sufism mainly by drawing together earlier theories expounded in Arabic into a single coherent system. Ibn 'Arabi named his system, or doctrine, *wahdat al-wujud* (Unity of Being), which he elaborated in a number of prose works, the voluminous *Al-Futuhat al-Makkiyya* (The Meccan Revelations) and the more concise *Fusus al-hikam* (The Bezels of Divine Wisdom) principal among them. Basically, he affirms by *wahdat al-wujud* that the phenomenal and the eternal are one, that creation is the outward aspect of the creator. "Multiplicity is due to different points of view," he explains of reality in *Al-Futuhat,* "not an actual division in the One Essence."[14]

Ibn 'Arabi stirred controversy in his own day, and he has stirred controversy ever since. The formidable legal scholar Ibn Taymiyya (d. 1328) two generations hence devoted part of his career to refuting him and exposing his doctrinal "perversity."[15] Ibn Taymiyya articulated a definitive response to Ibn 'Arabi, from the standpoint of the *fuqaha'*. The comprehensive vision of Ibn 'Arabi, however, has enduring appeal among Sufis, despite opposition to the vision by the strict orthodox and their invocation of Ibn Taymiyya's arguments.

In the recollection of later Arabs, Ibn 'Arabi is frequently located with his contemporary Ibn al-Farid, the great Arab Sufi poet (compare al-Ja'bari [d. 1288], who, in a dream cited by Ibn Taymiyya, saw "Ibn 'Arabi and Ibn al-Farid, both blind old men, stumbling around and crying out: 'Where is the way? Where is the way?'").[16] It is said that Ibn 'Arabi requested from Ibn al-Farid a commentary on the latter's mystical masterpiece, *Nazm al-suluk* (The Poem of the Sufi Way, otherwise known as *Al-Ta'iyya al-kubra,* The Great Ta'iyya/Poem in Ta'). "Your *Meccan Revelations* is a commentary on it," Ibn al-Farid supposedly replied.[17] Many Sufi commentators have sought to explain aspects of Ibn al-Farid's poetry by making reference to Ibn 'Arabi's theosophy. But to a certain extent Sufi sheikhs find their own paths to God, as we have indicated. Ibn al-Farid registers in his poetry his own psychological and spiritual experience. Furthermore, no evidence exists that the two ever met. Suffice it to say that they were both luminary Sufis drawing from the same abundance of predecessors' teaching and moving in the same cultural milieu.

Having reached our poet, let us deal first with his life. Indeed, not much is known of it. Ibn al-Farid was born in 1181, the son of a notary, in Ayyubid Cairo—the Ayyubi Salah al-Din, or Saladin, had put an end to Fatimid rule and made the city his capital ten years earlier. Ibn al-Farid studied jurisprudence in his youth, although he was wont to absent himself in the Muqattam hills east of Cairo, where he wandered and meditated. He went to Mecca when he was thirty-five, and in and around Mecca he stayed for fifteen years. He returned finally to Cairo. His poetry attests that, as an older man in Egypt, he felt very nostalgic for the Hejaz. He spent his last years living in seclusion near the Azhar Mosque, attending to his *Diwan*. He died at fifty-four and was buried at the foot of the Muqattam hills. There his shrine is still frequented.

As Th. Emil Homerin has shown, the general perception of Ibn al-Farid shifted over time: gradually he came to be viewed, by what seems to have been, until the previous century, a majority of Muslims, as not just a great poet but a saint.[18] His grandson 'Ali Sibt Ibn al-Farid, who in all probability never met his grandfather, deserves much of the credit for this sanctification. The prologue he wrote about the poet, to a new fourteenth-century edition of the *Diwan,* reads as hagiography. For instance, here is an included quotation of the poet, pertaining to his leaving Egypt for the central, religiously focal city of Mecca:

One day I ceased wandering and returned to Cairo, where I entered the Suyufiyah law school [so named because it was situated by the market for swords, *suyuf*]. I found an old greengrocer there at the door of the law school doing ablutions out of order; he washed his hands, then his legs, then he wiped his head and washed his face.[19] So I said to him, "O shaykh, you are this old, in the land of Islam, at the door of the law school, among the scholars of Muslim jurisprudence, yet you are doing the prayer ablutions out of the order prescribed by religion?" He looked at me and said, "'Umar! [Ibn al-Farid's first name] You will not be enlightened in Egypt. You will be enlightened only in the Hijaz, in Mecca—may God glorify it! So head for it, for the time of your enlightenment is near!"

Then I knew that the man was among the saints of God most high and that he disguised himself with this lifestyle and by feigning ignorance of the order of ablutions. So I sat before him and said, "Oh, sir, I am here but Mecca is so far away, and I will not find a mount or a travel companion in the non-pilgrimage months." Then he looked at me, pointed and said, "Here is Mecca before you!" And I looked with him and saw Mecca—may God glorify it! So I left him and sought Mecca whose image remained before me until I entered it almost instantaneously. Then as I entered, enlightenment came to me wave after wave and never left.[20]

His return to Cairo fifteen years later also had a supernatural aura: he heard the greengrocer sheikh summoning him—the man's death was at hand, and he desired Ibn al-Farid to visit him and see to his burial—and so the poet dutifully went back; he arrived just at the right time. Though 'Ali never explicitly claims that his grandfather was a saint, throughout the prologue on his life he gives this impression.

Similarly, 'Ali indicates that Ibn al-Farid composed—or at least composed his most celebrated work—extraordinarily, as one divinely inspired and abstracted from his fellow men. From the prologue again:

The shaykh . . . in most of his moments of inspiration was always perplexed, eyes fixed, hearing no one who spoke, not even seeing them. Sometimes he would be standing, sometimes sitting, sometimes he would lie down on his side, and sometimes he would throw himself down on his back wrapped in a shroud like a dead man. Ten consecutive days—more or less—would pass while he was in this state, he neither eating, drinking, speaking, nor moving, as has been said:

See the lovers felled in their encampments
like the youths of the Cave, not knowing how long they've lingered.

By God, had the lovers sworn to go mad from love or die,
then they would not break their oath![21]

Then he would regain consciousness and come to, and his first words would be a dictation of what God had enlightened him with of the ode *Nazm al-suluk*.[22]

We should be aware, on the other hand, that conservatives and *fuqaha'* vilified Ibn al-Farid and labeled his works as the deeds of an infidel. "Beneath the Sufi garb lurk vipers and pernicious philosophy," Ibn Hajar (d. 1449) warned of him. Al-Dhahabi, roughly a century before this last critic, commented: "He speaks of unification, by the most pleasing expressions and elegant metaphors; his words are like poisoned sweetmeat." In the fifteenth century al-Bulqini was more direct. "This is infidelity," he said upon hearing lines of the *Great Ta'iyya*. "This is infidelity."[23]

One of the first things we notice when reading the *Great Ta'iyya,* and Ibn al-Farid's verse generally, is how he invests poetic imagery with Sufi meanings, rendering the profane spiritual. The beloved he sings of is God (hence Beloved). And in his works, the poet's death before Her signifies the Sufi passing away of the self. It will be found, in particular, that Ibn al-Farid largely repeats the 'Udhri experience and represents his love in 'Udhri terms. In his pursuit of union, he eschews material things. Compare Jamil:

> Other than Buthayna, I want nothing of this world,
> not little or much.[24]

Ibn al-Farid also adores an authoritative Beloved, to Whom he surrenders. Moreover, his love defines his life:

> For me, love is the only way to go.
> Were I to stray, I would be leaving my religion.[25]

The parallel to 'Udhri love and experience can be drawn only so far, however. Ibn al-Farid's love remains the way, the mystical way, of a real religion—patently it is not worship of a lady—and union with his Beloved may be gloriously attained in this life, not just in the hereafter.

Looking specifically at the *Great Ta'iyya,* one finds that it outlines three stages in the experience of Sufi love. In the first stage, the poet and the Beloved are separate. He suffers at not being able to get close and yearns for Her constantly. At one point he exclaims:

> Where is repose? Far from a lover's life!
> The Garden of Eden is ringed by adversity.[26]

Steadily, he thins and becomes pallid. When he has been weakened by his intense, unrequited love, but not completely exhausted, She comes to him and relates:

Such is love: if you don't expire, you never reach your goal.
So choose extinction or give up the quest.[27]

So he continues to suffer and deny himself for Her sake.

Then, as the poem imparts to us, the magical moment arrives. It arrives, though, by grace only. After the Sufi has prepared himself unwearyingly to receive Her favor, She—providing this be Her will—freely grants him union. Al-Suhrawardi (d. 1234) has said in this regard that the beginning of the Sufi path is knowledge, the middle is action, and the end is a gift from God.[28] Our Sufi has now recovered his original unity with God (more on this original state below), what he has been yearning for all along. This union is the supreme bliss, the matchless intoxication, the total annihilation of self (*fana'*). Here individual boundaries dissolve, and the one loses itself in the Whole.[29]

This glorious second stage leads to the sublime third, the so-called second sobriety or sobriety of union, the abiding (*baqa'*) in God. Paradoxically, in this stage the Sufi recovers his sense of self, even while he abides in the Whole. He recognizes himself, on the one hand, as separate and distinct from the One and, on the other, as deeply connected to the One. In this stage he understands that God is all around him. The preponderance of the *Great Ta'iyya,* as Giuseppe Scattolin has noted, may be read as a meditation on the mysteries of this enduring state of union.[30] We quote here lines from another poem (in it God is referred to in the masculine), lines that express succinctly his enlightened apprehension of the last stage that divine beauty shows itself in all things beautiful:

Though He be gone, every sense perceives Him
in all that is fine and clear and pleasing:

In the sound of lute and pipe
when they come together in a melodious strain;

In the soft meadow where gazelles roam
in the cool of evening and morn's temperate warmth;

In the glistening moisture from thin clouds
on a large carpet woven of flowers.

In the train of a gentle breeze
that brings to me at dawn the sweetest of odors;

And in the kiss of the chalice, from whose mouth I sip wine
in a bright, cheerful place.[31]

In such lines we appreciate Ibn al-Farid's realization of the Qur'anic truth, namely, "Wheresoever you turn, there is the Face of God" (2:115).

The last stage also involves the Sufi's return to the world. Now, outwardly he follows religious law, while inwardly he follows Truth (compare the Sufi saying: "Law is worshipping God; Reality is seeing Him").[32] He possesses divine attributes at this stage, since he abides in union with God. These attributes in him are visible to others. As al-Junayd has said of those individuals who return, having been admitted to the Light:

They march in the unique glory of His attributes
trailing the robes of Unity.[33]

The Sufi who has come this far, we readily understand, feels enormous privilege. A great many strive for union, but few finally receive God's gift. Ibn al-Farid revels in being one of these select few: in much of the *Great Ta'iyya* he calls attention to his exalted status. There is no question, considering the poet's various affirmations about himself—which occur with increased frequency during this last stage—that the *Great Ta'iyya* belongs to the rich tradition of boasting in classical Arabic poetry.

But his boasting is not for the sake of self-glorification solely—partially, it should serve to inspire, for Ibn al-Farid addresses his poem to an anonymous aspirant. The Sufi poet, having attained union and gnosis, assumes the role of spiritual director, of sheikh. Certainly, he does point to his own glory as a successful lover, but he also describes in detail the way he pursued his love. The other may take him as a guide and embark on a like spiritual journey. The journey is extremely arduous, as Ibn al-Farid indicates. Yet if the aspirant persists, adhering to the path and struggling on, similarly in the end the person may, God willing, reach the Light.

Indeed, we can find inspiration for an aspirant in the lyrical center of the *Great Ta'iyya*, rendered below. The reader will promptly notice the way Ibn al-Farid reworks traditional love motifs, giving them religious coloration. Nor will it take long for the reader to detect a familiar vainglory (based on this passage, it should not come as a surprise that our poet came to be known as "the Sultan of Lovers"). Yet the reader also may well detect, beneath the grand talk of spiritual union, an element of enticement. An aspirant can find here encouragement to break from the herd and emulate the poet. The person may eventually receive, it is to be hoped, similar gratification.

> Due to Her, in every tribe each man is as dead,
> killed by love—the finest destruction.

> All passions tend to Her,
> so all you see are lovers longing to get close.

> When She goes abroad on a Feast day,
> from every quarter men crowd for a glimpse.

> Their souls yearn for the essence of Her beauty,
> while their pupils delight in Her fruit.

> But my Feast is every day that, with gratified eye,
> I regard Her comely visage.

> And to me every night She draws near is Laylat al-Qadr,
> just as every rendezvous is Friday.[34]

> My striving for Her is a pilgrimage: every stop at her door
> corresponds to a rite at a way-station.

> Any place in God's creation at which She alights,
> hence made pleasing to my sight, I see only as Mecca.

> Sacred is the area that encloses Her,
> and wherever She emigrates to I view as Medina.

> Every house She resides in is Jerusalem;
> there my insides are calm, my eyes glad.

My distant Aqsa Mosque lies at the trail of Her skirt;
my choice fragrance rises from the soil where She treads.[35]

Such are the homelands of my felicities, the summits of my aims,
my wants' limits, where my fears come to rest.

Abodes where Fate has never come between us,
where Time has never plotted a divide;

Nor where the days have endeavored to disorder our affairs,
or the nights seen fit to disturb us.

Misfortunes never greeted us roughly at dawn,
nor did chance sightings ever speak to us of disgrace.

A go-between never spoke horribly of a change of heart,
nor did a censurer ever harangue us about moving on.

The eye of Her watchman did not stay open, looking at me;
rather, during the transports of love, mine was the eye watching.

No time has been designated, at the exclusion of others, for lush pasturage;
with Her all my times are seasons of delight.

My whole day is cool evening if, at the sun's rising,
She returns my greeting with a smile.

And my whole night is enchantment
if the soft breeze carries Her perfume.

If, by night, She knocks at my door,
my whole month is resplendent Laylat al-Qadr.

If She approaches my tent,
my whole year is temperate spring in luxuriant meadows.

If She approves of me,
my whole life is love-cheered youth.

For when, in one image, She commingles the world's charms
I appreciate all the subtleties.

My breast encloses every deep affection for Her
and the constant ache that reveals to you all.

So why shouldn't I boast to one who claims that he loves Her,
and glory in my own happiness,

Having attained more than I wished for,
and gotten closer than I even imagined possible?

Her generous embrace exceeded my every desire
and spited separation to the utmost.

And at dawn, I was just as passionate as I had been at dusk,
and She looked every bit as beautiful.[36]

The *Great Ta'iyya* is a very long poem—761 lines—and a whole book, at least, would be needed for a careful interpretation of it. (In this connection, it is said that a scholar once came before Ibn al-Farid asking permission to write a two-volume commentary on the poem. "I could write two volumes of commentary on every single line," the poet supposedly replied.)[37] So let us turn to another celebrated work, one that can be conveniently discussed within a chapter: his *Khamriyya,* or Wine Ode. In extolling wine and outlining its effects, Ibn al-Farid takes a page from Abu Nuwas's book. The wine he sings of, though, is God's love. We shall start by reading the first section.

A

1   We drank a wine to the memory of the Beloved,
     and were drunk even before the vine was created.

2   A sun, that a crescent brings around in a full-moon cup;
     and when water is added, how many stars appear!

3   Were it not for the musk, I would not have located its tavern;
     were it not for the lightning-flash, my fancy would never have conceived it.
4   Time has preserved of it but the innermost flame,
     as if it were the beloved's name, hidden in the breasts of the wary.
5   Let it be mentioned in the tribe, and the people are ecstatic,
     though no shame or sin on their part.
6   From the abdomens of clay jars it emerged,
     and really all there was, by then, was a name.
7   If its thought should occur once to someone,
     joys stay with him, and cares go on their way.

The poem begins with a reference to the preeternal Day of Covenant (Qur'an 7:172), when human souls were in the presence of God and acknowledged Him as Lord. In preeternity they plentifully imbibed God's love, being in a state of union, but now that they have been born into the world, all that remains of God's love in them is a trace, a faint memory (see lines 4 and 6). By rigor and concentration, by reciting God's name (and, depending on the Sufi order, by performing a series of rituals), the mystic tries to return, if momentarily, to the primordial state of union. To quote al-Junayd, the mystic tries, by these means, to go back to that state "in which he was before he was."[38] If God grants this favor and allows the Sufi to taste divine love again, then the Sufi experiences incomparable joy (see lines 5 and 7).

    In line 2 Ibn al-Farid conjures an image of the cosmic wine of divine love being passed around among Sufis at their meeting place or tavern. He uses figurative language to evoke a scene, whereby the full moon, we interpret, represents a goblet; the sun, white wine; the crescent, a fair cupbearer bent in serving; and the stars, bubbles. Sufi commentators are inclined to take the interpretation further. For example, al-Nabulusi (d. 1731) finds that the full-moon cup stands for the Perfect Man, that is, the gnostic or saint in whom God reveals Himself totally and who is filled with God's love. The crescent he reads as the gnostic veiled by his own personality, so that he manifests only part of God's light. He passes around the wine of divine love, that is, he makes known God's names and attributes. Turning to al-Burini (d. 1619), with whom al-Nabulusi is in agreement on this point, "'When wine is mixed with water' means that when pure contemplation is blended with the element of religion, the seeker of God is guided by divine light and like a traveler directed by the stars during his night-journey."[39]

Like Nicholson, though, we would diverge from Sufi commentators "when they handle their text like philologists and try to fasten precise mystical significations upon individual words and phrases"—which they do often. Such commentators are helpful in putting us in mind of Ibn al-Farid's allegory, as Nicholson points out, if perhaps they go too far with many details.[40]

Having considered the main purport of the allegory in A, we would approach this section also from a literary angle and observe how Ibn al-Farid invokes the tradition and artfully manipulates its motifs to express religious meaning. The mood here recalls Abu Nuwas, whose golden beloved is a source of joy. In line 1 specifically, however, Ibn al-Farid recalls Imru' al-Qays; he alludes to the first line of the *Mu'allaqa*. Like Imru' al-Qays, Ibn al-Farid remembers his Beloved. Yet for the pre-Islamic poet, remembrance produces a downpour of tears. For the Sufi, it produces bliss. Ibn al-Farid closes the section with another allusion to pre-Islamic poetry. Normally, the poet, after weeping copiously, leaves his sadness at the abandoned encampment and goes off (the middle section being his recuperative *rahil*). But in this case it is the cares that go off, while happiness stays with the poet. In this manner with an allusion to a *rahil*, albeit one that dispenses with cares, Ibn al-Farid brings the first section to a fitting close.

B

8   Were the boon companions to look on its jar,
     the seal would intoxicate them.

9   Were they to sprinkle it on a person's grave,
     the spirit would return, and the body would quicken.

10   Were they to cast a seriously ill man in the shade of its vine's wall,
     the illness would leave him.

11   Were they to carry a cripple near its tavern, he would walk.
     And mutes, at the recollection of its taste, would speak.

12   Were its fragrance to waft in the East,
     and in the West was a person with a stopped nose, he would smell.

13   Were a man's palm dyed by its cup,
     he would not get lost at night, being in his hand the lodestar.

14   Were it unveiled, as a bride, to one born blind, next day he would emerge seeing.
     And at the sound of its filtering, the deaf would hear.

15   Were a riding party to make for its country,
     and one of the party were snake-bitten, the poison would not harm him.

16   Were a sorcerer to write its letters on the forehead of one possessed,
      the jinn would leave him.

17   Were its name inscribed on the army's banner,
      those under the banner would get drunk.

18   It chastens the boon companions,
      so that the companion with no restraint is led to firmness;

19   So that the one who closes his palm becomes liberal,
      and the one who flies into a rage learns composure.

20   Were the tribe's idiot to kiss its filter,
      the kiss would apprise him of its qualities.

21   People say to me: "Describe it, for you are surely able."
      Indeed, I have some knowledge of its features.

22   Clarity, but not of water, fineness, but not of air,
      light and no fire, spirit without body.

23   Features that guide the eulogists on description's right path,
      so beauty characterizes their poetry and prose.

Section B deals with the wondrous, transformative effects of the wine. The wine even causes writers' and poets' words to flow and be beautiful. The wine's identity, about which Sufi commentators are in agreement, has been explained above. Yet nowhere in the poem does the poet make the identity explicit. As if realizing that he will not be giving away secrets, the audience is represented as asking for a description. Complying, he gives them an esoteric one. The wine has attributes of the four elements—water, air, fire, and earth—without their materiality.

In this central section of the *Khamriyya*, therefore, we find Ibn al-Farid incorporating a tradition from love poetry. It became standard for poets in the 'Abbasid period, which was urban in character and thus conducive to the outbreak of scandals, to conceal the beloved's identity (the lover's breast was a tomb for the secret, it was commonly declared). Nevertheless, everyone wanted a suggestive description. Here Ibn al-Farid describes the wine, but preserves the secret.

A¹

24   At its mention, one unacquainted is thrilled,
      like Nu'm's lover whenever he hears of Nu'm.

25   And they said to me: "You drank sin!"
      No—sin is letting the cup go by.

26   Cheers to the people of the monastery! How often they became inebriated by it!
      They did not truly drink it, however, though that was their wish.

27   From imbibing, I was filled with ecstasy before I was born;
      and the feeling will last when my bones disappear.

28   So take it pure, or mixed with water if you please;
      since turning from the Beloved's mouth itself is the blatant wrong.

29   Behold it in the tavern; seek its light there;
      and by listening to the sweet melodies you will experience it as a gift.

30   For where it dwells, care never lodges,
      just as grief never cohabitates with song.

31   Lo, in a state of blessed intoxication—if only for an hour—
      Time is servant, and you are master.

32   In this world, then, he who stays sober misses the good life,
      and he falls short of resolution, who does not die drunk.

33   So let him weep for himself, whose life is wasted,
      who does not enjoy of it a measure or share.

In the last section we notice a clear return to the themes of the beginning. The mention of the wine elates the person who has never heard of it, as its thought ensures happiness for the person who happens to think of it (line 7). Again we hear of preeternal ecstasy and are informed of the tavern where divine love is now drunk, the Sufi meeting place. And in the last line, Ibn al-Farid calls back Imru' al-Qays, if only to leave him to his weeping. Like Abu Nuwas instead, the Sufis shall revel.

Censurers, we see, make their appearance in this last section. Who might these displeased observers—traditional figures in the poetry—be in this case? Surely, no ones other than the *fuqaha'*, who, given to interpreting literally and to passing judgment, would conclude he was talking about real wine and quickly call his drinking a sin. We may contrast their narrow and intolerant attitude with the broad-mindedness and charity that Ibn al-Farid exhibits in the next line toward the Christian monks. He raises his glass to them. Consider also, on Ibn al-Farid's tolerant attitude, these lines from near the end of the *Great Ta'iyya*:

Though the niche of a mosque be illuminated by the Qur'an,
the altar of a church is not made vain by the Gospel;

Nor vain is the Torah revealed to Moses for his people;
through it rabbis confide with God each night.

So if a devotee prostrates himself in a temple of idols,
do not rush to condemn him fanatically.

For more than one person seemingly removed from idolatry,
in private worships the Dinar.

My warning has reached those who are aware;
and before me the excuses of every people stand:

In no religion have sights been askew;
in no sect have thoughts been perverse.

Those who loved the sun with abandon were not dazed,
inasmuch as its brilliance they adored was from my unveiled splendor.

And if Magians worshiped the Fire—which did not go out
for a thousand years, as history tells us—

Even if they faced elsewhere, even if they did not reveal their intention,
they intended none but me.

They once saw the glow of my light and supposed it a fire,
so that they were led away from the radiance by the rays.[41]

Obviously, Ibn al-Farid recognizes Islam as the true religion, just as he knows Sufism to be the true way to experience God's love. Even so, he respects other faiths and finds commonality between himself and their earnest adherents. Only from those individuals who worship what is plainly worldly (e.g., money) does he disassociate himself; evidently, with all the others he feels a certain spiritual kinship.[42]

The *Khamriyya* ends, having been a celebration of this mysterious wine throughout. One encounters here no mention of asceticism or of the arduous quest. We realize that Ibn al-Farid is trying to excite our interest, to stir our desire, so that we will want to taste the wine. The ecstasy he speaks of here may be experienced: one must follow him on the Sufi Way. And by this poem, he is extending us an invitation.

SUMMARY: THE *KHAMRIYYA* OF IBN AL-FARID

Section	Lines	Structural and Thematic Elements
A	1–7	Sufis drinking divine wine in tavern remembrance of preeternal union with Beloved no shame associated with wine wine sends cares on their way (pre-Islamic poetry evoked)
B	8–23	*description of wondrous effects of wine* *and its marvelous qualities*
A¹	24–33	invitation to join Sufis in tavern recollection of preeternal drunkenness and anticipation of posthumous feeling of intoxication sin is not drinking the wine let person weep for himself who doesn't taste it (pre-Islamic poetry evoked)

13

To Egypt with Love

An Egyptian is whoever truly loves Egypt.
—NAJIB MAHFUZ, "Simsarat al-amir"
(The Prince's Broker, 1979)

OUR LAST POET is Baha' al-Din Zuhayr, a younger contemporary of Ibn al-Farid. He is not as well known as Ibn al-Farid nor as well known as any of the other poets from whose works we have read. In the past quarter century he has attracted scant scholarly attention, and perhaps by many readers and admirers of Arabic literature he has been forgotten. His poetry has a special charm, however, and it would seem that he deserves greater recognition and an acknowledged place in the first rank of poets from the classical period. In this chapter we will recall his life and suggest the milieu in which he operated, read a selection of his amatory and panegyrical verse, and study an extraordinary poem by him.

Baha' al-Din Zuhayr was born in 1186 at Mecca. We may assume that he began attending lessons there in such subjects as literature, history, and religion. At some time while still a young man, he emigrated to Qus, where he completed his formal education.

Qus, it may be pointed out, is located by the Nile some twenty miles north of Luxor at which place the river comes closest to the Red Sea. Egypt then was ruled by the Ayyubids (1171–1250) and was the center of Muslim power, Islam's richest territory,[1] and Qus was Egypt's way station en route to the Red Sea. In this period it was Egypt's third city, after Cairo and Alexandria. Andalusi traveler Ibn Jubayr sojourned there in 1183 and said: "This is a city of fine markets, and of ample amenities, and it has many beings in it because of the comings and goings of pilgrims and merchants from India, the Yemen, and Ethiopia. It is a place which all may come upon, a place of alighting for the traveler, a gathering place for companies of wayfarers, and a meeting-place for pilgrims from the Maghrib [North Africa and al-Andalus], from Misr [Cairo], from Alexandria and from adjoining lands. From here they go into the desert of 'Aydhab, and here they return on their way back from the Hajj."[2]

When Baha' al-Din was twenty-four, Ibn al-Lamti, an Ayyubid favorite, was appointed governor of Qus, and our poet addressed to him a poem of congratulation. He spent the next decade or so in this governor's service, although he also traveled to Cairo and Damascus and composed panegyrics for the sultans al-'Adil (r. 1200–1218) and al-Kamil (r. 1218–38). During this period he developed a close friendship with the Upper Egyptian native Ibn Matruh (d. 1251), who would become an important political poet for the Ayyubids and would remain Baha' al-Din's friend for life. Around the middle 1220s Baha' al-Din left Qus for Cairo and, there, was made secretary to the crown prince, al-Salih Ayyub.

Under the Ayyubids Cairo was thriving, and we may pause here to picture the environment into which Baha' al-Din settled. The city included at least eighteen principal markets. Urbanization was under way, and while the less fortunate were crowding into existing dwellings or adding small additions to them, the rich and well connected were building for themselves pavilions, complete with ample reception areas and Nile views. Numerous gardens lined the river; one of them was called, presumably in reference to the person who was often taken or met there, "Bustan al-Ma'shuq" (Garden of the Beloved). The atmosphere in Cairo was notably pleasant and festive from August to October, on account of high Nile. The atmosphere could also be dreadful this time of year, however, such as in 1201 and 1202, when the river did not rise much.[3] The opening, typically in August, of the canal, the Khalij, was annual cause for celebration. Yet authorities had reason for concern should this event fall during the holy month of Ramadan. For example, in 1198, as we are told: "The water in the Khalij flowed by the grace of God. . . . The people engaged in activities of depravity and idleness in boats on a day of the month of Ramadan and with them were whores who played upon lutes. One heard their voices, their lewdness, and their customers with them in their boats. These men kept neither their hands nor their looks from these women nor did they fear retribution from any emir or civil officer."[4] An enforcement of moral standards did in fact follow this event. However, from reading al-Maqrizi (d. 1442), we infer that such behavior was highly egregious because it was taking place at this time; *A History of the Ayyubid Sultans of Egypt* indicates that wine was prohibited only during Ramadan. Through the rest of the year, the sultan and his men collected a considerable tax sum from its sale.[5]

The 1220s stood out as a very good decade in Cairo. The Franks, who had designs on Egypt, were defeated by al-Kamil at the coastal town of Damietta in 1221. This defeat marked the end of a three-year conflict (the Fifth Crusade), and the expulsion of the Franks from Egypt in 1221 produced a general sense of relief. No major diseases spread through the city in this decade. Meanwhile, Egypt's soil was highly cultivated. And, as al-Maqrizi has said, "Learning and literature flourished under [al-Kamil], and men of distinction resorted to his court."[6]

Before proceeding with our discussion of Baha' al-Din Zuhayr, it might be of interest briefly to go into the subject of what the people around this time thought of those indelible features of the Cairene environment situated across the river: the pyramids, then some thirty-eight hundred years old. As wonders of the ancient world, we know that they were popular to visit. Indeed, something of a "tourist industry" existed at Giza, and guides were available to help visitors scale the pyramids and to lead visitors into a narrow passage dug at one of the bases.[7] The pyramids were described mostly by travelers from North Africa and al-Andalus, since Egypt was on the pilgrimage route. These travelers would disembark at Alexandria after a sea voyage and go south to Qus, passing through Cairo; similarly, they would pass through Cairo on their return.

So what, then, did people think of them? With hieroglyphics a big mystery—their interpretation long forgotten and the Rosetta Stone not yet discovered—people could only conjecture. Ibn Jubayr reports that some believed they were tombs for the tribe of 'Ad and that others disagreed.[8] Only God knows what is correct, he adds.[9] Though Rabbi Benjamin of Tudela, who visited ca. 1171, does not gives his opinion on their original purpose, he writes that they are unlike anything else in the world and remarks that they were constructed by witchcraft.[10] On the feeling of mystery at encountering monuments such as the pyramids, perhaps the most eloquent testament is the following by physician, scientist, and Aristotelian philosopher 'Abd al-Latif al-Baghdadi (d. 1231): "The more you contemplate the antiquities of Egypt, the more your wonder increases, and the more closely you examine them, the more delight you experience. No sooner do you think that you have discerned their meaning than a wilder idea springs into your mind, and just when you think you have learned something from them, you perceive a greater secret beyond it."[11] We cannot resist concluding this short discussion with some observations on the pyramids by the same al-Baghdadi, observations that reveal his admirable empiricism and appreciation for an ancient culture:

> The shape chosen for the pyramids and the sureness of their construction are wondrous, and it is for this reason that they have withstood time—or rather, one might say time has withstood them, so timeless are they. If you give the matter proper thought, you will reach the conclusion that noble minds devoted themselves to building them, pure geniuses dedicated themselves tirelessly to constructing them, brilliant souls put their finest efforts into them, and masters of engineering applied themselves to achieve the limit of possibility. It is as if the pyramids speak to us of their people, inform us of their condition, articulate their sciences and the extent of their genius, and interpret for us their life-stories and history.[12]

Thus, it was in a vibrant and exciting Cairo that Baha' al-Din began to reside. He continued composing—mostly short *ghazals*, as they constitute the bulk of his *Diwan,* although works in other genres were also composed. We shall read here just a few of his love poems to get a flavor for them. Often they take the form of letters or relate to correspondence. For example:

> O Mistress, my heart is with you.
> O Mistress, your servant misses you!
>
> Speak to me, O Mistress,
> and tell me when you'll fulfill your promise.
>
> Do you, I wonder, fondly recall
> the time we spent together, as I do?
>
> And do you, I wonder,
> protect and cherish our love, as I do?
>
> Come visit me!
> Or, if you like, I'll come visit you.
>
> I'm here at home, alone.
> So come over, alone![13]

And:

You're my love, and there's no getting over you,
though men and jinn raise a hue and cry.

Between us are things we've established,
as you know, and mutual faith.

Would that I knew when you'll be alone,
able to listen well, for my heart's full.

I've condensed my reproofs in my letters;
when we meet I'll provide commentary.

But beware lest anyone learn of our conversation—
as they say, "Walls have ears."

O Mistress, show some mercy—I can endure no longer!
Like you, I am flesh and blood.

Your absence has left me feeling chills,
and from sobbing all night my body is wracked.

To what higher authority can I complain of insomnia,
when sleep is said to be Sultan of all?

When will my eyeballs, hot and dry from staring,
look on your blessed face?

Yet perhaps I don't need to persist in asking;
perhaps my Mistress will recall my needs.

I've heard, meanwhile, she's been reproaching me—
how so, when I would give my life for her?

Let her send her phantom as a spy
to report whether my eyelids close at night!

O east wind, be my messenger to her,
and God knows I am jealous of you.

Give my regards to one I won't address—
truly, I'm angry at that angry one!

No, messenger—don't mention my anger!
That was an exaggeration, a lie.

How could I be mad? By God, I'm not mad;
I'm overjoyed that she wants to kill me.

I take pleasure in each pain from her;
her doing harm to me is benefaction.

Every day our envoys come back rebuffed;
every day brings another rebuke.

So I'll use the wind to send you greetings
and be like Solomon in this age.[14]

Usually, our poet is a victim of love, but sometimes his fortunes improve. Here he looks back on a happy occurrence:

God bless a night of union
pure and serene and lovely.

It came suddenly and passed quickly,
though for its shortness, it was complete.

Without fuss or ceremony it came;
no tryst had been arranged and awaited.

So I said when my heart, sensing her arrival,
practically took flight:

"O heart, do you know who's come to visit?
And O eye, do you know who's here?

And you, O moon in the sky, go back to your station—
a glorious moon is spending the night with me here!

And O night, keep on, keep on!
And by God, O daybreak, by God stay away!"

It was truly a night as we would want;
the sweet conversation lasted long.

And wonders came of our gentle reproaches,
wonders whose like are not found in any story.

And off we went together, trailing modesty behind us,
leaving no trace.

We enjoyed privacy—no third was there,
and at dawn our tale was known only to the breeze.[15]

Here he speaks of another positive occasion, a time of reconciliation:

We're acquainted as of today—
our past is rolled up!

Nothing happened or went by;
you didn't say anything, nor did I!

And now, if there must be reproach,
let it be fair and kind.

For I was told things about you,
and you were told things about me.

Absence lasted long enough;
you tasted it, and so did I.

Now, all that being no more,
how nice it is to meet anew![16]

The last *ghazal* we shall read describes quite a bold way of courtship, which he may have resorted to at times. The poem perhaps reminds one of Abu Nuwas:

If only you had seen me and my beloved
when she escaped from me like an excited fawn!

She started running, and I started running after her—
if only you had seen us traversing the town!

She said, "Stop following me." "No," I said.
"What do you want from me?" she asked. "Oh, a little something."

She blushed and lowered her head,
and pride turned her away.

I almost kissed her right there, in front of everyone.
Had I done so, it would not have been wrong.[17]

From this sample, one gets a sense for Baha' al-Din's love poetry. We are struck, in particular, by the theatricality of his verse. He represents emotion through situation and dialogue, evoking a scene. Even a *khamriyya* by him is apt to be less about the wine than the interaction between him and the cupbearer. For instance:

A friend, with whom I always find myself
feeling free and easy,

Came towards me with a bright goblet
that joined the moon's and Pleiades' light.

"Here," she said. "Take it."
"No, you," I replied. "Enjoy!

Don't compound my love-drunkenness
with intoxication from wine."

She lowered her head bashfully
and turned away.

"No no!" I said. "Here, by God,
give me a copious drink.

I shall not disobey your order
nor violate one of your prohibitions."

So she gave me a vintage
that turns a sheikh into a young man;

That shows you right as wrong
and wrong as right.

Time and again she refreshed me,
and I refreshed her.

We remained thus,
until morning revealed its bright face.

Oh, what a night it was,
one whose like we shall never see![18]

We may also point out the prevalence of short meters in his love poetry and
the simple diction. Furthermore, Baha' al-Din not uncommonly incorporates
in his love poetry proverbs and adapted colloquial expressions.[19] Though these
poems are still classical in form and language, they symbolize a bridge toward
popular poetry.

We need hardly add that they were very well liked. It was said, "Friends are not
reproached nor are beloveds addressed in correspondences as in the poetry of Baha'
al-Din Zuhayr."[20] His verse was called, in admiration, *al-sahl al-mumtani'* (the easy
poetry that's impossible to imitate). And one Sa'd al-Din Muhammad attested:

The poetry of Baha' al-Din Zuhayr has a special standing,
for it has claimed much of our hearts.

It's so elegant and fine that I've remarked,
"Perhaps he's trying to bring out meanings without using words."[21]

The initial residence in Cairo for Baha' al-Din, a golden period in his life, lasted about seven years. In 1232 he left Egypt, accompanying al-Salih Ayyub— who, because he had been exhibiting tyrannical tendencies and acquiring a personal guard of Mamluks, or Turkish slave-soldiers, was no longer the heir apparent—on an expedition to upper Mesopotamia. It had been decided that al-Salih should impose Ayyubid authority there and then stay as the sultan's vicegerent, while his younger brother 'Adil was groomed for the throne. Al-Salih took possession of the fortresses of Amid and Kayfa, located in what is now southeastern Turkey, and made the latter his base. As before, Baha' al-Din served as his secretary.

How Baha' al-Din felt at being away from Egyptian friends we may deduce from these lines, which he included in an epistle:

I write this letter from Amid
out of a surfeit of emotion.

By God, since I left you,
no watering hole I've come to has been clear.

So will my remaining time on earth
aid me and take me back?

How many vows I make in each mosque
for your sake!

I would give the rest of my life
to spend a single day with you.[22]

We gather that, often, he felt nostalgia for the place that had become his home. It is probable he composed these lines at this stage, while he was abroad:

God bless Egypt
and the memory of times spent there.

How lovely is the Nile,
with its myriad craft going upstream and down.

Sing no more of the Tigris and the Euphrates—
make your music of the Nile!

Sing to me of the nights passed on Roda,[23]
and at Giza, surrounded by delights;

Amid greenery and flowers resembling a peacock's plumage,
under an azure sky, gem-studded like a falcon's breast;

Where the Khalij winds like a speckled serpent,
through gardens and little paradises;

With a fine companion,
forthcoming with all we like.

She is everything you would want in a person:
accomplished, sweet-tempered, and beautiful.

Oh, how I sigh for those good times,
for those good times gone by![24]

After Sultan al-Kamil's death in 1238, Baha' al-Din's master, al-Salih Ayyub, was able to negotiate an exchange of territories with al-Jawad Yunus, the unpopular prince of Damascus and nominal deputy of the new sultan, al-'Adil II. This transfer, of course, brought al-Salih Ayyub closer to his ambition: Egypt. However, in 1239 he was captured in Palestine while staying there with a small contingent. His captor, al-Nasir Dawud, prince of Karak (east of the Jordan River), though no ally of the new sultan, sought to benefit in some way by holding al-Salih Ayyub. The former crown prince was kept at Karak and treated with courtesy. Baha' al-Din, meanwhile, waited loyally at Nablus. After seven months al-Nasir Dawud released al-Salih Ayyub, and just one month later, in May 1240, Sultan al-'Adil II, by now a recognized spendthrift and hedonist, was seized by his own men. Forthwith these men invited al-Salih Ayyub to mount the throne. Al-Salih Ayyub entered Cairo triumphantly and became the new sultan, and al-'Adil II was consigned to a secure place in the citadel (he was later strangled). Baha' al-Din, for his part, was made secretary of the chancery, a promotion to the level of vizier. As chancery secretary, he would be responsible for protocol and royal correspondence.

Pursuant to recalling the circumstances of Baha' al-Din's life, it is useful here to make a few remarks about the rule (1240–49) of his master. Al-Salih Ayyub was much given to building, and his reign saw significant changes to the landscape of Cairo. He demolished the pavilions on the island of Roda and built a palace complex there, evidently so he could be surrounded by water. He also constructed, in addition to other edifices, a large madrassa (named al-Salihiyya, after him) for the teaching of canon law. This monument, which includes his mausoleum at one end, remains partially standing today. Al-Salih Ayyub likewise changed the military significantly. He greatly increased, through procurement, the proportion of those Turkish slave-soldiers, the Mamluks, a move that would have major implications for the political future of Egypt. By the end of his rule, they numbered about a thousand and formed the core of the army. He quartered them on Roda. We last mention, regarding al-Salih Ayyub's rule, that the mood around him seems to have been serious. Al-Maqrizi relates:

> Al-Salih was a courageous and resolute king, but he was much dreaded because of his great severity and his haughty disposition, combined with a proud spirit and high ambition. He was highly decorous, chaste and innocent of obscenity, preserving his tongue from grossness of language, and shunning ribaldry and trifling. He was extremely grave, and compelled silence, so that when he came out from his harem to his Mamluks, they were seized with trembling at the sight of him, being in terror of him, and not one of them remained beside the other. When he sat with his companions he held silence, stirred by no motions, unmoving. Those who sat with him were as though they had birds on their heads. If he spoke to one of his close circle, his words were few, and his gravity extreme. . . . And when he went apart, no one might approach him. Documents were taken to him by slaves for his signing, and the slaves withdrew with them to the Secretary of the Chancery. No officer of state might deal himself with any matter, but had

to refer it to him by correspondence through a slave. With this acuteness and aloofness, he never looked the person to whom he was talking in the eye, because of his shyness and bashfulness. Nor was a foul expression ever heard from him against any of his slaves, and the most he would say, if reproaching anyone, was "Disobedient one," and he would not go beyond that term.[25]

During this decade, Baha' al-Din enjoyed prominence in Cairo. Biographer Ibn Khallikan (d. 1282), who describes him as "one of the most accomplished men of his time, and not only the best writer of prose and verse, but the best calligraphist," got to know Baha' al-Din in this period; the poet eventually gave him a certificate of proficiency in the study of his *Diwan*. About Baha' al-Din he says: "I found him far surpassing all that I heard of his good nature, and of his great affability and gentleness of disposition. He possessed great influence with his master, who esteemed him greatly, and never entrusted his secrets to any one else. But for all this, he never used his influence except for good, and he benefited many people by his kind intervention and good offices."[26] The poet also met the famous Ibn Sa'id al-Maghribi (d. 1286), compiler of *Kitab al-mughrib fi hula al-Maghrib* (The Extraordinary Account of the Ornaments of the West), and the two became friends. Ibn Sa'id informed him that his poetry was very popular in al-Andalus. During one of their literary meetings, incidentally, the conversation turned to Ibn Zaydun and his *Nuniyya*. "Your country of al-Andalus did not produce another amorous poet like him," Baha' al-Din reportedly said, "and he was, I believe, sincere in his love."[27]

Yet the decade was not all positive for our poet, and it did not end well. In 1246 he was sent on an important embassy to Aleppo to extradite al-Salih Isma'il, a dangerous rival of the sultan being held at the time by the prince al-Nasir Yusuf. Baha' al-Din returned months later, empty-handed. And around 1249 he somehow crossed the sultan. He was summarily dismissed from court.

Soon after, in November 1249, the sultan died of illness. He had been defending Egypt at the northern town of al-Mansura against another Crusade.[28] In the room where he died, it was suddenly obvious that Egypt had no leader. Shajarat al-Durr (Tree of Pearls), his wife, decided at this juncture to conceal the sultan's death from all but a select few until their son, Turanshah, could be recalled from Kayfa in upper Mesopotamia (amazingly, she succeeded in carrying out her plan, issuing forged decrees in her late husband's name, with the army commander, until Turanshah arrived). In February 1250 Turanshah reached Egypt and was proclaimed sultan, and al-Salih Ayyub was buried with ceremony in Cairo. Our poet was called back into service and dispatched to Aleppo to inform al-Nasir Yusuf of the death and the succession.

In April 1250 Egypt's army decisively defeated the Crusaders. Turanshah's hold on power would seem to have been ensured. As it turned out, he lasted only a month after the victory. He brusquely sidelined his father's officers and went about installing men from Kayfa in their places. Worse, and what proved fatal, however, was his hostility to the Mamluks, who had just played a central role in saving Egypt. That they lived in his palace complex does not seem to have deterred him from causing offense. On this subject, al-Maqrizi tells us, "When drunk at night, he would cause the candles to be collected before him and with his sword strike their tops so that they were severed, and say: 'Thus I will treat the Mamluks,' calling each one by his name."[29] After a banquet on May 2 in the Roda citadel, a number of them assassinated him. Thus ended the Ayyubid dynasty in Egypt and began the reign of the Turkish Mamluks, which would last more than two and a half centuries.

Baha' al-Din was in Damascus in July of this year when al-Nasir Yusuf swept down from Aleppo and took the city (previously it had been an Egyptian possession). The poet composed a panegyric of seventy-one lines for him. From the work we will read below, it would appear that Baha' al-Din was not well remunerated for his long panegyric. Yet we can appreciate, nevertheless, that al-Nasir Yusuf represented the poet's best hope at this stage. In 1250 Baha' al-Din was sixty-four years old. Al-Nasir Yusuf, the young prince and remaining Ayyubid strong actor, sought restoration of Ayyubid rule in Egypt (his attack there in 1251 failed, and in 1260 the dynasty came to a complete end when al-Nasir Yusuf was killed personally by the leader of the Mongols). Let us read, then, his subsequent, rather poignant, panegyric, which suggests that Baha' al-Din had become a needy poet. The poem was probably recited to al-Nasir Yusuf in the Damascus citadel.

Your illustrious road is most noble and exalted,
your kind action most beneficent and compassionate.

I know of your generosity, your self-control, your piety,
but by my life, you are more than what I know.

I am devoted, by God, in my allegiance to you,
and about this, by God, I do not need to swear.

I feel I should not ever complain to you:
I come forward and then go back again.

Yet your goodness to me, others have wished to pare;
and far be it that your goodness be called lacking!

Up to now I have never known detraction,
and surely your like will not allow detraction in a case such as mine.

So if you protect me from it, you will be to me a lofty fortress
where I am secure and raised above others.

Alas, but for affairs better left unmentioned,
I would turn from complaint and shun it.

For I know there is a side of you
that will always please and succor me.

Hopes speak to me of a single look directed my way
that would turn the world into a resplendent bride.

Indeed, it is not far-fetched you should bestow favor on me
that restores my former glory and doubles it.

And if you are affectionate, then loss of wealth is the easiest loss to bear;
boon from you easily compensates.

⁂

All I wish for is a small stronghold of my own;
no other deficiency do I lament.

My spirit, thank God, rejects degradation,
shedding not its resolve or its patience.

It raises edifices of power and distinction to inhabit,
and arms itself with the sword and the Qur'an.

But I also have wives and small children to consider,
and none but myself shows them any kindness.[30]

I grow concerned when the gentlest breeze blows on them;
out of pity my heart nearly breaks.

My joy is seeing them content and well-off,
while my sadness lies in seeing them poor.

I have stored for them, though, God's benevolence and al-Nasir Yusuf,
and by God, they shall not perish as long as Yusuf is Yusuf!

꙳ ꙳ ꙳

I impose difficulty on my poetry when I complain,
as if I am calling on it to do something foreign.

Heretofore its mode has been every love poem
whereat minds are ravished and hearts ache.

In lines of love it reveals magnificent splendor,
while in petitions it exhibits strain.

And still my poetry has in it a quiet place for the soul,
a retreat for the heart, and an outlet for emotion.

In it the fair and black-eyed gazelle meets you;
in it the slender branch bends your way.

Yes, I used to bemoan passion's throes
inflicted on me by each unjust beauty.

Here was one coming near flirtatiously;
there another haughtily strutting off.

Now I complain to you. And though doing so
is no shame, it irks me anyway.

To you, Salah al-Din, I've told my tale;
and whatever you say, my lord, is best.[31]

Unfortunately, life got no better for Baha' al-Din. He returned to Egypt in 1252 and spent the rest of his life there secluded in his house. It is said that he gradually sold all his possessions, including his library of roughly five thousand volumes, to feed himself. In 1258 a pestilence raged through Cairo, and Baha' al-Din was one of its victims. He was buried in the Qarafa Cemetery, southeast of the city.

We will now read and analyze a novel work (No. 237) by Baha' al-Din Zuhayr describing the Cairo experience of a merchant.[32] Apparently, this poem was composed during the last period of our poet's life.

A

1   I entered Cairo wealthy, hardly trying to hide:
2   With twenty loads of silk, ditto of colored cloth,
3   And an ample supply of pearls and gleaming jewels.
4   With me also were Mamluk Turks, handsome and clean.

B

5   Then I went forth, open-palmed, grandly requiting;
6   Settling affairs amid amaranth and choicest wine;
7   Fraternizing and befriending at every turn.
8   And with weighty merchants—my peers—I got involved.
9   Daily I offered them trays piled with goat and lamb.

A¹

10   Gradually, I sold every valuable I had.
11   The sale even consumed my mattress and blanket.
12   So I bade farewell in Cairo to all that wealth.
13   There I became poor and deprived of modesty.
14   Now here I am departing: bare, starved, and shoeless.

This poem is unique in Baha' al-Din's *Diwan* in that it tells a story from another person's perspective. Such a point of view, one finds, adds a semblance of credibility to the story. Unique also is the choice of subject—a merchant's experience. In fact, both the point of view and the subject matter make this poem very exceptional in classical Arabic poetry. One thinks here of popular literature, and of *The Thousand and One Nights* especially, whose text happens to come to us from the Mamluk period. *The Thousand and One Nights* includes numerous first-person stories about changes in fortune, stories involving merchants as well as others not belonging to the social elite.

Yet besides telling us a succinct, interesting story, what is this poem telling us? Why, indeed, did the poet compose it? We would note, as a basis for discussion, that the merchant embodies some classic Arabian values: generosity, bonhomie, hospitality. One might be reminded here of al-Khansa''s brother Sakhr, slaughtering camels and accommodating guests, or of Labid, exchanging his herd for wineskins so he and his friends can roister. Nor did these values, by the way, lose their importance in the Islamic era (although, of course, in the Islamic era, throwing drinking parties was no longer a condoned way to express one's congeniality).[33] But if we recall the pre-Islamic age for a moment and think of its warrior hero, we notice a big difference between his situation and the position of the merchant. The pre-Islamic hero, after giving away all his wealth, could always go on a raid and acquire more wealth. Our merchant, by contrast, must succeed in a competitive business environment. He should be generous, but he must also profit. The established moral code thus plainly conflicts with the contemporary urban reality and its climate of sharp business practice. With this poem, we find, Baha' al-Din is making an ironic commentary on tradition and change, on the incompatibility of classic values with life in contemporary Cairo.[34]

As James T. Monroe and Mark F. Pettigrew have observed in a recent article (cited in chapter 11), when literary conditions deteriorate at court, talented authors are apt to innovate. Ibn Quzman, we remember, developed the colloquial *zajal* at a time when the Berber-speaking Almoravids were ruling al-Andalus. It would seem that Baha' al-Din is innovating here with poetry in the form of personal narrative to convey effectively his ironic message. When the court fails to nurture Arabic literature, moreover, authors tend to write social criticism. One is reminded perhaps foremost of Badi' al-Zaman al-Hamadhani, who lived in the tenth and eleventh centuries when the Persian-speaking Buwayhids ruled Iraq.

"Men are asses," the trickster protagonist of his *Maqamat,* Abu al-Fath al-Iskan-dari, says. "Compete with, and excel them, till thou has obtained from them what thou desirest, then quit."[35] But when a knave like Abu al-Fath succeeds splen-didly, as he does in the *Maqamat,* then society is being criticized. By the same token, when a good, generous merchant fails dramatically, as in the case of this poem, society is being criticized.

Disgruntled authors are likewise apt to criticize authority figures, although usually obliquely. Ibn Quzman, we recall, faulted the jurists for their strict legal-ism through negative example.[36] Baha' al-Din, through the story of the merchant, similarly criticizes authority figures insofar as he implies they have not fostered an environment in which virtue prevails. Admittedly, his criticism of them (we suppose these figures to be Mamluks, as it is hard to imagine the poem's situation occurring to him and his writing of social criticism about contemporary Cairo except in the last period of his life) is muted; he even adds the detail about the new group of slave-soldiers being handsome and clean. Elsewhere, however, his criticism of authority, while still discreet, is more direct. These lines in the *Diwan* attract attention:

How often we used to pray
for a change in government!

And we rejoiced when that old one passed away,
only to find the new one even worse.[37]

Again, we would suppose he is referring to Mamluks, to a Mamluk government. During the last eight years of his life, power changed hands among them several times. Perhaps he was put in a frame of mind to write these lines after the first major change, which occurred in 1254.

By criticizing those persons in power, if discreetly, Baha' al-Din anticipates an important trend in Arabic literature. Ibn Daniyal (d. 1310), for example, would soon pointedly satirize the Mamluks. In one of his shadow plays, the character of a poet "eulogizes" the character of a Mamluk emir using language filled with double entendres. Because the emir does not understand Arabic well, he thinks the poet is flattering him, and so at the end he rewards him; actually, the poet has been tarring him with obscenities.[38] And in a witty poem composed following the 1267 crackdown on vice by Sultan Baybars, Ibn Daniyal elegizes Satan. He furthermore implies that, with Satan now dead, Egypt has become a dull paradise.[39] Nor would 'Ali al-Baghdadi (fl. ca. 1340), author of a collection of bawdy stories, be especially kind to the ruling Mamluks. In the stories, as Robert Irwin has pointed out, "The Turkish élite are portrayed as greedy and stupid—and some of them cannot speak Arabic properly."[40]

This discussion has led us into the literature of another era, however. Though the poem invites us to look forward, it seems fitting to return finally to our poet. In conclusion, therefore, we would say that this ironic, subtly critical work seems to reflect Baha' al-Din's attitude toward the end of his life, after having come to Cairo with excellent prospects some three decades before, and after having enjoyed so many good times there.

SUMMARY: NO. 237

Section	Lines	Structural and Thematic Elements
A	1–4	merchant enters Cairo in grand style; list of imports
B	5–9	merchant requites generously, enjoys sensual pleasures and befriends, hosts counterparts lavishly
A¹	10–14	sale of possessions; merchant departs Cairo bare

Conclusion

> What we call the beginning is often the end
> And to make an end is to make a beginning.
>
> —T. S. ELIOT, *Four Quartets*

HAVING THUS TRACED the course of classical Arabic poetry from the sixth century to the thirteenth, in locations from the East to the West, and through the major genres, we have reached a convenient stopping point. Proceeding chronologically, one crosses into what is considered the postclassical period. This age begins around 1250, with the establishment of Mamluk rule in Egypt in that year and the sack of Baghdad by the Mongols, which formally put an end to the 'Abbasid Caliphate, in 1258.

Literary historian H. A. R. Gibb, looking back at the classical period, has divided it into four ages: the Heroic Age (ca. 500–622), the Age of Expansion (622–750), the Golden Age (750–1055), and the Silver Age (1055–1258).[1] We would accept this division and naming of epochs, albeit with an important reservation. Applied to our poets, we see that it categorizes Imru' al-Qays, al-Shanfara, Labid, and al-Khansa' as poets of the Heroic Age; Jamil and Jarir as poets of the Age of Expansion; Abu Nuwas, Abu Tammam, al-Mutanabbi, and Ibn Zaydun as poets of the Golden Age; and Ibn Quzman, Ibn al-Farid, and Baha' al-Din Zuhayr as poets of the Silver Age. Our reservation concerns the last designation, which implies a clear decline in the said era from previous glory. Based on our reading of some of their works, any one of Ibn Quzman, Ibn al-Farid, and Baha' al-Din Zuhayr may reasonably be championed among the poets. Surely, their *Diwans*— innovative, engaging, meaningful—do not represent a decline in the quality of classical Arabic poetry; it would seem that, in terms of literary creativity, the Golden Age continued.

Other literary historians have been more severe, speaking of an "Age of Decadence" ('Asr al-Inhitat), a period of extreme conventionality and general bad taste, beginning after the death of the brilliant Syrian poet al-Ma'arri in 1058 and lasting approximately eight centuries until the dawn of the modern period (1850–present).[2] Yet the poetry dating from 1250 to 1850, the putative postclassical period, is by far the most neglected in Arabic literature. It may well be that this period will not seem so benighted after scholars shed light on it (in this regard, the recently published *Cambridge History of Arabic Literature in the Post-Classical Period* is a most welcome contribution and should prove to be an excellent starting point for further specialized research).

Moving forward into the modern period, we see that the classical poetic tradition in fact continues and remains very much a part of Arab culture. Poets such as al-Barudi (d. 1904), Ahmad Shawqi (d. 1932), Hafiz Ibrahim (d. 1932), al-Zahawi (d. 1936), al-Rusafi (d. 1945), al-Khuri (known as al-Akhtal al-Saghir, "the Little al-Akhtal" [d. 1968]), al-Jawahiri (d. 1998), and Fadwa Tuqan (d. 2004), while giving voice to personal feelings and responding to contemporary circumstances, have been clearly influenced by the ancient poets, exploited classical forms, and made use of classical themes in their work. In fiction classical motifs are also developed and famous lines frequently evoked by allusion.[3] In the area of drama classical poetry has inspired works such as Shawqi's *Majnun Layla* (Crazy about Layla [1931], about the legendary 'Udhri lover modeled after Jamil, Qays) and *Amirat al-Andalus* (The Princess of al-Andalus [1932], about the daughter of the renowned poet-king of Seville, al-Mu'tamid ibn 'Abbad [d. 1095]); the contemporary Palestinian al-Hakawati troupe has dramatized not uncommonly the romance based on the life of the pre-Islamic *Mu'allaqa* poet 'Antara. In the field of music new *qasidas* have featured prominently in the repertory of the supremely popular Egyptian singer Umm Kulthum; one of her best-loved songs is a *qasida* rendition titled "Al-Atlal" (The Encampment Traces [1966]).[4] The legacy of classical Arabic poetry endures, and continues to inspire the work of Arab artists, both literary and otherwise.

Stepping back and expanding our scope for a moment, we may observe the direct and extended influence of classical Arabic poetry on a number of other poetic traditions. Stefan Sperl and Christopher Shackle, in the introduction to their second edited volume of *qasida* poetry from Islamic Asia and Africa, discuss this widespread influence. The classical Arabic ode—as characterized by its monorhyme, single meter, Bedouin provenance and retention often of desert themes, and public performance typically—gave rise in the tenth century, they point out, to Hebrew and Persian *qasida* forms.[5] The Hebrew and Persian odes were generally panegyrical in nature, as were the Arabic *qasida*s at that time. Later, in the thirteenth century, the Arabic *qasida* began to be used extensively to convey religious meaning—notably in the hands of Ibn al-Farid—and this trend led to the emergence of devotional *qasida* poetry in other literatures. In modern times the *qasida* has been used also to express secular, nationalist, and humanist themes in a variety of literatures, Arabic among them. Altogether, the originally Arabic *qasida* has been adapted in Asia and Africa since the tenth century by poets working in Hebrew, Persian, Ottoman and modern Turkish, Kurdish, Pashto, Urdu, Punjabi, Sindhi, Malaysian, Indonesian, Swahili, Fulani, and Hausan literary traditions. Sperl and Shackle, describing all this adaptation through a conceit, speak of a great tree. Its roots are the ancient Bedouin tribal poetry, its trunk the *qasida* poetry of the 'Abbasid period, and its branches and foliage the various outgrowths in different literatures since that time.[6] Over the long course of history, the early verse created in the Arabian Peninsula turned out to be the beginning of one of the major poetic strands of world literature.

Returning to our subject, we affirm that it has been our belief that good poems in all literatures possess organic unity and indicate that we have merely tried to show, in accordance with this belief, that the Arabs during the classical period composed their share of good poems.

Yet it might be claimed, perhaps, that the poets were unaware of overall coherence, that if some poems hold together, it is due to fortune, not craft. We would respond first by exhibiting the poetry and asking a simple question. Is it by chance that, in the centers of the poems, we find telling personal statements (see the poems by Imru' al-Qays and Jamil); imagery of hungry, stoical wolves (see al-Shanfara's *su'luk* poem, *Lamiyyat al-'Arab*); a symbol of immortality (see Labid's ode about sacrificing the self for the good of the tribe); an image of a mountain with a fire blazing at the summit (see al-Khansa''s elegy for her eminent and hospitable brother Sakhr); a barb about being ignorant of Islam (see the satire by Jarir); transactional statements (see the apology/panegyric by Abu Tammam and the 'Id poems by Ibn Quzman); an allusion to impending doom for the enemy (see the panegyric by al-Mutanabbi); a description of conviviality and generous action (see the merchant poem by Baha' al-Din Zuhayr); and an attractive description of the poem's subject (see the *khamriyya*s by Abu Nuwas and Ibn al-Farid as well as Ibn Zaydun's love poem to Wallada)? These elements would seem to have been centered intentionally, insofar as thematically they are the nuclei of the poems.[7] Furthermore, we would bring in other evidence and ask a few more questions. Is it again a mere coincidence that Ibn Zaydun elegantly says, "Yours is the central jewel in the necklace of states,"[8] thereby expressing his essential message, in the middle of a panegyric? Also, should we make anything of the fact that elsewhere he boasts of the symmetry in his poems?[9] And is there any significance to the countless recurrences, in the utterances of poets and critics, of the comparison of a poem to a necklace? Could the comparison's perceived appropriateness to them have something to do with the expectation that, in picturing a necklace, one sees a number of individual elements that hang together as a single entity, a beginning and an end that connect, a symmetrical arrangement, and, in the center, a particular element that captures one's attention?[10] Last, concerning the poet Ibn al-Rumi (d. 896), what are we to make of his concluding a poem thusly, after he has returned to the theme of the introduction:

> Take, then, this as a pearl necklace well strung,
> whose ending resembles its beginning.[11]

Was he aware of what he was saying?

The evidence surely suggests that the composers of our sample of poems were conscious artists and that they carefully constructed integrated, whole works. Nor would we deny, for that matter, that original audiences and readers appreciated the organic unity in these poems. Samuel Taylor Coleridge has said, "The sense of beauty subsists in simultaneous intuition of the relation of parts, each to each, and of all to a whole."[12] Alexander Pope was of the same view. In "An Essay on Criticism" he writes:

> 'Tis not a lip, or eye, we beauty call,
> But the joint force and full result of all.

We would argue that Coleridge and Pope are speaking here of a universal way of perceiving beauty. Can we really suppose that Arabs during the classical period saw beauty instead in the constituent part?

What about, however, all those hyperfocused ancient critics, oblivious to everything beyond the line?[13] In their defense, we would submit that they doubtlessly thought it was more instructive to criticize by picking out concise, easily apprehensible examples—that is, examples contained in a single line. Their judgments, if pointedly referenced, would be more likely to be remembered and heeded by poets and readers alike. Perhaps, though, we should step aside briefly and let a few of these critics speak for themselves. The following passages have been quoted before—and discredited also in some cases because of a lack of lengthy, accompanying proof texts—but it may be that we see them in a new light after having read a number of poems. Here, first, is Ibn Tabataba (d. 934) on the subject of coherence:

> If poetry is based on independent passages [like those] of epistles, on self-contained maxims, and on proverbs marked by their conciseness, then its composition is not good. No, the whole *qasida* ought to be like one utterance in the resemblance of its beginning and its ending, in its texture, beauty, purity, the vigor of its diction, the accuracy of its motifs, and the correctness of its composition. The transition of the poet from each motif he produces to another should be subtle ... so that the *qasida* turns out as if it were cast in one piece ... without any contradiction between its motifs, nor any feebleness in its structures or artificiality in its texture; while every word requires what follows, and what follows is dependent on it and in need of it.[14]

Next, Abu Hilal al-'Askari (d. after 1010) on the same subject: "You ought to make your discourse [whether poetry or prose] such that its beginning resembles its end, its neck corresponding to its croup; its extremities should not disagree with one another, nor should its borders be incongruous. Let each word stand alongside its sister, paired with its counterpart."[15] We now cite from a commentary by philosopher Ibn Sina (d. 1037) on Aristotle's *Poetics*. Although these thoughts are the Stagirite's, Ibn Sina evidently considered them pertinent to his Arab audience so as to quote them:

> The structure of poetry, then, should be of this quality: it should be arranged with a beginning, middle and ending; the most important part should be in the middle; it should have a symmetrical measure; its theme should be limited, and

neither excessive nor mixed with what is not appropriate to that kind of verse; and it should be such that if one part was removed, the whole would be marred and incomplete. If the true nature of a thing lies in order, and if this order disappears, the thing will lose its effect, for it makes its effect through being a whole. A whole is a thing preserved through its parts; it is not a whole when one of its parts is not present.[16]

The Andalusi philosopher Ibn Rushd (d. 1198) made a new commentary on the *Poetics;* he likewise quoted the above passage. We will not read from his *Talkhis kitab Aristutalis fi al-shiʻr* (Summary of Aristotle's Book on Poetry), but rather from his preface to it, in which he underscores the Greek philosopher's broad relevance. He says: "The objective of this discourse is to select from Aristotle's book on Poetry those general rules that are common either to all peoples, or at least to their great majority."[17]

Turning from theoretical discussions to visible practice, in order to add a last point to this short defense in behalf of the critics, we mention the method of philologist al-Marzuqi (d. 1030), who inter alia wrote a commentary to Abu Tammam's *Hamasa* anthology. Andras Hamori has studied his scheme of reading as reflected in his commentary. He points out that "al-Marzuqi is clearly asking such questions as 'Why is this bit where it is?' and 'How does it go with the rest?'"[18] In sum, it seems that ancient critics were not necessarily obsessed with the poetic line. A goodly number of them, one gathers, had global concerns.

Nevertheless, we would not try, by any means, to defend all the early critics. Certainly, a percentage were, shall we say, nitpickers. Yet if some classical Arab critics did not see the forest for the trees, should we be at all surprised? To quote Samuel Johnson, "Some seem always to read with the microscope of criticism, and employ their whole attention upon minute elegance, or faults scarcely visible to common observation." His forceful elaboration on this remark, which leaves nothing else to be said about quibbling critics, is worth quoting in full:

The dissonance of a syllable, the recurrence of the same sound, the repetition of a particle, the smallest deviation from propriety, the slightest defect in construction or arrangement, swell before their eyes into enormities. As they discern with great exactness, they comprehend but a narrow compass, and know nothing of the justness of the design, the general spirit of the performance, the artifice of connection, or the harmony of the parts; they never conceive how small a proportion that which they are busy in contemplating bears to the whole, or how the petty inaccuracies with which they are offended, are absorbed and lost in general excellence.[19]

We would not, however, wish to approach the conclusion of our study while thinking about how a sharply critical minority looked on such poetry as we have been reading. So let us try to recall the reading (or listening) experience of the majority, a group that we can be assured was far more receptive to what the poets had to say. In *What is Art?* Tolstoy has proposed, "Art is a human activity consisting in this, that one man consciously, by means of certain external signs, hands on to others feelings he has lived through, that others are infected by these feelings and also experience them."[20] We would accept this succinct definition and suggest that it describes the reaction of our audiences to the poems. Critic Ibn Qutayba, in *Kitab al-shi'r wa-al-shu'ara'*, quotes an anonymous appreciator of poetry who says, "The best poet is the one in whose poetry you are currently engrossed."[21] This anonymous person, it can be observed, intimates the reaction Tolstoy has described to art. The same reaction, namely, becoming caught up in the work and feeling the author's emotions, is discernible also among the modern Bedouin tribe of Awlad 'Ali, located in northern Egypt near the border with Libya. Lila Abu-Lughod writes, disclosing the reaction of Awlad 'Ali and their critical perspective as well: "They attach special weight to the messages conveyed in poetry and are moved, often to tears, by the sentiments expressed. In fact, their definition of a good poem is that it moves the people who hear it. They say, 'Beautiful poetry makes you cry,' and note that poems can move others to change their minds and actions."[22] Such responses to beautiful poetry, presumably, have been occurring among Arab audiences through the centuries.

All this is to suggest that the early audiences, though admiring, to be sure, the poet's felicitous expression, were attuned to the poet's message. And this point brings us back to structure. Julie Scott Meisami has keenly perceived, in this regard, that "structure does not just keep the poem from falling apart, or the audience from losing track; it is, rather, a means by which the poet conveys meaning."[23] Hence the importance of James T. Monroe's contribution to the study of Arabic literature in alerting us to the incidence of ring composition. We now have clear understanding of a common way Arab poets chose to organize their poems. We may not have in our possession a master key, but we do possess a key that seems to open a great many doors. Simply stated: Understanding the structure of a particular work enables us to interpret its meaning. And interpreting meaning, of course, is what literary criticism is all about.

Finally, for those readers who may have found something appealing in these poems, we might add that the study of classical Arabic poetry remains largely an unexplored field. A great number of precious literary works lie waiting to be discovered. The only necessary skill to assist in bringing them to our awareness is a proficiency in Arabic, and acquiring this skill itself promises rich rewards. There is much work to be done.

Abbreviations

Notes

Glossary

Bibliography

Index

Abbreviations

ASQ	*Arab Studies Quarterly*
CHALABL	*Cambridge History of Arabic Literature: 'Abbasid Belles-Lettres.* Ed. Julia Ashtiany et al. Cambridge: Cambridge Univ. Press, 1990.
CHALLA	*Cambridge History of Arabic Literature: The Literature of al-Andalus.* Ed. María Menocal et al. Cambridge: Cambridge Univ. Press, 2000.
CHALUP	*Cambridge History of Arabic Literature: Arabic Literature to the End of the Umayyad Period.* Ed. A. F. L. Beeston et al. Cambridge: Cambridge Univ. Press, 1983.
EI¹	*Encyclopedia of Islam.* 1st ed. 4 vols. Leiden: Brill, 1913–38.
EI²	*Encyclopedia of Islam.* 2nd ed. 11 vols. Leiden: Brill, 1960–2002.
IJMES	*International Journal of Middle Eastern Studies*
IQ	*Islamic Quarterly*
JAL	*Journal of Arabic Literature*
JAOS	*Journal of the American Oriental Society*
JNES	*Journal of Near Eastern Studies*

Notes

INTRODUCTION

1. Jirji Zaydan (d. 1914) quoted in Vicente Cantarino, *Arabic Poetics in the Golden Age* (Leiden: Brill, 1975), epigraph.

2. Wilhelm Ahlwardt quoted in Jaroslav Stetkevych, "Arabic Poetry and Assorted Poetics," in *Islamic Studies: A Tradition and Its Problems,* ed. Malcolm H. Kerr (Malibu: Udena, 1980), 112; A. S. Tritton, s.v. "Shi'r," *EI¹.* The same negative evaluation has often been made by Western scholars about classical Persian poetry, although recently the validity of this evaluation has been cast in grave doubt. See Julie Scott Meisami, *Structure and Meaning in Medieval Arabic and Persian Poetry: Orient Pearls* (London: RoutledgeCurzon, 2003).

3. See translation and discussion of *Phaedrus* excerpts in G. M. A. Grube, *The Greek and Roman Critics* (London: Methuen, 1965), 58; *Aristotle's Poetics,* trans. S. H. Butcher (New York: Hill and Wang, 1961), 67.

4. Samuel Johnson, *Selected Essays* (London: Penguin, 2003), 101–2.

5. Wen-chin Ouyang, *Literary Criticism in Medieval Arabic-Islamic Culture: The Making of a Tradition* (Edinburgh: Edinburgh Univ. Press, 1997), 203.

6. Johnson stresses, though, that the critic is obligated to be open-minded and fair, "for the duty of criticism is neither to depreciate, nor dignify by partial representations, but to hold out the light of reason, whatever it may discover; and to promulgate the determinations of truth, whatever she shall dictate" (187).

7. Samuel Taylor Coleridge, *Biographia Literaria,* ed. J. Shawcross, vol. 2 (Oxford: Oxford Univ. Press, 1962), 10.

8. G. J. H. van Gelder, *Beyond the Line: Classical Arabic Literary Critics on the Coherence and Unity of the Poem* (Leiden: Brill, 1982), 201ff; G. J. H. van Gelder, "Genres in Collision: *Nasib* and *Hija',*" *JAL* 21 (1990): 22.

9. On ring composition, see Mary Douglas's important new study, *Thinking in Circles: An Essay on Ring Composition* (New Haven: Yale Univ. Press, 2007).

10. I am not suggesting that structure is variable. A distinction is to be made here between a work's structure, which is inherent, and its overall significance, which is subjectively determined.

Readers may well have their differences over the precise significance of a sonnet, for example, but the poem remains a sonnet.

11. Harold Bloom, *A Map of Misreading* (Oxford: Oxford Univ. Press, 1975), 3–4.

NOTE ON TRANSLATION AND TRANSLITERATION

1. See the translations, respectively, by A. J. Arberry (*The Seven Odes: The First Chapter in Arabic Literature* [London: Allen and Unwin, 1957], 61–66), Suzanne Pinckney Stetkevych (*The Mute Immortals Speak: Pre-Islamic Poetry and the Poetics of Ritual* [Ithaca: Cornell Univ. Press, 1993], 249–57), and Alan Jones (*Early Arabic Poetry*, vol. 2 [Oxford: Ithaca Press, 1996], 55–86); chapter 2: Michael Sells ("Shanfara's *Lamiyya*: A New Version," *Al-'Arabiyya* 16 [1983]: 5–25), Alan Jones (*Early Arabic Poetry*, vol. 1 [Oxford: Ithaca Press, 1992], 139–84), and Suzanne Pinckney Stetkevych (*Mute Immortals*, 143–50); chapter 3: A. J. Arberry (*Seven Odes*, 142–47), William R. Polk (*The Golden Ode* [Chicago: Univ. of Chicago Press, 1974], 3–177), Michael Sells (*Desert Tracings: Six Classic Arabian Odes* [Middletown, Conn.: Wesleyan Univ. Press, 1989], 35–44), Suzanne Pinckney Stetkevych (*Mute Immortals*, 9–18), and Alan Jones (*Early Arabic Poetry*, 2:166–202); and chapter 10: James T. Monroe (*Hispano-Arabic Poetry: A Student Anthology* [Piscataway, N.J.: Gorgias, 2004], 178–86) and Michael Sells ("The *Nuniyya* [Poem in N] of Ibn Zaydun," *Cambridge History of Arabic Literature: The Literature of al-Andalus*, ed. María Menocal et al. [Cambridge: Cambridge Univ. Press, 2000], 491–96). Although the renditions in these four chapters reflect my own readings of the poems—as do perforce the ones in the other chapters—at times they follow closely the previous renditions, particularly the ones by Michael Sells.

1. THE TRIUMPH OF IMRU' AL-QAYS

1. Abu al-Faraj al-Isfahani (d. 967), *Kitab al-aghani* [The Book of Songs], ed. Ibrahim al-Abyari, vol. 9 (Cairo: Dar al-Sha'b, 1969), 3207.

2. In reality, Emperor Justinian was childless.

3. Irfan Shahid, "The Last Days of Imru' al-Qays: Anatolia," in *Tradition and Modernity in Arabic Literature*, ed. Issa J. Boullata and Terri DeYoung (Fayetteville: Univ. of Arkansas Press, 1997), 207–22.

4. Arberry, *Seven Odes*, 39–41.

5. Salomon Gandz, "Die Mu'allaqa des Imrulqais," *Sitzungsberichte der Akademie der Wissenschaften in Wien* 170 (1913): 3, quoted in Michael Zwettler, *The Oral Tradition of Classical Arabic Poetry: Its Character and Implications* (Columbus: Ohio State Univ. Press, 1978), 42.

6. This theory has been refuted by Arberry (*Seven Odes*, 228–54) and, further, by Irfan Shahid ("The Authenticity of Pre-Islamic Poetry: The Linguistic Dimension," *Al-Abhath* 44 [1996]: 3–29).

7. Taha Husayn, *Fi al-shi'r al-jahili* (Damascus: Dar al-Mada lil-Thaqafa wa-al-Nashr, 2001), 135–39.

8. Kamal Abu-Deeb, "Towards a Structural Analysis of Pre-Islamic Poetry (II): The Eros Vision," *Edebiyat* 1 (1976): 3–69; Adnan Haydar, "The *Mu'allaqa* of Imru' al-Qays: Its Structure and Meaning," pts. 1 and 2, *Edebiyat* 2 (1977): 227–61 and 3 (1978): 51–82; Suzanne Pinckney Stetkevych, "Structuralist Interpretations of Pre-Islamic Poetry: Critique and New Directions," *JNES* 42 (1983): 85–107; S. P. Stetkevych, *Mute Immortals*, 241–85; Muhammad Siddiq, "Al-Qasida wa-al-dhat: Qira'a jamaliyya li-Mu'allaqat Imri' al-Qays," *Al-Karmil* 18–19 (1997–98): 231–58.

9. Ibn Rashiq (d. 1064), *Al-'Umda fi mahasin al-shi'r wa-adabihi wa-naqdihi* [The Chief Work on the Charms of Poetry and Its Rules and Criticism], 2 vols. (Cairo: Dar al-Hilal, 1996), 1:67.

10. Clinton Bailey, "The Narrative Context of the Bedouin *Qasidah*-Poem," *Folklore Research Center Studies* 3 (1972): 67.

11. Our text comes from al-Anbari (d. 940), *Sharh al-qasa'id al-sab' al-tiwal al-jahilyyat* [The Explication of the Seven Long Pre-Islamic Odes], ed. 'Abd al-Salam Muhammad Harun (Cairo: Dar al-Ma'arif, 1969), 15–112, which is based on the recension of al-Mufaddal (d. ca. 786). (Al-Mufaddal's was the older of the two original major recensions, the other being the text of al-Asma'i [d. 828]. Before the period when these two men lived, Arabic poetry was preserved orally.) Our only exception to the al-Anbari text concerns the four wolf lines, analyzed below. On the recensions and their slight differences, see Zwettler, 191–96.

12. An extremely bitter fruit. Splitting colocynth is a metaphor for shedding tears.

13. P. Marcel Kurpershoek has lately identified al-Dakhul as an ancient well located approximately halfway between Riyadh and Mecca and Hawmal as a large conical rock of basalt, which rises majestically out of the sand ten miles to the west of al-Dakhul (*Oral Poetry and Narratives from Central Arabia*, vol. 2, *The Story of a Desert Knight* [Leiden: Brill, 1995], xvii, 97–98, 513).

14. Ibn Rashiq, 1:356.

15. That is, her glances, in this case sad and remonstrating, mortally wound him. The topos in Arabic poetry that a beloved's glances are arrows may well have been adopted from Greek poetry. Consider the following by the Greek poet Meleager of Palestine (fl. ca. 95 BCE) in regard to one lost Cupid and a lady named Zenophile (trans. Peter Whigham in *The Greek Anthology and Other Ancient Greek Epigrams*, ed. Peter Jay [New York: Oxford Univ. Press, 1973], 135–36):

armed and certainly dangerous,
beware!
But a moment—
You say you have found him?
Where?
Lo! with fierce bow
who lurks below
her lashes, shoots
where eyen flash:
ZENOPHILE!

16. That is, in winter.

17. The poet is likening her to a palm tree, which he pulls down to get at its fruit.

18. Imru' al-Qays, *Diwan* (Beirut: Dar Sadir, 1958), No. 63, p. 173.

19. Ibn Qutayba, *Kitab al-shi'r wa-al-shu'ara'* [The Book of Poetry and Poets] (Beirut: Dar al-Thaqafa, 1964), 65–66.

20. Stith Thompson, *Motif-Index of Folk-Literature*, 6 vols. (Bloomington: Indiana Univ. Press, 1955), 4:387; Bailey, "Narrative Context," 69–70. Consider also Saad Abdullah Sowayan, *Nabati Poetry: The Oral Poetry of Arabia* (Berkeley and Los Angeles: Univ. of California Press, 1985), 125: "The listeners contribute to the shaping of the narrative and to some extent direct its development by asking for missing details and by injecting comments and expressions of approval or disapproval. Audience participation in developing the narrative contributes further to the divergence of one version from another."

21. Semha Alwaya, "Contemporary Bedouin Oral Poetry," *JAL* 8 (1977): 55.

22. Ibn Qutayba (d. 889) tells us that, from the poem, line 14 about the swaying howdah was part of the repertoire for 'Abbasid singing girls (*Kitab al-shi'r wa-al-shu'ara'*, 56).

23. See al-Nabigha al-Dhubyani, *Diwan*, ed. Karam al-Bustani (Beirut: Dar Sadir, 1963), No. 15, p. 41; and Bashshar ibn Burd in A. J. Arberry, ed., *Arabic Poetry: A Primer for Students* (Cambridge: Cambridge Univ. Press, 1965), 45.

24. Here is line 42 transliterated: "tasallat 'amayatu r-rijali 'ani s-siba / wa-laysa fu'adi 'an hawaki bi-munsali."

25. Nathalie Khankan, "Reperceiving the Pre-Islamic *Nasib*," *JAL* 33 (2002): 21; Renate Jacobi, "Time and Reality in *Nasib* and *Ghazal*," *JAL* 16 (1985): 5.

26. It will be noted that the *nasib* contains neither a description of the beloved nor a mention of her name. Consciously, our poet is trying to block out her memory. This explanation for the beloved's absence from the *Mu'allaqa* was provided to the author by Dina Aburous.

27. Johnson, 8.

28. Duwar was a sacred pillar that some of the pre-Islamic Arabs used to circumambulate. See al-Zawzani (d. 1093), *Sharh al-Mu'allaqat al-sab'* [The Explication of the Seven *Mu'allaqat*] (Beirut: Dar al-Thaqafa, 1966), 47; and Sir Charles Lyall, *Ancient Arabian Poetry* (Westport, Conn.: Hyperion, 1981), 93.

29. Imru' al-Qays, *Diwan*, No. 62, p. 170.

30. Sir Charles Lyall, ed. and trans., *The "Mufaddaliyyat": An Anthology of Ancient Arabian Odes*, 2 vols. (Oxford: Clarendon Press, 1918), 2:85, 386.

31. S. P. Stetkevych, *Mute Immortals,* 271.

32. No. 40, p. 140.

33. James E. Montgomery, "Dichotomy in Jahili Poetry," *JAL* 17 (1986): 13–14. This conclusion is in contrast to an elegy by Labid (d. ca. 661), which voices resignation to grief.

34. No. 30, p. 118.

35. Andras Hamori, *On the Art of Medieval Arabic Literature* (Princeton: Princeton Univ. Press, 1974), 3–30; Horace, *Art of Poetry,* trans. Walter Jackson Bate, in *Criticism: The Major Texts,* ed. Walter Jackson Bate (New York: Harcourt, 1970), 52–53.

36. Here is Arberry's translation:

Many's the water-skin of all sorts of folk I have slung
by its strap over my shoulder, as humble as can be, and humped it;

Many's the valley, bare as an ass's belly, I've crossed
a valley loud with the wolf howling like a many-bairned wastrel

To which, howling, I've cried, "Well, wolf, that's a pair of us,
pretty unprosperous both, if you're out of funds like me.

It's the same with us both—whenever we get aught into our hands
we let it slip through our fingers; tillers of our tilth go pretty thin."

37. Al-Anbari, 80. These transmitters attribute them instead to the pre-Islamic brigand poet Ta'abbata Sharran.

38. Abdulla el Tayib, "Pre-Islamic Poetry," in *CHALUP*, 95; Qudama ibn Ja'far, *Naqd al-shi'r* [Criticism of Poetry] (Cairo: Maktabat al-Khanji, 1979), 113; Lee T. Lemon and Marion J. Reis, trans., *Russian Formalist Criticism: Four Essays* (Lincoln: Univ. of Nebraska Press, 1965), 13. Consider Shklovsky's remarks in this location on Tolstoy: "He describes an object as if he were seeing it for the first time, an event as if it were happening for the first time. In describing something he avoids the accepted names of its parts and instead names corresponding parts of other objects."

39. Lemon and Reis, 12.

40. Cf. Montgomery, "Dichotomy," 4.

41. Siddiq, 254–55.

42. The names in this section, except Tayma', al-Ghabit, and Thabir, refer to mountains and hills in northwestern and central Arabia. Tayma' is an oasis in northwestern Arabia, and the depression of al-Ghabit lies just to the south of it; Mount Thabir is located near Mecca.

43. Kanahbals are of the oak family.

44. S. P. Stetkevych, *Mute Immortals*, 275–76, 278.

45. *Aristotle's Poetics*, 93.

46. Lyall, *Arabian Poetry*, xxi–xxii.

47. Alois Musil, *The Manners and Customs of the Rwala Bedouins* (New York: American Geographical Society, 1928), 14–15.

48. Al-Nabigha al-Dhubyani, *Diwan*, No. 19, p. 50, trans. el Tayib. Consider also these lines by Andalusi poet Ibn Shuhayd (d. 1035) (Ibn Shuhayd, *Diwan Ibn Shuhayd al-Andalusi wa-rasa'iluhu*, ed. Muhyi al-Din Dib [Beirut: Al-Maktaba al-'Asriyya, 1997], No. 22, p. 68):

Is it the dawn that has been seen, or a flash of lightning,
or the brightness of the beloved who exposed her forearms?

From bed she rises, blinking her eyes,
letting down her sleeves and trailing her robe.

And from the modern period, these lines from Swelim ibn Twem al-Dawway (Sowayan, 33):

I cry over my beloved,
whose neck shines like lightning from rain-laden clouds,

Auspicious lightning, presaging abundant rain
that will drench the land and fill the pools.

I only looked upon her, I never touched her;
for she is a chaste lady whose virtue is without doubt.

She is protected by valiant men,
supported by strong kinsmen.

I shall endure and hope for better days;
may the hard times end in joy.

49. Abu-Deeb, "Towards a Structural Analysis (II)," 43; Haydar, 237; Barbara Herrnstein Smith, *Poetic Closure: A Study of How Poems End* (Chicago: Univ. of Chicago Press, 1968), 4.

50. Johnson, 349.

2. AN OUTCAST REPLIES

1. Al-Isfahani, 24:8413–14, quoted in Lyall, *Arabian Poetry,* 83.

2. Francesco Gabrieli, "Ta'abbata Sharran, al-Shanfara, Khalaf al-Ahmar," *Atti della Academia Nazionale dei Lincei,* ser. 8 (1946): 56.

3. J. W. Redhouse, *The L-Poem of the Arabs* (London: Trübner, 1881), x, 13.

4. The claim was made by al-Qali (d. 967) on the authority of Ibn Durayd (d. 933) (F. Krenkow, "Al-Shanfara," in *EI¹*).

5. 'Abd al-Halim Hifni, *Shi'r al-sa'alik* (Cairo: Al-Hay'a al-Misriyya al-'Amma lil-Kitab, 1979), 162–73.

6. Lyall, *"Mufaddaliyyat,"* 2:68.

7. Jones, 1:140; Albert Arazi, "Al-Shanfara," in *EI².*

8. Sources for the poem: al-'Ukbari (d. 1219), *I'rab Lamiyyat al-'Arab,* ed. Muhammad Adib 'Abd al-Wahid Jumran (Beirut: Al-Maktab al-Islami, 1984); al-Shanfara, *Diwan,* ed. Imil Badi' Ya'qub (Beirut: Dar al-Kitab al-'Arabi, 1991).

9. Al-Zawzani, 183.

10. Al-Zawzani, 69.

11. Muhammad ʿAli Abu Hamda, *Fi al-tadhawwuq al-uslubi wa-al-lughawi li-Lamiyyat al-ʿArab lil-Shanfara* (Amman: Dar ʿAmmar, 1997), 35.

12. Yusuf al-Yusuf, *Maqalat fi al-shiʿr al-jahili* (Damascus: Wizarat al-Thaqafa wa-al-Irshad al-Qawmi, 1975), 216–17.

13. The young are starved because the she-camels cannot find sufficient pasture, and thus produce no milk. See Jones, 1:150–51.

14. Mark Twain, *Adventures of Huckleberry Finn,* chap. 43.

15. *Diwan,* No. 14, p. 54.

16. This is a reference to a pre-Islamic game of chance, played for the parts of a slaughtered beast. The body was divided into ten pieces, for which arrows were blindly drawn. Seven notched arrows won one or more pieces, while three or four unnotched, white-ended arrows won no meat (T. Fahd, "Al-Maysir," in *EI²*).

17. Ibn Rashiq, 2:125.

18. *Diwan,* No. 3, p. 34.

19. Uhaza was a branch of the poet's tribe, al-Azd (*Diwan,* No. 67).

20. Al-Maydani (d. 1124), *Majmaʿ al-amthal* [Collection of Proverbs], ed. Naʿim Husayn Zarzur, 2 vols. (Beirut: Dar al-Kutub al-ʿIlmiyya, 1988), 2:54.

21. Al-Zawzani, 162.

22. Jibrail S. Jabbur, *The Bedouins and the Desert,* trans. Lawrence I. Conrad (Albany: State Univ. of New York Press, 1995), 124.

23. The Mother of Dust, an epithet for war (referring to the dust that is kicked up).

24. An epithet for a snake.

25. Johnson, 490.

26. As noted by R. A. Nicholson in *A Literary History of the Arabs* (Cambridge: Cambridge Univ. Press, 1956), 79.

27. Henry David Thoreau, *Walden* (London: Penguin, 1986), 69, 135, 377.

28. Arazi, "Al-Shanfara."

29. Al-Zawzani, 150, 154–55.

30. Hadith No. 36 in al-Nawawi, *Al-Arbaʿin al-Nawawiyya,* trans. Ezzeddin Ibrahim and Denys Johnson-Davies (Damascus: Holy Koran Publishing House, 1976), 114. This is a well-attested tradition.

31. *Diwan,* No. 18.

32. See Qurʾan 2:178–79; and Mustansir Mir, "Qisas," in *Dictionary of Qurʾanic Terms and Concepts* (New York: Garland, 1987), 170–72.

33. F. Krenkow, "Al-Shanfara," in *EI¹*.

34. Cf. the ending of a poem by al-Shanfara's suʿluk colleague Taʾabbata Sharran, sensitively analyzed by Suzanne Pinckney Stetkevych (in *Hamasa* anthology section of *Abu Tammam and the Poetics of the ʿAbbasid Age* [Leiden: Brill, 1991], 306–7). Taʾabbata Sharran represents himself as becoming one of the wild gazelles. The implication of this development, which he accepts, is that like them he will now be hunted down and killed by humans. The ending of al-Shanfara's poem, we will see below, connotes something quite different.

35. *Diwan,* No. 3, p. 33.

36. On sacred pillars, see W. Robertson Smith, *The Religion of the Semites: The Fundamental Institutions* (New York: Schocken, 1972), 206–12.

37. Musil, 25.

38. Trans. Lyall in *"Mufaddaliyyat,"* 2:182.

39. Joseph J. Hobbs, *Bedouin Life in the Egyptian Wilderness* (Cairo: American Univ. in Cairo Press, 1990), 42.

3. THE PRICE OF GLORY

1. Labid ibn Rabiʻa, *Sharh Diwan Labid ibn Rabiʻa al-ʻAmiri,* ed. Ihsan ʻAbbas (Kuwait: Wizarat al-Irshad wa-al-Anbaʼ, 1962), 10.

2. Taha Husayn, *Hadith al-arbiʻa,* vol. 1 (Cairo: Dar al-Maʻarif, 1959), 28–39.

3. James T. Monroe, "Oral Composition in Pre-Islamic Poetry," *JAL* 3 (1972): 43; Kamal Abu-Deeb, "Towards a Structural Analysis of Pre-Islamic Poetry," *IJMES* 6 (1975): 148–84; S. P. Stetkevych, *Mute Immortals,* 8–54.

4. Nöldeke, *Fünf Moʻallaqat* (1900), 2:5, as cited in C. Brockelmann, "Labid," in *EI²;* Abu-Deeb, "Towards a Structural Analysis," 149.

5. Sources for the ode: al-Anbari, al-Zawzani, and Labid ibn Rabiʻa, *Diwan.*

6. The four months of peace were Muharram, Rajab, Dhu al-Qaʻda, and Dhu al-Hijja. During the other months intertribal hostilities were permitted.

Based on discussions of the seasons by Musil (7–19) and Lyall (*Arabian Poetry,* xxi–xxii), I would like to propose the following arrangement for the pre-Islamic lunar calendar (maintained approximately thus by the addition of an intercalary month every three years):

No.	Season	Constellation of Note	Status re: Hostilities	Name	Gregorian Equivalent
1	al-Sferi	Gemini	Peace	Muharram	December
2	al-Shitaʼ	Sirius	War permitted	Safar	January
3	"	Sirius/Arcturus	"	Rabiʻ al-Awwal	February
4	al-Smak	Arcturus	"	Rabiʻ al-Thani	March
5	al-Smak/al-Sayf	"	"	Jumada al-Ula	April
6	al-Sayf		"	Jumada al-Akhira	May
7	al-Qayz		Peace	Rajab	June
8	"		War permitted	Shaʻban	July
9	"		"	Ramadan	August
10	"		"	Shawwal	September
11	al-Sferi	Canopus	Peace	Dhu al-Qaʻda	October
12	"	Pleiades	"	Dhu al-Hijja	November

Though the existence of a fixed pre-Islamic calendar according to the seasons cannot be confirmed by ancient sources (for this reason, the *Encyclopedia of Islam* does not posit one), the above disposition has numerous recommendations to support it. By this arrangement:

- the three consecutive months of peace fall when the Bedouins are returning to the desert and once more camping adjacent to each other (October–December)
- the most important annual fair (Suq 'Ukaz) and the annual pilgrimage occur during two temperate months (October and November, respectively) after the long summer
- Rabi' al-Awwal and Rabi' al-Thani ("Spring the First," "Spring the Second") fall during the actual period of late winter and early spring
- Ramadan (from *ramada*, "to be burning hot") occurs during the month of August

Note: This proposed fixing of the lunar calendar pertains only to the pre-Islamic period. The Prophet abolished the practice of intercalation ca. 631, after which the lunar calendar, shorter than the solar calendar by eleven days, ceased to have any connection to the seasons.

7. Musil, 8.

8. As James T. Monroe has recently observed, "The pattern of seasonal separations and regroupings is not restricted exclusively to the Bedouins of Arabia, but is a feature of nomadic, pastoral life in general" ("Literary Hybridization in Ibn Quzman's 'Zajal 147' [The Poet's Repentance]," in *Medieval Oral Literature,* ed. Karl Reichl [Berlin: de Gruyter, in press], n. 40). See also M. N. Shahrani, *The Kirghiz and Wakhi of Afghanistan: Adaptation to Closed Frontiers* (Seattle: Univ. of Washington Press, 1979).

9. Cf. Hamori, *Art of Medieval Arabic Literature,* 17–18.

10. *Diwan,* No. 24, p. 168.

11. The rain trench encircled the camp, keeping floodwaters from inundating the living area, and the thatch was used to stuff holes in the tents.

12. Consider this opening from the famous ode by Ka'b ibn Zuhayr (d. after 630) (*Sharh al-Tibrizi 'ala Banat Su'ad li-Ka'b ibn Zuhayr,* ed. 'Abd al-Rahim Yusuf al-Jamal, trans. S. P. Stetkevych [Cairo: Maktabat al-Adab wa-Matba'atuha, 1990], 21–23):

Su'ad has departed, and today my heart is sick
A slave to her traces, unransomed, enchained.

On the morning of departure when her tribe set out,
Su'ad was but a bleating antelope with languid gaze and kohl-lined eyes.

13. Jabbur, 288.

14. Lyall, "*Mufaddaliyyat,*" 2:9–10.

15. Al-Anbari, 537.

16. Lyall, "*Mufaddaliyyat,*" 1:40.

17. Imru' al-Qays, *Diwan,* No. 44, pp. 151–52.

18. No. 17, p. 156.

19. Jaroslav Stetkevych, "In Search of the Unicorn: The Onager and the Oryx in the Arabic Ode," *JAL* 33 (2002): 87. See also Jaroslav Stetkevych, "The Hunt in the Arabic *Qasidah:* The Antecedents of the *Tardiyyah*," in *Tradition and Modernity in Arabic Language and Literature*, ed. J. R. Smart (Richmond, UK: Curzon, 1996), 103–5.

20. According to the lunar calendar used by the Bedouins, the diurnal cycle begins at nightfall. Day is regarded as an appendage of the night. See Musil, 4.

21. It will be noted, as regards the ending of the second simile, that the oryx doe now knows where the archers lurk; she will be able to exit the area safely.

22. J. Stetkevych, "In Search of the Unicorn," 116–20.

23. S. P. Stetkevych, *Mute Immortals,* 32–33; Suzanne Pinckney Stetkevych, "Intoxication and Immortality: Wine and Associated Imagery in al-Ma'arri's Garden," in *Homoeroticism in Classical Arabic Literature*, ed. J. W. Wright Jr. and Everett Rowson (New York: Columbia Univ. Press, 1997), 221–23.

24. Al-Jahiz, *Kitab al-hayawan* [The Book of Animals], ed. 'Abd al-Salam Muhammad Harun, vol. 2 (Cairo: Maktabat Mustafa al-Babi al-Halabi wa-Awladihi, 1965), 20.

25. See chap. 2, n. 16.

26. Charles Dickens, *Our Mutual Friend,* bk. 3, chap. 15.

27. El Tayib, 100.

28. Al-Anbari, 339, trans. el Tayib.

29. That is, al-Nu'man (Salma was his mother) (*Diwan,* No. 195).

30. *Diwan,* No. 26, pp. 194–96.

31. Al-Isfahani, 16:5738–39. Labid himself apparently did not agree with this assessment. When asked later in life to name the greatest poet, he named Imru' al-Qays. He rated himself as the third best, following Tarafa (author of the second *Mu'allaqa*) (Al-Isfahani, 16:5728).

32. Al-Anbari, 284.

33. Ibn Rashiq, 1:109, trans. Lyall.

34. Arberry, *Arabic Poetry,* 33.

35. *Diwan,* No. 36, p. 256.

36. Ibn Qutayba, *Kitab al-shi'r wa-al-shu'ara',* 195.

37. Jaroslav Stetkevych, *The Zephyrs of Najd: The Poetics of Nostalgia in the Classical Arabic "Nasib"* (Chicago: Univ. of Chicago Press, 1993), 33; S. P. Stetkevych, *Mute Immortals,* 24.

38. *Rasa'il al-Jahiz,* ed. 'Abd al-Salam Muhammad Harun, vol. 3 (Cairo: Maktabat al-Khanji, 1964), 3.

39. Alfred Lord Tennyson, "Ulysses," 68.

4. MAKING THE REMEMBRANCE DEAR

1. In the Greek literary tradition also, women's poetry is mostly confined to the lament. See Margaret Alexiou, *The Ritual Lament in Greek Literary Tradition* (Cambridge: Cambridge Univ. Press, 1974).

2. Deborah Wickering, "Experience and Expression: Life among Bedouin Women in South Sinai," *Cairo Papers in Social Science* 14, no. 2 (1991): 34.

3. Ahmad Muhammad al-Hufi, *Al-Mar'a fi al-shi'r al-jahili* (Cairo: Dar al-Fikr al-'Arabi, 1963), 660.

4. Al-Qali (d. 967), *Kitab al-amali* [The Book of Dictations], vol. 2 (Cairo: al-Matba'a al-Kubra al-Amiriyya, 1906), 200.

5. Lila Abu-Lughod, *Veiled Sentiments: Honor and Poetry in a Bedouin Society* (Berkeley and Los Angeles: Univ. of California Press, 1986), 234.

6. Wickering, 6, 43–44.

7. J. A. Bellamy, "Some Observations on the Arabic *Ritha'* in the Jahiliyah and Islam," *Jerusalem Studies in Arabic and Islam* 13 (1990): 44–61.

8. Arberry, *Arabic Poetry*, 31.

9. Hamasa anthology section of S. P. Stetkevych, *Abu Tammam*, 291–303; S. P. Stetkevych, *Mute Immortals*, 195.

10. *Diwan* (Beirut: Dar Sadir, 1963), No. 24, p. 43; No. 94, p. 144.

11. Lyall, *Arabian Poetry*, 42–43, slightly modified. See also al-Isfahani, 10:3485–89.

12. Al-Jahiz, attrib., *Al-Mahasin wa-al-addad* [Good Works and Qualities and Their Opposites] (Cairo: Maktabat al-Qahira, 1978), 104. The accounts indicate that she did wear such a blouse after his death, and continued to do so for the rest of her life.

13. Al-Isfahani, 15:5387–89.

14. Al-Isfahani relates that Sakhr died rather of a wound sustained during an attack on Banu Asad (15:5362). However, Isma'il al-Qadi argues persuasively that the Murrites were the ones who killed him (*Al-Khansa' fi mir'at 'asriha*, vol. 1 [Baghdad: Matba'at al-Ma'arif, 1962], 207–23).

15. Al-Khansa', *Diwan* (Beirut: Dar Sadir, 1963), No. 21, p. 40; No. 63, p. 99; No. 94, p. 144.

16. Bint al-Shati', *Al-Khansa'* (Cairo: Dar al-Ma'arif, 1963), 85–114.

17. No. 56, p. 91.

18. No. 26, p. 47.

19. No. 42, p. 73.

20. No. 15, p. 30.

21. Labid ibn Rabi'a, *Diwan*, No. 17, p. 155.

22. Hatim al-Ta'i, *Diwan Hatim Shi'r al-Ta'i ibn 'Abd Allah wa-akhbaruhu*, ed. 'Adil Sulayman Jamal (Cairo: Maktabat al-Khanji, 1990), No. 42, p. 211.

23. No. 53, p. 86.

24. The slaughtered calf alluded to here would be male. Jonathan Kingdon notes, "Managed herds tend to have very few males as there is a valuable saving in milk from the elimination of male calves. Adult males are also difficult to control during the rut, at which time they fight and indulge in noisy displays." By contrast, "the she-camel, Naqah, is the most valued animal in a nomad's flock because of her milk production which ranges between 2 and 14 litres a day and up to 3,600 litres per lactation" (*Arabian Mammals: A Natural History* [London: Academic Press, 1990], 128, 130).

25. Here is a transliteration of section D:

15   wa-inna Sakhran la-walina wa-sayyiduna
      wa-inna Sakhran idha nashtu la-nahharu
16   wa-inna Sakhran la-miqdamun idha rakibu
      wa-inna Sakhran idha ja'u la-'aqqaru
17   wa-inna Sakhran la-ta'tammu l-hudatu bihi
      ka-annahu 'alamun fi ra'sihi naru
18   jaldun jamilu l-muhahyya kamilun wari'un
      wa-lil-hurubi ghadata r-raw'i mis'aru
19   hammalu alwiyatin habbatu awdiyatin
      shahhadu andiyatin lil-jayshi jarraru
20   nahharu raghiyatin mija'u taghiyatin
      fakkaku 'aniyatin lil-'azmi jabbaru

26. Al-Jahiz, *Al-Mahasin*, 104.

27. 'Urwa ibn al-Ward, *Diwan* (Beirut: Dar al-Kitab al-'Arabi, 1994), No. 6, p. 22.

28. No. 52, p. 84.

29. In the Dar Sadir *Diwan*, line 8 is found after line 13. The order presented here is from the recension of Abu al-'Abbas Tha'lab in al-Khansa', *Sharh Diwan al-Khansa'*, ed. Fayiz Muhammad (Beirut: Dar al-Kitab al-'Arabi, 1993). See also Jones, 1:90.

30. See this statement from one of her laments (No. 34, p. 62): "Al-Khansa' weeps in the dark out of bitter sorrow, / calling for her brother who, cast in the ground, does not reply."

31. Imru' al-Qays describes his long night of despair in the section immediately following the *nasib* (see *Mu'allaqa*, lines 44–48). Typically, however, the motif of the poet enduring a sleepless, anxiety-filled night occurs at the beginning of the ode.

32. Abu Tammam, *Diwan al-hamasa*, ed. 'Abd al-Mun'im Ahmad Salih (Baghdad: Dar al-Shu'un al-Thaqafiyya al-'Amma, 1987), No. 266, p. 225. Mutammim reportedly annoyed his wife as well with his tearfulness, such that she could take no more of their marriage. He relates (al-Isfahani, 16:5656, trans. A. Kh. Kinany):

I said to Hind when I was displeased with her behavior:
"Is that a strange sort of coquetry or rather the conduct of the wife who hates her
    husband?

"Or do you want divorce? Yea, I can stand every separation,
after being separated from my brother."

It is said that thereafter she got what she wanted.

33. That is, the area comprising Mecca and its environs.

34. Here is one of two references in the *Diwan* to al-Khansa'''s father. Because the father is mentioned here in the context of fallen kinsmen, one supposes that he also died in battle.

35. No. 24, p. 43.

36. Ibn Qutayba, *Kitab al-shi'r wa-al-shu'ara'*, 261.

37. Al-Jahiz, *Al-Mahasin,* 104.

5. MARTYR TO LOVE

1. The pension system, based on precedence of conversion to Islam, had been set up by Caliph 'Umar.

2. Ibn Sa'd (d. 845), *Al-Tabaqat al-kubra* [The Major Classes], vol. 3 (Beirut: Dar Sadir, 1957), 110.

3. Waddah al-Yaman, *Diwan,* ed. Muhammad Khayr al-Biqa'i (Beirut: Dar Sadir, 1996), No. 9, pp. 46–48, trans. Kinany.

4. 'Umar ibn Abi Rabi'a, *Diwan,* ed. Qadri Mayu, 2 vols. (Beirut: 'Alam al-Kutub, 1997), No. 152, vol. 1, p. 250.

5. No. 86, vol. 1, pp. 148, 151.

6. Jamil, *Diwan,* ed. 'Adnan Zakiy Darwish (Beirut: Dar al-Fikr al-'Arabi, 1994), No. 10, p. 26.

7. No. 84, p. 87.

8. No. 88, p. 93.

9. No. 103, p. 106.

10. No. 105, p. 108, line 3.

11. No. 216, p. 217.

12. See, for example, No. 44, p. 51; and No. 110, p. 112.

13. See No. 170, p. 171; and No. 215, p. 213.

14. Cf. No. 56, p. 64, in which Jamil makes the same argument.

15. Al-Isfahani, 8:2875–76.

16. A. Kh. Kinany, *The Development of Gazal in Arabic Literature* (Damascus: Syrian Univ. Press, 1950), 179.

17. Ibn Dawud (d. 910), *Kitab al-zahra* [The Book of the Flower], ed. A. R. Nykl, *University of Chicago Studies in Ancient Oriental Civilization* 6 (1932): 283.

18. See No. 84, p. 86; and No. 86, p. 90.

19. The Night of Power and Excellence being Laylat al-Qadr, when the Qur'an was first revealed to the Prophet Muhammad. See Qur'an 97:3. *Diwan,* No. 84, p. 89.

20. No. 197, p. 192.

21. No. 86, p. 90.

22. Al-Saraqusti, *Al-Maqamat al-luzumiyah,* trans. James T. Monroe (Leiden: Brill, 2002), 34.

23. Kinany, 258.

24. No. 184, p. 182.

25. No. 45, p. 54.

26. For the wording of a few lines, Ibn Maymun's recension has also been consulted.

27. Al-Qali, 303.

28. Abu 'Ubayd al-Bakri, *Kitab al-tanbih 'ala awham Abi 'Ali fi amalihi* [The Book That Call Attention to the Errors of Abu 'Ali in His "Dictations"] (Cairo: Matba'at Dar al-Kutub al-Misriyya, 2000).

29. Respectively, No. 150, p. 157; and No. 175, p. 176.

30. See chap. 1, fourth excerpt.

31. Ibn Rashiq, 2:194.

32. *Diwan,* No. 319, vol. 2, pp. 174–75.

33. Johnson, 124.

34. Ibn Qutayba, *Kitab al-shi'r wa-al-shu'ara',* 351–52.

35. Al-Isfahani, 8:2836–900.

36. Charles Pellat, "Madjnun Layla," in *EI².*

37. Al-Isfahani, 8:2851. On these narratives, see Stefan Leder, "The 'Udhri Narrative in Arabic Literature," in *Martyrdom in Literature: Visions of Death and Meaningful Suffering in Europe and the Middle East from Antiquity to Modernity,* ed. Friedericke Pannewick (Wiesbaden: Reichert, 2004), 163–87; Ruqayya Yasmine Khan, *Self and Secrecy in Early Islam* (Columbia: Univ. of South Carolina Press, 2008), 72–125.

38. No. 233, p. 232.

39. No. 73, p. 77.

40. Paul Fussell, *Thank God for the Atom Bomb, and Other Essays* (New York: Summit, 1988), 183.

41. Wickering, 49–50.

42. J. Stetkevych, *Zephyrs of Najd,* 116.

43. Al-Hufi, 653. It is said that Mu'awiya, who was stout, did not appreciate this last reference and sent Maysun back whence she came, to live with those of her tribe who had remained in the desert. Cf. Nicholson, *Literary History,* 195–96; and 'Abd al-Badi' Saqr, *Sha'irat al-'Arab* (Doha, Qatar: Al-Maktab al-Islami, 1967), 396.

44. No. 135, p. 144.

45. No. 87, p. 90.

46. Renate Jacobi, "'Udhri," in *EI².* See also Renate Jacobi, "The 'Udhra: Love and Death in the Umayyad Period," in *Martyrdom in Literature: Visions of Death and Meaningful Suffering in Europe and the Middle East from Antiquity to Modernity,* ed. Friedericke Pannewick (Wiesbaden: Reichert, 2004), 137–47.

47. Al-Jahiz, *The Epistle on Singing-Girls of Jahiz,* ed. and trans. A. F. L. Beeston (Warminster, UK: Aris and Phillips, 1980), 17, 26.

6. FLYTING

1. Al-Isfahani, 2:605, quoted in G. J. H. van Gelder, *The Bad and the Ugly: Attitudes Towards Invective Poetry ("Hija'") in Classical Arabic Literature* (Leiden: Brill, 1988), 26.

2. Al-Isfahani, 2:610, quoted in van Gelder, *Bad and Ugly,* 29.

3. Salma Khadra Jayyusi, "Umayyad Poetry," in *CHALUP*, 409.

4. *The Naqa'id of Jarir and al-Farazdaq*, ed. Anthony A. Bevan, 3 vols. (Leiden: Brill, 1905), No. 50, vol. 1, p. 333.

5. Al-Isfahani, 25:8529.

6. *Naqa'id*, No. 31, vol. 1, p. 134.

7. The references to al-Ba'ith in the poem are not helpful in dating it, for biographical information is ambiguous as to when al-Ba'ith died. See Charles Pellat, "Al-Ba'ith," in *EI²*.

8. Jarir is referring to the fire of the beloved.

9. Al-Ba'ith's mother was a slave from Sijistan, the southeastern part of present-day Iran.

10. Jarir, *Diwan* (Beirut: Dar Sadir, 1964), No. 4, p. 15.

11. No. 129, p. 218.

12. 'Abd al-Malik, incidentally, was the caliph who gave the world the Dome of the Rock (691–92). On 'Abd al-Malik and the erection of this, the first major architectural monument of the Islamic era, see Oleg Grabar, "The Umayyad Dome of the Rock in Jerusalem," in *Early Islamic Art and Architecture*, ed. Jonathan M. Bloom (Hampshire, UK: Ashgate, 2002), 223–56.

13. No. 158, p. 277.

14. No. 155, p. 267.

15. See the expressions *bayyada wajhahu* ("he brightened his face," that is, he did himself honor) and *sawwada wajhahu* ("he darkened his face," that is, he disgraced himself).

16. No. 81, p. 126.

17. This is a reference to an attack by the Banu Sa'd (one of the principal tribes of Tamim) on Bakr ibn Wa'il of Yamama that probably occurred around 600, when Tamim was frequently clashing with Bakr (presumably, Yarbu' participated in it alongside Banu Sa'd). On the eve of the attack, it is related, Bakr was camping at the foot of a mountain. A young woman of Bakr, unable to sleep that night owing to a passion she was harboring, looked out in the darkness and saw "a man as tall as a tree" with a bow slung over his left shoulder. She alerted her father, who notified others in the tribe. The tribespeople were incredulous and said, "Your daughter has not revealed anything at this hour except that she is in love." The father returned abashed, but his daughter insisted on the danger and urged an immediate departure. So they left on their camels. Sure enough, in the early morning Banu Sa'd attacked Bakr, killing many of them and taking many prisoner. See *Naqa'id*, 1:335–36; and W. Caskel, "Bakr ibn Wa'il," in *EI²*.

18. A reference to the pre-Islamic Battle of al-Sara'im. On this day, Rabi'a of Tamim was surprised by a contingent from Banu 'Abs. Rabi'a managed to get word to nearby Yarbu', whose men came quickly and overwhelmed the 'Absis. They slew a number of them and then chased after the ones who tried to escape, capturing several (*Naqa'id*, 1:336–37).

19. That is, al-Farazdaq.

20. The patronymic and two matronymics in this section all refer to Mujashi'. The genealogy indicated for al-Farazdaq is discussed below, after the last section.

21. Nizar was the ancestor of the northern Arabian tribes.

22. From "A Post-script to the Reader" in Joseph Hall, *Collected Poems*, ed. A. Davenport (Liverpool: Liverpool Univ. Press, 1949), 97.

23. The detailed negative reference is to al-Farazdaq's mother. Arab women traditionally removed the hair.

Lines 35, 36, and 41 would appear to have been placed incorrectly in the original recension (in which they occur as lines 37, 42, and 38, respectively). The order here is submitted as a logical alternative. It should be noted, in any case, that the question of these three lines' proper placement within section A¹ does not have a significant bearing on the matter of the poem's overall structure.

24. According to the commentators, Wabar was a land filled with jinn. It seems that Jarir has Southeast Arabia in mind, inasmuch as elsewhere, to suggest a vast expanse, he speaks of what lies between Egypt and Oman. See, for example, *Diwan,* No. 279, p. 468; and No. 287, p. 480.

25. Qufayra was al-Farazdaq's great-grandmother, said to have been a slave. Jarir implies that the son, al-Farazdaq's grandfather, turned out weak and effeminate.

26. Al-Khatafa was Jarir's grandfather.

27. That is, cautious and unsuspected.

28. Presumably, she lost it during an encounter with a visitor to her abode.

29. Ji'thin being al-Farazdaq's sister (discussed later).

30. Our poet is wont to cite, among al-Farazdaq's ancestors, people with ludicrous names (for example, Jawkha, Khajkhaj, and al-Qidham; compare this line from *Diwan,* No. 106, p. 174: "So when you boast of the mothers of Mujashi', / boast of Qabqab, and be sure to mention al-Nikhwar").

31. *Diwan,* No. 124, p. 208.

32. *Diwan,* No. 81, p. 126.

33. Al-Farazdaq is referring to Jarir's mother (explained later).

34. Al-Farazdaq, *Diwan,* ed. Iliya al-Hawi, 2 vols. (Beirut: Dar al-Kitab al-Lubnani, 1983), No. 383, vol. 2, p. 185.

35. *Diwan,* No. 80, 1:176.

36. *Naqa'id,* 1:324.

37. Abu Hayyan al-Tawhidi (d. 1023), *Mathalib al-wazirayn: Akhlaq al-Sahib Ibn 'Abbad wa-Ibn al-'Amid* [The Vices of the Two Viziers: The Habits of al-Sahib Ibn 'Abbad and Ibn al-'Amid], ed. Ibrahim al-Kaylani (Damascus: Dar al-Fikr, 1961), 175.

38. See, for example, Ibn Sallam al-Jumahi (d. ca. 846), *Tabaqat al-shu'ara'* [The Classes of the Poets] (Leiden: Brill, 1913), 107; and al-Isfahani, 8:2827.

39. See *Diwan,* No. 133, p. 230; and No. 259, p. 432. Cf. al-Farazdaq (*Diwan,* No. 288, vol. 1, p. 574): "Verily in the horse race / Kulayb is the one riding on a donkey."

40. Adel Sulaiman Gamal, "The Ethical Values of the Brigand Poets in Pre-Islamic Arabia," *Bibliotheca Orientalis* 34, nos. 5–6 (1977): 291.

41. *Diwan,* No. 299, p. 497. A Hanifa member, by the way, was asked after the poem was recited to which group he belonged. "To the one not mentioned," he replied (that is, to the free men) (Qudama ibn Ja'far, 201).

42. Compare the following account (Ibn Sallam al-Jumahi, 86) of a conversation between a friend and the prestigious poet al-Farazdaq:

"A new poem by Jarir reached Mirbad today that people are reciting."

Al-Farazdaq turned pale.

"It's not about you, O Abu Firas al-Farazdaq!"

"Who is it about?"

"Ibn Laja' al-Tamimi."

"Did you memorize any of it?"

"Yes." And he began to recite.

43. *Diwan*, No. 155, p. 267.

44. *Diwan*, No. 242, p. 416.

45. Al-Isfahani, 8:2775–77, trans. Nicholson, *Literary History*, 245–46, slightly modified.

46. He glories through verse in his drinking and his sexual escapades, so we can assume that there was legitimacy to Jarir's criticisms of his behavior.

47. *Diwan*, No. 19, p. 43.

48. John Dryden, "Preface to the Fables," in *Essays*, ed. W. P. Ker, vol. 2 (New York: Russell, 1961), 260.

7. PLEASURE IN TRANSGRESSION

1. See Garth Fowden, *Qusayr 'Amra: Art and the Umayyad Elite in Late Antique Syria* (Berkeley and Los Angeles: Univ. of California Press, 2004), 85–141, 227–47 (Fowden has suggested the connection to Imru' al-Qays); Robert Hillenbrand, *"La Dolce Vita* in Early Islamic Syria: The Evidence of Later Umayyad Palaces," in *Early Islamic Art and Architecture,* ed. Jonathan M. Bloom (Aldershot, UK: Ashgate, 2002), 350.

2. Al-Walid II (al-Walid ibn Yazid), *Diwan,* ed. Husayn 'Atwan (Beirut: Dar al-Jil, 1998), No. 24, p. 39.

3. The wine was often mixed with water before being served. Compare the Greek tradition in which, at banquets, wine was mixed with water in bowls called "kraters" before being served.

4. No. 5, p. 17.

5. Quoted in Patricia Crone and Martin Hinds, *God's Caliph: Religious Authority in the First Centuries of Islam* (Cambridge: Cambridge Univ. Press, 1986), 132.

6. Al-Mas'udi (d. ca. 956), *Muruj al-dhahab* [The Meadows of Gold], ed. Charles Pellat, vol. 4 (Beirut: al-Jami'a al-Lubnaniyya, 1973), 234.

7. Al-Isfahani, 13:4604. Contrast this, however, with what the Umayyad poet Malik ibn Asma' said of his Persian singing girls (al-Isfahani, 18:6536, trans. after Kinany): "Their speech is correct; they sometimes make mistakes in Arabic, / yet the best speech in my opinion is that which has some mistakes in it."

8. Chosroes and Sasan are kings of the Persian dynasty that ruled much of western Asia from 224 CE until 651.

9. In Khurasan.

10. Aleppo has one river.

11. That is, al-ʿAbbas, uncle of the Prophet and ancestor of the ʿAbbasid line. Quraysh is the Prophet's tribe.

12. Bashshar ibn Burd, *Diwan,* ed. Husayn Hamwi, vol. 1 (Beirut: Dar al-Jil, 1996), No. 97, p. 342.

13. Albert Arazi, "Abu Nuwas fut-il šhuʿubite?" *Arabica* 26 (1979): 29, 39. Consider, for example, this line about former edifices in Yemen: "The palaces of Naʿit and Ghumdan belong to us, / with their royal halls emanating musk" (Abu Nuwas, *Diwan* [Beirut: Dar Sadir, 1980], No. 105, p. 86).

14. Jujube is an olive-shaped, dark-red fruit from a tree of this name, that is, she is striking her cheeks with the ends of henna-tinged fingers.

15. No. 50, p. 53.

16. No. 873, p. 617.

17. Maurice Lombard, *The Golden Age of Islam,* trans. Joan Spencer (Princeton: Markus Wiener, 2004), 116–45.

18. Cited in al-Khatib al-Baghdadi (d. 1071), *Tarikh Baghdad* [The History of Baghdad], vol. 1 (Cairo: Maktabat al-Khanji, 1931), 45.

19. No. 303, p. 239.

20. No. 198, p. 164.

21. No. 135, p. 111. See James E. Montgomery, "Revelry and Remorse: A Poem of Abu Nuwas," *JAL* 25 (1994): 116–34.

22. No. 334, p. 263.

23. No. 841, p. 594.

24. No. 474, p. 366.

25. No. 223, p. 181.

26. The style characterized by frequent use of rhetorical figures came to be called the *badiʿ* style, after these figures collectively.

27. Al-Isfahani, 29:9862.

28. Ibn Rashiq, 1:159. Compare the opinion of a critic named Ibn al-Aʿrabi (d. ca. 846): "The poems of those moderns like Abu Nuwas and others are like flowers of which one takes in the fragrance one day and which fade and are thrown away the next. The poems of the ancients, on the other hand, are like musk and ambergris which become more fragrant the more one stirs them" (quoted in Seeger A. Bonebakker, "Poets and Critics in the Third Century A.H.," in *Logic in Classical Islamic Culture,* ed. G. E. von Grunebaum [Wiesbaden: Otto Harrassowitz, 1970], 90).

29. M. A. A. El Kafrawy and J. D. Latham, "Perspective of Abu al-ʿAtahiya," *IQ* 17 (1973): 160–76.

30. Abi al-ʿAtahiya, *Diwan,* ed. Majid Tirad (Beirut: Dar al-Kitab al-ʿArabi, 1995), No. 39, p. 48.

31. Cf. Nicholson, *Literary History,* 260–61.

32. Al-Isfahani, 29:9906.

33. No. 626, p. 453.

34. No. 967, p. 673.

35. No. 380, p. 291.

36. No. 913, p. 635.

37. See the report of boys running away and seeking refuge when they hear that Abu Nuwas has come to town (al-Isfahani, 30:10106).

38. Philip F. Kennedy, *The Wine Song in Classical Arabic Poetry: Abu Nuwas and the Literary Tradition* (Oxford: Oxford Univ. Press, 1997), 242.

39. On this subject, see Everett K. Rowson, "The Traffic in Boys: Slavery and Homoerotic Liaisons in Elite 'Abbasid Society," *Middle Eastern Literatures* 11, no. 2 (2008): 193–204.

40. Everett K. Rowson, "The Categorization of Gender and Sexual Irregularity in Medieval Arabic Vice Lists," in *Body Guards: The Cultural Politics of Gender Ambiguity,* ed. Julia Epstein and Kristina Straub (London: Routledge, 1991), 65–66. When considering earlier representations of pederasty, it is thus important to dissociate ourselves from acquired sexual standards. James T. Monroe notes: "Sexual acts are universal in nature, only limited by the anatomical, gymnastic, and imaginative abilities of the species; however, the position they hold within the value system of any given society is culture-specific. What was viewed by both ancient Greeks and medieval Arabs as a perfectly normal kind of relationship was for Edwardians 'the unspeakable vice of the Greeks' and is for us . . . a particularly reprehensible form of child molestation" ("The Striptease That Was Blamed on Abu Bakr's Naughty Son: Was Father Being Shamed, or Was the Poet Having Fun? [Ibn Quzman's 'Zajal No. 133']," in *Homoeroticism in Classical Arabic Literature*, ed. J. W. Wright Jr. and Everett K. Rowson [New York: Columbia Univ. Press, 1997], 120).

41. Cf. No. 137, p. 116; No. 804, p. 568; and No. 894, p. 627.

42. No. 146, p. 126.

43. No. 611, p. 444.

44. Abu Nuwas's influence in the bacchic genre is not limited to Arabic literature. He had a significant impact on Hebrew wine poetry of al-Andalus. See Raymond P. Scheindlin, *Wine, Women, and Death: Medieval Hebrew Poems on the Good Life* (Oxford: Oxford Univ. Press, 1999), 19–33.

45. It will be recalled that Noah, after he left the Ark, planted a vine. See Gen. 9:20.

46. On the etiquette at these parties, compare this poem attributed to Abu 'Abd al-Rahman al-'Atawi by the poet and man of letters al-Husri (d. 1022) (*Zahr al-adab wa-thamar al-albab* [The Flower of Letters and the Fruit of Bright Minds], ed. 'Ali Muhammad al-Bajawi, vol. 1 [Cairo: Dar Ihya' al-Kutub al-'Arabiyya, 1953], 448; see also 'Abd al-Rahman Sidqi, *Alhan al-han* [Tunes of the Tavern] [Cairo: Dar al-Ma'arif, 1957], 262):

The rules of imbibing and boon-companionship are five:
the first is to maintain always a dignified mien.

The second is to be lenient towards the others—
how many a boon companion's reputation has been saved thanks to lenience!

The third—which applies even if the greatest desert sheikh were your father—
is to refrain from boasting.

The fourth—and boon companions are entitled to treatment
different from that of kin and neighbors—

Is to clothe your speech, when you express yourself,
in the garment of concision.

And the fifth, the observance of which
attests truly to noble origin and character,

Is to forget by day what was said by night—
the blame for all indiscretions belongs to the wine.

47. No. 32, p. 37.

48. Some of the wine evidently was effervescent.

49. No. 138, p. 116.

50. No. 31, p. 36.

51. The jars in which the wine was kept were sealed on top with clay. See David Storm Rice, "Deacon or Drink: Some Paintings from Samarra Re-examined," in *Early Islamic Art and Architecture*, ed. Jonathan M. Bloom (Aldershot, UK: Ashgate, 2002), 219.

52. They also maintained that He is unique and unitary, without resemblance to his creatures and without separable attributes (His attributes are identical with His essence). Because of their two main positions they were called the "Partisans of Unity and Justice."

53. Al-Nazzam's coming to Baghdad was a harbinger of the Muʻtazilites' increased influence at court. Their influence peaked under the next caliph, al-Maʼmun (r. 813–33), who adopted their rationalist views.

54. Contrast No. 785, p. 559, in which Jinan's look is said to make a stone lovesick.

55. Cited by al-Raghib al-Isfahani (d. ca. 1108) in *Muhadarat al-udaba' wa-muhawarat al-shu'ara' wa-al-bulagha'* [The Colloquies of the Litterateurs], ed. ʻUmar al-Tabbaʻ, vol. 2 (Beirut: Dar al-Arqam, 1999), 279, trans. Rowson.

56. The similar roots for medication and illness are *d-w-ya'* and *d-w-a'*.

57. See Montgomery, "Revelry and Remorse"; and James E. Montgomery, "For the Love of a Christian Boy: A Song by Abu Nuwas," *JAL* 27 (1996): 115–24.

58. P. Kennedy, 191–92.

59. Al-Maʼmun was the son of Harun al-Rashid and Persian concubine Marajil.

60. Abu Hiffan, *Akhbar Abi Nuwas,* ed. ʻAbd al-Sattar Ahmad Farraj (Cairo: Maktabat Misr, 1953), 99.

61. No. 440, p. 342; No. 998, p. 691.

62. Al-Hariri, *The Assemblies of al-Hariri,* trans. Thomas Chenery, vol. 1 (London: Williams and Norgate, 1867), 173 (translation slightly modified).

63. No. 307, p. 242.

8. THE POETICS OF PERSUASION

1. Al-Mas'udi, *The Meadows of Gold,* trans. and ed. Paul Lunde and Caroline Stone (London: Kegan Paul, 1989), 205.

2. Al-Suli (d. 946), *Akhbar Abi Tammam* [The Particulars Transmitted of Abu Tammam], ed. Muhammad 'Abduh 'Azzam (Cairo: Lajnat al-Ta'lif wa-al-Tarjama wa-al-Nashr, 1937), 104–5.

3. See chapter 3.

4. Suzanne Pinckney Stetkevych, *The Poetics of Islamic Legitimacy: Myth, Gender, and Ceremony in the Classical Arabic Ode* (Bloomington: Indiana Univ. Press, 2002), 34.

5. Abu Tammam, *Diwan Abi Tammam bi-sharh al-Khatib al-Tibrizi,* ed. Muhammad 'Abduh 'Azzam, 3 vols. (Cairo: Dar al-Ma'arif, 1964), No. 37, vol. 1, p. 384.

6. In 836 al-Mu'tasim had moved the 'Abbasid court to Samarra (the name is shortened from *surra man ra'a,* "Joy to the Beholder"). It remained there until 892, when it was moved back to Baghdad. Amorium, in Anatolia, was captured in 838 from the Byzantines.

7. Al-Suli, 146.

8. Mudar was the ancestor of the largest and most powerful confederation of tribes in ancient northern Arabia. Ibn Abi Du'ad traced his ancestry to Iyad, the brother of Mudar. The following tree illustrates the putative North Arabian genealogy:

By contrast Abu Tammam claimed descent, as mentioned above, from Tayyi', a Yemenite, or South Arabian tribe.

9. Al-Suli, 147–48. This incident probably occurred between 841 and 843, since Abu Tammam returned one year later to Ibn Abi Du'ad with a plea of intercession from Khalid ibn Yazid al-Shaybani (d. 844), the governor of Armenia under al-Wathiq (r. 842–47). Shayban, it may be noted, traced its ancestry to Rabi'a. See previous note.

10. No. 35, vol. 1, p. 369.

11. No. 36, vol. 1, p. 383.

12. No. 38, vol. 1, p. 400.

13. Julie Scott Meisami notes a similar analogy between the love for the lady and love for the patron in a panegyric by Bashshar ibn Burd ("The Uses of the *Qasida:* Thematic and Structural Patterns in a Poem of Bashshar," *JAL* 16 [1985]: 41–45).

14. Mas'ud ibn 'Amr al-Azdi. Al-Suli proposes that Abu Tammam refers rather to Mas'ud, the brother of Dhu al-Rumma, although this idea is unconvincing since the brother is mentioned in the *Diwan* not as crying but instead as expressing amazement that a dignified and reasonable man like Dhu al-Rumma should shed tears over a departed woman (Abu Tammam, *Sharh al-Suli li-Diwan Abi Tammam*, ed. Khalaf Rashid Nu'man, 3 vols. [Baghdad: Wizarat al-I'lam, 1972], 1:389). Cf. Dhu al-Rumma, *Diwan*, ed. Zuhayr Fath Allah (Beirut: Dar Beirut, 1995), No. 32, p. 233.

15. Labid ibn Rabi'a, *Diwan*, No. 28, p. 214.

16. The tribe of al-'Id from southern Arabia was known for its camels.

17. Ishmael and Hud were prophets (discussed later).

18. For example, he dispenses formally with both *nasib* and *rahil* in the Amorium poem, which deals with al-Mu'tasim's military victory.

19. Hadith No. 35 in al-Nawawi, 113.

20. Similarly, he promotes a collective identity to the Arab readers of the *Hamasa* anthology. On Abu Tammam's editorial practice, Suzanne Pinckney Stetkevych observes keenly, "The random mixing of poems relating to particular tribes, wars, battles, and eras has the effect of suppressing the specific heritage of a particular tribe or era and creating instead a panorama of seemingly timeless exemplars of 'Arabism'" (*Abu Tammam*, 287).

21. Ma'add is a collective name for the North Arabs; Iyad was a subset of Ma'add. See note 8.

22. Zuhr was Ibn Abi Du'ad's clan within the Iyad tribe.

23. The hero here mentioned is Ka'b ibn Mama of Iyad, who chose to share his supply of water with a companion and thereupon died of thirst (Abu Tammam, *Sharh al-Suli*, 1:392). Hatim al-Ta'i likewise immortalized himself by being extremely generous. He is remembered, for example, for giving away, as a youth, his father's entire herd of three hundred camels to three passing riders (the father, not being as generous, decamped with the family and would not let Hatim come along when he learned of it). See Nicholson, *Literary History*, 85–86.

24. At one point (ca. 835) in the period of al-Mu'tasim's rule, the orthodox population of Baghdad threatened to wreck the palace after their champion, Ahmad ibn Hanbal, had been flogged. Ibn Abi Du'ad had played a major role in the inquisition that led to this punishment, and we may assume that he was inside the palace. Later, the Mu'tazilites found themselves increasingly isolated and under attack. The succeeding caliph, al-Wathiq, finally withdrew his support from them and, in 851–52, under al-Mutawakkil, their doctrine was officially pronounced heretical. Cf. M. Hinds, "Mihna," in *EI²*; Walter M. Patton, *Ahmad ibn Hanbal and the Mihna* (Leiden: Brill, 1897), 91–123; and Hugh Kennedy, *The Prophet and the Age of the Caliphates: The Islamic Near East from the Sixth to the Eleventh Century* (London: Longman, 1986), 164, 168–69. On later manifestations of Mu'tazilism, see D. Gimaret, "Mu'tazila," in *EI²*.

25. Here is a transliteration of D:

30   fa-sma' maqalata za'irin lam tashtabih
      ara'uhu 'inda -shtibahi l-bidi

31   yastamu baʿda l-qawli minka bi-fiʿlihi
      kamalan wa-ʿafwa ridaka bi-l-majhudi

26. Khalid ibn Yazid al-Shaybani, governor of Armenia and advocate for Abu Tammam. See note 9.

27. Al-Walid ibn ʿAbd al-Malik (al-Walid I), Umayyad caliph (r. 705–15). Yazid ibn al-Muhallab served periodically between 702 and 720 as governor of Khurasan and of Iraq.

28. Although the "happy king" has been traditionally thought to be Sulayman ibn ʿAbd al-Malik (r. 715–17), al-Walid would seem to be the person intended (see later explanation).

29. Ayyub and ʿAbd al-ʿAziz were, respectively, sons of Sulayman and al-Walid.

30. The use of taha'im, plural of Tihama (a region in Arabia), suggests western outlying areas specifically.

31. Whether because of his relatives' gratitude or not, Yazid apparently enjoyed Sulayman's esteem subsequently, as he was appointed governor of Iraq upon Sulayman's accession in 715 and of Khurasan as well a short time later.

32. ʿAbid ibn al-Abras, pre-Islamic poet said to have been slain by the Lakhmid king Mundhir III (d. 554). According to the story of ʿAbid's demise, the king, in remorse for burying alive two boon companions, had designated for commemorative rites two days of the year: the "Day of Delight," on which he would give the first person he saw one hundred black camels, and the "Day of Sorrow," when he would sacrifice the first person he saw. ʿAbid encountered him first on the latter day. Al-Isfahani, 28:9669–72.

33. S. P. Stetkevych, Abu Tammam, 153.

34. Abu Tammam's alteration of the facts raises the issue of sidq, or truthfulness. Whatever one thinks of his ethics, one cannot, at least according to the standards of some classical Arab theorists, fault his poetics. Qudama ibn Jaʿfar (d. ca. 932) found that a poet should not be taxed for insincerity, so long as he combined skillfully the wording, meaning, rhyme, and meter to suit the immediate context, and related that the best poetry was thought to be the least truthful. In Al-ʿIqd al-farid [The Peerless Necklace], 4 vols. (Cairo: al-Matbaʿa al-Jamaliyya, 1913), Ibn ʿAbd Rabbihi (d. 940) quotes an authority who articulates this last position explicitly: "A man of letters was once asked who, in his opinion, was the greatest of all poets (ashʿar al-nas). To this he answered: He who can present what is false under the appearance of truth, and what is true under the appearance of falsehood, through the charm of his poetic concept and the delicacy of an appealing expression, in such a way that he may be able to deface the most perfect beauty and to embellish even utter ugliness" (quoted in Cantarino, 37). By such standards, the lie told in this section certainly qualifies as great poetry, and Abu Tammam as a master poet.

35. The land of the Mahra tribe stretched between Hadramawt and Oman in southern Arabia. Tazid belonged to the Qudaʿa federation of tribes, believed to be of Yemenite origin. From the regions of Mahra and Tazid came distinctive, high-quality garments (Abu Tammam, Diwan Abi Tammam bi-sharh al-Tibrizi, 1:398).

36. Al-Nabigha al-Dhubyani, *Diwan*, No. 34, p. 81.

37. No. 41, 1:423.

38. During the pre-Islamic era and later as well, poetry was widely believed to be inspired by the jinn and sometimes as having magical properties.

9. THE WOULD-BE PROPHET

1. Certain of the jinn were given to Solomon (the same as the biblical king) as workers. They constructed for him shrines, statues, and large pools. See Qur'an 34:12–13.

2. The Queen of Sheba, ruler of an unbelieving folk of Yemen, was brought to Solomon's palace in Jerusalem by means of a jinni. Upon entering the palace, the queen mistook the floor for a pool and bared her legs to step in. Solomon, seated at his throne, spoke out and informed her that what she thought was a pool was a floor of glass. Amazed, she surrendered to Solomon's God, the Lord of mankind, jinn, and all that exists. See Qur'an 27:15–44; J. Walker, "Sulayman ibn Dawud," in *EI²*; and E. Ullendorf, "Bilkis," in *EI²*.

3. Two stars.

4. Al-Buhturi, *Diwan*, ed. Karam al-Bustani, 2 vols. (Beirut: Dar Sadir, 1966), No. 14, vol. 1, pp. 35–36. The achievement of the Ja'fari Palace complex is discussed by Alastair Northedge in "The Palaces of the 'Abbasids at Samarra," in *A Medieval Islamic City Reconsidered: An Interdisciplinary Approach to Samarra*, ed. Chase F. Robinson (Oxford: Oxford Univ. Press, 2001), 39–41.

5. No. 92, vol. 1, p. 190.

6. The full poem is translated and discussed by Richard A. Serrano in "Al-Buhturi's Poetics of Persian Abodes," *JAL* 28 (1997): 68–87; Akiko Motoyoshi Sumi in *Description in Classical Arabic Poetry: Wasf, Ekphrasis, and Interarts Theory* (Leiden: Brill, 2004), 100–112; and Samer M. Ali in "Reinterpreting al-Buhturi's Iwan Kisra Ode: Tears of Affection for the Cycles of History," *JAL* 37 (2006): 46–67.

7. Ibn Rashiq, 1:174.

8. From Bahrain; the movement was started by Hamdan Qarmat (d. ca. 874). On their revolt against the 'Abbasids, see W. Madelung, "Karmati," in *EI²*.

9. Al-Mutanabbi, *Diwan* (Beirut: Dar Sadir, 1964), No. 10, p. 16.

10. No. 12, p. 21.

11. No. 28, p. 40.

12. No. 12, p. 22; Ibn Jinni, *Al-Fasr* [The Clear Explanation], ed. Safa' al-Khalusi, vol. 2 (Baghdad: Wizarat al-Thaqafa wa-al-Funun, 1977), 322. Salih was an ancient Arab prophet sent to the people of Thamud. They did not listen to his tidings, and so God destroyed them. See Qur'an 7:73–79. Others (see Ibn Jinni, 2:314) maintained that the nickname was for the poem's center line: "What is my status among Nakhla's folk, / but like that of Jesus among the Jews."

13. Quoted in 'Abd Allah al-Juburi, *Abu al-Tayyib al-Mutanabbi fi athar al-darisin* (Baghdad: Wizarat al-Thaqafa wa-al-Funun, 1977), 21. Other accounts include this communication, part of

what he supposedly cited as holy revelation: "By the traveling star, and the revolving firmament, and the night and the day—Behold: mankind is in jeopardy. Proceed on your way, and follow the footsteps of those prophets who came before you. For God, through you, is bringing into line those who have swerved from the religious path and are going astray" (215, and elsewhere with slight variation).

14. A version may be found in al-Juburi, 13. This translation, from a slightly different version, is by Wolfhart Heinrichs in "The Meaning of Mutanabbi," in *Poetry and Prophecy: The Beginnings of a Literary Tradition,* ed. James L. Kugel (Ithaca: Cornell Univ. Press, 1990), 126.

15. No. 36, p. 55; Ibrahim 'Awad, *Al-Mutanabbi: Dirasa jadida li-hayatihi wa-shakhsiyyatihi* (Cairo, 1987), 118–27.

16. Cf. Lyall, "*Mufaddaliyyat,*" 2:295–97.

17. Not all the patrons proved themselves worthy of the praise. One gave al-Mutanabbi, for a forty-line work (No. 64, p. 109), a single dinar; the work came to be known as "The Dinar Qasida." Here is a line from it: "He is like the sea, casting pearls generously before the man at the shore / and sending clouds over the man inland."

18. No. 109, p. 198.

19. No. 62, p. 101.

20. No. 73, p. 142.

21. No. 145, p. 239.

22. No. 111, p. 205.

23. No. 149, p. 245.

24. No. 58, p. 85.

25. See the following from Hilal al-Sabi' (d. 1056), *Rusum dar al-khilafa* [The Rules and Regulations of the 'Abbasid Court], trans. Elie A. Salem (Beirut: American Univ. of Beirut, 1977), 29–32: "In the past it was the practice of the caliph sometimes to offer his hand, covered with his sleeve, to an amir or a wazir to kiss. The caliph did this to honor him and to acknowledge his high position and to do him a special favor. The reason he covered it with his sleeve was to protect it from being touched by mouth or lip. This practice has now been replaced by kissing the ground, and to this rule all people now comply." And from the same, on the demeanor before the caliph:

> The wazir must minimize turning to his sides or his back, and minimize the movements of his hands or of any of his members; and must not lift his leg and rest it on the other if he should get tired. His attention should be focused on the caliph alone, particularly on his mouth. He may not whisper to anyone else in the caliph's presence nor point to anyone by hand or by look. He may not read a note or a letter / delivered to him, except those which the caliph asks him to read. . . .
>
> From the moment he enters to the moment he leaves the caliph's presence, the wazir must stand in the place assigned to him according to his rank. He may not stop short of it, or go beyond it, unless he is asked by the caliph to draw near for a secret conversation. He should not leave as long as the caliph is talking to him or is showing interest in him,

nor should he stay when their conversation comes to an end. If, upon his departure, the caliph is watching him, he must leave walking backwards lest he show his back to him. When he disappears from his sight, he may then walk straight.

26. No. 160, p. 259.

27. Yusuf al-Badiʻi (d. ca. 1662), *Al-Subh al-munbi ʻan haythiyyat al-Mutanabbi* [The Revealing Dawn as to the Distinction of al-Mutanabbi] (Damascus: Matbaʻat al-Iʻtidal, 1931), 45.

28. See al-Thaʻalibi, quoted in al-Juburi, 99. For example, al-Mutanabbi openly says in one poem (No. 190, p. 321), "I love you, O sun and full moon of the age." As regards the beloved, he contrasts himself apparently with the Don Juans of Arabic literature. In the same poem he continues:

This because your excellence shines,
not because life with you is pleasant and easy.

Loving one person wisely is sound;
loving many unthinkingly is corrupt.

29. Consider this sentiment of his (from No. 194, p. 333): "If you leave a people, and they allow it, / then really they are the ones leaving."

30. No. 248, p. 466. Ibn Jinni confided to him about the *nasib* (al-Badiʻi, 53–54):

"It's hard for me to read this poetry as being about anyone but Sayf al-Dawla."

"He was the one who gave me to Kafur by his mishandling of affairs and lapse in judgment," al-Mutanabbi replied.

31. Al-Badiʻi, 62.

32. The caliph normally was concealed from general observation by a curtain. When he was formally addressed, the curtain was raised (al-Sabiʼ, 66).

33. No. 252, pp. 480–81.

34. No. 265, p. 512.

35. Quoted in Seeger A. Bonebakker, *Hatimi and His Encounter with Mutanabbi: A Biographical Sketch* (Amsterdam: North-Holland, 1984), 17–18.

36. In his treatise, al-Hatimi reveals himself as sharply focused on niceties. In considering al-Hatimi's very close-up approach, the critical question discussed in *On the Sublime* by the author called Longinus, thought to be of the first century CE, is pertinent (trans. G. M. A. Grube [New York: Liberal Arts Press, 1957], 44–45):

Which is to be preferred in poetry or in prose, great writing with occasional flaws or moderate talent which is entirely sound and faultless? . . . I am well aware that supreme genius is certainly not at all free from faults. Preciseness in every detail incurs the risk of pettiness, whereas with the very great, as with the very rich, something must inevitably be neglected. It is perhaps also inevitable that inferior and average talent remains for the most part safe and faultless because it avoids risk and does not aim at the heights, while great qualities are always precarious because of their very greatness. . . .

I have myself drawn attention to not a few faults in Homer and other very great writers. These faults displeased me, yet I did not consider them to be willful mistakes but rather lapses and oversights due to the random carelessness and inattention of genius. In any case, it is my conviction that greater talents, even if not sustained throughout, should get our vote for their nobility of mind if for no other reason.

37. Quoted in ʿAbd al-Wahhab ʿAzzam, *Dhikra Abi al-Tayyib baʿd alf ʿam,* 2nd ed. (Cairo: Dar al-Maʿarif, 1968), 172.

38. The name of al-Mutanabbi's wife, or otherwise the woman who bore his son, is not mentioned in the sources. It seems reasonable to believe, according to the chronology, that al-Mutanabbi met her and fathered the child in Syria.

39. The line is from No. 278, p. 539, a panegyric to ʿAdud al-Dawla.

40. Al-Badiʿi, 90. For more on al-Mutanabbi's life and poetry, see Margaret Larkin's excellent recent study, *Al-Mutanabbi: Voice of the ʿAbbasid Poetic Ideal* (Oxford: Oneworld, 2008).

41. In 926 the Byzantines repulsed an attack by the Bulgarian czar Symeon. The next year they signed a treaty with his successor and began to devote their attention to their Muslim adversaries.

42. The accounts relating to this expedition are contained in Marius Canard, ed., *Sayf al-Daula: Recueil de textes relatifs à l'émir Sayf al-Daula le Hamdanide* (Algiers: Carbonel, 1934), 87–92. Canard has constructed a comprehensive narrative based on these accounts (see his *Histoire de la dynastie des Hʾamdanides de Jazîra et de Syrie,* vol. 1 [Paris: Presses Universitaires de France, 1953], 763–70). The description of events provided here is a summary of Canard's narrative.

43. Probably a Byzantine spy had been among the Muslims and had reported the return itinerary. Cf. Canard, *Histoire,* 769.

44. The poem is No. 188, p. 311. It is also the subject of a recent article by Majd Yaser al-Mallah. See "A Victory Celebration after a Military Defeat? Al-Mutanabbi's ʿAyniyyah of 339/950," *JAL* 40 (2009): 107–28.

45. That is, in the first phrase, glory in the form of a sword; the sword was hung from the shoulder in a suspensory.

46. No. 226, p. 375.

47. That is, a chain.

48. He often begins his chronicles with a verb of motion in the past tense. See the discussion of chronicle openings in Andras Hamori, *The Composition of Mutanabbi's Panegyrics to Sayf al-Dawla* (Leiden: Brill, 1992), 6–18.

49. Compare the diagram of this poem in Julie Scott Meisami, "Al-Mutanabbi and the Critics," *Arabic and Middle Eastern Literatures* 2, no. 1 (1999): 31–33.

50. Ibn Rashiq, 1:381, quoted in Meisami, "Al-Mutanabbi," 24.

10. LETTER TO A PRINCESS

1. The story of 'Abd al-Rahman I is one of the most dramatic in Arab history. In 750, when he was twenty years old, the successful 'Abbasid revolt spelled doom for his family. He was the only one to escape the general massacre. He initially took refuge, along with his thirteen-year-old brother, in a Bedouin camp along the left bank of the Euphrates. Then one day the black 'Abbasid standards appeared on the horizon, at which point the two dashed into the water. The younger believed his pursuers' assurances of amnesty and returned from midstream to the bank (perhaps he was a weak swimmer), whereupon he was slaughtered; 'Abd al-Rahman kept going and reached the other side. Over the next five years, despite being the most wanted man in the empire, he was able to work his way incognito back through Syria, then across Palestine, Egypt, and North Africa, before crossing into al-Andalus via Gibraltar (from the Arabic "Jabal Tariq," "Tariq's Mountain," after one of the conquering generals). Thence he built his own Andalusi empire. His accomplishment won admiration even from his worst enemies. A historian relates (Ibn al-'Idhari [fl. 1310], *Al-Bayan al-mughrib* [The Extraordinary Explanation], quoted in Nicholson, *Literary History*, 407):

> One day, the 'Abbasid Caliph Mansur [r. 754–75] asked his courtiers, "Who is the Falcon of the Quraysh [the Meccan tribe of the Umayyads and the 'Abbasids]?" They replied, "O Commander of the Faithful, that title belongs to you who have vanquished mighty kings and have put an end to civil war." "No," said the Caliph, "it is not I." "Mu'awiya [r. 661–80], then, or 'Abd al-Malik [r. 685–705]?" "No," said Mansur, "the Falcon of the Quraysh is 'Abd al-Rahman, he who traversed alone the deserts of Asia and Africa, and without any army to aid him sought his fortune in an unknown country beyond the sea. With no weapons except judgment and resolution he subdued his enemies, crushed the rebels, secured his frontiers, and founded a great empire. Such a feat was never accomplished by any one before."

2. Quoted in Reinhart Dozy, *Spanish Islam: A History of the Moslems in Spain,* trans. Francis Griffin Stokes (London: Chatto and Windus, 1913), 268.

3. Philip K. Hitti, *History of the Arabs,* 10th ed. (New York: St. Martin's, 1970), 524–26; Philip K. Hitti, *Capital Cities of Arab Islam* (Minneapolis: Univ. of Minnesota Press, 1973), 144, 154.

4. T. S. Eliot, "Tradition and the Individual Talent," in *Selected Essays: 1917–1932* (New York: Harcourt, 1932), 5–6.

5. Ibn Zaydun, *Diwan,* ed. Karam al-Bustani (Beirut: Dar Sadir, 1964). References are to this edition, unless otherwise indicated.

6. Ibn Zaydun, *Diwan Ibn Zaydun wa-rasa'iluhu,* ed. 'Ali 'Abd al-'Azim (Cairo: Dar Nahdat Misr lil-Tab' wa-al-Nashr, 1980), 30.

7. Ibn Bassam (d. 1147), *Al-Dhakhira fi mahasin ahl al-Jazira* [The Rich Repository of the Merits of the People of the Iberian Peninsula], ed. Ihsan 'Abbas, vol. 1, pt. 1 (Beirut: Dar al-Thaqafa, 1975), 430.

8. Ibn Zaydun, *Diwan Ibn Zaydun wa-rasa'iluhu,* 779.

9. No. 77, p. 94.

10. No. 149, pp. 283–84. Cf. Ibn Zaydun, *Diwan Ibn Zaydun wa-rasa'iluhu,* 92–93.

11. Ibn Bassam, 431–32.

12. No. 28, p. 51.

13. No. 41, p. 59.

14. Ibn Bassam, 432. The line is from a panegyric by Abu Nuwas.

15. No. 61, p. 70.

16. 'Ali 'Abd al-'Azim, *Ibn Zaydun* (Cairo: Dar al-Katib al-'Arabi lil-Tiba'a wa-al-Nashr, 1967), 217. It will be noted that Saturn is smaller than Jupiter and farther from Earth.

17. No. 18, p. 34.

18. No. 76, pp. 91, 93.

19. No. 157, p. 288.

20. Ibn Hazm, *The Ring of the Dove: A Treatise on the Art and Practice of Arab Love,* trans. A. J. Arberry (London: Luzac, 1994), 85.

21. Ibn Zaydun, *Diwan Ibn Zaydun wa-rasa'iluhu,* 33.

22. Ibn Zaydun, *Diwan Ibn Zaydun wa-rasa'iluhu,* 667. Normally, in the figurative expressions about sexual intercourse, men are the ones described as riding horseback. However, sexually assertive women may also be described as riding horseback. See Rowson, "Medieval Arabic Vice Lists," 56–57, 68, 71–72.

23. Ibn Zaydun, *Diwan Ibn Zaydun wa-rasa'iluhu,* 34.

24. This line is translated in James T. Monroe, "Hispano-Arabic Poetry During the Caliphate of Córdoba: Theory and Practice," in *Arabic Poetry: Theory and Development,* ed. G. E. von Grunebaum (Wiesbaden: Otto Harrassowitz, 1973), 145. On the sentiment expressed here, compare the anecdote related by Ibn Rashiq: "The poet Dhu al-Rumma (d. 735) was once asked, 'What would you do if your genius did not help you to compose poems?' That could not happen, he answered, since he knew an ever-effective means to stir his genius up. 'It is,' he said, 'just to remember your beloved when you are alone'" (quoted in Kinany, 60).

25. No. 25, pp. 48–49.

26. The assistance of the ruler's son is conjectured by 'Ali 'Abd al-'Azim in Ibn Zaydun, *Diwan Ibn Zaydun wa-rasa'iluhu,* 44.

27. Al-Safadi (d. 1363), *Tamam al-mutun fi sharh risalat Ibn Zaydun* [The Comprehensive Text in the Explication of Ibn Zaydun's Letters], ed. Muhammad Abu al-Fadl Ibrahim (Cairo: Dar al-Fikr al-'Arabi, 1969), 13.

28. Ibn Rashiq, 1:356.

29. Here is the first line transliterated: "adha t-tana'i badilan min tadanina / wa naba 'an tibi luqyana tajafina."

30. This aspect of the poem has been highlighted in Monroe, *Hispano-Arabic Poetry,* 20.

31. Ibn Dawud, 66.

32. Ibn Hazm, 59.

33. Monroe, "Caliphate of Córdoba," 145–46. Cf. Emil L. Fackenheim, "A Treatise on Love by Ibn Sina," *Medieval Studies* 7 (1945): 208–28, esp. 220–21.

34. Ibn Hazm, 156.

35. Monroe, "Caliphate of Córdoba," 153.

36. Wallada had a beauty spot on her cheek.

37. Eglantine, native to Europe, has bright-pink flowers. The poet is referring here to ruddy cheeks.

38. As noted in el Tayib, 48.

39. This because it comes from Najd, the plateau region in the Arabian Peninsula where Bedouin tribes traditionally camped during the winter and spring. During the long summer months, the various tribes remained by permanent water sources, generally to the west, in the Hejaz. On the east wind, see J. Stetkevych, *Zephyrs of Najd,* 123–34.

40. *Diwan,* No. 19, p. 96.

41. Al-Zawzani, 184.

42. Nadia Lachiri, "Andalusi Proverbs on Women," in *Writing the Feminine: Women in Arab Sources,* ed. Manuela Marín and Randi Deguilhem (London: I. B. Tauris, 2002), 44, 47.

43. Ibn Hazm, 89.

44. Cf. Teresa Garulo, "Women in Medieval Classical Arabic Poetry," in *Writing the Feminine: Women in Arab Sources,* ed. Manuela Marín and Randi Deguilhem (London: I. B. Tauris, 2002), 30–35.

45. Al-'Abbas ibn al-Ahnaf, *Diwan* (Beirut: Dar Sadir, 1965), No. 193, p. 132.

46. Ibn Dawud, 66.

47. Sidra, or Sidrat al-Muntaha, is a lote tree in Paradise; Kawthar is a river there. Zaqqum is a tree in hell producing a bitter, skull-shaped fruit; Ghislin is the perspiration from the bodies of the damned. Qur'an 53:14, 16, 108, 44:43, 56:52, 69:36.

48. Ibn Hazm, 154.

49. One finds evidence of such unrequited love in Ibn Zaydun's poem (No. 23, p. 46) that opens, "In al-Zahra', I remembered you longingly. . . ." Composed after the *Nuniyya*—Ibn Zaydun later returned anonymously to the Córdoba environs and revisited their old haunts—it bears an interesting intertextual relation to the longer and more famous poem. The poem begins with a recollection of the beloved Wallada in the intimate *ki* form, after which there is a description of the al-Zahra' gardens, probably their favorite purlieu. In this case, nature appears to empathize with the poet rather than be called to his aid, for the period of their mutual pleasure is long past. The pronominal suffix *kum* replaces *ki* in the last third of the poem, since more detached relations have taken the place of intimacy. Wallada has found consolation for the times lost, and the poet, preserving the bond, remains her devoted lover.

50. Renate Jacobi, "The *Khayal* Motif in Early Arabic Poetry," *Oriens* 32 (1990): 50–64.

51. No. 112, p. 219.

52. No. 26, p. 49.

53. James T. Monroe, "The Structure of an Arabic *Muwashshah* with a Bilingual *Kharja*," *Edibiyat* 1 (1976): 122.

11. SEASON'S GREETINGS

1. Suzanne Pinckney Stetkevych, *Poetics of Islamic Legitimacy,* 229. See her discussion of 'Id poems in *Poetics of Islamic Legitimacy,* 185–209, 223–37, 243–81.

2. Ibn Quzman, *Diwan: Isabat al-aghrad fi dhikr al-a'rad* [Hitting the Mark in Recalling the Good Reputations], ed. Federico Corriente (Cairo: Consejo Superior de Cultura, 1995); Ibn Quzman, *Diwan (Todo Ben Quzman),* ed. Emilio García Gómez, 3 vols. (Madrid: Gredos, 1972); Ibn Quzman, *Diwan* (manuscript facsimile), ed. David de Gunzburg (Berlin: Calvary, 1896). Page references are to Corriente's edition.

3. See James T. Monroe's *Structural Coherence and Organic Unity in the Poetry of Ibn Quzman* (Leiden: Brill, forthcoming).

4. Al-Marrakushi, *Al-Mu'jib fi talkhis akhbar al-Maghrib* [The Amazing Summary of Information on the Maghrib], ed. Muhammad Sa'id al-'Aryan and Muhammad al-'Azbi al-'Almi (Casablanca: Dar al-Kitab, 1978), 252–54. Al-Marrakushi, by the way, was employed by the dynasty that replaced the Almoravids, so we should be aware that his history has a negative slant.

5. Ibn al-Qasim (d. 806) was Malik's disciple and the principal transmitter of his opinions. Ibn al-Qasim's *Al-Mudawwana al-kubra* is a basic text for the Malikite school of jurisprudence. Ibn al-Banni's lines are quoted in Marrakushi, 253.

6. Al-Maqqari (d. 1632), *Nafh al-tib min ghusn al-Andalus al-ratib* [The Diffusion of Fragrance from the Tender Branch of al-Andalus], ed. Ihsan 'Abbas, vol. 3 (Beirut: Dar Sadir, 1968), 448.

7. Marcel Mauss, *The Gift: Forms and Functions of Exchange in Archaic Societies,* trans. Ian Cunnison (New York: Norton, 1967), 72. Cf. S. P. Stetkevych, *Poetics of Islamic Legitimacy,* 33–34, 76–79, 181–84.

8. The *musalla* was an open space outside the city where the entire community would perform prayers during 'Id al-Fitr (Feast of the Fast-Breaking, following the month of Ramadan) and 'Id al-Adha.

9. Quoted in George Makdisi, *Ibn 'Aqil, Religion, and Culture in Classical Islam* (Edinburgh: Edinburgh Univ. Press, 1997), 210–11.

10. Edward W. Lane, *Manners and Customs of the Modern Egyptians* (New York: Dutton, 1966), 486. Compare "Cemetery Turns into Brothel" from twenty-first-century Kuwait, published on the third day of 'Id al-Fitr: "Away from the sight of security forces, a group of female prostitutes have reportedly turned the Sulaibikhat cemetery into a safe haven for their trade. After being alerted, security forces immediately rushed to the area but the alleged culprits managed to escape by pretending to be among the mourners at a funeral service. Security forces are reportedly exerting concerted efforts to apprehend the culprits" (*Al-Watan Daily,* Oct. 2, 2008, 1).

11. Mikhail Bakhtin, *Rabelais and His World,* trans. Helene Iswolsky (Cambridge: MIT Press, 1968), 18.

12. L. J. McLoughlin, *A Learner's Dictionary of Classical Arabic Idioms* (Beirut: Librarie du Liban, 1988), 115. Al-Maydani lists instead the variant *al-hurru takfihi al-isharatu* (Allusion Suffices the Noble Man) (1:296).

13. No. 148, p. 420.

14. No. 15, p. 69.

15. G. J. H. Van Gelder, *Of Dishes and Discourse: Classical Arabic Literary Representations of Food* (Richmond, UK: Curzon, 2000), 18.

16. Al-Ghazali (d. 1111), *Ihya' 'ulum al-din* [The Revival of the Religious Sciences], 4 vols. (Cairo: Mu'assasat al-Halabi wa-Shuraka'ihi, 1967), 3:105.

17. Ikhwan al-Safa', *Rasa'il,* ed. 'Arif Tamir, vol. 1 (Beirut: Manshurat 'Uwaydat, 1994), 333–35; Abu Hayyan al-Tawhidi, *Kitab al-imta' wa-al-mu'anasa* [The Book of Enjoyment and Sociability], ed. Ahmad al-Tuwayli (Tunis: Dar Bu Salama lil-Tiba'a wa-al-Nashr wa-al-Tawzi', 1988), 297–300.

18. *Diwan,* ed. Corriente, No. 17 (unpublished trans. by James T. Monroe).

19. Al-Isfahani, 8:3033–34, 3036–37, 11:3814; al-Mutanabbi, *Diwan,* No. 197, p. 339, line 40; cf. al-Mutanabbi, *Diwan al-Mutanabbi wa-fi athna' matnihi sharh al-Wahidi,* ed. Friedrich Dieterici (Berlin, 1861), 493.

20. James T. Monroe and Mark Pettigrew, "The Decline of Courtly Patronage and the Appearance of New Genres in Arabic Literature: The Case of the *Zajal,* the *Maqama,* and the Shadow Play," *JAL* 34 (2003): 138–77.

21. *The Maqamat of Badi' al-Zaman al-Hamadhani,* trans. W. J. Prendergast (London: Luzac, 1915), 30.

22. Badi' al-Zaman al-Hamadhani, 71.

23. Fedwa Malti-Douglas, "Structure and Organization in a Monographic *Adab* Work: *Al-Tatfil* of al-Khatib al-Baghdadi," *JNES* 40, no. 3 (1981): 234, 240–42. Malti-Douglas goes on to say that "tatfil represents the abuse by a guest of his rights in a hospitality situation" (242). Though the *tufayli* exists in classical Arabic literature as a humorous character type, the egregious *tatfil* behavioral pattern also surfaces occasionally in modern Arabic literature. For instance, when the character Sa'id in Najib Mahfuz's *Al-Liss wa-al-kilab* [The Thief and the Dogs, 1961], in vol. 6 of *Al-A'mal al-kamila* (Beirut: Al-Maktaba al-'Ilmiyya al-Jadida, 1981), 783–884, gets out of prison, he makes an unexpected visit to an old friend, who now lives in a posh villa. There he appalls the friend by his partiality for the hors d'oeuvres. However, in contrast to the stereotypical *tufayli,* Sa'id does not outwit his host, and when he later returns to the villa to steal objets d'art, he gets caught.

24. Badi' al-Zaman al-Hamadhani, 155.

25. In the *maqama,* Abu al-Fath's personal conduct raises a question about the priorities of literate society, since the learned guests at the feast are able to overlook his fundamental boorishness because they find his postprandial speech so charming. For an analysis of these *maqamas,* see James T. Monroe, *The Art of Badi' az-Zaman al-Hamadhani as Picaresque Narrative* (Beirut: American Univ. of Beirut, 1983).

26. S. A. Hussain, *A Guide to Hajj* (Lahore: Ashraf, 1972), 60.

27. In the Old Testament version, the father and son are Abraham and Isaac.

28. Al-Ghazali, 1:30. Cf. *Hamlet,* 3.3.97: "Words without thoughts never to heaven go."

29. Al-Ghazali, 1:61, 2:189.

30. Al-Ghazali, 1:214.

12. ECSTASY

1. Cited in Mahmud 'Abd al-Khaliq, *Shi'r Ibn al-Farid fi daw' al-naqd al-adabi al-hadith* (Cairo: Dar al-Ma'arif, 1984), 26.

2. From *Al-Kamil fi al-adab* [The Complete Literary Anthology] by al-Mubarrad (d. 898), quoted in Nicholson, *Literary History,* 226–27.

3. Cited in Muhammad Mustafa Hilmi, *Ibn al-Farid wa-al-hubb al-ilahi* (Cairo: Dar al-Ma'arif, 1971), 141. Compare the apocryphal story of Jesus (cited in R. A. Nicholson, *The Mystics of Islam* [London: Routledge and Kegan Paul, 1963], 10–11):

> Jesus passed by three men. Their bodies were lean and their faces pale. He asked them, saying, "What has brought you to this plight?" They answered, "Fear of the Fire." Jesus said, "You fear a thing created, and it behooves God that He should save those who fear." Then he left them and passed by three others, whose faces were paler and their bodies leaner, and asked them, saying, "What has brought you to this plight?" They answered, "Longing for Paradise." He said, "You desire a thing created, and it behooves God that He should give you that which you hope for." Then he went on and passed by three others of exceeding paleness and leanness, so that their faces were as mirrors of light, and he said, "What has brought you to this?" They answered, "Our love of God." Jesus said, "You are the nearest to Him, you are the nearest to Him."

4. Quoted in Margaret Smith, *Rabi'a the Mystic* (San Francisco: Rainbow Bridge, 1977), 10, 13.

5. Saqr, 126.

6. Quoted in M. Smith, *Rabi'a the Mystic,* 3–4.

7. Quoted in R. A. Nicholson, *The Idea of Personality in Sufism* (Cambridge: Cambridge Univ. Press, 1923), 9–10.

8. Al-Hallaj, *Diwan,* ed. 'Abduh Wazin (Beirut: Dar al-Jadid, 1998), No. 69, p. 161. Compare this famous saying of his: "There is nothing under my cloak but God."

9. Quoted in Louis Massignon, *Hallaj: Mystic and Martyr,* trans. and ed. Herbert Mason (Princeton: Princeton Univ. Press, 1994), 276.

10. Al-Hujwiri (fl. 1057), *Kashf al-mahjub* [Exposing the Veiled], trans. R. A. Nicholson (London: Luzac, 1959), 176.

11. Quoted in Nicholson, *Idea of Personality,* 39–40. See A. J. Arberry, *Sufism: An Account of the Mystics of Islam* (London: Allen and Unwin, 1969), 80.

12. Quoted in Margaret Smith, *Al-Ghazali the Mystic* (Lahore: Hijra International, 1983), 201.

13. His domed shrine in a Damascus suburb still attracts visitors today.

14. Quoted in S. H. Nadeem, *A Critical Appreciation of Arabic Mystical Poetry* (Lahore: Islamic Book Service, 1979), 142. Cf. Coleridge, "Religious Musings":

'Tis the sublime of man,

Our noontide Majesty, to know ourselves

Parts and proportions of one wondrous whole!

This fraternizes man, this constitutes

Our charities and bearings. But 'tis God

Diffused through all, that doth make all one whole.

15. See Alexander D. Knysh, *Ibn 'Arabi in the Later Islamic Tradition: The Making of a Polemical Image in Medieval Islam* (Albany: State Univ. of New York Press, 1999), 87–111.

16. Knysh, 100.

17. Cited in Hilmi, 8.

18. Th. Emil Homerin, *From Arab Poet to Muslim Saint: Ibn al-Farid, His Verse, and His Shrine* (Columbia: Univ. of South Carolina Press, 1994). In popular Islam, saints are believed to the intercessors with God on behalf of ordinary people. They are called Awliya' Allah, literally "God's Friends." Of the saint's office, al-Ghazali has said (quoted in Margaret Smith, *Readings from the Mystics of Islam* [London: Luzac, 1950], 72):

It is for the saint to descend from the mountain of transfiguration to the lower levels of this world, so that the weak may seek out his company and may kindle their lights at the radiance which the saint has brought from the heavenly places. . . . It is the glory of the saint to spend himself for those in need and to undertake the task of shepherding them into Paradise. Again, it is the mark of saintship to show compassion to all God's servants, to be pitiful towards them, and to fight for them, and with them, against the forces of evil.

It should be noted, however, that the idea of sainthood is not acceptable to conservative religious scholars. "If the learned are not God's saints," al-Biqa'i (d. 1480) protested during an Ibn al-Farid controversy in Egypt, "then God has no saint!" (quoted in Homerin, *From Arab Poet,* 119).

19. The correct order is: (1) washing the face, (2) washing the hands, (3) wiping the head, and (4) washing the feet.

20. *'Umar Ibn al-Farid: Sufi Verse, Saintly Life,* trans. Th. Emil Homerin (Mahwah: Paulist, 2001), 305.

21. The "youths of the Cave" refers to "the Seven Sleepers" (Qur'an 18:10–27) who took refuge from persecution in a cave. God preserved them in a sleep for a several hundred years, but when they awoke, they thought they had been sleeping for a day or a part of a day.

22. Ibn al-Farid, *Diwan,* ed. Giuseppe Scattolin (Cairo: Institut Français d'Archéologie Orientale, 2004), 13–14, quoted in *'Umar Ibn al-Farid,* 313.

23. Cited in Hilmi, 121–22.

24. Jamil, *Diwan,* No. 50, p. 61.

25. No. 4, p. 72.

26. No. 4, p. 72.

27. No. 4, p. 76.

28. Cited in M. Smith, *Al-Ghazali the Mystic,* 207.

29. Cf. Emily Dickinson, No. 76:

Exultation is the going
Of an inland soul to sea,
Past the houses—past the headlands—
Into deep Eternity—

30. Giuseppe Scattolin, "The Experience of the Divine in the Poetry of the Egyptian Sufi Poet 'Umar Ibn al-Farid," in *Representations of the Divine in Arabic Poetry,* ed. Gert Borg and Ed de Moor (Amsterdam: Rodopi, 2001), 98–110.

31. No. 10, p. 164.

32. Cited in Hilmi, 113.

33. Trans. in Nadeem, 48.

34. Laylat al-Qadr (the Night of Power and Excellence) being the night when the Qur'an was first revealed to the Prophet Muhammad (see Qur'an 97:3), as noted in chapter 5; Friday is the day of communal prayer.

35. The Aqsa Mosque (literally, "the Farthest Mosque") stands in Jerusalem very close to the Dome of the Rock.

36. No. 4, pp. 101–4.

37. *Diwan,* No. 12.

38. Quoted in Arberry, *Sufism,* 57. Cf. Ibn Abi al-Khayr (d. 1048): "God created the souls four thousand years before He created their bodies and placed them near to Himself, and there He shed His Light upon them" (M. Smith, *Readings,* 51). See also this statement from the modern period (quoted in Nicholson, *The Mystics of Islam,* 15–16):

Seventy Thousand Veils separate God, the One Reality, from the world of matter and of sense. And every soul passes before his birth through these seventy thousand. The inner half of these are veils of light: the outer half, veils of darkness. For every one of the veils of light passed through, in this journey towards birth, the soul puts off a divine quality: and for every one of the dark veils, it puts on an earthly quality. Thus the child is born weeping, for the soul knows its separation from God, the One Reality. And when the child cries in his sleep, it is because the soul remembers something of what it has lost. Otherwise, the passage through the veils has brought with it forgetfulness (nisyan): and for this reason man is called insan. He is now, as it were, in prison in his body, separated by these thick curtains from God.

But the whole purpose of Sufism, the Way of the dervish, is to give him an escape from this prison, an apocalypse of the Seventy Thousand Veils, a recovery of the original unity with The One, while still in this body. The body is not to be put off; it is to be refined and made spiritual—a help and not a hindrance to the spirit. It is like a metal that has to be refined by fire and transmuted. And the shaykh tells the aspirant that he has the secret of this transmutation. "We shall throw you into the fire of Spiritual Passion," he says, "and you will emerge refined."

39. Quoted in Nadeem, 203. Cf. R. A. Nicholson, *Studies in Islamic Mysticism* (Cambridge: Cambridge Univ. Press, 1921), 184.

40. Nicholson, *Studies,* 169.

41. No. 4, pp. 140–41.

42. Compare Ibn 'Arabi (quoted in Nicholson, *Mystics,* 87–88):

Do not attach yourself to any particular creed exclusively, so that you disbelieve in all the rest; otherwise you will lose much good, nay, you will fail to recognize the real truth of the matter. God, the omnipresent and omnipotent, is not limited by any one creed, for He says, "Wheresoever you turn, there is the Face of God." Every one praises what he believes; his god is his own creature, and in praising it he praises himself. Consequently he blames the beliefs of others, which he would not do if he were just, but his dislike is based on ignorance.

Compare also the great Persian mystical poet Jalal al-Din Rumi (d. 1273) (trans. from the Persian by Nicholson in *Mystics,* 100):

Oh, cry not that all creeds are vain! Some scent
of truth they have, else they would not beguile.

Say not, "How utterly fantastical!"
No fancy in the world is all untrue.

Amongst the crowd of dervishes hides one,
one true faqir [mystic]. Search well and thou wilt find!

13. TO EGYPT WITH LOVE

1. Iraq, meanwhile, which had been ruled by the Saljuq Turks (r. 1055–1194), was now controlled by the Khwarizm Turks. In Baghdad the 'Abbasid caliph retained nominal authority.

2. *The Travels of Ibn Jubayr,* trans. R. J. C. Broadhurst (London: Camelot, 1952), 58.

3. Low Niles resulted in poor crop irrigation. In 1201 and 1202 Cairo was afflicted with disease and severe famine.

4. From al-Maqrizi, *Al-Mawa'iz wa-al-i'tibar fi dhikr al-khitat wa-al-athar* [Sermons and Learning by Example in an Account of the New Settlements and the Remains], quoted in Neil D. MacKenzie, *Ayyubid Cairo: A Topographical Study* (Cairo: American Univ. in Cairo Press, 1992), 40.

5. Al-Maqrizi, *A History of the Ayyubid Sultans of Egypt,* trans. R. J. C. Broadhurst (Boston: Hall, 1980), 120, as noted in Broadhurst, xxiv–xxv.

6. Al-Maqrizi, 187–88, 229–30.

7. Mark F. Pettigrew, "The Wonders of the Ancients: Arab-Islamic Representations of Ancient Egypt" (Ph.D. diss., Univ. of California, Berkeley, 2004), 172–73.

8. 'Ad was a prosperous ancient tribe that perished because they disbelieved the prophet Hud. See Qur'an 11:53–60.

9. Ibn Jubayr, 45.

10. *The Itinerary of Rabbi Benjamin of Tudela,* ed. and trans. A. Asher, vol. 1 (New York: Hakesheth, 1900), 153.

11. From 'Abd al-Latif al-Baghdadi, *Kitab al-ifada wa-al-i'tibar fi al-umur al-mushahada wa-al-hawadith al-mu'ayana bi-ard Misr* [The Beneficial and Morally Instructive Book on Matters Observed and Events Witnessed in the Land of Egypt], quoted in Pettigrew, 146.

12. Quoted in Pettigrew, 173.

13. Baha' al-Din Zuhayr, *Diwan* (Beirut: Dar Sadir, 1964), No. 108, p. 105.

14. No. 382, p. 347. Solomon was given power over the wind, to set it blowing in the direction he intended. See Qur'an 21:81, 38:36.

15. No. 163, p. 157.

16. No. 371, p. 340.

17. No. 445, p. 397.

18. No. 452, p. 401, trans. after E. H. Palmer.

19. Two examples of proverbs in the poems above are "Walls have ears" and "Sleep is the Sultan of all." For examples of colloquial expressions in his poetry, see 'Abd al-Fattah Shalabi, *Al-Baha' Zuhayr* (Cairo: Dar al-Ma'arif, 1960), 67–71; and Sa'ida Muhammad Ramadan, *Baha' al-Din Zuhayr* (Cairo: Dar al-Ma'arif, 1982), 143–44.

20. Al-Safadi, *Al-Wafi bi-al-wafayat* [The Complete Work on Eminent Persons], ed. S. Dedering, vol. 14 (Wiesbaden: Bibliotheca Islamica, 1982), 232.

21. Al-Safadi, *Al-Wafi,* 232.

22. No. 93, p. 93.

23. Roda is an island in the Nile next to Cairo. Ibn Jubayr wrote of it as an island "with fine houses and commanding belvederes, which is a resort for entertainment and diversion" (47).

24. No. 51, p. 55.

25. Al-Maqrizi, 294–95.

26. Quoted in Baha' al-Din Zuhayr, *The Poetical Works of Behá-ed-Dín Zoheir of Egypt,* ed. and trans. E. H. Palmer, 2 vols. (Cambridge: Cambridge Univ. Press, 1876), 1:xxviii.

27. Al-Safadi, *Al-Wafi*, 235.

28. It was the Seventh Crusade, led by Louis IX of France.

29. Al-Maqrizi, 311.

30. A son named Salah al-Din is the only dependent known to us from the sources.

31. No. 235, p. 219. The patron's full name was al-Nasir Salah al-Din Yusuf. He was the great-grandson of Salah al-Din (r. 1171–93).

32. No. 237, p. 222.

33. Regarding this merchant's closeness to the Islamic standard for someone of his occupation, compare al-Ghazali, *Al-Adab fi al-din* [Fitting Conduct Within the Framework of Religion]: "When a nobleman stops at the shop, the merchant should show him due honor; if a neighbor drops in, he should be received with politeness; if a poor man comes, he should be treated with compassion. . . . The merchant should not turn away beggars nor prevent folks from seeking favors with him" (quoted in John S. Badeau, "They Lived Thus in Baghdad," in *Medieval and Middle Eastern Studies in Honour of Aziz Suryal Atiya*, ed. Sami A. Hanna [Leiden: Brill, 1972], 45).

34. What befalls the merchant brings to mind the experience of someone in fifteenth-century Cairo who gradually becomes reliant on the baker for bread credit. He remarks on the change: "In the past I resembled a lion, devouring raw meat. / But now I have turned into a nibbling rat" (quoted in Boaz Shoshan, *Popular Culture in Medieval Cairo* [Cambridge: Cambridge Univ. Press, 1993], 64).

35. Badi' al-Zaman al-Hamadhani, 58.

36. Baha' al-Din does not seem to have been sympathetic to the *fuqaha'*, either. In Nos. 294 and 329 (pp. 275, 306), for example, he satirizes unnamed dreary clerics. Here he addresses someone who has reviled a Sufi sheikh (No. 378, p. 344):

Do you abuse someone whom God has honored,
and who deserves special praise?

By your life, you've not done right,
nor is saying ugly things a trifle.

O one whose talk displeases,
we repudiate foul expression.

You opened your mouth rather than keeping it shut,
erring in the choice of action.

Leave these people alone: they have nothing to do with you,
and there's no need to say what you said.

They're men devoted solely to God.
You're not of their kind, and neither am I.

You pretend to be a holy man—
woe to you for your pious show!

You lean to the sensual world while affecting to stay away,
and are not counted as being here or there.

37. No. 417, p. 377.

38. This shadow play is discussed by Pettigrew in "Decline of Courtly Patronage" (with Monroe). See also Cyrus Ali Zargar, "The Satiric Method of Ibn Daniyal: Morality and Anti-Morality in *Tayf al-Khayal*," *JAL* 37 (2006): 68–108.

39. See Li Guo, "Paradise Lost: Ibn Daniyal's Response to Baybars' Campaign Against Vice in Cairo," *JAOS* 121 (2001): 219–35.

40. Robert Irwin, "'Ali al-Baghdadi and the Joy of Mamluk Sex," in *The Historiography of Islamic Egypt (c. 950–1800),* ed. Hugh Kennedy (Leiden: Brill, 2001), 55.

CONCLUSION

1. H. A. R. Gibb, *Arabic Literature: An Introduction* (Oxford: Oxford Univ. Press, 1963). He marks the end of the Golden Age by the fall of the Buwayhids in Iraq.

2. One wonders if the initial proponents of this traditional view were influenced by the following famous line by al-Ma'arri, to the extent that they looked no further and indeed regarded him as the final member admitted to the club of great ones: "Behold: though I may be the last to come along, / I bring forth what my earliest predecessors could not" (*Saqt al-zand* [The Flint's Spark] [Beirut: Dar Sadir, 1957], No. 45, p. 193).

3. Concerning the development of an important motif, see Hilary Kilpatrick, "Literary Creativity and the Cultural Heritage: The *Atlal* in Modern Arabic Fiction," in *Tradition, Modernity, and Postmodernity in Arabic Literature: Essays in Honor of Professor Issa J. Boullata,* ed. Kamal Abdel-Malek and Wael Hallaq (Leiden: Brill, 2000), 28–44. One example of allusion, in this case ironic, occurs in Najib Mahfuz's *Al-Sukkariyya* [Sugar Street] (Cairo: Dar Misr lil-Tiba'a, 1957), chap. 9, when the character Hilmi 'Izzat calls to mind about 'Abd al-Rahim Pasha, a politician of dubious morality, the following: "Is there anyone to be found of whom the attributes all are pleasing? / It suffices, as regards nobility, that a man's shortcomings can be counted." The line, of unknown authorship, is proverbial.

4. The Sudanese poet al-Majdhub here offers insight about Umm Kulthum's popularity, related as it is to her selection of source material: "Umm Kulthum, in her perfect pronunciation of Arabic, in her choice of excellent Arabic qasidas, and in her rendition . . . can arouse something deep and basic in the hearts of Sudanis" (quoted in Virginia Danielson, "The Qur'an and the *Qasidah*: Aspects of the Popularity of the Repertory Sung by Umm Kulthum," *Asian Music* 19, no. 1 [1987]: 32).

5. The Hebrew *qasida* form emerged in Iraq and was later transmitted to al-Andalus.

6. Stefan Sperl and Christopher Shackle, eds., *"Qasida" Poetry in Islamic Asia and Africa,* vol. 2 (Leiden: Brill, 1996), 1–5, 13–32.

7. In a poem composed according to the principles of ring composition, the center, being unique, attracts attention. Because of its structural prominence, it is a logical place for a poet, employing this form, to choose for the expression of a key message or the evocation of a significant image. See Mary Douglas, who finds a prime test of a well-turned ring as "the loading of meaning on the center and the connections made between the center and the beginning; in other words, the center of a polished ring integrates the whole" (31–32).

8. Ibn Zaydun, *Diwan Ibn Zaydun wa-rasa'iluhu,* No. 83, p. 127.

9. No. 98, p. 170.

10. The Arabic term for this last-mentioned element is *al-wasita* ("the best, the central part of the necklace"); compare the construction *wasitat al-'iqd* (literally, "the center of the necklace"): "the focus, highlight, chief attraction, pièce de résistance."

11. Ibn al-Rumi, *Diwan,* vol. 2 (Beirut: Dar al-Jil, 1998), No. 412, p. 188.

12. Coleridge, 239.

13. It appears that the Arab critics were not the only ones during this period who examined literature from an extremely close-up position, contrary to general current practice. In *A History of Byzantine Literature (650–850)* (Athens: National Hellenic Research Foundation, 1999), Alexander Kazhdan notes that the "twelfth-century exegetes of Damaskenos and Kosmas [Byzantine poets of the eighth century] concentrated on minutiae and rare words, thereby side-stepping what is now regarded as literary criticism" (138).

14. From Ibn Tabataba, *'Iyar al-shi'r* [The Measure of Poetry], quoted in van Gelder, *Beyond the Line,* 56–57.

15. From Abu Hilal al-'Askari, *Kitab al-sina'atayn* [The Book of the Two Crafts, that is, poetry and prose], quoted in van Gelder, *Beyond the Line,* 91.

16. Trans. from Arabic by Ismail M. Dahiyat in *Avicenna's Commentary on the "Poetics of Aristotle": A Critical Study with an Annotated Translation of the Text* (Leiden: Brill, 1974), 99.

17. Quoted in Cantarino, 177.

18. Andras Hamori, "Some Schemes of Reading in al-Marzuqi, al-Iskafi, and Fakhr al-Din al-Razi," in *Israel Oriental Studies,* vol. 11, *Studies in Medieval Arabic and Hebrew Poetics,* ed. Sasson Somekh (Leiden: Brill, 1991), 19.

19. Johnson, 295–96.

20. Leo Tolstoy, *What Is Art?* trans. Almyer Maude (New York: Liberal Arts Press, 1960), 51.

21. Ibn Qutayba, *Kitab al-shi'r wa-al-shu'ara',* 26.

22. Abu-Lughod, 177. Compare the opinion cited by al-Jahiz in *Kitab al-bayan wa-al-tabyin* [The Book of Eloquence and Exposition], ed. 'Abd al-Salam Muhammad Harun, vol. 1 (Cairo: Maktabat al-Khanji, 1960), 83–84: "If it's from the heart, it goes straight to the heart. If it's merely from the mouth, it never gets past the ears."

23. Meisami, *Structure and Meaning,* x.

Glossary

atlal: encampment traces

Diwan: collected poetry by a single poet

fakhr: self-praise

ghazal: love poetry

hamasa: manly verve and courage

hasab wa-nasab: nobility, acquired by outstanding deeds and superior lineage

hija': satire

hikma: wisdom; a maxim

hilm: self-control

jinas: paronomasia, or employing different words from the same root

khamriyya: wine poem

madih: panegyric

maqama: a picaresque genre composed in rhymed prose, invented by Badi' al-Zaman
   al-Hamadhani

matla': opening lines of a poem

Mu'allaqa: prized ode from the pre-Islamic period, supposedly inscribed in gold letters
   and hung on the Ka'ba in Mecca

muwashshaha: a strophic form native to al-Andalus, composed in classical Arabic

naqada: to criticize

nasib: amatory prelude

niyaha: ancient lament for the dead, originally uttered in rhymed prose

qasida: ode

radd al-'ajuz 'ala al-sadr: repetition of the first word at the end of the line

rahil: poet's resumption of travel on his she-camel away from the abandoned encampment

ritha': elegy

sabr: patience

saj': rhymed prose

sha'ir (fem. sha'ira; pl. shu'ara'): poet

shi'r: poetry

su'luk: brigand

tahrid: incitement

tayf: dream image of the beloved

tibaq: antithesis

wasf: descriptive poetry

zajal: a strophic form native to al-Andalus, composed in colloquial Arabic

za'n: caravan departure

Bibliography

'Abbas, 'Abd al-Halim. *Abu Nuwas.* Cairo: Dar al-Ma'arif, 1966.

al-'Abbas ibn al-Ahnaf. *Diwan.* Beirut: Dar Sadir, 1965.

'Abd al-'Azim, 'Ali. *Ibn Zaydun.* Cairo: Dar al-Katib al-'Arabi lil-Tiba'a wa-al-Nashr, 1967.

'Abd al-Khaliq, Mahmud. *Shi'r Ibn al-Farid fi daw' al-naqd al-adabi al-hadith.* Cairo: Dar al-Ma'arif, 1984.

'Abd al-Raziq, Mustafa. *Al-Baha' Zuhayr.* Cairo: Dar al-Kutub al-Misriyya, 1930.

Abu al-'Ala, Mustafa Muhammad. *Shi'r al-Mutanabbi: Dirasa fanniyya.* Cairo: Maktabat Nahdat al-Sharq, 1986.

Abu al-'Atahiya. *Diwan.* Ed. Majid Tirad. Beirut: Dar al-Kitab al-'Arabi, 1995.

Abu-Deeb, Kamal. "Towards a Structural Analysis of Pre-Islamic Poetry." *IJMES* 6 (1975): 148–84.

———. "Towards a Structural Analysis of Pre-Islamic Poetry (II): The Eros Vision." *Edebiyat* 1 (1976): 3–69.

Abu Hamda, Muhammad 'Ali. *Fi al-tadhawwuq al-uslubi wa-al-lughawi li-Lamiyyat al-'Arab lil-Shanfara.* Amman: Dar 'Ammar, 1997.

Abu Hiffan. *Akhbar Abi Nuwas.* Ed. 'Abd al-Sattar Ahmad Farraj. Cairo: Maktabat Misr, 1953.

Abu-Lughod, Lila. *Veiled Sentiments: Honor and Poetry in a Bedouin Society.* Berkeley and Los Angeles: Univ. of California Press, 1986.

Abu Nuwas. *Diwan.* Beirut: Dar Sadir, 1980.

Abu Tammam. *Diwan Abi Tammam bi-sharh al-Khatib al-Tibrizi.* Ed. Muhammad 'Abduh 'Azzam. 3 vols. Cairo: Dar al-Ma'arif, 1964.

———. *Diwan al-hamasa.* Ed. 'Abd al-Mun'im Ahmad Salih. Baghdad: Dar al-Shu'un al-Thaqafiyya al-'Amma, 1987.

———. *Sharh al-Suli li-Diwan Abi Tammam.* Ed. Khalaf Rashid Nu'man. 3 vols. Baghdad: Wizarat al-I'lam, 1972.

Agha, Saleh Said, and Tarif Khalidi. "Poetry and Identity in the Umayyad Age." *Al-Abhath* 50–52 (2002–3): 55–120.

Alexiou, Margaret. *The Ritual Lament in Greek Literary Tradition.* Cambridge: Cambridge Univ. Press, 1974.

Ali, Samer M. "Reinterpreting al-Buhturi's Iwan Kisra Ode: Tears of Affection for the Cycles of History." *JAL* 37 (2006): 46–67.

Allen, Roger. *An Introduction to Arabic Literature.* Cambridge: Cambridge Univ. Press, 2000.

Almagro, Martin, Luis Caballero, Juan Zozaya, and Antonio Almagro. *Qusayr 'Amra: Residencia y baños omeyas en el Desierto de Jordania.* Madrid: Instituto Hispano-Arabe de Cultura, 1975.

Alwaya, Semha. "Contemporary Bedouin Oral Poetry." *JAL* 8 (1977): 48–76.

al-Amidi. *Al-Muwazana bayna Abi Tammam wa-al-Buhturi.* Ed. Muhammad Muhyi al-Din 'Abd al-Hamid. Cairo: Maktabat al-Sa'ada, 1980.

al-Anbari. *Sharh al-qasa'id al-sab' al-tiwal al-jahilyyat.* Ed. 'Abd al-Salam Muhammad Harun. Cairo: Dar al-Ma'arif, 1969.

al-Antaki. *Tazyin al-aswaq.* Ed. Muhammad al-Tunji. Vol. 1. Beirut: 'Alam al-Kutub, 1993.

Arazi, Albert. "Abu Nuwas fut-il šhu'ubite?" *Arabica* 26 (1979): 1–61.

———. "Al-Shanfara." In *EI².*

———. "Shi'r." In *EI².*

Arberry, A. J., ed. *Arabic Poetry: A Primer for Students.* Cambridge: Cambridge Univ. Press, 1965.

———. *The Seven Odes: The First Chapter in Arabic Literature.* London: Allen and Unwin, 1957.

———. *Sufism: An Account of the Mystics of Islam.* London: Allen and Unwin, 1969.

Aristotle. *Aristotle's Poetics.* Trans. S. H. Butcher. New York: Hill and Wang, 1961.

Arnander, Primrose, and Ashkhain Skipwith, eds. *The Son of a Duck Is a Floater, and Other Arab Sayings.* London: Stacey International, 1995.

Ashtiany, Julia. "Mutanabbi's Elegy on Sayf al-Dawla's Son." In *Festschrift Ewald Wagner zum 65. Geburtstag,* ed. Wolfhart Heinrichs and Gregor Schoeler, 362–72. Beirut: Verlag, 1994.

Assis, Elie. "Chiasmus in Biblical Narrative: Rhetoric of Characterization." *Prooftexts* 22, no. 3 (2002): 273–304.

'Awad, Ibrahim. *Al-Mutanabbi: Dirasa jadida li-hayatihi wa-shakhsiyyatihi.* Cairo, 1987.

'Azzam, 'Abd al-Wahhab. *Dhikra Abi al-Tayyib ba'd alf 'am.* 2nd ed. Cairo: Dar al-Ma'arif, 1968.

Badeau, John S. "They Lived Thus in Baghdad." In *Medieval and Middle Eastern Studies in Honour of Aziz Suryal Atiya,* ed. Sami A. Hanna, 38–49. Leiden: Brill, 1972.

Badi' al-Zaman al-Hamadhani. *The Maqamat of Badi' al-Zaman al-Hamadhani.* Trans. W. J. Prendergast. London: Luzac, 1915.

al-Badi'i, Yusuf. *Al-Subh al-munbi 'an haythiyyat al-Mutanabbi.* Damascus: Matba'at al-I'tidal, 1931.

Baha' al-Din Zuhayr. *Diwan.* Beirut: Dar Sadir, 1964.

———. *The Poetical Works of Behá-ed-Dín Zoheir of Egypt.* Ed. and trans. E. H. Palmer. 2 vols. Cambridge: Cambridge Univ. Press, 1876.

Bailey, Clinton. *Bedouin Poetry from Sinai and the Negev.* Oxford: Clarendon Press, 1991.

———. "The Narrative Context of the Bedouin *Qasidah*-Poem." *Folklore Research Center Studies* 3 (1972): 67–105.

Bakhtin, Mikhail. *Rabelais and His World.* Trans. Helene Iswolsky. Cambridge: MIT Press, 1968.

al-Bakri, Abu 'Ubayd. *Kitab al-tanbih 'ala awham Abi 'Ali fi amalihi.* Cairo: Matba'at Dar al-Kutub al-Misriyya, 2000.

Bardenstein, Carol. "Stirring Words: Traditions and Subversions in the Poetry of Muzaffar al-Nawwab." *ASQ* 19, no. 4 (1997): 37–63.

Bashshar ibn Burd. *Diwan.* Ed. Husayn Hamwi. Vol. 1. Beirut: Dar al-Jil, 1996.

———. *Selections from the Poetry of Bashshar.* Ed. A. F. L. Beeston. Cambridge: Cambridge Univ. Press, 1977.

Bauer, Thomas, and Angelika Neuwirth, eds. *Ghazal as World Literature.* Vol. 1, *Transformations of a Literary Genre.* Beirut: Verlag, 2005.

Beissel, Daniela. "'Abbas b. al-Ahnaf, the Courtly Poet." *JAL* 24 (1993): 1–10.

Bellamy, J. A. "Some Observations on the Arabic *Ritha'* in the Jahiliyah and Islam." *Jerusalem Studies in Arabic and Islam* 13 (1990): 44–61.

Benjamin of Tudela. *The Itinerary of Rabbi Benjamin of Tudela.* Ed. and trans. A. Asher. Vol. 1. New York: Hakesheth, 1900.

Bianquis, Th. "Sayf al-Dawla." In *EI².*

Blachère, Régis. *Histoire de la littérature arabe.* Vol. 3. Paris: Librairie Adrien Maisonneuve, 1966.

———. *Un poète arabe du IVe siècle de l'Hégire (Xe siècle de J.-C.): Abou t-Tayyib al-Motanabbî.* Paris: Adrien-Maisonneuve, 1935.

Blachère, Régis [and Charles Pellat]. "Al-Mutanabbi." In *EI².*

Bloom, Harold. *A Map of Misreading.* Oxford: Oxford Univ. Press, 1975.

Bonebakker, Seeger A. *Hatimi and His Encounter with Mutanabbi: A Biographical Sketch.* Amsterdam: North-Holland, 1984.

———. "Poets and Critics in the Third Century A.H." In *Logic in Classical Islamic Culture,* ed. G. E. von Grunebaum, 85–111. Wiesbaden: Otto Harrassowitz, 1970.

Boullata, Issa J. "Toward a Biography of Ibn al-Farid." *Arabica* 28 (1981): 38–46.

———. "Verbal Arabesque and Mystical Union: A Study of Ibn al-Farid's *Al-Ta'iyya al-Kubra*." *ASQ* 3 (1981): 152–69.

Brockelmann, C. "Labid." In *EI²*.

al-Buhturi. *Diwan*. Ed. Karam al-Bustani. 2 vols. Beirut: Dar Sadir, 1966.

———. *Diwan*. Ed. Hasan Kamil al-Sayrafi. 4 vols. Cairo: Dar al-Maʿarif, 1963.

Cambridge History of Arabic Literature: ʿAbbasid Belles-Lettres. Ed. Julia Ashtiany et al. Cambridge: Cambridge Univ. Press, 1990.

Cambridge History of Arabic Literature: Arabic Literature to the End of the Umayyad Period. Ed. A. F. L. Beeston et al. Cambridge: Cambridge Univ. Press, 1983.

Cambridge History of Arabic Literature: The Literature of al-Andalus. Ed. María Menocal et al. Cambridge: Cambridge Univ. Press, 2000.

Canard, Marius. *Histoire de la dynastie des H'amdanides de Jazîra et de Syrie*. Vol. 1. Paris: Presses Universitaires de France, 1953.

———, ed. *Sayf al-Daula: Recueil de textes relatifs à l'émir Sayf al-Daula le Hamdanide*. Algiers: Carbonel, 1934.

Cantarino, Vicente. *Arabic Poetics in the Golden Age*. Leiden: Brill, 1975.

Caskel, W. "Bakr ibn Wa'il." In *EI²*.

"Cemetery Turns into Brothel." *Al-Watan Daily*, Oct. 2, 2008, 1.

Chejne, Anwar G. "The Boon-Companion in Early ʿAbbasid Times." *JAOS* 85, no. 3 (1965): 327–35.

Coleridge, Samuel Taylor. *Biographia Literaria*. Ed. J. Shawcross. Vol. 2. Oxford: Oxford Univ. Press, 1962.

Coope, Jessica A. "Muslim-Christian Relations in Ninth-Century Córdoba." Ph.D. diss., Univ. of California, Berkeley, 1988.

Corriente, Federico. *A Dictionary of Andalusi Arabic*. Leiden: Brill, 1997.

———. "Textos andalusíes de cejeles no quzmanianos en Alhilli, Ibn Saʿid Almaghribi, Ibn Xaldun y en la *Genizah*." *Foro Hispánico* 7 (1994): 61–104.

Cour, Auguste. *Un poète arabe d'Andalousie: Ibn Zaïdoûn*. Constantine, Algeria: Boet, 1920.

Cowell, Dustin. "Narrative Art in ʿUmar ibn Abi Rabiʿa." In *30th International Congress of Human Sciences in Asia and North Africa*, ed. Graciela de la Lama, 78–93. Mexico City: El Colegio de Mexico, 1982.

———. "The Poetry of Ibn ʿAbd Rabbihi." Ph.D. diss., Univ. of California, San Diego. 1975.

Creswell, K. A. C. *Early Muslim Architecture: Umayyads, ʿAbbasids, and Tulunids*. Vol. 2. Oxford: Clarendon Press, 1940.

Crone, Patricia. "Mawla." In *EI²*.

Crone, Patricia, and Martin Hinds. *God's Caliph: Religious Authority in the First Centuries of Islam.* Cambridge: Cambridge Univ. Press, 1986.

Culler, Jonathan. *Structuralist Poetics: Structuralism, Linguistics, and the Study of Literature.* Ithaca: Cornell Univ. Press, 1975.

Dahiyat, Ismail M. *Avicenna's Commentary on the "Poetics of Aristotle": A Critical Study with an Annotated Translation of the Text.* Leiden: Brill, 1974.

Danielson, Virginia. "The Qur'an and the *Qasidah*: Aspects of the Popularity of the Repertory Sung by Umm Kulthum." *Asian Music* 19, no. 1 (1987): 26–45.

———. *The Voice of Egypt: Umm Kulthum, Arabic Song, and Egyptian Society in the Twentieth Century.* Chicago: Univ. of Chicago Press, 1997.

Dhu al-Rumma. *Diwan.* Ed. Zuhayr Fath Allah. Beirut: Dar Beirut, 1995.

Djedidi, Tahar Labib. *La poesie amoueuse des Arabes: Le cas des 'Udhrites.* Algiers: Société Nationale d'Edition et de Diffusion, 1974.

Douglas, Mary. *Thinking in Circles: An Essay on Ring Composition.* New Haven: Yale Univ. Press, 2007.

Dozy, Reinhart. *Spanish Islam: A History of the Moslems in Spain.* Trans. Francis Griffin Stokes. London: Chatto and Windus, 1913.

Dryden, John. *Essays.* Ed. W. P. Ker. Vol. 2. New York: Russell, 1961.

Eliot, T. S. "Tradition and the Individual Talent." In *Selected Essays: 1917–1932,* 3–11. New York: Harcourt, 1932.

Elliott, Robert C. *The Power of Satire: Magic, Ritual, Art.* Princeton: Princeton Univ. Press, 1960.

Encyclopedia of Islam. First ed. 4 vols. Leiden: Brill, 1913–38.

Encyclopedia of Islam. New ed. 11 vols. Leiden: Brill, 1960–2002.

Fackenheim, Emil L. "A Treatise on Love by Ibn Sina." *Medieval Studies* 7 (1945): 208–28.

Fahd, T. "Al-Maysir." In *EI².*

al-Farazdaq, *Diwan.* Ed. Iliya al-Hawi. 2 vols. Beirut: Dar al-Kitab al-Lubnani, 1983.

Fatima, Rais. *Ghazal under the Umayyads.* New Delhi: Kitab Bhavan, 1995.

Fowden, Garth. *Qusayr 'Amra: Art and the Umayyad Elite in Late Antique Syria.* Berkeley and Los Angeles: Univ. of California Press, 2004.

Fussell, Paul. *Thank God for the Atom Bomb, and Other Essays.* New York: Summit, 1988.

Gabrieli, Francesco. "Ta'abbata Sharran, al-Shanfara, Khalaf al-Ahmar." *Atti della Academia Nazionale dei Lincei,* ser. 8 (1946).

Gamal, Adel Sulaiman. "The Ethical Values of the Brigand Poets in Pre-Islamic Arabia." *Bibliotheca Orientalis* 34, nos. 5–6 (1977): 290–98.

Gandz, Salomon. "Die Mu'allaqa des Imrulqais." *Sitzungsberichte der Akademie der Wissenschaften in Wien* 170 (1913): 3–125.

Garcin, J.-Cl. "Qus." In *EI²*.

Garulo, Teresa. "Women in Medieval Classical Arabic Poetry." In *Writing the Feminine: Women in Arab Sources,* ed. Manuela Marín and Randi Deguilhem, 25–40. London: I. B. Tauris, 2002.

al-Ghadeer, Moneera. "The Inappropriable Voice." Ph.D. diss., Univ. of California, Berkeley, 1999.

al-Ghazali. *Ihya' 'ulum al-din.* 4 vols. Cairo: Mu'assasat al-Halabi wa-Shuraka'ihi, 1967.

Gibb, H. A. R. *Arabic Literature: An Introduction.* Oxford: Oxford Univ. Press, 1963.

——. *Studies on the Civilization of Islam.* Boston: Beacon, 1968.

Giffen, Lois Anita. *Theory of Profane Love among the Arabs: The Development of the Genre.* New York: New York Univ. Press, 1971.

Gimaret, D. "Mu'tazila." In *EI²*.

Goldziher, Ignaz. "Bemerkungen zur arabischen Trauerpoesie." In vol. 4 of *Gesammelte Schriften,* ed. Joseph Desomogyi, 361–93. Hildesheim, Germany: Olms, 1970.

——. *Muslim Studies.* Ed. S. M. Stern. Trans. C. R. Barber and S. M. Stern. Vol. 1. London: Allen and Unwin, 1967.

Gómez, Emilio García. "Un eclipse de la poesía en Sevilla: La época almorávide." *Al-Andalus* 10 (1945): 285–343.

——. "Nuevos testimonios del 'odio a Sevilla' de los poetas musulmanes." *Al-Andalus* 14 (1949): 143–48.

Grabar, Oleg. "The Umayyad Dome of the Rock in Jerusalem." In *Early Islamic Art and Architecture,* ed. Jonathan M. Bloom, 223–56. Hampshire, UK: Ashgate, 2002.

Grube, G. M. A. *The Greek and Roman Critics.* London: Methuen, 1965.

Gruendler, Beatrice. *Medieval Arabic Praise Poetry: Ibn al-Rumi and the Patron's Redemption.* London: Routledge, 2003.

Gruendler, Beatrice, and Louise Marlow, eds. *Writers and Rulers: Perspectives on Their Relationship from 'Abbasid to Safavid Times.* Wiesbaden: Reichert, 2004.

Guo, Li. "Paradise Lost: Ibn Daniyal's Response to Baybars' Campaign Against Vice in Cairo." *JAOS* 121 (2001): 219–35.

al-Hadidi, 'Abd al-Latif Muhammad. *Bayn al-ana wa-al-akhar fi madhiyyat al-Mutanabbi.* Cairo: Al-Azhar Univ. Press, 1998.

Hall, Joseph. *Collected Poems.* Ed. A. Davenport. Liverpool: Liverpool Univ. Press, 1949.

al-Hallaj. *Diwan.* Ed. 'Abduh Wazin. Beirut: Dar al-Jadid, 1998.

Hammud, Muhammad. *Abu Nuwas: Sha'ir al-khati'a wa-al-ghufran.* Beirut: Dar al-Fikr al-'Arabi, 1994.

Hamori, Andras. *The Composition of Mutanabbi's Panegyrics to Sayf al-Dawla.* Leiden: Brill, 1992.

———. "Did Medieval Readers Make Sense of Form? Notes on a Passage of al-Iskafi." In *In Quest of an Islamic Humanism: Arabic and Islamic Studies in Memory of Mohamed al-Nowaihi,* ed. A. H. Green, 39–47. Cairo: American Univ. in Cairo Press, 1984.

———. *On the Art of Medieval Arabic Literature.* Princeton: Princeton Univ. Press, 1974.

———. "Reading al-Mutanabbi's Ode on the Siege of al-Hadath." In *Studia Arabica et Islamica: Festschrift for Ihsan 'Abbas,* ed. Wadad al-Qadi, 195–206. Beirut: American Univ. of Beirut, 1981.

———. "Some Schemes of Reading in al-Marzuqi, al-Iskafi, and Fakhr al-Din al-Razi." In *Israel Oriental Studies.* Vol. 11, *Studies in Medieval Arabic and Hebrew Poetics,* ed. Sasson Somekh, 13–20. Leiden: Brill, 1991.

al-Hariri. *The Assemblies of al-Hariri.* Trans. Thomas Chenery. Vol. 1. London: Williams and Norgate, 1867.

al-Hatimi. *Al-Risala al-mudiha fi dhikr sariqat Abi al-Tayyib al-Mutanabbi wa-saqit shi'rihi.* Ed. Muhammad Yusuf Najm. Beirut: Dar Sadir, 1965.

Hatim al-Ta'i. *Diwan Shi'r Hatim al-Ta'i ibn 'Abd Allah wa-akhbaruhu.* Ed. 'Adil Sulayman Jamal. Cairo: Maktabat al-Khanji, 1990.

Haydar, Adnan. "The *Mu'allaqa* of Imru' al-Qays: Its Structure and Meaning." Pts. 1 and 2. *Edebiyat* 2 (1977): 227–61; 3 (1978): 51–82.

Heath-Stubbs, John. *The Pastoral.* Oxford: Oxford Univ. Press, 1969.

Heinrichs, Wolfhart. "The Meaning of Mutanabbi." In *Poetry and Prophecy: The Beginnings of a Literary Tradition,* ed. James L. Kugel, 120–39, 231–39. Ithaca: Cornell Univ. Press, 1990.

Hifni, 'Abd al-Halim. *Lamiyyat al-'Arab lil-Shanfara.* Cairo: Maktabat al-Adab wa-Matba'atuha, 1981.

———. *Shi'r al-sa'alik.* Cairo: Al-Hay'a al-Misriyya al-'Amma lil-Kitab, 1979.

Highet, Gilbert. *The Anatomy of Satire.* Princeton: Princeton Univ. Press, 1962.

Hillenbrand, Robert. "*La Dolce Vita* in Early Islamic Syria: The Evidence of Later Umayyad Palaces." In *Early Islamic Art and Architecture,* ed. Jonathan M. Bloom, 333–71. Aldershot, UK: Ashgate, 2002.

Hillenbrand, Robert, and A. J. Wensinck. "Musalla." In *EI².*

Hilmi, Muhammad Mustafa. *Ibn al-Farid wa-al-hubb al-ilahi.* Cairo: Dar al-Ma'arif, 1971.

Hinds, M. "Mihna." In *EI².*

Hitti, Philip K. *Capital Cities of Arab Islam.* Minneapolis: Univ. of Minnesota Press, 1973.

———. *History of the Arabs.* 10th ed. New York: St. Martin's, 1970.

Hobbs, Joseph J. *Bedouin Life in the Egyptian Wilderness.* Cairo: American Univ. in Cairo Press, 1990.

Hogga, Mustafa. *Orthodoxie, subversion et réforme en Islam: Gazali et les Seljudiqes.* Paris: J. Vrin, 1993.

Homerin, Th. Emil. "Echoes of a Thirsty Owl: Death and Afterlife in Pre-Islamic Poetry." *JNES* 44, no. 3 (1985): 165–84.

———. *From Arab Poet to Muslim Saint: Ibn al-Farid, His Verse, and His Shrine.* Columbia: Univ. of South Carolina Press, 1994.

———. "In the Gardens of al-Zahra': Love Echoes in a Poem by Ibn Zaydun." In *The Shaping of an American Islamic Discourse: A Memorial to Fazlur Rahman,* ed. Earle H. Waugh et al., 215–32. Atlanta: Scholars Press, 1998.

———. "'Tangled Words': Toward a Stylistics of Arabic Mystical Verse." In *Reorientations/Arabic and Persian Poetry,* ed. Suzanne Pinckney Stetkevych, 190–98. Bloomington: Indiana Univ. Press, 1994.

———, ed. and trans. *The Wine of Love and Life: Ibn al-Farid's 'al-Khamriyah' and al-Qaysari's Quest for Meaning.* Chicago: Middle East Documentation Center, 2005.

L'Hôpital, Jean-Yves. "Le vocabulaire amoureux dans les poèmes de 'Umar b. al-Farid." *Annales Islamologiques* 36 (2002): 77–116.

Horace. *Art of Poetry.* Trans. Walter Jackson Bate. In *Criticism: The Major Texts,* ed. Walter Jackson Bate, 51–58. New York: Harcourt, 1970.

al-Hufi, Ahmad Muhammad. *Al-Mar'a fi al-shi'r al-jahili.* Cairo: Dar al-Fikr al-'Arabi, 1963.

al-Hujwiri. *Kashf al-mahjub.* Trans. R. A. Nicholson. London: Luzac, 1959.

Humphreys, R. Stephen. *From Saladin to the Mongols.* Albany: State Univ. of New York Press, 1977.

al-Hurr, 'Abd al-Majid. *Jarir: Riqqat al-siyagha wa-'udhubat al-lafz wa-jazalat al-shi'r.* Beirut: Dar al-Fikr al-'Arabi, 1998.

Husayn, Muhammad Muhammad. *Al-Hija' wa-al-hajja'un fi sadr al-Islam.* Beirut: Dar al-Nahda al-'Arabiyya, 1970.

Husayn, Taha. *Fi al-shi'r al-jahili.* Damascus: Dar al-Mada lil-Thaqafa wa-al-Nashr, 2001.

———. *Hadith al-arbi'a.* Vol. 1. Cairo: Dar al-Ma'arif, 1959.

———. *Ma'a al-Mutanabbi.* Cairo: Dar al-Ma'arif, 1962.

al-Husri. *Zahr al-adab wa-thamar al-albab.* Ed. 'Ali Muhammad al-Bajawi. Vol. 1. Cairo: Dar Ihya' al-Kutub al-'Arabiyya, 1953.

Hussain, S. A. *A Guide to Hajj.* Lahore: Ashraf, 1972.

Ibn 'Abbad, al-Sahib. *Al-Kashf 'an masawi al-Mutanabbi.* Ed. Muhammad Hasan Al Yasin. Baghdad: Maktabat al-Nahda, 1965.

Ibn 'Abd Rabbihi. *Al-'Iqd al-farid.* 4 vols. Cairo: Al-Matba'a al-Jamaliyya, 1913.

Ibn Abi Usaybi'a. *'Uyun al-anba' fi tabaqat al-atibba'.* Ed. Nizar Rida. Beirut: Dar Maktabat al-Hayat, 1965.

Ibn al-'Adim. *Bughyat al-talab fi tarikh Halab.* Ed. Suhayl Zakkar. Vol. 9. Damascus, 1988.

Ibn 'Asakir. *Al-Ta'rikh al-kabir.* Ed. 'Abd al-Qadir Badran. Vol. 4. Damascus: Rawdat al-Sham, 1912.

Ibn Bassam. *Al-Dhakhira fi mahasin ahl al-Jazira.* Ed. Ihsan 'Abbas. Vol. 1, pt. 1. Beirut: Dar al-Thaqafa, 1975.

Ibn Dawud. *Kitab al-zahra.* Ed. A. R. Nykl. *University of Chicago Studies in Ancient Oriental Civilization* 6 (1932): 1–406.

Ibn al-Farid. *Diwan.* Ed. Giuseppe Scattolin. Cairo: Institut Français d'Archéologie Orientale, 2004.

———. *'Umar Ibn al-Farid: Sufi Verse, Saintly Life.* Trans. Th. Emil Homerin. Mahwah: Paulist, 2001.

Ibn Hajar al-'Asqalani. *Al-Isaba fi tamyiz al-sahaba.* Ed. 'Ali Muhammad al-Bahawi. Vol. 7. Cairo: Dar Nahdat Misr lil-Tab' wa-al-Nashr, 1970.

Ibn Hazm. *The Ring of the Dove: A Treatise on the Art and Practice of Arab Love.* Trans. A. J. Arberry. London: Luzac, 1994.

Ibn Iyas. *Bada'i' al-zuhur fi waqa'i' al-duhur.* Ed. Muhammad Mustafa. Vol. 2. Cairo: Al-Hay'a al-Misriyya al-'Amma lil-Kitab, 1984.

Ibn al-Jawzi. *Talbis Iblis.* Ed. and trans. D. S. Margoliouth. *Islamic Culture* 9–12 (1935–38).

Ibn Jinni. *Al-Fasr.* Ed. Safa' al-Khalusi. Vol. 2. Baghdad: Wizarat al-Thaqafa wa-al-Funun, 1977.

Ibn Jubayr. *The Travels of Ibn Jubayr.* Trans. R. J. C. Broadhurst. London: Camelot, 1952.

Ibn Khaqan. *Qala'id al-'iqyan.* Ed. Muhammad al-Tahir ibn 'Ashur. Tunis: Al-Dar al-Tunisiyya, 1990.

Ibn Maymun. *Muntaha al-talab.* Ed. Muhammad Nabil Tarifi. Vol. 2. Beirut: Dar Sadir, 1999.

Ibn al-Mu'tazz. *Tabaqat al-shu'ara'.* Ed. 'Abd al-Sattar Ahmad Farraj. Cairo: Dar al-Ma'arif, 1956.

Ibn al-Qasim. *Al-Mudawwana al-kubra.* 16 vols. Cairo: Maktabat al-Sa'ada, 1905.

Ibn Qutayba. *Kitab al-shi'r wa-al-shu'ara'.* Beirut: Dar al-Thaqafa, 1964.

———. *'Uyun al-akhbar.* Vol. 1. Cairo: Dar al-Kutub, 1925.

Ibn Quzman. *Cancionero andalusí.* Ed. and trans. Federico Corriente. Madrid: Hiperión, 1996.

———. *Diwan* [manuscript facsimile]. Ed. David de Gunzburg. Berlin: Calvary, 1896.

———. *Diwan: Isabat al-aghrad fi dhikr al-a'rad.* Ed. Federico Corriente. Cairo: Consejo Superior de Cultura, 1995.

———. *Diwan (Todo Ben Quzman).* Ed. Emilio García Gómez. 3 vols. Madrid: Gredos, 1972.

Ibn Rashiq. *Al-'Umda fi mahasin al-shi'r wa-adabihi wa-naqdihi.* 2 vols. Cairo: Dar al-Hilal, 1996.

Ibn al-Rumi. *Diwan.* Vol. 2. Beirut: Dar al-Jil, 1998.

Ibn Sa'd. *Al-Tabaqat al-kubra.* Vol. 3. Beirut: Dar Sadir, 1957.

Ibn Sallam al-Jumahi. *Tabaqat al-shu'ara'.* Leiden: Brill, 1913.

Ibn Shuhayd. *Diwan Ibn Shuhayd al-Andalusi wa-rasa'iluhu.* Ed. Muhyi al-Din Dib. Beirut: Al-Maktaba al-'Asriyya, 1997.

————. *Risalat at-Tawabi' wa z-zawabi': The Treatise of Familiar Spirits and Demons by Abu 'Amir ibn Shuhaid al-Ashja'i, al-Andalusi.* Trans. James T. Monroe. Near Eastern Studies 15. Berkeley and Los Angeles: Univ. of California Press, 1971.

Ibn Simak. *Al-Hulal al-mawshiyya fi dhikr al-akhbar al-Marrakushiyya.* Ed. Suhayl Zakkar and 'Abd al-Qadir Zamama. Casablanca: Dar al-Rashad al-Haditha, 1979.

Ibn Taghribirdi. *Al-Manhal al-safi.* Ed. Nabil Muhammad 'Abd al-'Aziz. Vol. 5. Cairo: Al-Hay'a al-'Amma lil-Kitab, 1988.

Ibn Tayfur. *Al-Manthur wa-al-manzum.* Ed. Muhsin Ghayyad. Beirut: Turath 'Uwaydat, 1977.

Ibn Zaydun. *Diwan.* Ed. Karam al-Bustani. Beirut: Dar Sadir, 1964.

————. *Diwan Ibn Zaydun wa-rasa'iluhu.* Ed. 'Ali 'Abd al-'Azim. Cairo: Dar Nahdat Misr lil-Tab' wa-al-Nashr, 1980.

Ikhwan al-Safa'. *Rasa'il.* Ed. 'Arif Tamir. Vol. 1. Beirut: Manshurat 'Uwaydat, 1994.

Imru' al-Qays. *Diwan.* Beirut: Dar Sadir, 1958.

Irwin, Robert. "'Ali al-Baghdadi and the Joy of Mamluk Sex." In *The Historiography of Islamic Egypt (c. 950–1800),* ed. Hugh Kennedy, 45–57. Leiden: Brill, 2001.

al-Isfahani, Abu al-Faraj. *Kitab al-aghani.* Ed. Ibrahim al-Abyari. 31 vols. Cairo: Dar al-Sha'b, 1969–82.

'Izz al-Din, Hasan al-Banna. *Al-Kalimat wa-al-ashya'.* Cairo: Dar al-Fikr al-'Arabi, 1988.

Jabbur, Jibrail S. *The Bedouins and the Desert.* Trans. Lawrence I. Conrad. Albany: State Univ. of New York Press, 1995.

Jacobi, Renate. "The Camel Section of the Panegyrical Ode." *JAL* 13 (1982): 1–22.

————. "The *Khayal* Motif in Early Arabic Poetry." *Oriens* 32 (1990): 50–64.

————. "Theme and Variations in Umayyad *Ghazal* Poetry." *JAL* 23 (1993): 109–19.

————. "Time and Reality in *Nasib* and *Ghazal*." *JAL* 16 (1985): 1–17.

————. "The 'Udhra: Love and Death in the Umayyad Period." In *Martyrdom in Literature: Visions of Death and Meaningful Suffering in Europe and the Middle East from Antiquity to Modernity,* ed. Friedericke Pannewick, 137–47. Wiesbaden: Reichert, 2004.

————. "'Udhri." In *EI².*

al-Jahiz. *The Book of Misers*. Trans. R. B. Serjeant. Reading, UK: Garnet, 1997.

———. *The Epistle on Singing-Girls of Jahiz*. Ed. and trans. A. F. L. Beeston. Warminster, UK: Aris and Phillips, 1980.

———. *Kitab al-bayan wa-al-tabyin*. Ed. 'Abd al-Salam Muhammad Harun. Vol. 1. Cairo: Maktabat al-Khanji, 1960.

———. *Kitab al-hayawan*. Ed. 'Abd al-Salam Muhammad Harun. Vol. 2. Cairo: Maktabat Mustafa al-Babi al-Halabi wa-Awladihi, 1965.

———. *The Life and Works of Jahiz: Selected Texts*. Trans. Charles Pellat. Trans. from the French D. M. Hawke. London: Routledge and Kegan Paul, 1969.

———, attrib. *Al-Mahasin wa-al-addad*. Cairo: Maktabat al-Qahira, 1978.

———. *Rasa'il al-Jahiz*. Ed. 'Abd al-Salam Muhammad Harun. Vol. 3. Cairo: Maktabat al-Khanji, 1964.

Jamil. *Diwan*. Ed. 'Adnan Zakiy Darwish. Beirut: Dar al-Fikr al-'Arabi, 1994.

———. *Diwan*. Ed. Husayn Nassar. Cairo: Dar Misr lil-Tiba'a, 1967.

Jamil, Nadia. "Playing for Time: *Maysir*-Gambling in Early Arabic Poetry." In *Islamic Reflections, Arabic Musings*, ed. Robert G. Hoyland and Philip F. Kennedy, 48–90. Oxford: Gibb Memorial Trust, 2004.

Jarir. *Diwan*. Beirut: Dar Sadir, 1964.

Jay, Peter, ed. *The Greek Anthology and Other Ancient Greek Epigrams*. New York: Oxford Univ. Press, 1973.

Jayyusi, Salma Khadra. "Nature Poetry in al-Andalus and the Rise of Ibn Khafaja." In *The Legacy of Muslim Spain*, ed. Salma Khadra Jayyusi, 367–97. Leiden: Brill, 1992.

———. "Umayyad Poetry." In *CHALUP*, 387–432.

Johnson, Samuel. *Selected Essays*. London: Penguin, 2003.

Jones, Alan. *Early Arabic Poetry*. 2 vols. Oxford: Ithaca Press, 1992–96.

al-Juburi, 'Abd Allah. *Abu al-Tayyib al-Mutanabbi fi athar al-darisin*. Baghdad: Wizarat al-Thaqafa wa-al-Funun, 1977.

Ka'b ibn Zuhayr. *Sharh al-Tibrizi 'ala Banat Su'ad li-Ka'b ibn Zuhayr*. Ed. 'Abd al-Rahim Yusuf al-Jamal. Cairo: Maktabat al-Adab wa-Matba'atuha, 1990.

El Kafrawy, M. A. A., and J. D. Latham. "Perspective of Abu al-'Atahiya." *IQ* 17 (1973): 160–76.

Kazhdan, Alexander. *A History of Byzantine Literature (650–850)*. Athens: National Hellenic Research Foundation, 1999.

Kennedy, Hugh. *The Prophet and the Age of the Caliphates: The Islamic Near East from the Sixth to the Eleventh Century*. London: Longman, 1986.

Kennedy, Philip F. *The Wine Song in Classical Arabic Poetry: Abu Nuwas and the Literary Tradition*. Oxford: Oxford Univ. Press, 1997.

Khairallah, As'ad E. *Love, Madness, and Poetry: An Interpretation of the Majnun Legend.* Beirut: Orient-Institut der Deutschen Morgenlandischen Gesellschaft, 1980.

Khan, Ruqayya Yasmine. *Self and Secrecy in Early Islam.* Columbia: Univ. of South Carolina Press, 2008.

Khankan, Nathalie. "Reperceiving the Pre-Islamic *Nasib.*" *JAL* 33, no. 1 (2002): 1–23.

al-Khansa'. *Diwan.* Beirut: Dar Sadir, 1963.

———. *Sharh Diwan al-Khansa'.* Ed. Fayiz Muhammad. Beirut: Dar al-Kitab al-'Arabi, 1993.

al-Khatib al-Baghdadi. *Tarikh Baghdad.* Vol. 1. Cairo: Maktabat al-Khanji, 1931.

Kilpatrick, Hilary. "Literary Creativity and the Cultural Heritage: The *Atlal* in Modern Arabic Fiction." In *Tradition, Modernity, and Postmodernity in Arabic Literature: Essays in Honor of Professor Issa J. Boullata,* ed. Kamal Abdel-Malek and Wael Hallaq, 28–44. Leiden: Brill, 2000.

Kinany, A. Kh. *The Development of Gazal in Arabic Literature.* Damascus: Syrian Univ. Press, 1950.

Kingdon, Jonathan. *Arabian Mammals: A Natural History.* London: Academic Press, 1990.

Knysh, Alexander D. *Ibn 'Arabi in the Later Islamic Tradition: The Making of a Polemical Image in Medieval Islam.* Albany: State Univ. of New York Press, 1999.

Krenkow, F. "Kasida." In *EI'.*

———. "Al-Shanfara." In *EI'.*

Kurpershoek, P. Marcel. *Oral Poetry and Narratives from Central Arabia.* Vol. 2, *The Story of a Desert Knight.* Leiden: Brill, 1995.

Labid ibn Rabi'a. *Sharh Diwan Labid ibn Rabi'a al-'Amiri.* Ed. Ihsan 'Abbas. Kuwait: Wizarat al-Irshad wa-al-Anba', 1962.

Lachiri, Nadia. "Andalusi Proverbs on Women." In *Writing the Feminine: Women in Arab Sources,* ed. Manuela Marín and Randi Deguilhem, 41–48. London: I. B. Tauris, 2002.

Lane, Edward W. *Manners and Customs of the Modern Egyptians.* New York: Dutton, 1966.

Larkin, Margaret. *Al-Mutanabbi: Voice of the 'Abbasid Poetic Ideal.* Oxford: Oneworld, 2008.

———. "Two Examples of *Ritha'*: A Comparison Between Ahmad Shawqi and al-Mutanabbi." *JAL* 16 (1985): 18–39.

Larsson, Göran. *Ibn García's Shu'ubiyya Letter: Ethnic and Theological Tensions in Medieval al-Andalus.* Leiden: Brill, 2003.

Latham, J. D. "The Elegy on the Death of Abu Shuja' Fatik by al-Mutanabbi." In *Arabicus Felix: Essays in Honour of A. F. L. Beeston on His Eightieth Birthday,* ed. Alan Jones, 90–107. Oxford: Oxford Univ. Press, 1991.

————. "Al-Mutanabbi: Some Reflections and Notes on His Egyptian Valedictory." In vol. 1 of *Studies in Honour of Clifford Edmund Bosworth,* ed. Ian Richard Netton, 15–31. Leiden: Brill, 1999.

————. "Towards a Better Understanding of al-Mutanabbi's Poem on the Battle of al-Hadath." *JAL* 10 (1979): 1–22.

Leder, Stefan. "The 'Udhri Narrative in Arabic Literature." In *Martyrdom in Literature: Visions of Death and Meaningful Suffering in Europe and the Middle East from Antiquity to Modernity,* ed. Friedericke Pannewick, 163–87. Wiesbaden: Reichert, 2004.

Lemon, Lee T., and Marion J. Reis, trans. *Russian Formalist Criticism: Four Essays.* Lincoln: Univ. of Nebraska Press, 1965.

Liebhaber, Sam. "Al-Shanfara and 'The Mountain Poem' of Ibn Khafaja: Some Observations on Patterns of Intertextuality." *JAL* 34, nos. 1–2 (2003): 107–21.

Lings, M. "Mystical Poetry." In *CHALABL,* 235–64.

Lombard, Maurice. *The Golden Age of Islam.* Trans. Joan Spencer. Princeton: Markus Wiener, 2004.

Longinus. *On Great Writing (On the Sublime).* Trans. G. M. A. Grube. New York: Liberal Arts Press, 1957.

Lug, Sieglinde. *Poetic Techniques and Conceptual Elements in Ibn Zaydun's Love Poetry.* Washington, D.C.: Univ. Press of America, 1982.

Lyall, Sir Charles. *Ancient Arabian Poetry.* Westport, Conn.: Hyperion, 1981.

————, ed. and trans. *The "Mufaddaliyyat": An Anthology of Ancient Arabian Odes.* 2 vols. Oxford: Clarendon Press, 1918.

Lyons, M. C. *Identification and Identity in Classical Arabic Poetry.* Warminster, UK: Aris and Phillips, 1999.

Maalouf, Amin. *The Crusades Through Arab Eyes.* Trans. Jon Rothschild. New York: Schocken, 1985.

al-Ma'arri. *Saqt al-zand.* Beirut: Dar Sadir, 1957.

MacKenzie, Neil D. *Ayyubid Cairo: A Topographical Study.* Cairo: American Univ. in Cairo Press, 1992.

Madelung, W. "Karmati." In *EI².*

Mahfuz, Najib. *Al-Liss wa-al-kilab.* In vol. 6 of *Al-A'mal al-kamila,* 783–884. Beirut: Al-Maktaba al-'Ilmiyya al-Jadida, 1981.

————. *Al-Sukkariyya.* Cairo: Dar Misr lil-Tiba'a, 1957.

Makdisi, George. *Ibn 'Aqil, Religion, and Culture in Classical Islam.* Edinburgh: Edinburgh Univ. Press, 1997.

————. *The Rise of Humanism in Classical Islam and the Christian West.* Edinburgh: Edinburgh Univ. Press, 1990.

Makki, Tahir Ahmad. *Imru' al-Qays: Amir shu'ara' al-jahiliyya*. Cairo: Dar al-Ma'arif, 1968.

Al-Mallah, Majd Yaser. "A Victory Celebration after a Military Defeat? Al-Mutanabbi's 'Ayniyyah of 339/950." *JAL* 40 (2009): 107–28.

Malti-Douglas, Fedwa. "Structure and Organization in a Monographic *Adab* Work: *Al-Tatfil* of al-Khatib al-Baghdadi." *JNES* 40, no. 3 (1981): 227–45.

Mansur, Sa'id Husayn. *Al-Tajriba al-insaniyya fi Nuniyyat Ibn Zaydun*. Dubai: Dar al-Mutanabbi, 1984.

al-Maqqari. *Nafh al-tib min ghusn al-Andalus al-ratib*. Ed. Ihsan 'Abbas. Vol. 3. Beirut: Dar Sadir, 1968.

al-Maqrizi. *A History of the Ayyubid Sultans of Egypt*. Trans. R. J. C. Broadhurst. Boston: Hall, 1980.

Margoliouth, D. S. "The Origins of Arabic Poetry." *Journal of the Royal Asiatic Society* (1925): 417–49.

al-Marrakushi. *Al-Mu'jib fi talkhis akhbar al-Maghrib*. Ed. Muhammad Sa'id al-'Aryan and Muhammad al-'Azbi al-'Almi. Casablanca: Dar al-Kitab, 1978.

al-Marzuqi. *Sharh mushkilat Diwan Abi Tammam*. Ed. 'Abd Allah Sulayman al-Jarbu'. Mecca: Maktabat al-Turath, 1986.

Mason, Herbert. *Al-Hallaj*. Surrey: Curzon, 1995.

Massignon, Louis. *Hallaj: Mystic and Martyr*. Trans. and ed. Herbert Mason. Princeton: Princeton Univ. Press, 1994.

al-Mas'udi. *The Meadows of Gold*. Trans. and ed. Paul Lunde and Caroline Stone. London: Kegan Paul, 1989.

———. *Muruj al-dhahab*. Ed. Charles Pellat. Vol. 4. Beirut: Al-Jami'a al-Lubnaniyya, 1973.

Mauss, Marcel. *The Gift: Forms and Functions of Exchange in Archaic Societies*. Trans. Ian Cunnison. New York: Norton, 1967.

al-Maydani. *Majma' al-amthal*. Ed. Na'im Husayn Zarzur. 2 vols. Beirut: Dar al-Kutub al-'Ilmiyya, 1988.

McLoughlin, L. J. *A Learner's Dictionary of Classical Arabic Idioms*. Beirut: Librarie du Liban, 1988.

Meisami, Julie Scott. "Al-Mutanabbi and the Critics." *Arabic and Middle Eastern Literatures* 2, no. 1 (1999): 21–41.

———. *Structure and Meaning in Medieval Arabic and Persian Poetry: Orient Pearls*. London: RoutledgeCurzon, 2003.

———. "The Uses of the *Qasida*: Thematic and Structural Patterns in a Poem of Bashshar." *JAL* 16 (1985): 39–60.

Memon, Muhammad Umar. *Ibn Taimiya's Struggle Against Popular Religion.* The Hague: Mouton, 1976.

Meyerhof, Max. "New Light on Hunayn ibn Ishaq and His Period." In *Studies in Medieval Arabic Medicine,* 685–724. London: Variorum, 1984.

Mir, Mustansir. *Dictionary of Qur'anic Terms and Concepts.* New York: Garland, 1987.

Monroe, James T. *The Art of Badiʿ az-Zaman al-Hamadhani as Picaresque Narrative.* Beirut: American Univ. of Beirut, 1983.

———. *Hispano-Arabic Poetry: A Student Anthology.* Piscataway, N.J.: Gorgias, 2004.

———. "Hispano-Arabic Poetry During the Almoravid Period: Theory and Practice." *Viator* 4 (1973): 65–98.

———. "Hispano-Arabic Poetry During the Caliphate of Córdoba: Theory and Practice." In *Arabic Poetry: Theory and Development,* ed. G. E. von Grunebaum, 124–54. Wiesbaden: Otto Harrassowitz, 1973.

———. "Ibn Quzman's 'Zajal 118': An Andalusi 'Ode to the Onion.'" In *Proceedings of "Los quilates de su Oriente": La pluralidad de culturas en la Península Ibérica durante la Edad Media y en los albores de la Modernidad, a Conference in Honor of Francisco Márques Villaneuva.* Newark, Del.: Juan de la Cuesta, in press.

———. "Improvised Invective in Hispano-Arabic Poetry and Ibn Quzman's 'Zajal 87' (When Blond Meets Blonde)." In *Voicing the Moment: Improvised Oral Poetry and Basque Tradition,* ed. Samuel G. Armistead and Joseba Zulaika, 135–60. Reno: Center for Basque Studies, 2005.

———. "Literary Hybridization in Ibn Quzman's 'Zajal 147' (The Poet's Repentance)." In *Medieval Oral Literature,* ed. Karl Reichl. Berlin: de Gruyter, in press.

———. "Literary Hybridization in the *Zajal:* Ibn Quzman's 'Zajal 88' (The Visit of Sir Gold)." *JAL* 38 (2007): 324–51.

———. "The Mystery of the Missing Mantle: The Poet as Wittol? (Ibn Quzman's 'Zajal 20')." *JAL* 37 (2006): 1–45.

———. "Oral Composition in Pre-Islamic Poetry." *JAL* 3 (1972): 1–53.

———. "Prolegomena to the Study of Ibn Quzman: The Poet as Jongleur." In *El Romancero hoy: Historia, comparatismo, bibliografía crítica,* ed. Samuel G. Armistead, Diego Catalán, and Andonio Sánchez Romeralo, 78–128. Madrid: Gredos, 1979.

———. *The Shuʿubiyya in al-Andalus: The Risala of Ibn García and Five Refutations.* Trans. James T. Monroe. Near Eastern Studies 13. Berkeley and Los Angeles: Univ. of California Press, 1970.

———. "The Striptease That Was Blamed on Abu Bakr's Naughty Son: Was Father Being Shamed, or Was the Poet Having Fun? (Ibn Quzman's 'Zajal No. 133')." In *Homoeroticism in Classical Arabic Literature,* ed. J. W. Wright Jr. and Everett K. Rowson, 94–139. New York: Columbia Univ. Press, 1997.

———. *Structural Coherence and Organic Unity in the Poetry of Ibn Quzman.* Leiden: Brill, forthcoming.

———. "The Structure of an Arabic *Muwashshah* with a Bilingual *Kharja.*" *Edibiyat* 1 (1976): 113–23.

———. "The Underside of Arabic Panegyric: Ibn Quzman's (Unfinished?) '*Zajal* No. 84.'" *Al-Qantara* 17 (1996): 79–115.

———. "Wanton Poets and Would-Be Paleographers (Prolegomena to Ibn Quzman's '*Zajal* No. 10')." *La Corónica* 16 (1987): 1–42.

———. "Which Came First, the *Zajal* or the *Muwashshaha*? Some Evidence for the Oral Origins of Hispano-Arabic Strophic Poetry." *Oral Tradition* 4, nos. 1–2 (1989): 38–74.

Monroe, James T., and Mark Pettigrew. "The Decline of Courtly Patronage and the Appearance of New Genres in Arabic Literature: The Case of the *Zajal,* the *Maqama,* and the Shadow Play." *JAL* 34 (2003): 138–77.

Montgomery, James E. "Arkhilokhos, al-Nabigha al-Dhubyani, and a Complaint Against Blacksmiths; or, A Funny Thing Happened to Me . . ." *Edebiyat* 5 (1994): 15–49.

———. "Dichotomy in Jahili Poetry." *JAL* 17 (1986): 1–20.

———. "For the Love of a Christian Boy: A Song by Abu Nuwas." *JAL* 27 (1996): 115–24.

———. "Al-Mutanabbi and the Psychology of Grief." *JAOS* 115 (1995): 285–92.

———. "Of Models and Amanuenses: The Remarks on the *Qasida* in Ibn Qutayba's *Kitab al-Shi'r wa-l-Shu'ara'.*" In *Islamic Reflections, Arabic Musings: Studies in Honour of Professor Alan Jones,* ed. Robert G. Hoyland and Philip F. Kennedy, 1–47. Oxford: Gibb Memorial Trust, 2004.

———. "Revelry and Remorse: A Poem of Abu Nuwas." *JAL* 25 (1994): 116–34.

Morray, David. "Egypt and Aleppo in Ibn al-'Adim's *Bughyat al-talab fi tarikh Halab.*" In *The Historiography of Islamic Egypt (c. 950–1800),* ed. Hugh Kennedy, 13–21. Leiden: Brill, 2001.

Mottahedeh, Roy P. "The Shu'ubiyah Controversy and the Social History of Early Islamic Iran." *IJMES* 7 (1976): 161–82.

Mumayiz, Ibrahim. "Imru' al-Qays and Byzantium." *JAL* 36 (2005): 135–51.

Musil, Alois. *The Manners and Customs of the Rwala Bedouins.* New York: American Geographical Society, 1928.

al-Mutanabbi. *Diwan.* Beirut: Dar Sadir, 1964.

———. *Diwan.* Ed. 'Abd al-Rahman al-Barquqi. 4 vols. Beirut: Dar al-Kitab al-'Arabi, 1965.

———. *Diwan.* Ed. Friedrich Dieterici. Baghdad: Maktabat al-Muthana, 1964.

————. *Diwan al-Mutanabbi wa-fi athna' matnihi sharh al-Wahidi*. Ed. Friedrich Dieterici. Berlin, 1861.

al-Nabigha al-Dhubyani. *Diwan*. Ed. Karam al-Bustani. Beirut: Dar Sadir, 1963.

Nadeem, S. H. *A Critical Appreciation of Arabic Mystical Poetry*. Lahore: Islamic Book Service, 1979.

The Naqa'id of Jarir and al-Farazdaq. Ed. Anthony A. Bevan. 3 vols. Leiden: Brill, 1905.

al-Nawaji, Muhammad. *Halbat al-kumayt*. Cairo: Matba'at Idarat al-Watan, 1881.

al-Nawawi. *Al-Arba'in al-Nawawiyya*. Trans. Ezzeddin Ibrahim and Denys Johnson-Davies. Damascus: Holy Koran Publishing House, 1976.

Neale, Harry. "The *Diwan* of al-Sharif al-Taliq." *JAL* 34, nos. 1–2 (2003): 20–44.

Nicholson, R. A. *The Idea of Personality in Sufism*. Cambridge: Cambridge Univ. Press, 1923.

————. *A Literary History of the Arabs*. Cambridge: Cambridge Univ. Press, 1956.

————. *The Mystics of Islam*. London: Routledge and Kegan Paul, 1963.

————. *Studies in Islamic Mysticism*. Cambridge: Cambridge Univ. Press, 1921.

Noorani, Yaseen. "Heterotopia and the Wine Poem in Early Islamic Culture." *IJMES* 36 (2004): 345–66.

Norris, H. T. "*Shu'ubiyyah* in Arabic Literature." In *CHALABL*, 31–47.

Northedge, Alastair. "The Palaces of the 'Abbasids at Samarra." In *A Medieval Islamic City Reconsidered: An Interdisciplinary Approach to Samarra*, ed. Chase F. Robinson, 29–67. Oxford: Oxford Univ. Press, 2001.

————. "The Racecourses at Samarra'." *Bulletin of the School of Oriental and African Studies* 53, no. 1 (1990): 31–56.

Nuwayhi, Muhammad. *Nafsiyyat Abi Nuwas*. Cairo: Maktabat al-Nahda al-Misriyya, 1953.

Nyberg, H. S. "Mu'tazila." In *EI¹*.

Nykl, A. R. *Hispano-Arabic Poetry and Its Relations with the Old Provençal Troubadours*. Baltimore: Furst, 1946.

Ouyang, Wen-chin. *Literary Criticism in Medieval Arabic-Islamic Culture: The Making of a Tradition*. Edinburgh: Edinburgh Univ. Press, 1997.

Patton, Walter M. *Ahmad ibn Hanbal and the Mihna*. Leiden: Brill, 1897.

Pellat, Charles. "Al-Ba'ith." In *EI²*.

————. "Al-Buhturi." In *EI²*.

————. "Madjnun Layla." In *EI²*.

Pettigrew, Mark F. "The Wonders of the Ancients: Arab-Islamic Representations of Ancient Egypt." Ph.D. diss., Univ. of California, Berkeley, 2004.

Polk, William R. *The Golden Ode*. Chicago: Univ. of Chicago Press, 1974.

Preminger, Alex, and T. V. F. Brogan, eds. *The New Princeton Encyclopedia of Poetry and Poetics.* Princeton: Princeton Univ. Press, 1993.

al-Qadi, Isma'il. *Al-Khansa' fi mir'at 'asriha.* Vol. 1. Baghdad: Matba'at al-Ma'arif, 1962.

al-Qadi al-Jurjani. *Al-Muntakhab min kinayat al-udaba' wa-isharat al-bulagha'.* Ed. Muhammad Shams al-Haqq Shamsi. Hyderabad: Da'irat al-Ma'arif al-'Uthmaniyya, 1983.

al-Qali. *Kitab al-amali.* Vol. 2. Cairo: Al-Matba'a al-Kubra al-Amiriyya, 1906.

Qudama ibn Ja'far. *Naqd al-shi'r.* Cairo: Maktabat al-Khanji, 1979.

al-Raghib al-Isfahani. *Muhadarat al-udaba' wa-muhawarat al-shu'ara' wa-al-bulagha'.* Ed. 'Umar al-Tabba'. Vol. 2. Beirut: Dar al-Arqam, 1999.

Ramadan, Sa'ida Muhammad. *Baha' al-Din Zuhayr.* Cairo: Dar al-Ma'arif, 1982.

Redhouse, J. W. *The L-Poem of the Arabs.* London: Trübner, 1881.

Rice, David Storm. "Deacon or Drink: Some Paintings from Samarra Re-examined." In *Early Islamic Art and Architecture,* ed. Jonathan M. Bloom, 195–221. Aldershot, UK: Ashgate, 2002.

Rikabi, Jawdat. *La Poésie profane sous les Ayyûbides et ses principaux représentants.* Paris: GP Maisonneuve, 1949.

Rosenthal, Franz. *The Classical Heritage in Islam.* London: Routledge, 1992.

———. *Gambling in Islam.* Leiden: Brill, 1975.

Rowson, Everett K. "The Categorization of Gender and Sexual Irregularity in Medieval Arabic Vice Lists." In *Body Guards: The Cultural Politics of Gender Ambiguity,* ed. Julia Epstein and Kristina Straub, 50–79. London: Routledge, 1991.

———. "The Traffic in Boys: Slavery and Homoerotic Liaisons in Elite 'Abbasid Society." *Middle Eastern Literatures* 11, no. 2 (2008): 193–204.

al-Sabi', Hilal. *Rusum dar al-khilafa.* Trans. Elie A. Salem. Beirut: American Univ. of Beirut, 1977.

al-Safadi. *Tamam al-mutun fi sharh risalat Ibn Zaydun.* Ed. Muhammad Abu al-Fadl Ibrahim. Cairo: Dar al-Fikr al-'Arabi, 1969.

———. *Al-Wafi bi-al-wafayat.* Ed. S. Dedering. Vol. 14. Wiesbaden: Bibliotheca Islamica, 1982.

Sallam, Muhammad Zaghlul. *Al-Adab fi al-'asr al-Ayyubi.* Alexandria: Munsha'at al-Ma'arif, 1990.

Saqr, 'Abd al-Badi'. *Sha'irat al-'Arab.* Doha, Qatar: Al-Maktab al-Islami, 1967.

al-Saraqusti. *Al-Maqamat al-luzumiyah.* Trans. James T. Monroe. Leiden: Brill, 2002.

Scattolin, Giuseppe. "The Experience of the Divine in the Poetry of the Egyptian Sufi Poet 'Umar Ibn al-Farid." In *Representations of the Divine in Arabic Poetry,* ed. Gert Borg and Ed de Moor, 85–118. Amsterdam: Rodopi, 2001.

———. "More on Ibn al-Farid's Biography." *Mélanges de l'Institut Dominicain d'Études Orientales (MIDEO)* 22 (1994): 197–242.

———. "Towards a Critical Edition of Ibn al-Farid's *Diwan*." *Annales Islamologiques* 35 (2001): 503–47.

———. "The Translations of Ibn al-Farid's *Al-Ta'iyya al-Kubra:* Past Essays and New Proposal." In *Comparative Literature in the Arab World,* ed. Ahmed Etman, 309–37. Cairo: Al-Dar al-'Arabiyya, 1998.

Scheindlin, Raymond. *Form and Structure in the Poetry of al-Mu'tamid Ibn 'Abbad.* Leiden: Brill, 1974.

———. *Wine, Women, and Death: Medieval Hebrew Poems on the Good Life.* Oxford: Oxford Univ. Press, 1999.

Schimmel, Annemarie. *Mystical Dimensions of Islam.* Chapel Hill: Univ. of North Carolina Press, 1978.

Schoeler, G. "Bashshar b. Burd, Abu al-'Atahiyah, and Abu Nuwas." In *CHALABL,* 275–99.

———. "Muwashshah." In *EI².*

Sells, Michael. *Desert Tracings: Six Classic Arabian Odes.* Middletown, Conn.: Wesleyan Univ. Press, 1989.

———. "Love." In *CHALLA,* 126–58.

———, trans. "The *Nuniyya* (Poem in N) of Ibn Zaydun." In *CHALLA,* 491–96.

———. "The *Qasida* and the West: Self-Reflective Stereotype and Critical Encounter." *Al-'Arabiyya* 20 (1987): 307–57.

———. "Shanfara's *Lamiyya:* A New Version." *Al-'Arabiyya* 16 (1983): 5–25.

Semah, David. *Four Egyptian Literary Critics.* Leiden: Brill, 1974.

Serrano, Richard A. "Al-Buhturi's Poetics of Persian Abodes." *JAL* 28 (1997): 68–87.

Shaban, M. A. *The 'Abbasid Revolution.* Cambridge: Cambridge Univ. Press, 1970.

al-Shabushti. *Kitab al-diyarat.* Ed. Gurgius 'Awwad. Baghdad: Maktabat al-Muthanna, 1966.

Shahid, Irfan. "The Authenticity of Pre-Islamic Poetry: The Linguistic Dimension." *Al-Abhath* 44 (1996): 3–29.

———. "Byzantium and Kinda." *Byzantinische Zeitschrift* 53 (1960): 57–73.

———. *Byzantium and the Arabs in the Fourth Century.* Washington, D.C.: Dumbarton Oaks, 1984.

———. *Byzantium and the Arabs in the Sixth Century.* 2 vols. Washington, D.C.: Dumbarton Oaks, 1995–2002.

———. "The Composition of Arabic Poetry in the Fourth Century." In vol. 2 of *Studies in the History of Arabia,* 87–93. Riyadh: King Saud Univ. Press, 1984.

———. "The Last Days of Imru' al-Qays: Anatolia." In *Tradition and Modernity in Arabic Literature,* ed. Issa J. Boullata and Terri DeYoung, 207–22. Fayetteville: Univ. of Arkansas Press, 1997.

———. *Rome and the Arabs: A Prolegomenon to the Study of Byzantium and the Arabs.* Washington, D.C.: Dumbarton Oaks, 1984.

Shahrani, M. N. *The Kirghiz and Wakhi of Afghanistan: Adaptation to Closed Frontiers.* Seattle: Univ. of Washington Press, 1979.

Shakir, Mahmud Muhammad. *Al-Mutanabbi.* 2 vols. Cairo: Matba'at al-Madani, 1978.

Shalabi, 'Abd al-Fattah. *Al-Baha' Zuhayr.* Cairo: Dar al-Ma'arif, 1960.

al-Shanfara. *Diwan.* Ed. Imil Badi' Ya'qub. Beirut: Dar al-Kitab al-'Arabi, 1991.

al-Shati', Bint. *Al-Khansa'.* Cairo: Dar al-Ma'arif, 1963.

Shoshan, Boaz. *Popular Culture in Medieval Cairo.* Cambridge: Cambridge Univ. Press, 1993.

Siddiq, Muhammad. "Al-Qasida wa-al-dhat: Qira'a jamaliyya li-Mu'allaqat Imri' al-Qays." *Al-Karmil* 18–19 (1997–98): 231–58.

Sidqi, 'Abd al-Rahman. *Abu Nuwas.* Cairo: Al-Dar al-Qawmiyya, 1965.

———. *Alhan al-han.* Cairo: Dar al-Ma'arif, 1957.

Smith, Barbara Herrnstein. *Poetic Closure: A Study of How Poems End.* Chicago: Univ. of Chicago Press, 1968.

Smith, Margaret. *Al-Ghazali the Mystic.* Lahore: Hijra International, 1983.

———. *Rabi'a the Mystic.* San Francisco: Rainbow Bridge, 1977.

———. *Readings from the Mystics of Islam.* London: Luzac, 1950.

Smith, W. Robertson. *Kinship and Marriage in Early Arabia.* London: Black, 1903.

———. *The Religion of the Semites: The Fundamental Institutions.* New York: Schocken, 1972.

Sowayan, Saad Abdullah. *Nabati Poetry: The Oral Poetry of Arabia.* Berkeley and Los Angeles: Univ. of California Press, 1985.

Sperl, Stefan. "Islamic Kingship and Arabic Panegyric Poetry in the Early 9th Century." *JAL* 8 (1977): 20–35.

———. *Mannerism in Arabic Poetry: A Structuralist Analysis of Selected Texts (3rd Century A.H./9th Century A.D.–5th Century A.H./11th Century A.D.).* Cambridge: Cambridge Univ. Press, 1989.

Sperl, Stefan, and Christopher Shackle, eds. *"Qasida" Poetry in Islamic Asia and Africa.* Vol. 2. Leiden: Brill, 1996.

Stern, Samuel M. *Hispano-Arabic Strophic Poetry.* Oxford: Clarendon Press, 1974.

Stetkevych, Jaroslav. "Arabic Poetry and Assorted Poetics." In *Islamic Studies: A Tradition and Its Problems,* ed. Malcolm H. Kerr, 103–23. Malibu: Udena, 1980.

————. "Arabism and Arabic Literature: Self-View of a Profession." *JNES* 28, no. 3 (1969): 145–56.

————. "The Hunt in Classical Arabic Poetry: From Mukhadram *Qasidah* to Umayyad *Tardiyyah.*" *JAL* 30, no. 2 (1999): 107–27.

————. "The Hunt in the Arabic *Qasidah*: The Antecedents of the *Tardiyyah.*" In *Tradition and Modernity in Arabic Language and Literature,* ed. J. R. Smart, 102–18. Richmond, UK: Curzon, 1996.

————. "In Search of the Unicorn: The Onager and the Oryx in the Arabic Ode." *JAL* 33, no. 2 (2002): 79–130.

————. "Toward an Arabic Elegiac Lexicon: The Seven Words of the *Nasib.*" In *Reorientations/Arabic and Persian Poetry,* ed. Suzanne Pinckney Stetkevych, 58–129. Bloomington: Indiana Univ. Press, 1994.

————. *The Zephyrs of Najd: The Poetics of Nostalgia in the Classical Arabic "Nasib."* Chicago: Univ. of Chicago Press, 1993.

Stetkevych, Suzanne Pinckney. *Abu Tammam and the Poetics of the 'Abbasid Age.* Leiden: Brill, 1991.

————. "From Text to Talisman: Al-Busiri's *Qasidat al-Burdah* (*Mantle Ode*) and the Supplicatory Ode." *JAL* 37 (2006): 145–89.

————. "Intoxication and Immortality: Wine and Associated Imagery in al-Ma'arri's Garden." In *Homoeroticism in Classical Arabic Literature,* ed. J. W. Wright Jr. and Everett Rowson, 210–32. New York: Columbia Univ. Press, 1997.

————. *The Mute Immortals Speak: Pre-Islamic Poetry and the Poetics of Ritual.* Ithaca: Cornell Univ. Press, 1993.

————. *The Poetics of Islamic Legitimacy: Myth, Gender, and Ceremony in the Classical Arabic Ode.* Bloomington: Indiana Univ. Press, 2002.

————. "Structuralist Interpretations of Pre-Islamic Poetry: Critique and New Directions." *JNES* 42, no. 2 (1983): 85–107.

Stewart, Devin J. "Ibn Zaydun." In *CHALLA,* 306–17.

Stoetzer, W. "Zadjal." In *EI²*.

al-Suli. *Akhbar Abi Tammam.* Ed. Muhammad 'Abduh 'Azzam. Cairo: Lajnat al-Ta'lif wa-al-Tarjama wa-al-Nashr, 1937.

Sumi, Akiko Motoyoshi. *Description in Classical Arabic Poetry: Wasf, Ekphrasis, and Interarts Theory.* Leiden: Brill, 2004.

al-Tabari. *The History of al-Tabari.* 38 vols. Albany: State Univ. of New York Press, 1985.

Taha, Nu'man Muhammad Amin. *Jarir: Hayatuhu wa-shi'ruhu.* Cairo: Dar al-Ma'arif, 1968.

al-Tanukhi. *The Table-Talk of a Mesopotamian Judge.* Trans. D. S. Margoliouth. Vol. 2. London: Royal Asiatic Society, 1922.

al-Tawhidi, Abu Hayyan. *Kitab al-imta' wa-al-mu'anasa.* Ed. Ahmad al-Tuwayli. Tunis: Dar Bu Salama lil-Tiba'a wa-al-Nashr wa-al-Tawzi', 1988.

———. *Mathalib al-wazirayn: Akhlaq al-Sahib Ibn 'Abbad wa-Ibn al-'Amid.* Ed. Ibrahim al-Kaylani. Damascus: Dar al-Fikr, 1961.

el Tayib, Abdulla. "Pre-Islamic Poetry." In *CHALUP,* 27–109.

al-Tha'alibi. *The Book of Curious and Entertaining Information.* Trans. C. E. Bosworth. Edinburgh: Edinburgh Univ. Press, 1968.

———. *Yatimat al-dahr.* Ed. Muhammad Muhyi al-Din 'Abd al-Hamid. Vol. 1. Cairo: Matba'at al-Sa'ada, 1956.

Thompson, Stith. *Motif-Index of Folk-Literature.* 6 vols. Bloomington: Indiana Univ. Press, 1955.

Thoreau, Henry David. *Walden.* London: Penguin, 1986.

al-Tibrizi. *Sharh al-qasa'id al-'ashr.* Cairo: Idarat al-Tiba'a al-Muniriyya, 1964.

Tolstoy, Leo. *What Is Art?* Trans. Almyer Maude. New York: Liberal Arts Press, 1960.

Tritton, A. S. "Shi'r." In *EI¹.*

al-'Ukbari. *I'rab Lamiyyat al-'Arab.* Ed. Muhammad Adib 'Abd al-Wahid Jumran. Beirut: Al-Maktab al-Islami, 1984.

Ullendorf, E. "Bilkis." In *EI².*

'Umar ibn Abi Rabi'a. *Diwan.* Ed. Qadri Mayu. 2 vols. Beirut: 'Alam al-Kutub, 1997.

'Urwa ibn al-Ward. *Diwan.* Beirut: Dar al-Kitab al-'Arabi, 1994.

Vadet, Jean-Claude. *L'esprit courtois en Orient.* Paris: Maisonnneuve et Larose, 1968.

Van Ess, Josef. *Theologie und Gesellschaft im 2. und 3. Jahrhundert Hidschra.* 6 vols. Berlin: Walter de Gruyter, 1991–97.

———. "Wrongdoing and Divine Omnipotence in the Theology of Abu Ishaq al-Nazzam." In *Divine Omniscience and Omnipotence in Medieval Philosophy: Islamic, Jewish, and Christian Perspectives,* ed. Tamar Rudavsky, 53–67. Dordrecht, Netherlands: Reidel, 1985.

Van Gelder, G. J. H. *The Bad and the Ugly: Attitudes Towards Invective Poetry ("Hija'") in Classical Arabic Literature.* Leiden: Brill, 1988.

———. *Beyond the Line: Classical Arabic Literary Critics on the Coherence and Unity of the Poem.* Leiden: Brill, 1982.

———. "Genres in Collision: *Nasib* and *Hija'.*" *JAL* 21 (1990): 14–25.

———. *Of Dishes and Discourse: Classical Arabic Literary Representations of Food.* Richmond, UK: Curzon, 2000.

———. "Street Arabs, Satire, and the Status of Poetry." *Arabist: Budapest Studies in Arabic* 15–16 (1995): 121–32.

Von Grunebaum, G. E. "Aspects of Arabic Urban Literature Mostly in Ninth and Tenth Centuries." In *Themes in Medieval Arabic Literature*, ed. Dunning S. Wilson, 281–300. London: Variorum, 1981.

Waddah al-Yaman. *Diwan*. Ed. Muhammad Khayr al-Biqa'i. Beirut: Dar Sadir, 1996.

Wagner, E. "Abu Nuwas." In *EI²*.

al-Walid II (al-Walid ibn Yazid). *Diwan*. Ed. Husayn 'Atwan. Beirut: Dar al-Jil, 1998.

Walker, J. "Sulayman ibn Dawud." In *EI²*.

Watt, W. Montgomery. *Free Will and Predestination in Early Islam*. London: Luzac, 1948.

———. *A History of Islamic Spain*. Edinburgh: Edinburgh Univ. Press, 1965.

———. *Muslim Intellectual: A Study of al-Ghazali*. Edinburgh: Edinburgh Univ. Press, 1963.

Wickering, Deborah. "Experience and Expression: Life among Bedouin Women in South Sinai." *Cairo Papers in Social Science* 14, no. 2 (1991): 1–70.

al-Yusuf, Yusuf. *Maqalat fi al-shi'r al-jahili*. Damascus: Wizarat al-Thaqafa wa-al-Irshad al-Qawmi, 1975.

al-Zamakhshari. *Qasidat Lamiyyat al-'Arab*. Istanbul: Matba'at al-Jawa'ib, 1883.

Zargar, Cyrus Ali. "The Satiric Method of Ibn Daniyal: Morality and Anti-Morality in *Tayf al-Khayal*." *JAL* 37 (2006): 68–108.

al-Zawzani. *Sharh al-Mu'allaqat al-sab'*. Beirut: Dar al-Thaqafa, 1966.

al-Zuhayri, Mahmud Ghannawi. *Naqa'id Jarir wa-al-Farazdaq*. Baghdad: Dar al-Ma'rifa, 1954.

Zwettler, Michael. *The Oral Tradition of Classical Arabic Poetry: Its Character and Implications*. Columbus: Ohio State Univ. Press, 1978.

Index